Anthropology & Education

The major objective of this series is to make the knowledge and perspective of anthropology available to educators and their students. It is hoped and believed, however, that it will also prove valuable to those in other professions and in the several disciplines that compose the behaviorial sciences.

In recent years some educators have discovered that anthropology has much to offer the areas of professional training and educational theory and practice. In its cross-cultural comparisons of human behavior and in its inductive, empirical method of analysis is found a conceptual freshness that is intellectually liberating.

There are four major areas of anthropological theory that have direct relevance for education. These are the regularities of behavior and belief that we call culture; the transmission of culture and learning processes; the ways in which individuals group themselves for the accomplishment of communal purposes, from which comes organization theory; and the processes by which transformations occur in human behavior and groupings that can be explained by a theory of change. In addition, there are the subject-matter areas of child rearing; community and the relationships among institutions within it; the rites of passage; the cultural categories of social class, ethnic group, age, grading, and sex; and others. These several areas of theory and substance provide a rich source for this series. It is believed that the availability of such a storehouse of knowledge in the several volumes in the series will contribute immensely to the further improvement of our educational system.

SOLON T. KIMBALL, GENERAL EDITOR

Anthropology & Education

Series

THE WAY TO MODERN MAN
Fred T. Adams

PERSPECTIVES FROM ANTHROPOLOGY
Rachel Reese Sady

BECOMING A TEACHER
Elizabeth M. Eddy

THE CULTURE OF CHILDHOOD
Mary Ellen Goodman

LEARNING TO BE ROTUMAN
Alan Howard

Functions of Language in the Classroom

Edited by
Courtney B. Cazden
Vera P. John
Dell Hymes

Teachers College Press
Teachers College, Columbia University
New York and London

Foreword

Solon T. Kimball
University of Florida

The publication of *Functions of Language in the Classroom* marks another in the progression of steps that make the findings of behavioral science available to professional educators. Indeed it is possible that the message and the insights that constitute the substance of this volume may prove to be one of the most significant contributions of this decade to the transformation of the teaching-learning process. Such a felicitous consequence may be hoped for, however, only if the basic importance of language as behavior is understood by those who are responsible for the curriculum in our schools and if they heed and apply the knowledge that is available here. That is their responsibility.

This book constitutes a new and significant addition to the Anthropology and Education series. Although the authors are representative of several disciplines, they achieve unity through their common focus upon language behavior in the communication between teachers and students in classrooms. They demonstrate that the meaning language conveys cannot be divorced from the behavioral context in which it originates or in which it is used. Unfortunately, there is little evidence that such knowledge now exists or is used in current educational practices.

The editors of this book, Courtney B. Cazden, Vera P. John, and Dell Hymes, are to be commended for their labors in assembling and preparing this collection for publication. Through their efforts, the pioneering accomplishments of themselves and of a number of their colleagues have been brought together for the edification of a scientific and professional audience. But with the incorporation of this new knowledge into the schooling process, students are the ones who will reap unanticipated rewards. The children in our schools, particularly those from minority groups who deserve better than they have thus far received, may well become the greatest beneficiaries and, if so, this is indeed a noteworthy accomplishment.

Preface

Courtney B. Cazden
Harvard University

Like every other book, this one has a biography. In October 1965, when the first summer of Head Start was just over, a small group of anthropologists, linguists, psychologists, and sociologists was called together at West Farms, New York, by Edmund Gordon, then of Yeshiva University. Our task was to suggest priorities to the U.S. Office of Education for research on children's language and its relation to school success. The three editors of this volume and four other authors—Joshua Fishman, Joan Gussow, John Gumperz, and Vivian Horner—were among the participants.

During the second day, Alfred Hayes of the Center for Applied Linguistics summarized much of our discussion by calling for "contrastive sociolinguistic" research. More was known then, as it still is today, about the structure of child language than about how children use language in particular social settings. We believed that school problems could be better explained by differences in language use between home and school, and the need for such research became a nagging theme throughout our discussions.

The following June, a larger follow-up conference, chaired by Beryl Bailey, was held at Yeshiva University. At the opening session, Dell Hymes gave the first presentation of his paper "On communicative competence,"[1] which since then has influenced many of the contributors to this book. When the small West Farms group met over coffee, we returned to the need for research, and a book was suggested. Could we assemble a set of papers on the "functions

[1]In M. Wax, S. Diamond, and F. Gearing (Eds.), *Anthropological perspectives on education* (New York: Basic Books, 1971), pp. 51-66. An expanded version with more discussion of linguistic theory appears in R. Huxley and E. Ingram (Eds.), *Language acquisition: models and methods* (New York: Academic Press, 1971), pp. 3-28.

of language in the classroom" that would illuminate the communicative demands of the school and the sociolinguistic discontinuities between a child's home community and his school culture? Such a volume could report the substantive knowledge that existed, interest other researchers in this area, and—as Hymes argues so well in his Introduction—encourage teachers to become their own ethnographers.

A year later, Sol Kimball suggested that a book on language would be appropriate for his series on Anthropology and Education at Teachers College Press, and work on the book began in earnest. With two exceptions, all papers have been written especially for this book. The chapters by Basil Bernstein and Susan Philips have been previously published and are reprinted here in somewhat different versions with permission and thanks.

The authors in this book come from many disciplines. We believe this inter-disciplinary quality is an important source of the book's strength. But it may cause problems for the reader. Each discipline has its own conceptual framework, and each chapter must be understood within the framework of its author. Across the chapters there will be shared ideas labeled in different terms, and shared terms used to refer to different phenomena. An example of the latter is the term *code,* whose different usage by Basil Bernstein and Claudia Mitchell-Kernan is pointed out by Hymes in his Introduction. Because of this lack of consistent relationship between terms and ideas throughout the book, we feared that an Index might be more misleading than helpful and so decided not to include one. Each chapter has its own list of references, through which the reader can trace back to the source of particular ideas.

Because research on children is so often done by outsiders to their communities, the relationship between our authors and the children they have studied is as important to mention as their scholarly background. Robert Dumont is an Assiniboin-Sioux, Eduardo Hernández-Chavez is Chicano, and Claudia Mitchell-Kernan is black; Robert Boese is the hearing child of deaf parents who himself learned "sign" as his native language; and Susan Philips' work, for example, was done with the approval, and indeed the encouragement, of the Warm Springs Inter-Tribal Council.

In the division of editorial labors, Courtney Cazden took primary responsibility for editorial work, assisted from beginning to end by Vera John. Dell Hymes provided the integrating organization for the book through his outline for the Contents and his Introduction. The collaboration this book represents has been, both intellectually and personally, a deeply rewarding experience.

Introduction

Dell Hymes
University of Pennsylvania

I

This is a hopeful book, and, its authors hope, a helpful one. I stress *hopeful,* because such a book might be read as merely another criticism of the present state of affairs. There is criticism here, a good deal of it, but it is criticism linked with painstaking efforts to understand what does go on in classrooms; and it is criticism directed at scholars as much as at anyone.

In endeavoring to provide useful information and perspectives on the functions of language in the classroom, we cannot but realize how remiss those who study language scientifically have been in this matter. True, for many years linguists have combated misguided prescriptivism, if perhaps sometimes not too wisely but too well; important contributions to the teaching of reading and usage have been made; many linguists have worked diligently and well on the teaching of English and of other languages. Too often, however, linguistics has been taken to be a source of truths already revealed, needing only to be packaged and applied; very seldom have linguists said of problems of language in the classroom: If we are to say something valid and helpful, we must undertake new research. And now that linguistics has become established, prominent, and fashionable, there has been a dizzying succession of books claiming a scientific authority to replace the authority of tradition. "Linguistics" has become a magic name. Partly in response, some linguists, whether in disgust, disdain, despair, or some combination of motives, have come to deny any claim to authority in classroom matters, saying that the present state of linguistic theory is so confused that linguists can tell teachers nothing useful at all.

There is something to the view that linguistics does not have much to offer education, but lack of an agreed dogma does not seem to us (if I may speak for the contributors to this book) the most important reason. There are two main reasons, one external to the study of language, about which scholars cannot do very much, and one internal to the study of language, about which scholars can and should do a great deal. The first reason is that much of the difficulty in schooling today is the result of social relationships and social changes that are beyond the power of the school, let alone the teacher, to affect much. Many of the things that are needed require changes in the allocation of resources, on the one hand, and in community attitudes and practices, on the other, and can change only as those things change. The second reason is that those things within the power of the school to affect or change—centrally, here, the relations between styles of teaching and styles of learning vis-à-vis language—have not been considered part of their concern by most linguists. There may be a severe limitation to what can be accomplished within the classroom—certainly that is so from a thoroughgoing egalitarian standpoint, such as that espoused by Ivan Illich (1971)—but Illich himself admits that many current efforts have some good effects. The primary difficulty for linguistics is that such improvements do not depend on language alone, but on language in social context. What is crucial is not so much a better understanding of how language is structured, but a better understanding of how language is used; not so much what language is, as what language is for. Linguists have generally taken questions of use and purpose for granted. They have not related the structure of language to the structure of speaking. Yet if one thing is abundantly clear, it is that the problems in many American classrooms have to do precisely with this relationship.

So far, the net effect of the current prestige of linguistics may have been more to sell books advertised as embodying a "linguistic" approach than to help teachers and children. Yet the helpfulness of the study of language can be greatly increased. The answer does not lie in retreat from educational problems, in pursuit of a unified linguistic theory to present to the world at some later time. Diversity of theory and approach may be a very healthy thing as an antidote to the faddish misuse of some one brand of linguistics as "the" authority. The answer lies in scholars as citizens doing what each can about allocation of resources, and community attitudes and practices, and in scholars as scholars tackling the things we need to know about. For language in the classroom, what we need to know goes far beyond how the grammar of English is organized as something to be taught. It has to do with the relationship between a grammar of English and the ways in which English is organized in use by teachers, by children, and by the communities from which they come; with the features of intonation, tone of voice, rhythm, style, that escape the usual grammar and enter into the essential meaning of speech; with the meanings of all those means of speech to those who use them and those who hear them, not in the narrow sense of meaning, as naming objects and stating relationships, but in the fuller sense, as conveying respect or disrespect, concern or indifference, intimacy or distance, seriousness or play, etc.; with the appropriateness of one or another means of speech, or way of speaking, to one or another topic, person, situation; in short, with the relation of the structure of language to the structure of speaking.

We realize how little we know about this relationship, and how far we are from an adequate theory of explanation for it. Yet we are hopeful, because a serious beginning has at last been made, drawing together people from many backgrounds — linguistics, sociology, psychology, anthropology—to take part in the kind of work that is needed. It is because there was almost nothing of this sort a few years ago that the initial studies and analyses presented here are not only helpful now, but also encouraging for the future.

II

Having said that papers such as these should be written, let me say something about why and how they should be read. Obviously each teacher and educator will have to decide for herself or himself what aspects of this book have relevance. In some cases there may be a close parallel to one's own situation. In other cases relevance may lie in a perspective whose detailed implications remain to be worked out. *This is very much as it should be.* Teachers and educators are no doubt somewhat inured to being lectured right and left by experts and authorities, and to being made whipping boys for the general ills of society. And obviously the contributors to this book believe that there are things badly in need of change in some classrooms—no one closely familiar with the education of American Indian children, for example, could, I think, conclude other-wise. Obviously the contributors believe that they have something useful to say. But nothing in the book is to be taken as a self-suffi-cient formula or surefire remedy. Quite the contrary. The book offers perspectives, arguments, information, analyses, to be reflected upon and made use of. But the use depends upon the user. Any other reading of the papers would be contrary to the book's inten-tion.

A principle that runs through those papers is that of starting where the children are. To adapt a phrase from the ministry, the principle is that one should "speak to their condition." More must be said about this shortly. The point here is that it is those in the particular classroom and community who can best know what the condition is. The authors of this book do not. If those in a particu-lar situation are blind to its nature, the authors of these papers can-not see for them. The papers may offer helpful perspectives and insights, but for them to be effective in a classroom, they must be articulated in terms of the features of that classroom and its com-munity context. The participants in the situation must themselves in effect be ethnographers of their own situation. These papers can suggest new things to notice, reflect upon, and do; an outsider and another situation can contribute an element of distance and objec-tivity; where feasible, consultations and workshops (such as those that Roger Shuy of Georgetown University has been conducting with teachers in Norfolk, Virginia) can make available some of the results of sociolinguistic research. In the last analysis, it is the under-standing and insight of those in the concrete situation that will deter-mine the outcome.

Such a book as this, and research such as it presents, can only be part of a general process. The point is obvious enough, but one of the implications may not be. If linguistics and ethnography are to contribute to a democratic way of life, their knowledge and perspec-tive must be gained and used in democratic ways. Indeed, it has been realized that linguistics and ethnography presuppose a kind of "participatory democracy" for their success, with regard both to their scientific findings and to their practical use.

There is such a thing as the authority that accrues to an inves-tigator from knowledge of a wide range of relevant materials, from mastery of methods of analysis, from experience with a type of problem. But the authority also accrues from mastery of activities and skills, from experience with a variety of language, in a community. An investigator depends upon the abilities of those in a situation, whether it is a question of scientific inquiry or practical application. Both inquiry and application are processes that involve mutuality and sharing of knowledge; neither can succeed as a one-way application of *a priori* method or knowledge.

This standpoint is one that I think most, if not all, of the contributors to this book would accept. It is familiar to linguists and ethnographers engaged in basic research on the structure of a language or the structure of life in a community. Their task can be described as that of making explicit and objectively systematic what speakers of the language, or members of the community, in a sense already know. There is more to linguistic and ethnographic analysis than that—the form of the systematization comes ultimately from the investigator, for one thing, and men in society bring about more than they can be said in any reasonable sense to know; but this description of the task goes to the heart of the work. There is more, but this is the core. To take a linguistic example: a speaker of English in some sense knows that in a sentence such as

Sue was induced to do it after all,

Sue has the same relationship to *was induced* and to *to do it,* so far as the surface form of the sentence is concerned—one would commonly say that *Sue* is the "subject" of both. A speaker also in some sense knows that the relationships of *Sue* to *was induced* and to *to do it* are not identical, in terms of some underlying structure. He or she knows that *Sue* is what has been called the "logical subject" only of *to do it,* and is what has been called the "logical object" of *was induced;* that in this respect *Sue was induced* stands in a systematic relationship to *Someone induced Sue* and other sentences of that form. The speaker may not have brought such relationships to consciousness, indeed, usually has not done so, and may lack a terminology in which to talk about them, let alone a frame of reference in which to analyze them. Terminology and analytic framework may be contributed by the linguist, but the process of developing an explicit analysis of the language is a collaboration in the true sense of the word.

Similarly, a user of English in the United States in some sense knows that the person who picks up a ringing telephone is the first to speak (whereas in Norway the person who has called speaks first to identify himself); that the answerer should speak within a few seconds; and that the answer is in effect a response to the ring as a summons, such that the person who issues a summons, whether by causing a phone to ring, by ringing a doorbell, or by calling a name (e.g., "Sylvia!") has the right and obligation to say the next thing, after the response, but not to repeat the summons. (If Sylvia says "Yes?" and I say nothing, she has the right to complain, e.g., "Well, what do you want?"; if Sylvia says "Yes?", and I say again, "Sylvia!", she has the right to complain, e.g., "Yes, yes, didn't you hear me?" If a phone or doorbell continues to ring, and we know we have already begun to respond, we may utter annoyedly, "I'm coming, I'm coming," on the same principle: once is enough.) One may not reflect on such patterns in one's behavior, let alone analyze them —indeed, some of these aspects of summoning as a pattern in American life were made explicit for the first time, so far as I know, only recently by the sociologist Emanuel Schegloff (1968). Yet much of our communicative conduct is regular in such respects, and disruption of these accustomed regularities can affect our well-being, from momentary annoyance to avoidance of persons or situations, as disturbing, or disturbed.

Again, a child raised in a Cherokee community in Oklahoma in some sense knows that certain kinds of conduct show respect for others, regard for others' personal worth, and that other kinds of conduct show disrespect, and are shaming. The child may not have brought such patterns to consciousness, and may not have a terminology and frame of reference in which to analyze them closely; neither may the child's teachers; yet seemingly small details may make a classroom a subtle battleground of silence (see Dumont's paper in this book). The general principle has been phrased by Goffman in a fundamental paper (1956, p. 475):

When a rule of conduct is broken we find that two individuals run the risk of becoming discredited: one with an obligation (perhaps imputed), who should have governed himself by the rule; the other with an expectation (perhaps imputed), who should have been treated in a particular way because of this governance. Both actor and recipient are threatened.

Those considerations are essential to a concern with communication, and with language as an element of communication, in classrooms as elsewhere, because, as Goffman goes on to point out (p. 475):

An act that is subject to a rule of conduct is, then, a communication, for it represents a way in which selves are confirmed—both the self for which the rule is an obligation (again, perhaps, imputed). An act that is subject to rules of conduct, but does not conform to them is also a communication—often even more so—for infractions make news and often in such a way as to disconfirm the selves of the participants. Thus rules of conduct transform both action and inaction into expression, and whether the individual abides by the rules or breaks them, something significant is likely to be communicated.

An observer can be aware of the significance of covert aspects of communication, and can see and document their consequences in a classroom; he or she may seek the sources of the patterns of communication in the community outside the classroom, and thus bring something new in the way of knowledge of the classroom situation, since the teacher may not have experience of the children's cultural community, nor the children experience of that of the teacher. Nevertheless, the observer's analysis ultimately stands or falls on its success in understanding the values and meanings that inhere in the observed behavior. Aversion of the eyes, for example, like silence, is an act of many meanings, and only the implicit knowledge of participants can disclose whether it is due to apprehension, hostility, disinterest, or respect. So also with a speech act, such as talking when another is talking: it may be disrespect (but to the person talking, or to the person listening, or both?); it may be a show of solidarity (cf. Boggs' paper in this book); it may be a normal way of eventually being heard (as Karl Reisman [forthcoming] has shown for a Caribbean community, Antigua).

Ultimately the participants in a setting have the most experience, the most access to evidence, as to the nature of the situation and the meanings and problems it contains. Moreover, if identification of meanings and problems is to wait upon outside observers, it will never occur for most classrooms. There are thousands upon thousands of classrooms, but only a handful of interested and capable observers. Sheer logistics would dictate a democratization of linguistic and ethnographic approaches, a general, collaborative sharing of them, even if principle did not. Most important of all, interpreting the world of the classroom does not suffice to change it. If information and ideas from this book are found useful and are implemented, it will be because the participants in an actual situation, through their observations and insight, have made them their own.

Let me repeat the point in order to bring out one final implication. I do not stress the theme of sharing out of courtesy alone, nor to give a veneer of mutuality to a concealed position of my own. I do hold strongly to a particular view of the way in which language should be studied, namely, that it must be studied in its social context, in terms of its organization to serve social ends. Such a view pervades this book, and some of the reasons for such a view have been given. In the next section, I will develop the reasons why such a view seems necessary. The point here is that to stress the importance of the participants in a situation is a matter, not of courtesy or rhetoric, but of scientific principle. To understand language in its social context requires understanding the meanings that social contexts and uses of language have for their participants (as several papers in this book show); and students of language are to a large extent in the same boat as participants in classrooms in this matter. As several of the contributors point out, linguistics has not gotten very far in this respect. The problem of the functions of language in the classroom is a challenge and an opportunity for the advancement of linguistics itself. Studying language in the classroom is not really "applied" linguistics; *it is really basic research.* Progress in understanding language in the classroom is progress in linguistic theory.[1] If those who participate in classrooms contribute to such understanding, they are contributing to a scientific as well as to a practical goal. Theoretical and practical concerns here are interdependent.

Those who maintain that linguistic theory has nothing to say to classrooms now are right, insofar as they mean that the prestige of linguistics should not be abused by pretending to tell more than linguistics knows. They are wrong insofar as they mean that linguistics must be excused from concern with classrooms, that its nature is

---

[1]The term "linguistic theory" is used by some linguists to refer just to that part of the study of language concerned with formal grammar. I use the term in the normal, general sense, in which it is equivalent to "theory of language."

such that it has nothing to learn from confronting the problems of classrooms.

Many linguists consider themselves to be concerned with characterizing the knowledge that a speaker has of his or her language, and with understanding the way in which there is a "creative aspect" to language use. They associate their work with intimations of the true nature of man as a being capable of creative growth and deserving of the freedom and dignity conducive to such growth. Just these matters are at stake in the classroom experience of children day after day. To deal with them requires cooperative effort of both those in the classroom and those who visit it, and an extension of concepts and understanding on the one side as much as the other.

III

The functions of language in the classroom are a special case of the general problem of the study of language in its social context. The key to understanding language in context is to start, not with language, but with context. Such a statement may strike one as perverse, and indeed it is true that an adequate theory of the functioning of language would not "start" from either language or context, but would systematically relate the two within a single model. The reason for starting with context now is that our present models of language leave out much, not only of context, but also of features and patterns of speech itself. Only by viewing the relationship from the side of contexts can we see an essential part of what is going on when language is taught and used.

The dominant models of language in linguistics today bespeak a neutral, affectless use of language for information and report. Considerable success has been gained in understanding some of the general properties of languages in this way, and in the systematic analysis of many individual languages, in terms of the way in which language is organized to serve what may be broadly called a "referential" function. The ways in which language is organized to serve what may broadly be called "social" functions have remained marginal. A number of excellent linguists have attended to these functions and work on them now, but most associate such work with a pursuit of diverse, ad hoc, superficial phenomena external to the heart of language, and secondary to the true goal of linguistics. The goal that leading theorists hold out to themselves today is to disclose universal structures underlying all language and presumably inherent in the human mind. This goal inspires (and sometimes rationalizes) most of the linguists and most of the work in the United States at the present time. It is a noble goal, and it speaks to the problem of language in the classroom in one essential respect. It highlights the long-standing assumption, and experience, of linguists that all normal human beings are gifted with a capacity for language, a capacity that is fundamentally equivalent in all, a capacity that has a complexity and potentiality for creative use beyond our scientific ability as yet to assess fully. Current work informs and supports this conception, giving explicit content to it. If some kinds of children are found to be disadvantaged linguistically vis-à-vis others, the causes are presumed to be not innate but social. Ability for some of the specialized creative uses of language in science, art, and social life no doubt varies widely among individuals, in part due to genetic inheritance, but the realization of such ability depends upon social opportunities. Individual differences due to inherited ability indeed are most likely to become realized in good environments, and to be suppressed in poor ones (Scarr-Salapatek, 1972). There is no basis for assuming differences in fundamental linguistic ability or for imputing to inherited differences between ethnic, racial, or other groups. The vernacular speech of every society or social group, when studied, has been found to be based on complex, profound structures of the same kind (Labov, 1969, 1972).

The presumption, moreover, is that the true ability of children who are found to be disadvantaged may not be accurately perceived. Certainly it is scientifically absurd to describe children as coming to school "linguistically deprived," so far as the presence of regular grammar and the capacity for creative use of language in social life are concerned.

But there is the rub. Children may indeed be "linguistically deprived" if the language of their natural competence is not that of the school; if the contexts that elicit or permit use of that competence are absent in the school; if the purposes to which they put language, and the ways in which they do so, are absent or prohibited in the school. The situation of the children, indeed, is much worse than "deprivation" if their normal competence is punished in the school. One could speak more appropriately of "repression." Such has been the fate of many American Indians, who as children were whipped if the language of their parents and home was heard in the classroom. Such is the fate of many children in classrooms today if the accent, grammatical characteristics, or style of their normal community are heard. The punishment may be merely disapproval, but even that may be cumulatively disastrous. (One classroom was observed in which about 90% of the teacher's communication to each child was negative.) I have heard a teacher in a Boston school exclaim to her principal that she was going to correct one grammatical fault (from the standpoint of the standard language) in a certain black child if it took all year. Will that be the sum of what the standard language means to a child at the end of a year of school—one grammatical propriety? In my own institution a teacher in training has shown himself marvelously effective because of his ability to make use of a style of repeating, responsive verbal performance common in churches and other occasions of admired public speech in the black community. He has shown he can involve children and make sure a point has gotten across. Those who are training him say they are reluctant to send him out into regular classrooms because of his "illogical" manner of presentation. "Illogical" here can only mean cultural style not their own; and, of course, hang the evidence before one's eyes of effectiveness.

Actual punishment or repression of differences may not exist, but rather inadequate mutual comprehension that frustrates the verbal growth the teacher may seek and of which the children are capable. Such is the case in many American Indian schools, as described in the papers by Dumont and Philips below.

As has been pointed out, linguistics today does not have much to say about social, institutional, interactional causes of deprivation, or lack of creative growth, except perhaps to deplore them. Many of the papers in this book point to ways in which these causes of failure in communication and communicative growth, frustrating to teachers and children alike, can be comprehended. In this respect the papers are part of an emerging trend of work, called "sociolinguistics." The considerations involved in comprehending these problems, and that underlie sociolinguistic research, are so obvious as to be common sense; but this is not the first time that the trained incapacity of a profession has had to be overcome by recognizing the obvious.

We start, as said, with context. In models of "linguistic theory" in the narrow sense, language is socially context-free; it is an all-purpose, and hence purposeless, source of any and all sentences. The units and structures that are counted as part of language are defined from the standpoint of "referential" function, and are analyzed in terms of canons of formal simplicity and generality. But the units and structures that count as part of language in social life do not come defined and organized in just that way. When language is used, it is commonly used in a situation and for a purpose; its use has some point.

In basing his later conception of language on this view, the philosopher Wittgenstein discussed the use of language in terms of a series of "games." Today a number of researchers speak in terms of "verbal strategies" (cf. Gumperz and Hernández-Chavez, and Mishler, in this volume). There is a growing body of work that investigates the organization of language according to styles, genres, and speech acts. We do not have a comprehensive theory of these things, nor even a standard set of terms in which to discuss them. What is encouraging is the growing recognition of the basis of such research, namely, that there is a structure in the use of language that goes beyond the aspect of structure dealt with in grammars; that formal simplicity and generality in language must be sought in more complex, comprehensive terms than hitherto. To recognize that language comes organized in terms of use is to recognize that language has more than a referential function, more than a single kind of meaning.

Here is the heart of the perspective on language that underlies the papers in this book. Language is polymorphous, even if to a linguist pursuing a standard theory its variety may appear perverse. Not only is language put to a multiplicity of purposes, but the linguistic resources available to people are organized in terms of a multiplicity of purposes. Indeed, if we are to understand what people are doing when they speak, we must recognize that "language" is not an adequate concept. We need to think of language in the classroom, and elsewhere, in terms of a concept that is at once more specific and more general. The concept must be more specifie than "language," because often a person is not adequately described as "speaking English," but as speaking in some variety of English, "standard," "dialect," "vernacular," etc.; as speaking in some recognizable manner, according to a general type of situation, "formally," "consultatively," "informally," etc.; or according to some specific type of scene or genre, a public lecture, a revivalistic sermon, a bureaucratic decision, etc.; according to some particular role or relationship, that of parent, lover, friend, boss, etc. At the same time the concept that we need must be more general than that of "language," because in many communities the available means of speech extend beyond any one language, or one linguistic norm, to comprise a variety of levels (cf. the paper by Fishman and Lueders-Salmon), even, often enough, a number of distinct languages. In many communities not only is it normal for the language of the classroom and the language of the home to be different; they may be mutually unintelligible. Both may differ from the language of religious worship. And all this without difficulty, if each language is accepted and approved in the role it serves. Finally, the concept must be more general than "language" because in all communities language is but one means of communication among others. (The paper by Byers and Byers brings home this point, as does Dumont's study of particular classrooms, in this volume.)

Common to all of these considerations is the general point that since every community has a variety of linguistic means, speaking always entails a choice (deliberate, spontaneous, automatic) among them. From the standpoint of communication in general, this extends to the choice of speech itself, as opposed to other means (vocal, gestural—a whistle, a scream, a nod, a turning away), and as opposed to silence. Silence itself is a specific message, of course, as a response within discourse, and, within gatherings, a generalized message about one's relation to a group and its rules for interaction: interrupting, speaking out of turn (cf. Boggs' paper below), breaking a long silence, greeting someone defined as "not on speaking terms," versus refusing to answer, failing to contribute to a discussion, etc. Whether one speaks, and, if one speaks, the way in which one speaks, are elements of choice and hence of the meaningfulness of language.

To deal with language from this standpoint, we may make use

of a concept that has come to prominence in large part through the work of John Gumperz: the concept of *verbal repertoire*. The concept is presented below by Fishman and Lueders-Salmon in their paper, and an essential aspect of it is explored below in detail by Gumperz and Hernández-Chavez. The term properly implies that people have available a variety of ways of speaking. We may understand *verbal repertoire* more precisely in terms of two interrelated aspects of speech. There are the *means of speech* that people have available, including the meanings associated with the use of one or another of these; and there are the *contexts of situation* in which speech is used, including meanings associated with these. To give one example: Among the Zuni Indians, one variety of language is characterized by circumlocutions that are substituted for certain ordinary words; this variety has the connotation of sacredness. Although recognized by all Zuni, it is best known by old people; it is used in prayers, myths, songs, and traditional sayings, and required in conversations within the underground ceremonial structure, the *kiva*. Another variety is characterized by the use of ordinary words with specialized and ephemeral meanings, as a kind of slang, and has the connotation of frivolous "nonsense"; it is said to be understood and used only by children and young adults; old people are supposed to ignore it (Newman, 1955). The set of patterns relating means of speech and contexts of situation may be said to constitute the *ways of speaking* of a person, a group, or a community.

Means of speech may be differentiated from one another in many ways, of course, indeed, by any and all of the elements that go to make up language and discourse. There is no way to decide except by discovering empirically just what features have been so used. The difference may be a matter of pronunciation or manipulation of sounds (as in student "op-talk," formed by inserting the syllable "op" after an initial consonant of a word); a matter of vocabulary (as in the Zuni examples); a matter of grammar, of morphology and syntax (as in the distinctive pattern of negative concord in Black English); or of two or all three of these. The difference may not be a matter of sheer presence or absence of features, but of proportion or degree. Sometimes only a few occurrences of a feature may stamp a way of speaking; an occurrence of *d* for *th* in forms such as *the, this, that* may suffice to class a style (and person) as lower-class vernacular; ethnic identities and archaic literary styles may be suggested by a few vestigial features, as in stereotypes used by public performers and comic strips. In other cases, a few occurrences of a feature may be ignored. Everything depends, not on the presence of variation in speech—there is always that—but on whether, and to what extent, difference is invested with social meaning.

This point is of utmost importance to understanding ways of speaking, and to efforts to learn, impart, and change them. To deal with these practical implications (as will be done in the following section), we need some further account of the principle involved. It is a principle fundamental to linguistics, namely, that the meaningfulness of language is interwoven of two kinds of meaning, "referential" and "social."

In both ordinary linguistics and sociolinguistics one seeks the differences that "make a difference" to users of a form of speech. Only the scope of the question is different. In ordinary grammar one may ask, does this difference in sound make this sentence different from that one? In English, for example, one finds that managing one's vocal chords in a way that is called "voicing" makes telling someone "Drop dead" a different thing from telling someone (without "voicing" the first sound of the second word) "Drop Ted." Again, in English, a difference between a heavy and a light release of breath after the first consonant in *Ted* does not make it a different name, or any other English word. In ordinary grammar, one stops there. A difference of "voicing" will differentiate sentences and entries in the dictionary in terms of "referential" function; a difference of aspiration will not. Meaning, however, does not stop there. Just those features that are not used in one function in a given context may be used for another. Depending on social context and other linguistic features (e.g., intonation), "I'm Ted," with heavy aspiration of the *t,* may convey clarification ("I'm *T*ed, not *N*ed"); disgust ("What part in the play do you have? I'm *T*ed"); delight ("What part do you have? I'm *T*ed"); etc.

In terms of means of speech, generally, we ask, does this difference make this sentence different from another in respect to what kind of attitude is conveyed, what kind of situation it is (intimate, formal), what kind of act it is (request, a command), what kind of person is talking (a Southerner from Charlottesville or Atlanta, an

Indiana resident from Brown County or northern Indianapolis), etc. In sum, what does the difference convey about identity, intent, or definition of the situation by the speaker? To keep to an example from pronunciation, in New York City the degree to which an *r*-sound is present after the vowel in fact does not affect what English word it is. (Technically, different degrees of constriction of the back of the tongue are not referentially significant.) Thus, differences in the degree of *r*-ness are available as a way of signalling other differences, and have come to be so used. New York City speakers constitute a speech community in part because they have come to share an evaluation of *r*-ness as prestigeful. The proportion of *r*-ness varies directly with social class, but also within a class according to the self-consciousness of the situation. If someone says "On the fourth floor" and is asked to repeat, the repetition is likely to have more *r*-ness; this and much other evidence show that *r*-ness enters not only into social levels of speech but into contextual styles as well (Labov, 1966). Nor, to repeat a point, is *r*-ness all or nothing; the levels and styles are defined in terms of relative frequencies of *r*-constriction. The indications are that this feature has become socially significant in New York City within this century, spreading in a detectible pattern among ethnic and age groups, as well as among classes.

Another way of putting the linguistic principle is in terms of repetition. For two generations or more linguists have built their science on the assumption that in any speech community some utterances are the same in form and meaning, i.e., count as repetitions (Bloomfield, 1933, p. 144; Swadesh, 1948, p. 257, n.11; Postal, 1968, pp. 7, 12, 217). We have seen that there are two standpoints, not one, from which one must ask if two utterances are the same in form and meaning. In the example just given, "on the fourth floor," said twice, is a repetition from the standpoint of referential meaning; from the standpoint of social meaning, it is not.

Our examples from pronunciation conceal a difficult and important step, for linguistics and those in classrooms alike. Features of pronunciation are made manifest in speech; one can hear them, or learn to hear them. True, they do not announce their meanings, which must be explained or inferred; but the physical presence of a feature is a great advantage and keeps us within the ordinary realm of linguistics. So also do alternative realizations of a common syntactic relationship, as when we note that whereas "Roger liked Barbara" and "Barbara liked Roger" are in contrast referentially, as to who did the liking and who was liked, "Roger liked Barbara" and "Barbara was liked by Roger" are the same referentially with respect to that relationship. If we consider a wider range of alternatives, such as "It was Barbara Roger liked" and "It was Roger who liked Barbara," we are still within a realm in which the social, or stylistic contrast, against the base of common referential meaning, is expressed "syntagmatically" in the linguistic form itself. Clearly there is a contrast in emphasis, focusing, or the like. Some schools of linguistics analyze the formal nature of such relationships without much considering their functions, whereas others pay a good deal of attention to such functions. And if we consider the set of alternatives for identifying Roger, such as "Roger," "Rog," "Mr. Adams," "Dr. Adams," "Professor Adams," and the like, we have a range also familiar to teachers and linguistics, and to which linguists, social psychologists, and anthropologists have made increasing contribution in recent years: what may be called "paradigmatic sets" of alternatives, for which we know modes of elicitation and analysis. Indeed it is just because the study of these things is so much a matter of orientation and interests, rather than a radical break with familiar materials and methods, that it is easy enough to extend linguistic practice, and ordinary linguistic conceptions of meaning, to include them.

There are aspects of meaning, however, that go beyond alternatives within grammar and lexicon, and that involve alternatives within the larger sphere of speech. From a "paradigmatic" standpoint, the set of alternatives by which English speakers may express negation includes not only certain words and constructions, but also intonation, head-shaking, standing (or remaining seated) when a vote is called, turning the back, etc. The deictic words of a language ("this," "that," et al.) are integrated with its other means of pointing and indicating, including, among many American Indians, pointing with the lips. And so on. From a "syntagmatic" standpoint, relationships of sequence and the rules that govern them go beyond sentences to sequences of sentences, and to sequences of interaction. These considerations again show that our perspective on language in the classroom should be that of communication as a whole, both to understand what is being conveyed and to understand the specific place of language within the process; I shall try to consider this consequence more fully in the next section as a prelude to the papers below that focus upon it (Byers and Byers, Cicourel and Boese). Here let me take up a notion that promises to help integrate the analysis of language with the analysis of communication, the concept of *speech act*.

The very notion of *act* takes us beyond the sphere of referential meaning, inasmuch as an act is itself the doing of something, not merely a way of referring to something. If I say, "Get me another cup of coffee while you're up," the words "cup of coffee" no doubt stand in a relation of reference to something non-linguistic, and we would verify this by finding that other members of the community would agree that the non-linguistic entity was indeed properly so designated, but the status of the words as a whole as a request (or command) is not a matter of finding out if members of the community agree in applying them to some non-linguistic object. That what was said was a request (or command) is to be verified by finding that members of the community would agree that the utterance is itself such an act (by virtue of the relationship between its features and those of its context).

The interpretation of an utterance as a particular act depends in an important part upon aspects of communication beyond language in the narrow sense—upon intonation, tone of voice, gesture, and the like—so that one ultimately needs the more general notion of *communicative act,* in keeping with what has just been said above. For many American Indian children, for example, a tone of voice that is normal to many white teachers can define something that is said as angry; for many white Americans, the aversion of the eyes that expresses respect among many black people is taken as an evasion, dishonesty, or whatever other construction may be put upon "won't look me in the eye." Here I should like to concentrate on the role of social relationships and norms of interaction in defining the status of what is said as an act of a certain kind.

Questions of the status of something as an act arise frequently, not only between persons of different ethnic backgrounds, but also between persons of somewhat different regional or even simply family backgrounds. Sometimes a marriage of many years is frozen into unwillingness to budge on the definition of minor acts of speech. Is what is done or said a neutral statement, a request, a command? a compliment or an insult? a spontaneous act or a quotation? and to what genre of speech-acts does it belong? is it a greeting or a taking leave? is it self-revelation or copping a plea? The difficult and important point is that one often cannot tell the act from the form of the message. One and the same sentence, the same set of words in the same syntactic relationship, may be now a request, now a command, now a compliment, now an insult, depending upon tacit understandings within a community. These understandings, or presuppositions, or norms of interpretation, involve recognition of certain sentences as conventional ways of expressing or accomplishing certain things—from long-established proverbs to lines from popular songs and currently established idioms; involve recognition of some utterances as pertaining to certain genres (e.g., as the opening move in a verbal duel, as bringing a situation under a religious heading); and involve specific ways of interpreting speech in relation to its verbal and social context. The place of something said in a sequence of things said, the scene, and the rights and obligations that are recognized as obtaining between participants in speech, all may enter into defining the status of what is said.

Sometimes it is thought that one can equate sentence-forms, such as interrogative, imperative, declarative, with the status of sentences as acts: questions and requests, commands, statements and reports. A moment's observation shows this to be false. We are familiar with rhetorical questions, which are embarrassed by an answer. If the relationship between two persons is such that one commands the services of the other, or that each feels mutual concern and obligation to the other, then a statement can serve as a polite request, or even command. Employer: "This desk is very littered." Secretary: "I'll clean it up right away." Wife: "The garbage can is very full." Husband: "I'll empty it right away." The meaning of request or command comes not from the sentence form, but from the relation of the sentence (specifically, the mention of the topic) to the relationship between the participants in the situation. Sometimes, of course, the participants do not share, or manipulate, that relationship. In a recent comic strip, the first panel shows Dagwood napping on the couch, with his wife's voice asking: "Dagwood, will you please come here a minute?" The second panel shows Blondie and Dagwood in the kitchen, with Blondie pointing to the garbage can and saying, "Look how full the garbage can is — it needs emptying." In the third panel Dagwood looks at the can and says, "You're right—it certainly needs emptying." In the fourth and final panel, Blondie regards Dagwood again napping on the couch, and says, "Well, at least he agreed with me." Perhaps we can say that the first panel shows a Request-as-Summons, which the second panel shows to have been complied with. Given this first act, perhaps we can say that the request status carries over to the second utterance by the requester, a Polite Deictic Instruction and Description-as-Request (or Further Instruction). In the third panel Dagwood responds by taking his wife's utterance as a Request-for-Confirmation, rather than as a Request- (or Instruction)-for-Action. The fourth panel shows Blondie settling for Confirmation.

This incident is immediately intelligible and amusing to millions of American readers of newspaper comic strips, showing that we do share some sort of knowledge of the status of utterances as acts in terms of rights and duties. The need for ad hoc descriptive labels shows how far we are from being able to explicate our knowledge in a confident and systematic way. And many cases in daily life are not amusing, but frustrating and tension-producing. If backgrounds differ, what is an unsettling fight to one may be an argument showing that one cares to the other. If we are to understand what children from a community are saying, and how they hear what we say to them, we must come to be able to recognize more than the language of what is said. We must recognize how the community norms of interpretation are embodied in speech. It is conflict and confusion as to norms of interpretation that the papers in this book show to be at the root of much of the difficulty in American classrooms today.

To a considerable extent, then, the use of language that is of concern in the classroom has to do with stylistic or social, rather than referential, meaning. It is not that a child does not know a word, but that he pronounces it in one social dialect, rather than another. Not that a child cannot express himself or that a thought cannot be required of him, but that he expresses it in one style of expression rather than another. Not that a child cannot answer questions, but that questions and answers are defined for him in terms of one set of community norms rather than another, as to what count as questions and answers, and as to what it means to be asked or to answer. The papers in this book are largely concerned with these dimensions of the meanings and functions of language in the classroom. In these dimensions, if we can understand them and deal with them well, lie not only much present difficulty and frustration, but also much hope for change. For—this is part of the principle to which reference was made early in this section—*social meanings need not be a bar to full command of the cognitive possibilities of language.* In regard to pronunciation, "dese" and "dose" for "these" and "those" in no way impairs command of vocabulary, syntax, and the logic of discourse. The voiced fricative (*th*) that begins "these" and "those" is relatively rare in English, and at least at the beginning of words occurs in pronominal forms such that it can hardly contrast with *d*. Negative concord (i.e., multiple negation) is quite normal in a number of languages, and entirely clear to those to whom it is normal. In these and many other cases the concern is not with something that is cognitively necessary to the child's intellectual growth, but with something that is considered socially necessary. When one teaches a variety of language to children for whom it is not a normal variety, one is engaged, not in logic, or reasoning, or cognitive growth, but in social change.

Many in the communities from which children come to school want such social change. Many, especially children responding to the norms of peer-groups, resist it. If sheer exposure to a variety of language sufficed, then, as many teachers have observed, children's exposure to radio and television, and to teachers who themselves speak a standard variety, should bring out acquisition of that variety. Obviously it frequently does not. The varieties, those of the media and school, and those of the peer-group, have social meanings involving identities and self-conceptions (cf. Cazden, Bryant, and Tillman, 1972). If children identified with speakers of the standard variety, expected and wished to be like them, to be of them, they could readily enough acquire the variety. If economic and social realities deny children that expectation, there is not much an individual teacher can do to provide it. But a teacher can do much to shape the environment surrounding language and its use in the classroom. The essential elements would appear to be not only knowledge, but also attitude.

As Fishman and Lueders-Salmon indicate, a situation embracing a number of language varieties is perfectly viable, and, indeed, not uncommon, in the world. The problem is not in the existence of multiple varieties of language, nor even in the stratification of these varieties, from locally to nationally acceptable, from least to most present elaboration for literature and technical discourse. The problem is in the attitude held toward the varieties. Is it one of approval or disapproval? Are the several varieties judged in terms of appropriateness to situations, or categorically (bad or good per se)?

I suppose that no one would insist on using the language of an inaugural address to console a hurt child, or very readily believe in the love of someone whose intimate speech resounded as from a platform. We generally have some sense of the verbal analogue of what W. H. Auden put visually:

> Private faces
> in public places
> are wiser and nicer
> Than public faces
> in private places.

In our lives, friendships, marriages, our sense of well-being and moral worth may depend on communications of which utterances that are less than grammatical, less than complete, are essential means. We seek out and avoid persons and places, sense acceptance or rejection, in ways that may depend upon the interpretation put upon speech, as welcome or not, as sincere or not, as honoring or dishonoring the self whose ability to maintain demeanor and offer deference in a state of social grace in inextricable from everyday life (cf. Goffman, 1958). Was I interrupted? unintentionally? Who has the right to speak now? how are turns taken in conversation? Are my rights, or authority, being challenged? Is what is happening a challenge, or enthusiasm? And what effect does my conduct have on the self-understanding of others, as having something to say, as being allowed to use speech creatively? Are the terms of communication that have grown up such as to leave others no way to tell me things I should hear, or they should say?

The ethnography of a situation is not for a non-participant to say. But many instances, in these papers and elsewhere, imply a lesson that is terrifyingly simple. If one rejects a child's speech, one probably communicates rejection of the child. In rejecting what one wishes to change (or to which one wishes to add), one probably is throwing away the chance of change. In accepting what one wishes to change (or to which one wishes to add) for what it is to the child, one probably is maximizing one's opportunity for change.

Herein lies a poignant and powerful implication of the principle that the cognitive possibilities of a variety of language are distinct from its social meanings. What man has made man can understand, said the great eighteenth-century precursor of the study of human language as a part of human culture, Giambattista Vico. Others have added, what man has made, man can change. If such things as social stereotypes, self-deprecating images derived from servitude and subordination, mistaken equations of intelligence and character with pronunciation, rejection of unfamiliar forms of verbal skill, bear responsibility for failures with language in the classroom, then stereotypes can be exposed, superficial traits distinguished from intrinsic worth, capacities for appreciation of one's own and other ways of speaking enlarged. A vernacular can accommodate the vocabulary of science. The language of mathematics has no accent. What is at stake is not logic, rationality, reasoning power, but what we think of each other and ourselves. Insofar as the concern of the classroom is with intellect, there is no necessary obstacle, no cost, to change. But of course the classroom is an expression of community norms, beliefs, values, aspirations, as well; often enough it is a battlefield of contention between conflicting conceptions of such things. And these conceptions run deep, beyond the classroom. If, as Kochman indicates in his paper, Lyndon Johnson need not change his accent to become president, but a black must do so to get an ordinary job, we are dealing with pervasive racism. (Not that white Southerners do not themselves sometimes suffer from individuous attitudes toward their accents, however.) It was and will seem reasonable to many for the stigmatized individual to make the adaptation. When we see the great limitations of this approach, what might be considered its large-scale failure, we may find it reasonable to insist on adaptation as well on the part of those who stigmatize. Without such adaptation, there is little if any hope for the functions of language in the classroom to be sources of intellectual and creative growth for many children.

IV

Attitudes are fundamental, but good will obviously is not enough. The best of teachers can unconsciously convey rejection to a black child while favoring a white, simply through differences in accustomed cues for gaining and giving attention. (Such was the case in the videotaped interaction mentioned by Byers and Byers below.) Hence the need for ethnography of the classroom, as urged earlier. Papers such as these cannot provide the specific knowledge, so much as stimulation to it (a point also urged earlier); and an introduction can hope only to provide a useful orientation to the ethnography that gains specific knowledge. In the next, and final, section of the introduction, I shall comment on the individual papers, but there are general concepts, *competence* and *performance,* and *speech* and *community,* important both to linguistic research and to practical affairs, about which something needs to be said. Let me introduce them by returning for a moment to the concept of verbal repertoire, or, as it should more generally be called, *communicative repertoire.*

The notion of repertoire is recent in this field, and we do not yet know much about the kinds of repertoires to be found in the world, nor much about how best to describe and interpret them. From the standpoint of orienting one's ethnography, the aspects of repertoire noted earlier can be taken as defining general questions to be asked, whether with reference to persons, groups, or communities:

(1) What is the set of means available (to the person, group, or community)? What are the meanings associated with these means?

(2) What are the contexts of situations for communication, including speaking, as defined by the person, group, or community? What meanings are associated with these contexts?

(3) What relations of appropriateness (and inappropriateness) obtain between means of communication and situations (again, for persons, groups, the community)? Eg., as to a means' being obligatory, preferred, optional, or proscribed in a given context? In particular, what is the meaning of the use of one means as against another?

The idea of communicative repertoire can help in identifying, understanding, and, hopefully, aiding what is brought to classrooms and what occurs there. As the parenthetic alternatives—person, group, community—suggest, however, the *locus* of repertoire has been left somewhat in the air. Indeed, one can reasonably speak of repertoire in reference to any of the three. On the one hand, one can (and should) consider the community as a whole, in terms of its contexts, roles, and activities, allowing for a diversity of means, not all of which need be within the command of any one person. On the other hand, one can (and should) consider the repertoires of particular persons, as these develop and change. So much would seem obvious enough. Yet to a considerable extent these characteristics of persons and of communities have been misrepresented in linguistic theory, and the basic terms for them misleadingly used, both by linguists and by others.

The basic term for the abilities of a speaker-hearer has come to be *competence*. In ordinary use, the term "competence" refers directly to what one is capable of doing. In linguistic theory, however, the leading contemporary figure, Noam Chomsky, has defined "competence" in a different, quite restricted sense. The word has been limited to a speaker's knowledge of grammar, thus severing it at once both from knowledge and from whatever else besides knowledge (e.g., motivation, identification, experience) may be involved in using knowledge. These other components of ability to speak appropriately (other kinds of knowledge, aspects of ability other than knowledge) have been subsumed under a common term, *performance* (Chomsky, 1965). And "performance" has been given a somewhat derogatory connotation, as a residual category, and as a term for what to a theorist of grammar is the "mere" event of realizing speech in behavior. It is valuable to have the term *competence*, since it directs the attention of linguists beyond grammar to the abilities of language users, but the definition must fit the term. In sociolinguistic research, the necessary scope of the term has come to be expressed by referring to *communicative competence*. And the term "performance" has come to be used with reference to characteristics of communicative events that go beyond what can be said to be due to the abilities of persons, and that emerge in the course of a particular event or interaction (how it "goes," so to speak), as when one speaks of performances as lively or dragging, perfunctory or meticulous, and the like.

One sense of *performance* is particularly important. This has to do with the uses of language for which a speaker takes (or is assigned) responsibility, and is subject to evaluation by others. Not all uses of language are performances in this sense. A person may disclaim ability to narrate a story or myth, to relate a set of events, to explain or instruct, even though he may say something about the matter in question. In many informal situations among friends, what is said may be regarded as something that can be taken back if misconstrued or inept. In other situations there may be no such recourse. One of the interesting and important characteristics of a personality or community is the set of circumstances under which it regards speech as performance. The extent to which occasions are so regarded may vary greatly from one community to another, as of course may conceptions of what constitutes good performance. The papers on "Black Uses of English," "First-Grade Classrooms," and "The 'Silent' Indian Child" below offer a variety of insights into ways in which classroom definitions of situations as performances pose difficulties.

These notions of *communicative competence* and *performance* readily allow for aspects of communication that go beyond language, and are flexible and dynamic enough to allow for diversity and change in the relations between persons' abilities and classroom contexts. But just as the notion of competence, as formulated in grammatical theory, requires critical revision, so also does the notion of community. The two in fact are connected, competence having been initially defined in terms of an ideal speaker-listener in a homogeneous speech community (Chomsky, 1965). Such a speaker, if actual, of course would have none of the problems that make such a book as this relevant. More precisely, we are concerned with the ways in which persons differ in their abilities, not only in the sense that individuals always do differ in ability, but also in the sense that there are socially patterned differences in ability in any community. Differences in age and sex role are apparently universal, with regard to speech as with regard to other forms of conduct. The forms of competence expected and *allowed* to women as opposed to men are often sharply different. In general it is impossible to deal with linguistic and communicative competence apart from social role (Bernstein is forceful on this point in his paper below), even in reference to a perfectly harmonious community. In an ideal community, perhaps the abilities of speakers and the occasions for them to speak would perfectly match. In known communities, speakers may have abilities for which there is no occasion, and lack abilities for occasions into which they are forced.

One difficulty to be overcome with common linguistic usage of the notion of *speech community,* then, is that it may imply a lack of differentiation, a community of interchangeable parts. A second difficulty is that it may imply that a community is constituted by a common language alone. To belong to the same speech community has been taken as the same thing as speaking, or knowing, the same language. Such a conception was possible only so long as it was not seriously examined. It has become rapidly apparent that such a conception is inadequate. What members of a community share with regard to speech, to be sure, includes knowledge of a variety of a language, but not that alone. Not every speaker of English in the world today can reasonably be said to belong to one and the same speech community; to a common *language* community, perhaps, in virtue of shared knowledge of English, but not to a single community in which members know how to speak to each other.

The source of the difficulty is that knowledge of a common language has been taken as equivalent to common understanding, or, as linguists say, mutual intelligibility. It has become clear that mutual understanding depends not only on common linguistic means, in the narrow sense, but also on common ways of using and interpreting speech. People who know the same sounds, words, and syntax may not know the same rules for interpreting utterances as requests or commands; the same rules for the topics that can be introduced among people not intimate with each other; for taking turns and getting the floor; for making allusions, avoiding insults, showing respect and self-respect in choice of words, etc. In sum, mutual intelligibility is a function of shared means of speech, but the requisite means of speech include not only some variety of language, but also its mode of use.

It follows from such considerations that a person may belong to more than one speech community. This is often the case, a fact recognized by the first great American linguist, William Dwight Whitney:

Nor must the word community, as used with reference to language, be taken in a too restricted or definite sense. It has various degrees of extension, and bounds within bounds: the same person may belong to more than one community, using in each a different idiom (1867, p. 156).

We can begin to analyze this fact more precisely. The verbal repertoire of a person or group may comprise several varieties of language (including varieties of more than one language); sometimes the alternation among these varieties will be according to patterns shared within a group, so that belonging to the corresponding speech community will entail knowledge of both a home and a market-place language, say, together with their appropriate uses. In other cases different varieties and their uses may link different persons, groups, within a larger community, each in different directions.

Those brought together in classrooms, even though having the language of the classroom in common, may not be wholly members of the same speech community. They may share a speech situation, but bring to it different modes of using its language and of interpreting the speech that goes on there (cf. the papers below by Mitchell-Kernan, Kochman, Boggs, John, Dumont, Philips). It may even be that the impression of a shared variety of language is only partly true. Children, for example, may have difficulty judging what is grammatical in the English of a teacher, and a teacher may have difficulty recognizing what is grammatical in the normal English of the children (cf. Labov, 1969; Shuy, 1972). There is no community without a basis in the knowledge and abilities that we have been discussing. Questions of identification and attitude both return. There may be shared rules for a variety and its use, but a simple refusal to count others as members of the community among whom those rules obtain. Many neighboring societies, for example, enjoin honesty and truth-telling, and expect strict adherence to these rules in dealings between members, but do not define these rules as applying to their neighbors. To take an exotic example concerning speech, there is a New Guinea group, the Busama, that comprises two historically distinct groups, alike in basic language and rules of speech; but neither group extends the rules for polite intercourse to the other, and there is constant friction when members of the different groups meet. Ignorance and conflict of rules breed unintentional insult; knowledge of the same rules may make intentional insult unmistakable and sure.

Much of the crisis in schools in the United States today comes from changes in relations between classrooms and speech communities. The conception of speech community presented here, and its attendant notions of competence, performance, and repertoire, may be helpful in thinking realistically about situations. It may help concerning a point made in many of the papers in this book, namely, that it is not just language, but use of language, that counts, and that participation in context, and mutuality, are the routes to effective change. In his paper, Bernstein puts the point in these words: "If the culture of the teacher is to become part of the consciousness of the child, then the culture of the child must first be in the consciousness of the teacher." Put in linguistic terms, if the child is to participate in the community of the teacher, then the teacher must be able to participate in the community of the child. In achieving this joint result, knowledge, such as this book can hope to suggest, and attitudes, for which it can only hope, are, to use a well-known linguistic analogy, two sides of the same sheet of paper.

Let me now turn to the individual papers in order.

V

Perspectives from Nonverbal Communication

To understand the functions of language in the classroom, we need to consider more than language, and the paper by Byers and Byers introduces the general perspective of communication in a clear and telling way. The notion of competence employed is that of *communicative competence;* and notice that the paper is not at all retricted to non-verbal communication as something over against language and apart from it. Nonverbal aspects of communication are emphasized in order to provide a more general understanding in which the verbal and nonverbal are integrated (cf. the examples of teacher-child interaction in the latter part of the paper). Notice too the emphasis on the *process* of communication as the crucial thing, and on mutual interaction, and participation in relevant contexts, as essential to successful growth and change. A further important point is that verbal abilities are often evaluated on the basis of other things, appearance, demeanor, and the like. We know too little as yet about the ways in which such factors are unconsciously woven together in judgments expressed in terms of the language skills, but it is clear that extrinsic factors commonly enter (cf. Seligman, Tucker, and Lambert, 1972).

Cicourel and Boese provide a perspective on the functions of language by considering a language use that is neither oral nor written; this enables them to explore the conditions of all communication, including verbal, more profoundly. Their stress is most particularly on the kinds of knowledge and interpretation persons bring to an interaction, enabling them to understand more than is overtly signaled. The meaning of an act of communication, verbal or visual, is necessarily always incomplete in the overt signs; the meaning is not simply "read off," but completed to the extent that it can be placed in terms of the interpretive procedures that ultimately are basic to all human communication. The argument for the dependence of meaning and function in language on context is here given its most general form.

Cicourel and Boese provide perspective also by attending to the ways in which for a deaf child using sign language one of its modes of communication is a "second language." They consider this problem from several sides, according to whether oral language or signing is first acquired, according to which is dominant, and in relation to the acquisition of signing by those who communicate with the child. The language of the classroom is not the language of competence for a signing child in a special way, but one that illuminates the general problem of disparity in this regard. Cicourel and Boese, like Kochman later, stress the development of the primary variety, which is vital to self-conceptions and personal growth. Like Byers and Byers, Cicourel and Boese stress participation in context as means of change, the need to learn to manage the role to manage the speech, and the need for the teacher to be able to participate in the child's code. It is perhaps not extreme to see an analogy between classrooms in which signing children are taught orally, and classrooms in which children with Indian or Afro-American ways of speaking are taught with white middle-class ways of speaking. Perhaps the children might as well be signing—we see from the studies by Dumont and Philips that they do not speak when taught according to alienating norms by persons who have not perceived or entered into the norms the children already have.[2]

Varieties of Language and Verbal Repertoire

Social Repertoires. Fishman and Lueders-Salmon bring a comparison to bear on the American situation. In the Schwaben area around Stuttgart, why is there almost no concern over the minority who cannot switch into a more prestigeful linguistic variety, and how do the majority acquire this ability? Fishman and Lueders-Salmon suggest that the answers to both questions have to do with specific differences between Swabian classrooms and many urban situations in the United States. In the Swabian case the speech community relationship has long been stable, whereas it has rapidly changed in the United States; and the approach in the Swabian case has long been one of emphasis on the spoken word, starting with the child's condition, with recognition of a functional role for the child's own speech. The attempt has not been replacement or even progressive modification; gaining education is not equated with acquiring the standard variety of language. Language norms are viewed, not in an all or nothing way, as a matter of correct or wrong, good or bad, but in terms of contexts. A variety has the meaning of a kind of situation, or topic, more than of a kind of person. In short, the attitude that informs the meaning of language varieties is *appropriateness,* rather than *correctness.*

Fishman and Lueders-Salmon introduce the notion of verbal

[2] It should be noted that this paper's account of transformational grammar in the section on "Theoretical Foundations" is a personal interpretation of such notions as "acceptable" (distinguished by Chomsky [1965] from grammatical correctness), "deep structure," and the relation between deep structure and intentions (Chomsky does not suggest any such relation).

repertoire, which is taken up and explored in close detail by Gumperz and Hernández-Chavez, first vis-à-vis the meaning of switching between Spanish and English among Mexican-Americans, and then vis-à-vis Black English. What may seem merely interference of one variety with another is shown on close examination to have pattern and meaning, as in the Spanish instances first examined. (It might be highly useful to have close studies of switching among majority group members, too, so as to bring out the common bases of adaptation of speech to context.) The analysis highlights the existence and importance of social meaning. Note especially the findings that the two language codes alternate only as long as all participants are Chicanos, and while the conversation revolves around personal experiences. Such embedding of one's most meaningful experiences in a particular means of speech is common in the world. To succeed in eradicating the means of speech that children bring to schools might be to succeed in denying them access to sources of their own identity and feeling. Note also that Gumperz and Hernández-Chavez suggest, toward the end of their paper, that members of minority groups (who generally have some command of the dominant variety as well as of their own vernacular) may be especially sensitive to the relationship among language, social meaning, and context—a sensitivity that can be in some respects a very desirable outcome of experience with language, and must be taken carefully into account in language programs. Indeed, whereas a teacher might regard use of other than the standard variety as deleterious, the extent of code-switching in her classroom may be a measure of her success in creating an environment of personal involvement and mutual trust in the use of language! To develop a creative and elaborated use of language requires building on situations containing the very phenomena some would think must first be stamped out.

Note finally the observations of two classroom groups with the same teacher and the implications drawn from them by Gumperz and Hernández-Chavez.

Cognitive Repertoires. Most of the attention devoted to differences in language has been concentrated on differences in language and dialect, marked by differences of grammatical elements, vocabulary, and pronunciation. Leacock and Bernstein take up differences in language that are often associated with the kind of difference just described, but that are in fact independent. Within one and the same language or dialect there may be ways of making use of its resources that are significantly distinct in their cognitive nature. Leacock attacks a false dichotomy in this area, whereas Bernstein considers the implications of a very real distinction.

Leacock takes up the relation between conceptions of languages and language varieties as different in cognitive adequacy, and shows correctly that Benjamin Lee Whorf, whose name is often associated with such views (unfortunately even by so considerable a scholar as Fishman, as quoted by Leacock in her paper), held quite different ones. Whorf argued strongly for a determining role of language in cognition, but he rejected any notion of the superiority of any one language in this regard. Rather, Whorf believed that a kind of study that he called "contrastive linguistics" (1956, p. 240) could enable men to transcend the determinism and limitations of particular languages, as obstacles to mutual understanding and as obstacles to deeper understanding of reality. His true view on this is well expressed in a final essay (1956, p. 263):

The scientific understanding of very diverse languages . . . is a lesson in brotherhood which is brotherhood in the universal human principle —. . . . It causes to transcend the boundaries of local cultures, nationalities, physical peculiarities dubbed "race," and to find that in their linguistic systems, though these systems differ widely, yet in the order, harmony, and beauty of the systems, and in their respective subtleties and penetrating analysis of reality, all men are equal.

Leacock stresses the situational nature of abstract thinking, both in our own society and elsewhere. A major study on this point has just appeared (Cole, Gay, Glick, and Sharp, 1971), and it is a powerful demonstration of this point through experimental psychological research among the Kpelle of Liberia. Like Fishman, Leacock notes that the English of black Americans has become a prominent subject in this regard, as segregation of black children's schooling has been overcome, especially in cities. Her analysis of group differences in style of speech vis-à-vis abstractness is further supported by Labov's (1969) analysis of the "logic of nonstandard English." An essential point of Labov's analysis is that not only is nonstandard

English capable of logical cogency, but that Standard English is capable of illogical use. Pungency and point are often on the side of the nonstandard, flaccid pleonasm on the side of the standard. Our contemporary bureaucratic society's greatest danger is lack of logic in the accumulation of standard official language. The point was made some years ago by George Orwell, and his illustration is the best I know (Orwell, 1946). He first observes that:

> As soon as certain topics are raised [in modern English prose], the concrete melts into the abstract and no one seems able to think of turns of speech that are not hackneyed; prose consists less and less of *words* chosen for the sake of their meaning, and more and more of *phrases* tacked together like the sections of a pre-fabricated hen-house.

Orwell then provides a "catalogue of swindles and perversions," summing it up by translating a well-known verse from *Ecclesiastes* into the kind of writing to which the typical tricks lead. First, *Ecclesiastes:*

> I returned, and saw under the sun, that the race is not to the swift, nor the battle to the strong, neither yet bread to the wise, nor yet riches to men of understanding, nor yet favor to men of skill; but time and chance happeneth to them all.

Then in modern English:

> Objective considerations of contemporary phenomena compel the conclusion that success or failure in competitive activities exhibits no tendency to be commensurate with innate capacity, but that a considerable element of the unpredictable must invariably be taken into account.

Is that what one wants as the outcome of the acquisition of correctness? The passage from *Ecclesiastes* shares concreteness, grace, and point with many users of nonstandard English. And apt use of figurative language, such as metaphor, in fact requires a level of abstraction and creativity much higher than the accumulation of bloodless adjectives. Orwell himself entitled his essay "Politics and the English language," because he believed that political democracy was abused by the abstract devices he attacked, and dependent for its health on concrete uses of language.

Leacock's closing example from Scheffler documents the point made by other contributors, that participation in relevant contexts is the key to success with language skills.

Work that calls to differences in language is liable to be taken as asserting inferiority for one term of the difference. This has happened to Bernstein as to Whorf. The present article should dispel such an interpretation.

Bernstein's work brings sharply into focus the diverse functions to which one and the same language can be put, and the impossibility of divorcing the form of messages and conduct from the sub-stratum of cultural meanings (or as this Introduction has put it, social meanings). He stresses the effect of attitudes and expectations on children's success, the necessity of starting from where the children are and of recognizing the situational nature of modes of language use. Bernstein is of course noted for his concepts of *restricted* and *elaborated* codes. Here he makes clear that the difference is not such that some have only a restricted code. The potentialities of both are present and may be used among people of any sort. The true difference is that some groups, including some children, preponderantly make use of one type of code and others of another. In this paper the essential difference between "restricted" and "elaborated" codes is taken as the predominant use of particularistic, relatively context-specific, meanings in the former, and of universalistic, relatively context-free, meanings in the latter.

Bernstein is at pains to stress that the difference is not a matter of formal grammar or dialect. The cognitive differences are not there, but the mode of use of whatever variety, standard or sub-standard, is involved.

It would be easy to conclude that the "elaborated" code, with its universalistic meanings, is simply superior to the "restricted" code, which many of the children Bernstein has studied bring to school, and that the task of the school is to replace the one by the other. This conclusion would distort Bernstein's meaning. Context-dependent meanings are essential to many kinds of communication that make social life, a meaningful personal life, possible. All of us seek out people we can "talk to," with whom much can be taken for granted. It is in the nature of man to need symbolic interaction of this kind. One of the great dangers of modern society is the rapid encroachment of technocratic-bureaucratic modes of communication upon spheres formerly reserved for symbolic communication of the particularistic kind. A life in which all meanings had to be made explicit by the norms of some external rationality, where there was no one to whom one could say, "you know what I mean," would be intolerable.

Bernstein is in the complex, difficult position both of defending the value of the kind of communication he calls a "restricted code" and of insisting on its limitations. His position will please few. Those who defend children by placing all blame on the schools, and those who explain the failures of schools by blaming the language of the children, will both be offended. For Bernstein maintains that one must respect, understand, and maintain the culture of the child, including its "restricted code," but that one must also give the child the essential elements of the "elaborated code" and its universalistic meanings. He maintains that the latter is not "compensatory education," it is education pure and simple.

Let me repeat. Bernstein is not talking about social acceptability, about negative concord, pronunciation, or other traits of language varieties, and he is not saying that some children lack language or cognitive skills. In demanding that all children have access to the universalistic meanings of the "elaborated code," he is arguing for a revolution in power relationships. For in his conception it is the "elaborated code" that contains an elaboration of means for "talking about talk," a meta-language, in other words, for objectifying and analyzing the forms, school, and society at large. Bernstein is saying that the purpose of teaching this mode of language use is not to preserve existing forms of social control and inequality (as it appears to many who see the schools as instruments of repression), but to aid those who are unequal to analyze and transform their situations.

Philips' paper at the end of the book documents a specific case, wherein there is need for respect for and understanding of the culture and speech community of the children, one valid and valuable in its own right, and at the same time need for the children to acquire the mode of language use that will enable them to defend and have control over their own lives in relation to the larger society.

This dual need, for personalistic and public modes of communication, for communication in the sphere of love and in the sphere of power, and to change in the light of them, being different for each person, is not surprisingly very difficult for communities and institutions.

Black Uses of English. Horner and Gussow note the need to go beyond linguistic form to understand actual verbal competence, and present the results of naturalistic observation of the development of language functions in two children, three-year-olds, in a lower-class black neighborhood. Although linguists are right in rejecting the psychology of Skinner, insofar as it claims to be able to explain language, they are wrong in dismissing Skinner's insistence upon considering language from the standpoint of behavioral function (cf. Hymes, 1964). Following Sapon's approach, Horner and Gussow stress that, from a functional standpoint, a verbal repertoire is both controlled and controlling.

The special importance of the study is that it shows the necessity of knowing what goes on outside school settings, even for the purpose of assessing the school itself. (Thus Horner and Gussow note Houston's finding that utterances of black children in rural Florida were shorter, slower, differently pitched and stressed, and relatively emotionless in the "School Register" or variety, as compared to the "Non-School Register," which the children used informally.) Contrary to preconceptions, Horner and Gussow found a great deal of talk with the two three-year-olds in the poor black neighborhood, and much verbal interaction with adults; they also found strong individual differences. Although the two children *sound* alike (in terms of standard versus nonstandard features), their modes of language use are quite distinct, although both are effective. From their behavioral perspective, Horner and Gussow go on to raise, in a new and important way, the question of the relation between the functioning of language for the child in its own community and in the school. How are the novel aspects of language and communication that the child should acquire in school to be tied to supports in the real world? Theory and experience indicate that, without such supports, success is unlikely.

Mitchell-Kernan considers the black community as a whole, in terms of an essential task of ethnography—the characteristics that define varieties and uses of language for the members of the community itself. (Note that Mitchell-Kernan uses the term *code* to refer to language in the narrow sense, and not in Bernstein's sense of a mode of language use.) She knows the situation to be more complex than a contrast between "Black English" and "Standard English," as defined from outside. Within the black community there is a distinction between standard and nonstandard usage, but the standard section need not conform to the prescriptions of the schools; and within the nonstandard sphere there is some regional differentiation. And these "code" factors cannot be considered in the abstract, for Mitchell-Kernan goes on to point out the importance of communicative style, where such "code" features figure less in evaluation than artistry and expressive effect. There is a hierarchy of functions, here as in any community, and aptness outranks correctness. As a number of the papers below suggest, such hierarchy too may be a point of conflict between the patterns of speaking in the community and those in the school, where correctness may supersede.

The nonstandard features persist, of course, not through more error or ignorance, but in important part because they carry meanings of identity and solidarity in many contexts. Features that might be embarrassing in some settings are employed in others to signal personal relationships and for expressive effect (cf. Gumperz and Hernández-Chavez). Kernan introduces a special term, *monitoring,* to reflect the fact that this does not have to do with switching between entire codes, but with selective use of features in terms of perceptions of another's place on a continuum between the most and the least standard usage. Such sensitive ranging from one level of style to another underscores the status of Black English features as bearers of social meaning.

Mitchell-Kernan suggests that Black English norms will approach the non-black standard more closely in grammatical and phonological features, but retain some distinctiveness, perhaps primarily in performance style. It is clear that a few features may suffice to symbolize a separate ethnic identity (cf. Barth, 1969). And there is increasing acceptance of the view that Black English in the United States must be seen in the light of Creole–Standard English relationships in the New World as a whole. It seems highly likely that many distinctive features of Black English in the United States stem from an earlier form of language, created by blacks in the early period of colonization. In a country such as Surinam, where the dominant European language is Dutch, the Black Creole English (Sranam Tongo) has developed its own church variety and literature, and has become a focus of national aspirations (see Voorhoeve's paper in Hymes, 1970). In areas where Black Creole English has continued cheek-by-jowl with other forms of English, the pattern of a continuum, such as Mitchell-Kernan remarks, is commonly found, with a tendency for movement toward the standard end, but, again as Mitchell-Kernan remarks, with individual speakers commanding a range of styles with centers at different points along it. The larger historical and social characteristics of Black English in the United States are to be understood in this New World context (cf. papers by De Camp, Bailey, Craig, and Dillard in Hymes, 1971). The methods of discovering the structure underlying such continua are becoming a matter of major importance in current liguistics (cf. Labov in Hymes, ed. 1971; and Bickerton, 1971). But just because social meaning is involved, the outcome in a given situation cannot be predicted from general trends. The particular social and political attitudes of those involved may vary and change, and upset any *a priori* extrapolation. Mitchell-Kernan draws attention to the variation in attitude among members of the black community in the United States, and the desire among young people for some basis of distinctness.

Kochman focuses primarily on the aesthetic aspect of Black English, and the conflict in aesthetics that can occur in the classroom. His paper is a comprehensive argument for an educational policy based on the use and development of Black English itself. It deserves to be read thoughtfully and thoroughly, and a summary would do it a disservice. The main comment to be made is that there is nothing linguistic that stands in the way of the program Kochman advocates. Vernaculars in every part of the globe have been developed as he advocates, as indeed has English itself in earlier times (recall its subordinate status under the Normans, and the need consciously felt by sixteenth- and seventeenth-century writers to raise its capacities and status). Such a program, however, is a proposal for social change (just as the proposals acted on by many schools now are), and success depends upon political, economic, and social factors, including attitudes most of all. The greatest difficulty may be the opposition of many blacks themselves (Roy Wilkins and the NAACP being a prominent example). The Ford Foundation recently felt it necessary to explain that a program it supported was designed entirely to help black students use the mainstream dialect, and not for reinforcement of nonstandard English, "as some hasty

(NAACP) critics have thought" (Ford, 1971, p. 2). A few years ago one largely black union in Philadelphia threatened to strike at the report that the local school system intended to teach "Black English." As in so many other colonial and quasi-colonial situations, the liberal impulse to value the cultural characteristics of subordinated people may be perceived by them as an attempt to deny them a route out of subordination. Nevertheless, to repeat, if enough black people wish it and make it, American Black English can and will have a standard of its own legitimacy and acceptability, such as Kochman urges. The irony and dialectic of such a situation is that full legitimation and acceptance may be the surest way to motivate black children to acquire the non-black standard as well, as a situational option. Kochman himself would seem to imply that the approach of pluralism is best even if one's goal is assimilation.

In a section on "A Brief Ethnography of Black American Speech Events," Kochman elaborates upon the kinds of uses of speech characteristics of the black community, as noted by Mitchell-Kernan. This section of his paper is particularly valuable. It is important to note that equivalents of "shucking" and the like, under other names, may be found among working-class white youths in urban areas (Beth Lewis, personal communication). The styles and values of Afro-American speech are undeniably distinctive, but we do not in fact know whether there has been stimulus diffusion to adjacent white communities as well, or whether analogous circumstances of subordination may have given rise to analogous modes of communication.

In a section on "Developing a Language Program," Kochman begins with the fundamental point that an oral language program that attempts to replace non-standard forms with socially preferred forms does not develop the child's ability to use language beyond what he is already capable of doing. It is concerned only with how a child says something, not with how well he or she says it. This section is rich with suggestions and ideas; the discussion of Bernstein's notions of elaborated and restricted codes is particularly important. Kochman presents evidence and arguments against any equation of non-standard English with "restricted code."

In sum, Kochman's comprehensive analysis may be read at two levels. It is a compelling presentation of the reasons why any program concerned with language must understand and come to terms with the language of the children and their community, providing fresh evidence and insight for points made in this Introduction and throughout the book. The paper is also a strong argument for a program whose goal is the use and elaboration of the child's variety of language; but here one can only show that such a thing *can* be done. On Kochman's own democratic principles, it is for communities to decide what is to be done.

Varieties of Communicative Strategies

First-Grade Classrooms. The papers by Mishler and Boggs, like that of Horner and Gussow, are empirical studies of speech patterning in concrete situations. Horner and Gussow report on the development of children prior to school, raising the question as to what such children encounter in school itself. Mishler and Boggs provide answers to the question in complementary ways, Mishler studying types of verbal strategies employed by teachers, and Boggs analyzing the consequences of teachers' strategies confronted by the strategies of children of a particular cultural background.

Mishler contrasts a focus on content to a focus on control in two classrooms. There is a parallel to the point that has been made about varieties of language, dialects, and the like, namely, whether the focus is on how well something is said, or merely on how it is said (to use Kochman's phrase); whether the focus is on elaboration of the functions of language, or on their management and control. Mishler goes beyond Bernstein's analysis of the relation of modes of language use to subcultural worlds of meaning, showing diverse modes of language use in the school itself. In Bernstein's terms, the first teaching style (employing a "tree"), in which language is related to meaning as to an ordered universe waiting to be explored, might be described as universalizing in communication about authority. The norms apply to the teacher as well. The second style (employing a "region"), in which language is related to meaning in terms of right and wrong, with the teacher herself as authority, is highly context-bound. There is little elaboration of syntactic and semantic resources, little structure. The third style (employing a "matrix"), in which language is related to meaning in terms of convergence on one correct answer, involves authority, but an authority more independent of the teacher, and located in language itself. The third style might be described as having universalizing and elaborating characteristics, but not as fully as the first. Only the first involves children's knowledge of language too.

Mishler goes on to discuss authority in the classroom more generally. (On this problem, cf. Roberts, 1971.) He contrasts the first teacher as task-centered and the second as directive, with the third teacher again being intermediate. And he contrasts "why" versus "what," to infer the way in which each teacher places herself vis-à-vis the group: the first within it, the second apart from it, the third within it within a yet larger group beyond the classroom. In sum, Mishler brings out sharply the significance of personal strategies and norms, different from each other, yet all within the limits of the general group and community norms.

Boggs turns to the strategies of children themselves. The case is a revealing one, not to be explained in terms of prejudice or poverty. The strikingly poor performance of children in these classrooms must be attributed to conflict in ways of speaking, particularly with regard to performance. Presumably the pattern that is inferred has roots in patterns of communication in Hawaiian families and social life generally. Boggs shows clearly that there is a pattern of relating to adults collectively, and to other children individually, but not to adults individually, in terms of answering questions. The common complaint that teachers just scold them reflects the struggle between teacher and children to define the rules of performance, or *participant structures* (see Philips' paper below), that will prevail.

The 'Silent' Indian child. In their accounts of four different groups of Indian children, the papers in the last section tell a common story, the problem of interference between the patterns of communication of children and those of the classroom, which Boggs' paper has so clearly brought out. Each of the three papers speaks to the image of the Indian child as "shy," and shows the image to be a question of situation. Indian children are alert and vocal when Indian conditions for speaking obtain.

John contrasts the usual schools encountered by Navajo children with the approach of the Rough Rock Demonstration School, where development of the native language and bilingual instruction are fundamental. Another innovation, involving parents, is the home-study week. John brings out the importance to Navajo children of visual and tactile relations to the evironment (an analogous observation is made by Horner and Gussow), and argues for attention to alternative styles of learning. A style of teaching stressing overt verbal performance is alien to such a child. In sum, the Navajo children are doubly disadvantaged, when neither the language of concaptual learning nor the norm of language use is their own.

Dumont follows out the consequences of such a situation with observations of Sioux and Cherokee classrooms. He notes the sharp contrast between the verbal behavior of children inside and outside the classroom. Like Boggs, he draws attention to the strategies of the children, here a matter of excluding the teacher, of exercising control by silence (rather than by interruption and forcing a group relationship). All of this is in a context in which there is no question of children's and families' not taking school seriously. The children are indeed attentive, well disciplined, restrained, and cautious. What is at stake is the students' self-respect, their sense of worth as Cherokee. (Note that here, as in many other situations, identity by birth and by culture are not the same thing. Many Indians are "white" culturally just as there are blacks who do not share in vernacular black culture.)

Like Mishler, Dumont is able to contrast two classrooms, and the strategies of the teachers in each. The key to the relative success of the second is that matters are not wholly predetermined; the other participants in the classroom (the students) have a part in what is done and how it is done. Again, whereas one teacher regards *what* he says as carrying the moral weight, the Cherokee also consider the *way* in which he says it as part of morality too. The words are not only about content, but also a way in which people relate to each other. No doubt this duality of meaning is fundamentally true in every society, but it is often not part of the consciousness of individuals. This teacher's way of moralizing might be acceptable, taken as he intends it, in another context, but it is not among Cherokee, and he appears not to know this. The Cherokee norm of sharing and mutuality in a situation such as a classroom comes out most strikingly when Dumont finds the children to reject indignantly the suggestion that they be taught in Cherokee, because use of Cherokee would exclude their teacher, who did not know it! (Dumont's findings on silence are supported in a related study by Dickerman, 1971. For a contrasting case, cf. Darnells' [1971] observations among the Cree of Alberta.)

The situation studied by Philips is more complex because both Indian and white children, and alternative structures of participation, are found within the same classroom. As does Dumont, she finds the contradiction that schools whose aim is to teach language and to teach through language instead train children into increasing silence the longer they are in school.

Philips' analysis of classroom structures of participation is precise and penetrating. She goes on to show the sources of conduct of the Indian children in the norms governing communicative performances in the community from which they come. Notice that it is not a matter of difference in language, since the children come to school knowing English. But a common language is not enough to make a common speech community. This is a point of importance, since such problems are often thought of in terms of bilingualism alone. Philips shows how deeply rooted and how fundamentally democratic and respectful of individual growth are the Indian norms. At the same time she faces the issue of the prevalence of other norms outside the community. Teachers in the lower grades have some success in adapting to the needs of the Indian children, but this does not teach the children the patterns of communication they will require in the high school levels, where, outnumbered greatly by white children, there is no adaptation to their needs at all. Here in a concrete case is the problem defined in Bernstein's paper: how to combine two sets of values, two speech communities, so as not to repress personal community and worth, yet give access to means made necessary by forces outside the local community's control.

These papers broach what might be called the ethnography of communication in classrooms. We hope that many users of this book will join in carrying it further.

Bibliography

Barth, Fredrik (ed.). *Ethnic Groups and Boundaries: The Social Organization of Culture Differences.* Bergen and London: Universitets Forlaget and George Allen and Unwin, 1969.

Bickerten, Derek. "Inherent Variability and Variable Rules." *Foundations of Language* 7, No. 4 (1971): 457-492.

Bloomfield, Leonard. *Language.* New York: Henry Holt, 1933.

Cazden, C. B.; Bryant, B. H.; and Tillman, M. A. "Making it and going home: the attitudes of Black people toward language education." In J. Griffeth and L. E. Miner (eds.), *Proceedings of the Second and Third Lincolnland Conferences on Dialectology.* University, Alabama: University of Alabama Press, 1972. Shorter version in *Harvard Graduate School of Education Association Bulletin* 14, No. 3 (1970): 4-9.

Chomsky, Noam. *Aspects of the Theory of Syntax.* Cambridge, Mass.: M.I.T. Press, 1965.

Cole, Michael: Gay, John; Glick, Joseph A.; and Sharp, Donald W. *The Cultural Context of Learning and Thinking: An Exploration in Experimental Anthropology.* New York: Basic Books, 1971.

Darnell, Regna. "The Bilingual Speech Community: A Cree Example." In Regna Darnell (ed.), *Linguistic Diversity in Canadian Society.* Edmonton and Champaign: Linguistic Research, Inc., 1971. Pp. 155-172.

Dickeman, Mildred. "The Integrity of the Cherokee Student." In Eleanor Burke Leacock (ed.), *The Culture of Poverty: A Critique.* New York: Simon and Schuster, 1971. Pp. 140-179.

Ford Foundation Letter. "Which English?" Vol. 2, No. 7 (October 15, 1971): 2.

Goffman, Erving. "The Nature of Deference and Demeanor." *American Anthropologist* 58 (1956): 473-502.

Gumperz, John J. *Language in Social Groups.* Stanford: Stanford University Press, 1971.

Hymes, Dell. "Formal Comment." In Ursula Bellugi and Roger Brown (eds.), *The Acquisition of Language.* Lafayette: Child Development Publications, Purdue University, 1964.

Hymes, Dell (ed.). *Pidginization and Creolization of Languages.* Cambridge: Cambridge University Press, 1971.

Illich, Ivan. "After Deschooling, What?" *Social Policy* 2, No. 3 (1971): 5-13.

Labov, William. *The Social Stratification of English in New York City.* Washington, D.C.: Center for Applied Linguistics, 1966.

———. "The Logic of Non-standard English." In James E. Alatis (ed.), *Linguistics and the Teaching of Standard English.* Monograph Series on Languages and Linguistics, No. 22. Washington, D.C.: Georgetown University Press, 1969. Reprinted in Frederic Williams (ed.), *Language and Poverty: Perspectives on a Theme* (Chicago: Markham, 1970); and in Pier Paoli Giglioli (ed.), *Language and Social Context: Selected Readings* (Baltimore: Penguin Books, 1972).

———. "Statement and Resolution on language and intelligence." *LSA Bulletin* 52 (1972): 19-22.

Newman, S. S. "Vocabulary Levels: Zuni Sacred and Slang Usage." *Southwestern Journal of Anthropology* 11 (1955): 345-354.

Orwell, George. "The Politics of the English Language." In Sonia Orwell and Ian Angus (ed.), *The Collected Essays and Letters of George Orwell,* Vol. 4, *In Front of Your Nose (1945-1950).* London: Penguin Books, 1970. Pp. 156-170.

Postal, Paul. *Aspects of Phonological Theory.* New York: Harper and Row, 1968.

Reisman, Karl. "Contrapuntal Conversation in an Antiguan Village." In William Gage (ed.), *Language in Society.* Washington, D.C.: Anthropological Society of Washington, forthcoming.

Roberts, Elsa. *Report on Workshop on Student-Teacher Communication.* Cambridge, Mass.: Language Research Foundation, 1971.

Scarr-Salapatek, Sandra. "Race, Social Class, and IQ." *Science* 174, No. 4016 (December 24, 1971): 1285-1295.

Schegloff, Emanuel A. "Sequencing in Conversational Openings." *American Anthropologist* 70 (1968): 1075-1095.

Seligman, C.; Tucker, R.; and Lambert, W. "The Effects of Speech Style and Other Attributes on Teachers' Attitudes Towards Pupils." *Language in Society* 1, No. 1 (1972): 131-142.

Shuy, Roger W. "Sociolinguistics and Teacher Attitudes in a Southern School System." In David M. Smith (ed.), *Symposium on Sociolinguistics in Cross-Cultural Analysis.* Washington, D.C.: Georgetown University Press, 1972.

Swadesh, Morris. "On Linguistic Mechanism." *Science and Society* 12, No. 2 (1948): 254-259.

Whitney, William Dwight. *Language and the Study of Language.* New York: Charles Scribners' Sons, 1867.

Whorf, Benjamin Lee. *Language, Thought, and Reality: Selected Writings of Benjamin Lee Whorf,* John B. Carroll, Ed. New York and Cambridge, Mass.: John Wiley and M.I.T. Press.

Contents

Series Editor's Foreword   **v**
    Solon T. Kimball

Preface   **vii**
    Courtney B. Cazden

Introduction   **xi**
    Dell Hymes

Part I
PERSPECTIVES FROM NONVERBAL COMMUNICATION

*Nonverbal Communication and the Education
of Children*   **3**
    Paul Byers and Happie Byers

*Sign Language Acquisition and the Teaching
of Deaf Children*   **32**
    Aaron V. Cicourel and Robert J. Boese

Part II
VARIETIES OF LANGUAGE AND VERBAL REPERTOIRE

Social Repertoires

*What has the Sociology of Language to Say
to the Teacher? On Teaching the Standard
Variety to Speakers of Dialectal or
Sociolectal Varieties*   **67**
    Joshua A. Fishman and Erika Lueders-Salmon

*Bilingualism, Bidialectalism, and Classroom
Interaction*   **84**
    John J. Gumperz and Eduardo Hernández-Chavez

Cognitive Repertoires

*Abstract Versus Concrete Speech: A False
Dichotomy*   **111**
    Eleanor Burke Leacock

A Critique of the Concept of Compensatory Education   **135**
  Basil B. Bernstein

Black Uses of English

John and Mary: A Pilot Study in Linguistic Ecology   **155**
  Vivian M. Horner and Joan D. Gussow

On the Status of Black English for Native Speakers: An Assessment of Attitudes and Values   **195**
  Claudia Mitchell-Kernan

Black American Speech Events and a Language Program for the Classroom   **211**
  Thomas Kochman

Part III
VARIETIES OF COMMUNICATIVE STRATEGIES

First-Grade Classrooms

Implications of Teacher Strategies for Language and Cognition: Observations in First-Grade Classrooms   **267**
  Elliot G. Mishler

The Meaning of Questions and Narratives to Hawaiian Children   **299**
  Stephen T. Boggs

The 'Silent' Indian Child

Styles of Learning—Styles of Teaching: Reflections on the Education of Navajo Children   **331**
  Vera P. John

Learning English and How to be Silent: Studies in Sioux and Cherokee Classrooms   **344**
  Robert V. Dumont, Jr.

Participant Structures and Communicative Competence: Warm Springs Children in Community and Classroom   **370**
  Susan U. Philips

PART I

Perspectives from Nonverbal Communication

Nonverbal Communication and the Education of Children

Paul Byers
Columbia University
Happie Byers

In this essay the authors will describe some of the insights that have emerged from the study of human communication in general and nonverbal communication in particular.[1] We will suggest some of the implications of this new understanding for education in general and for the classroom teacher in particular.

One of the authors (P.B.) is an anthropologist concerned with the comparative study of human communication. The other (H.B.) has spent many years in early childhood classrooms, in teacher-training and parent-education programs, and was the director of a community cooperative school in New York's East (Spanish) Harlem. Our own discussions persuade us that the communication model or framework can be useful in redefining or restating some

[1] The authors are particularly indebted to Gregory Bateson, Ray L. Birdwhistell, Edward T. Hall, and Eliot Chapple, whose research and insights have contributed most to our thinking about human communication. Each of these men would doubtless prefer a more precise representation of his work than the nature and length of this essay permits. We accept the responsibility for omitting and restating much in our effort to relate anthropological thinking about human communication to the education of children. We suggest the following original sources for further reading: Ruesch and Bateson (1968), Birdwhistell (1968), Hall (1963, 1968), Chapple (1940), and Chapple and Arensberg (1940).

3

of the concepts of education and can provide new, or perhaps only more direct, approaches to some of the problems in education.

We will (1) contrast an older and a newer view of human communication, (2) show how we arrive at our present view by making observations of imaginary communication situations, (3) describe and analyze actual communication situations involving children and classrooms and discuss the broader implications of these examples, and (4) relate our present understanding of human communication to the present and future of education in general by way of suggestions about "what to do about it."

I

In the recent past the so-called behavioral sciences were focused more on behaviors or parts of people than on whole people. Doctors were concerned with diseased organs or organ systems; psychologists studied reactions to stimuli; psychiatrists looked for and exorcised neuroses; teachers were trained to get the information into children that would enable them to score high on assorted tests and to perform well in assorted subject areas. Human communication was taken to be the study of messages, and almost always these were language messages. While animals might howl, growl, bristle, or dance, people were thought to use language as their principal, if not their only, important communication system.

The stuff of communication was information, organized as facts, concepts, or beliefs and taught as packaged knowledge. Each person was seen to have a kind of filing cabinet where this information or knowledge was stored. Ideally, each person's filing cabinet should contain the greatest possible amount of this knowledge in a well-ordered and usefully cross-indexed filing system. Much of a person's social worth and perhaps all of his education was assessed in terms of his capacity to produce this information, competently encoded, on demand. If some children were difficult to teach, it was because their filing cabinets (at the onset of education) were both impoverished and chaotic or because they suffered from a motivation deficiency.

However one looked at communication or education, the key seemed to be language. Parents competed to have their children speak and read early. Schools still use reading scores as their most significant index of success or failure in the early years. We have come to put such great emphasis on language as our chief communication modality, and we offer such great rewards to children who can construct and perform elaborate and sophisticated messages, that it is possible for some people to believe that even human relations is a verbal-message enterprise.

Talk (and reading and writing) can serve the communication requirements of science, technology, and elaborate civilization-building, but talk alone cannot engender interpersonal warmth, openness, or intimacy. The growing feeling of alienation in our society will not be dispelled by teaching people better language skills.

Today the human sciences are broadening their focus to include the "whole man," and the milieu of his life is not only the environment and the technological extensions of man but a human environment of other live people organized into a complex society. Where once doctors specialized in organs or organ systems, they now also specialize in family and community medicine. Psychiatrists and psychologists are increasingly concerned with a person's relationship to his family and society as the milieu for his mental health. Teachers are now reading about and attending conferences concerned with "open education," where children learn in an interactional milieu more nearly resembling a socially interacting world of people engaged in discovery. Human communication is coming to be seen as the processes by means of which people relate to each other.

With the older approach to communication we tended to think that a message belonged to its sender, who sent it to another person. Our communication research told us a great deal about the human capacity to generate, encode, transmit, receive, decode, and act upon messages as though messages *caused* behavior. But it told us little about human relations. Since the easiest messages to find and analyze were verbal messages, we tended to suppose that verbal messages alone caused behavior and that nonverbal communication was only the unlearned reflection of inner emotional states. It was difficult if not impossible to discover the "meaning" of nonverbal behavior, and without "meaning" it was difficult to think of messages or communication. Even today one finds popular articles that discuss language use in great and even scientific detail, but the same publications do little more with the so-called nonverbal behavior than amuse (or embarrass) the reader with psychological interpretations based on flimsy correlations.

When we study communication as the process by means of which people relate to each other, we must look at the context in which it occurs—the human relationship. And when we examine a human relationship, such as a simple conversation between two people, we almost immediately discover that there are multiple modalities or channels operating in addition to language. We discover that the modalities, verbal and nonverbal, are learned as patterns of the culture (as language is learned) and that they are systematic (as language has grammar, for example). Furthermore we discover that they all fit together; they are systematically interrelated.

A mother holds and feeds her baby; two people enjoy "talking to each other"; a community of mathematicians contributes articles and books to the academic community; a whole society maintains a particular political system. Each of these is a communication enterprise requiring the participation of two or more people who have learned the required cultural codes with some degree of code competence. A person's competence in using the cultural patterns or codes *is* his ability to participate in society's life. When we use this point of view or model of human communication, we can say that all of education is a matter of teaching children to participate in the communication of their human world. And we can begin to see that *the fact of participation, the process itself, is more deeply and interpersonally important than the content of the messages involved.* When we teach children how to participate in communication with others, we are teaching them how to learn. And whatever is learned serves to provide the child or person with the process for learning still more through increasingly higher levels of participation. This is a chicken-and-egg relationship in which the content learned at one point becomes the process for learning on the next step upward. One must know numbers (quantity symbols) to learn to count; he must know how to count (sequence) to learn arithmetic; he must know arithmetic (operations) to learn algebra—and so on to become a mathematician who must master the forms of participation in the scholarly community of mathematicians. But before any of this the basic processes of human communication through all verbal and nonverbal modalities must be learned with an appropriate competence before any subject matter can be placed in an appropriate human context.

If we look at the *content* as the end product of learning, we see people as filing cabinets of information with which to perform certain behavior. But when we focus, instead, on the process, we see people as increasingly competent participants in the human society. When we focus on content, we can stay within the frame of language. But when we are concerned with processes, we must consider the full range of verbal and nonverbal communication.

II

It is not possible to discuss nonverbal communication by translating nonverbal messages into words. This is, admittedly, often tried in popular writing, with the caution that "something is lost in the translation." But for our purposes it cannot be done without destroying the very structure of human communication and forcing nonverbal communication into the special structure and syntax of language. Indeed, the anthropologist who studies human communication never divides communication into verbal and nonverbal, since this division has no scientific significance or utility. He sees human communication as a process involving all modalities or channels of which one (or perhaps more) is called language, speech, or verbal communication. We will use the term nonverbal communication because it conveniently draws attention to those aspects of human communication which are nonlanguage and which are often overlooked as part of the total process. In face-to-face interpersonal communication, these so-called verbal and nonverbal modalities are interrelated, interdependent, and are used simultaneously.

In order to compare and contrast these verbal and nonverbal components of communication, we will imagine that we have a sound film of two people (adult Americans of roughly similar cultural backgrounds) talking to each other for several minutes. Since we are concerned with the nature of the process and the distribution of modalities or channels and are not concerned with particular people or their messages, it does not matter very much which people or what situation the reader imagines. And it does not matter much what they are talking about.

We can divide this sound-film record of human interaction or communication into four sub-records: (1) we can make a transcript of the speech; (2) we can listen to a tape of the speech without the visual part; (3) we can look at the film, the visual part, without the sound; and (4) we can look and listen to the full sound-film record. If the first two records are the language or verbal communication, then the third, the silent film, is the nonverbal part. This is artificial, but it will allow us to make some interesting observations.

When we have only the *written transcript* as our sole access to the interaction in our film, we can do little more than study language messages. We can make some inferences about the intelligence, the education, or the language skill of the people in the film, but not much of their personalities would come through. We could not get underneath the language and *feel* much about them as people.

When we listen to the *voices,* we can get much closer to the personalities of the people. We can listen to the words and their meaning, but we can also hear tones of voice, hesitations, and the rates and rhythms of the speech. As Eliot Chapple (1940) demonstrated many years ago, personality can be described in terms of certain ways in which a person manages his talk with others. Chapple used a recording machine and a controlled test interview to make measurements. But all of us subjectively relate to others in terms of the rate of speech, the amount of talk in relation to the other person (or ourselves), the degree to which one person adapts to the speech rhythms of another, the amount of pause a person allows before speaking after the other person (or the extent to which one person interrupts or overrides the other), the loudness relationship between people talking, etc. Except for the amount of talk, none of these things is in the transcript. These aspects of personality can be heard but not read, and thus the sound record of the speech gives us more information than the transcript. This also shows us that there is more to talk than language alone when we think in terms of the larger frame of communication.

When we look at the *silent film,* we have no access to the speech but we can see two people behaving their personalities. We may not be able to make inferences about their intelligence, education, or verbal skill, but we can see other kinds of information. We can see age, sex, and dress. These tell us something about the subjects in the film and tell them something about each other. We can see their facial expressions, gestures, personal styles of movement, the distance between them and how each person attempts (or does not attempt) to change this distance. We can see how their heads and bodies are oriented toward or away from each other, and when, how often, and for how long they maintain (or avoid) eye contact. We can not only observe these single items, but we can see how they are put together by each person into an individual pattern of behavior, and, most importantly, we can see how the two people weave these individual patterns of behavior together. A conversation is quite literally a dance, and we can watch how the two people do it together. We can see whether or not they fall into common or complementary rhythms, whether their gestures mirror each other, whether the postural configurations of one person follow or are in contrast to those of the other. From all this we can infer something of how they liked each other, whether they regarded the occasion as formal or intimate, what their status relationships were. And when we relate what we can see to ourselves, we will have some (emphathic) feelings about each of the people in the film.

In the silent film we would find some of the same information that we found in the voice recording, but most of the information on which we would base our inferences would be a different kind of information. This communication would come from the use of bodies, which are much more elaborately expressive instruments than vocal apparatuses.

When we look at the *full sound-film record* we can see the people and hear them simultaneously. If we examine this full sound-film record on a projector that allows us to look repeatedly at selected parts of the film and to see it very slowly if we choose, we discover that the verbal and nonverbal parts are closely interrelated. When a person is speaking, his head and often other body parts move to mark the stresses in his speech, and his gestures or body movements mark off phrases, sentences. and even longer speech units. The listener must nod his head slightly or make other movements to signal that he is listening. Even eye-blinks are made at regular points of speech.[2] These elements of communication are interwoven in such a way that two normal people talking together and visible to each other do not (and cannot) break them into separate parts. One cannot talk to another person without moving parts of his body in a regular relationship to his own speech and to that of the other person. And one cannot have a comfortable or pleasant conversation with another person without participating with the other person in an elaborate although microscopic communication "dance" that both people have learned from their culture.

There is, then, a grammar of nonverbal communication that enables members of the same culture to achieve (or avoid) a particular degree or kind of interpersonal relatedness. The degree to which two people can achieve an intellectual relatedness through language depends on learned competence in nonverbal communication.

A person's language skill is often judged by looking (or listening) almost solely at that person alone. A person's nonverbal communication competence can be seen only by examining the communication that is taking place *between* (or among) the people in communication. We are not saying that the great competence in nonverbal communication results in intimate or good human relationships. We are saying that such competence allows people to be predictable to each other and thereby to achieve whatever relationships they find appropriate.

Imagine now that one of the people in the sound film asked the other a question to which the spoken answer was "Okay." In the transcript this "okay" might be ambiguous. In the spoken record we might discover that the "okay" was sarcastic and, therefore, the opposite of the meaning we read in the transcript. But when we see and hear this interchange in the full sound film we might infer (i.e., decode the full range of verbal and nonverbal messages) that

[2] There are many studies of behavior-stream punctuation or segmentation, language-body motion relationships, intra- and interpersonal synchrony in communication, and eye behavior. Two suggested references: Condon and Ogston (1967) and Kendon (1970).

the speaker didn't like being asked the question, that he was ill or depressed, or perhaps that he was really lying. And when we take into consideration a somewhat longer piece of the conversation, we might infer that the person was in a hurry, did or did not like meeting and talking to the other person, was self-conscious about being filmed, was trying to promote (or avoid) a more intimate relationship with the other, etc. And the other person could, if he chose, let the speaker know how he felt about all that was being said—all nonverbally.

One might suppose that this nonverbal behavior was "just natural," and that people do not have to learn how to communicate tiredness, illness, self-consciousness, or many of the other things we observed. But if we were watching two Chinese having a conversation we could make almost none of these observations correctly. The Chinese learn and use a different cultural system of communication, one that is unfamiliar to us, and we have, therefore, called the Chinese "inscrutable." We cannot decode their nonverbal communication. In the past it was not uncommon to believe that an unfamiliar and culturally distant people were primitive or even stupid when the observer was unable to decode the unfamiliar communication behavior. Sometimes people in an unfamiliar culture were thought sneaky or even magical when they could communicate with each other in ways that were incomprehensible to the observer. Africans once complained that Peace Corps volunteers were inscrutably hiding their real feelings because "all they do is smile."

We supposed in the example above that the spoken "okay" was sarcastic. To be sarcastic, it is necessary for the speaker to signal this reversal of meaning by a meta-message, i.e., a message about the message. This signal is only partly in the voice; we can also find it in the nonverbal behavior. Now, on top of the sarcasm it is possible to put a meta-meta-message carrying the information that this spoken "okay" is actually being quoted from someone else and is not the speaker's own word. This requires a separate nonverbal piece of behavior. Then, on top of all that, the speaker who is quoting someone else's sarcastic remark may put a third meta-message—to the effect that he agrees (or disagrees) with the person he is quoting. This may sound complicated when it is broken into components and levels this way, but this simultaneous multi-level, multiple message-sending is a part of everyday human communication. One does not need to *think* about it.

All this multilevel, multiple message-sending that is going on in both verbal and nonverbal channels could not be successful communication unless the listener could keep it all sorted out. He must also be able to keep the speaker informed, nonverbally, that he has comprehended each signal or message on each level, and he must be able to signal the precise point at which he missed something so that the speaker can make the necessary corrections until the listener does understand (or thinks he does). This corrective feedback process is characteristic of all human *vis-à-vis* communication. Without it human communication would be as slow and laborious as two people trying to achieve an intimate relationship by communicating only through teletypewriters.

Imagine, for example, that a person has somehow been reared apart from any other people, in isolation, but has been taught his culture's language by tapes and teaching machines. Then he is brought out of his isolation and presented with another person to talk to. He can speak sentences with meaning and he can understand the word-meaning of other people's sentences. But he cannot carry on a normal conversation and he is certainly not able to get human value-sense into or out of a conversation. He does not know his nonverbal codes of communication, and we would say that "he isn't human."

This bizarre and impossible example is instructive if one thinks of a child who has learned language skills, even perhaps in an educated and highly verbal family, but whose nonverbal competence is poor because adults rarely engaged the child in *full* human communication so that he could learn it. This child's capacity to learn from a teacher would be impaired, and his capacity to relate subject matter (factual information) to the lives of people, including his own, would be limited. When he first comes to school, this child may appear to be intellectually superior but socially immature. He may have difficulty playing the games of other children or he may prefer to sit on the sidelines and watch, and he is likely to engage the teacher primarily through his best communication skill—language. Later on in school the boy or girl may be seen as the shy or easily embarrassed person who does not relate easily to others in face-to-face situations. When people avoid face-to-face communication, we see them as shy or embarrassed when it might be more useful to see that they are uncomfortable simply because they have too little nonverbal communication competence. It is perhaps for these children that the opportunities for communication involvement in the open classroom will be most useful, provided, of course, that teachers do not perpetuate a home situation in which children are talked *to* and not involved in the full range of adult communication.

We have already observed that the rates of speech of two communicating people tend to move toward a common rate (when they move toward feeling good about each other). We could look at the tiniest movements of the two people in our film and find numerous instances in which some parts of the two people moved together in almost perfect synchrony and in a continuing steady rhythm (see Condon and Ogston, 1968).

Present research[3] suggests that cultural patterns of communication are organized on a base of culturally specific patterns of rhythmic organization. It would then follow that individual (personality) variations are varying from cultural patterns. And, of course, there are species-specific rhythms such as heart and breathing rate and the multitude of internal rhythms subsumed under the term *biological clocks*. Individual and cultural time-qualities in human communication are reflected in such things as the time relationship between eye-blinks and other behavior, the rate of blinking, the duration that one remains in eye contact with another person. When walking down a city street, for example, one may sweep his eyes across oncoming people and come briefly into eye contact with strangers, but if one is to maintain the appropriate "stranger" relation to others, this eye contact cannot last more than a small fraction of a second. If this eye contact is prolonged by perhaps half a second, the person being looked at is immediately alerted to a possible threatening change. At the other end of the scale, one can signal a desire for greater intimacy by prolonging eye contact in other interpersonal situations. (Eye contact has been taken out of a pattern involving other accompanying behaviors for the sake

---

[3] The author's (P.B.'s) current research.

of highlighting the time element of a single item. Any *meaning* of eye-contact behavior would have to include the other behavior in the pattern and the context in which it was performed.)

In our imaginary film, then, we would find that if the two people were moving toward closeness or intimacy, we would find this reflected in certain patterns of coinciding rhythms. And, conversely, if they were contradicting each other, we would find rhythmic contrasts—not in words but in communication intent or style. The words have little to do with communication at this level. People can agree in words and dislike each other or they can disagree lovingly.

We can, then, literally see the nature of a human relationship, although at a level that we usually report as *feeling*. We believe that this kind of rhythmic underlayer of communication behavior is the basis for the intuitive talk about "good waves" or "bad vibrations." The waves or vibrations concept may turn out to be quite real, although it is only observable in any explicit detail when it is examined carefully from a film (or possibly TV) record.

We will now look at an example of a child learning to communicate.

<h1 style="text-align:center">III</h1>

The authors visited friends who had a twenty-month-old son. During the visit the child approached the male visitor and with appropriate behaviors got the visitor to accompany him to the kitchen, where, with other behaviors, he got the visitor to find a glass, put water in it, and hand it to him. The child took a small drink, handed back the glass, and returned to the living room with a look on his face that the visitors interpreted as one of great satisfaction and delight.

When the incident was finished, it was clear that the child did not undertake the "get me a drink" enterprise because he was thirsty. He had only a very small drink. We believe that his pleasure was derived from the self-evident proof that he could participate in this communication enterprise. We were told that this was the first time he had done this with people other than his parents.

This incident could be discussed in terms of psychological or cognitive development, but it will be discussed here as a communication enterprise. It will be convenient for the participating author (P.B.) to describe the incident in the first person.

I could not know what was in the child's head, but I could observe that the incident he directed was a sequence of events requiring the participation of two people. To accomplish the "get me a drink of water," the child had to:

1. Get my attention—i.e., get me into communication with him.

2. Establish the particular kind of communication—i.e., I was not simply to acknowledge him but to accept the "listen to me and do what I tell you" relationship.

3. Monitor my behavior so that he could correct my misinterpretations of his signals or messages and let me know when I was right and when I was wrong.

We can also observe that the incident had a beginning and an end. It began when he undertook to get me into communication with him, and it ended as he handed me back the glass. At that moment he broke the almost continuous eye contact with me abruptly, stopped vocalizing, turned away, and walked out of the kitchen.

To get me into communication with him the child stood in front of me, looked at my face, and vocalized loudly. All three elements were required. If he had not stood in front of me I wouldn't have noticed that he was confronting me, searching my face, and "talking" to me. If he had not looked continuously at my face I would not have known that his "talking" was directed at me. If he had not vocalized loudly, I might have assumed that he was merely staring at a visitor. He had learned, then, to combine three nonlanguage elements: (1) a body orientation in relation to me that was close enough for him to touch me and facing me with his body; (2) a search of my face so that he could "catch my eye"; and (3) vocalization, which was loud before we made eye contact and which dropped the moment we made eye contact. That is, the voice change had the effect of telling me when I was doing the expected thing with my eyes. Since he kept repeating the same sounds, I took them to be words. But I did not understand them. His parents understood the words, I discovered later, but they did not translate them for me. The child and I did not share a useful amount of language at the level of word-meaning.

When I first acknowledged the confronting, eye-searching, vocalizing child I quickly looked away, back to his parents, with whom I had been talking. But the child grasped my hand and vocalized loudly again. This served the purpose of bringing me quickly back into eye contact with him, this time to try to figure out what he wanted. That is, he was able to change my brief glance of acknowledgment into a different kind of communication. What I first perceived as "acknowledge me," I now perceived as "pay attention to what I want to tell you." The child had to know his nonverbal communication well enough to know how to correct my misinterpretation and to know when my prolonged eye contact with him meant that he could then proceed to direct me.

Having established the particular kind of communication relationship required for him to proceed, the child tugged at my hand and looked intermittently at me and away from me. This, plus his insistent tone of voice, got me to stand up. Then his voice and movements guided me to the kitchen. He led me to the sink and began saying a new but equally incomprehensible word. I thought he wanted a cookie, but his facial expressions and his tone of voice told me that I was wrong. When I looked at him and watched his gestures, I eventually realized that I was being directed to a water glass and, subsequently, to the idea that he wanted not milk or juice but water in the glass. As I put water in the glass he held out his hand. He took a sip of water, handed back the glass, and abruptly walked away with the broad smile.

It took two of us to carry out this enterprise, which I see as a testing out of the child's capacity to participate in a communication enterprise of this complexity. He had to succeed at several crucial points. He had to initiate communication. He had to correct the encounter into a particular kind of communication. He had to know how to send signals or emit messages and to observe me to know whether they were the appropriate signals and to change his own behavior, his signals, to correct my behavior.

No doubt the child's sense of himself in relation to his human world emerges from his successful participation in such enterprises.

But in addition to his own possession of and competence in these communication skills, there is one further requirement for this learning process. He must find people who will participate with him, people willing to engage in the full range of these communication processes with him. He can learn no more from his adult world than members of that world will share with him. In our enterprise we can say that he had already learned how to organize the various modalities of vocalization, face and eye use, space and body orientation, and body (hand) contact. But only by participating with me could he learn that he had learned. Participation with his parents would not suffice in the same way, since parents and young children share private codes—i.e., his parents understood his very imperfectly spoken words and a single word to them could have evoked the entire performance. This would give him no opportunity to test his communication competence against the larger world of people. Performances that are coded and organized by someone else and rote-learned by the child offer him a quite different and less useful opportunity to discover his own place in the world of other people.

One of the authors (H.B.) recalls a morning at school when a child came into the classroom "with a chip on his shoulder." She apparently picked this up without realizing it in a way that started the day off badly between herself and the child. It is possible that the child had no "chip on his shoulder" but that, in fact, it got there in the first moment of the encounter. We have no way of knowing this, and for practical purposes it is irrelevant, since both teacher and student, in fact, found themselves in communication of this kind. After several minutes of unpleasant and even hostile interaction between herself and the child, the teacher called the child over and said, "Billy, we started all wrong today, didn't we? Please go outside and come in again and we'll start over again." Billy went out the door, closed it behind him, and after a few seconds opened the door again. This time the teacher greeted him with a smile and a cheery "Hi, I'm glad to see you this morning." Billy grinned broadly and the day started again, quite differently.

We believe that the success of this procedure may be possible only when it is clear that the teacher does not blame the child. If she had said, "Go out and when you come in again have a smile on your face," it is probable that the child would have gone outside and cried. But when the nature of the communication about the situation was acknowledged as something *between* the teacher and child, when it was acknowledged as a matter of participation, then the child could expect to participate in the new beginning. In popular language this is called "trusting the teacher." In communication terms it means that the teacher is not dealing with particular messages from the child but proceeds as though the situation is something that exists between them and to which they have both contributed.

In large-scale social behavior we easily recognize that certain kinds of communication behavior are appropriate for certain contexts and inappropriate for others. Every parent is aware of the problem of teaching children that certain things may be said or done at home that are inappropriate elsewhere. Part, then, of the competence a child learns in communication concerns the relation of message to context. It is often easy to recognize the message-context confusion when it is a matter of obvious inappropriateness, but less easy to recognize when the confusion is of a different order. The following example will illustrate this.

A group of children were playing near some adults. There was much whispering and giggling; they were telling each other "dirty" words and knew that such words had to be whispered if adults were near. But among them was a younger child, who learned one of the new "dirty" words and went to his parents and whispered the word to them. The older children had learned that dirty words had to be whispered *in the presence of adults,* i.e., in a certain context. But the younger child had not yet learned that the whispering was related to the context, and assumed that certain words were simply "whisper words." The mastery of the hierarchy of contexts is probably learned in a developmental progression.

As the child proceeds through life he will be required to learn increasingly specialized behavior-context relationships, to learn how to perceive the mistakes he will make, and to learn how to produce the appropriate corrections. At whatever point this is poorly learned, the child or adult is seen by others as gauche, deviant, or uneducated, and his opportunity for further learning is impaired insofar as his world now communicates with him in terms of this deviance.

In a parent cooperative school in East Harlem (New York City) where parents work in the classrooms, a boy in nursery school, Juan, walked up to another boy sitting at a table, Leroy, and hit him. The teacher, who saw the incident and what preceded it, went to Juan and Leroy and asked Juan if he wanted to play with Leroy. Juan nodded yes. The teacher then told Juan that there was a better way. He should *ask* Leroy to play with him, and she told him the words to say. She had seen Juan silently looking at Leroy and recognized that he was uncertain of his language but had a certain repertoire of encounter behaviors that he had learned and which worked satisfactorily in the streets. It is more useful to recognize that the behavior, the attempt to establish a relationship with another child, was learned as appropriate at an earlier age or in another context and that it is not bad; it is simply inappropriate in the context of the classroom and the social situations the classroom represents.

At another time, in the same school, there were two boys who, at the beginning of the year, often behaved wildly and "tore up the classroom." By midyear their relation to the other people in the classroom was proceeding more peacefully. Then, one morning the two boys suddenly swept all the large building blocks off the shelf onto the floor. The teacher recalls asking herself, "Why did they do that? What is different in the room today?" When she looked around the room she saw an adult who was new and a stranger to the class. So she went up to the boys and said, "Do you want to know who that person is?" They nodded yes. The teacher said, "I think you know the words to ask that question. Now please put the blocks back, come over and sit down, and I'll tell you who she is." The boys put the blocks back and went to the teacher, and she introduced them to the newcomer.

Since the behavior of the children in the last two examples could be seen as communication behavior—i.e., related to other people—and since the function of communication is to implement, maintain, or change human relationships in some way, it was possible to discover what interpersonal relationship was sought and to arrange for that relationship to be implemented. Teachers sometimes say, in relation to problem behavior, "What is he trying to tell us?" It may be even more useful to ask, "What kind of a relationship is the person trying to achieve with whom?"

Children must learn how to behave appropriately when being instructed or chastised by parents, teachers, or other adults entitled to instruct or chastise them. American children are required to look at the instructing or chastising adult. If the child looks away, he may be accused of not "paying attention" to the teacher or of "being disrespectful" to a chastising parent. The authors have seen American parents hit children who have violated this rule of behavior. The Puerto Rican child, however, may be expected to look at a teacher or other instructing person, but he is expected to look "respectfully" down when being chastised by a parent or teacher. To look a chastising person "in the eye" would be seen as disrespectful, challenging, or arrogant. This difference in the meaning assigned to a particular behavior is, then, a source of cross-cultural communication conflict. Many Puerto Rican children in mainland schools have been thought disrespectful for doing the very thing that signaled respect in their own culture.

The African child (this is a generalization that is not true always and everywhere in Africa) is taught to respect people of higher status by not looking directly at them. Higher-status people in colonial Africa included fathers, chiefs, and all white people. This meant that when schools were introduced and white teachers were brought in, the teachers often faced classes of students who could not and did not look at them. It is possible that the different significance of eye contact to white Americans and people from African societies has played a part in the history of the relationships between white and black Americans—and continues to play some part today. No doubt the slaves brought to America did not look directly at or make eye contact with their white masters. Insofar as they were excluded from full participation in white society, this cultural practice could continue and would continue to be a source of hidden conflict. That is, the whites could observe that the blacks were "shiftless, untrustworthy, and unreliable" on the evidence of their avoidance of eye contact. This would also support the social mythology that accompanied slavery and the American evaluation of blacks. And it would be thought to have no special prejudicial or discriminatory significance, since whites also interpreted avoidance of eye contact as evidence of mistrust even when whites did it. The problem is, then, a circular one. Blacks cannot participate in white society because they are thought to be untrustworthy or stupid on the basis of their communication behavior. But this is a systematic, culturally learned difference, and it is not possible to take on the cultural practices of another group except through participation in the other culture.[4]

This is not to say that race prejudice stems from different cultural use of eye contact. But it is probably true that differing cultural practices that are quite out of the awareness of the people involved may act as the seeds of misunderstanding or conflict. When one of the authors once told a class of graduate students that Arabs tend to stand closer to each other in certain communication contexts, and that they look more "piercingly" into the other's eyes and can smell each other's breath, one of the students expressed his relief on realizing that a former Arab roommate had not actually been homosexual (an American interpretation of the behavior) but had been only a normal Arab. It is perhaps worth remembering that for every misinterpretation of non-American communication behavior by Americans there is a commensurate possibility of misinterpretation the other way. To the "inscrutable" Chinese the American is equally "inscrutable."

A final example will illustrate certain aspects of cross-cultural communication in particular and will set the stage for a discussion of the part a teacher can play in helping children with the matter of learning his culture's communication codes and enterprises generally.

Some years ago a teacher-training institution was asked to arrange for a teacher and four children in her nursery school class to come to the classroom on a Saturday morning to be filmed while going through a series of customary nursery school activities.[5] The teacher is considered by the institution to be a good nursery school

---

[4] For research showing that certain aspects of the cultural behavior of black Americans is or may be derived from an African background by normal processes of cultural transmission, see McDavid and McDavid (1951), Whitten and Szwed (1970), and Lomax and Abdul (1970).

[5] We are grateful to Dr. Joseph Schaeffer for permission to examine and cite these film records.

teacher. Of the four children, two were from white middle-class backgrounds and two were black children from Harlem. All of the children were four-year-old girls and all were regular members of the nursery school class. They were filmed (and the sounds were recorded) for an uninterrupted thirty-three minutes. Two simultaneous film records were made by two cameras, facing into the scene from opposite corners of the room. In this way the scene was recorded from two opposite directions, and any person moving out of range of one camera could be recorded by the other.

The observations we have made from this film record are not the result of intensive or complete analysis of the behavior. They are the product of many hours of repeated viewing at both normal and slow speeds. We examined this film only to describe contrasts we might find between (1) white children and teacher and (2) black children and teacher. We assumed that there would be cultural differences between the communication behavior of the white and black children and that the teacher's cultural background would be closer to the white children than to the black children. The available information on the five people supported this assumption.

It is important to understand that the people in our film record cannot be taken as typical of (i.e., a valid sample of) white behavior, black behavior, nursery school behavior, etc. We will observe, describe, and discuss only an example of contrasting nonverbal communication that is observable in the film.

Since, as we have said, all behavior in interpersonal interaction is at least potentially communication behavior, we limited our observations in this film to two kinds of events. Since eye-to-eye contact is, in most contexts in white American society, a necessary element in initiating communication, we examined occasions in which each child looked at the teacher and related this to those occasions in which eye contact was achieved and followed immediately by some exchange of expressions. We also examined those instances in which there was any form of physical contact between a child and the teacher. There are, additionally, some general observations.

Observations: The children are sitting around a small table and the teacher moves around the table, often bending down at the waist and sometimes crouching beside a child for a while. Her movements—walking, gesturing, moving chairs, etc.—are smooth, even, and unhurried. The rhythmic character of her movements and the rate at which she walks, moves, gestures, nods, smiles, etc., vary little throughout the thirty-three minutes. All the children exhibit a greater variety of movement than the teacher, but the white children's rhythms are more nearly those of the teacher. The black children follow this general pace but punctuate it often with small, quick movements. When walking or moving around the room, the white children occasionally jump or run and the black children, in addition, break intermittently into what appears to be dancing movement. On several occasions a white child appears to try bits of dance movement in imitation of the black children.

In the first ten minutes of the film the children are seated around a table cutting, pasting, and drawing. The teacher, after moving around the table behind the children, sits first at one side of the table for a while and then moves to the other side. The children have about equal opportunity to see the teacher in this period. One white child is considerably more active than the other, and one of the black children is considerably more active than the other. In the first ten minutes (at the table) the more active black child looks or glances at the teacher thirty-five times and "catches her eye" and exchanges facial expressions with the teacher four of those times. Each of these exchanges lasts from one to three seconds. The more active white girl looks or glances at the teacher fourteen times and "catches her eye" and exchanges expressions eight of those times.

Comments: At first it appears that the teacher does not pay as much attention to the black child as she does to the white child (and that she does not pay as much attention to the less active children of either color). This is true insofar as one is looking at the number and length of interpersonal engagements. Actually, the teacher appears to be trying to distribute her attentions equally among the children. But if one looks closely at the black girl's attempts to establish communication, it appears that they are not timed to catch the pauses or general "searching the scene" behavior of the teacher. When the active white child appears to want to get into communication with the teacher she either will characteristically wait for pauses, or, after glancing at the teacher, will then watch the person with whom the teacher is talking. By watching the person to whom the teacher is listening, she is not only being polite in American terms but she can anticipate the moment when it will be appropriate for her to initiate her own communication with the teacher.

Both the black girl and the teacher look toward each other often (more often, in fact, than the white girl and the teacher) but rarely achieve eye contact and the exchange of expressions that would follow. Although this behavior may be summed up by a casual observer as "the black child gets less attention," it is more useful to see that there is a mismatching or difference in communication systems. We are not prepared, as yet, to try to describe the difference in detailed process terms. Research in human communication is not sufficiently advanced for such a detailed process description. But we can observe that the white child's monitoring of the total scene and her initiations into it are both quite different from and more successful than those of the black child in terms of the subsequent communication involvements.

Observations: Throughout the film the teacher occasionally touches, pats, strokes, or otherwise makes physical contact with the children. When we look at those occasions between the teacher and the white child there is little "search" or trial-and-error behavior. Touching occurs in a smooth flow of events. As the teacher, for example, stands and leans over the table to look into a small terrarium, the white girl snuggles slowly between the teacher and the table and the teacher's hand moves to the girl's waist and rests there for a while. But the teacher and the black girl almost never manage to achieve this. A common sequence is one in which the black girl approaches the teacher, the teacher reaches out tentatively, and the girl jiggles or twists and the contact is broken; the teacher tries again, brushes the girl lightly, and the encounter ends with only fleeting physical contact.

Comments: If we ask "who is doing what to whom?" we can say with equal justification that the teacher avoids contact with the girl or that the girl resists contact by the teacher. But neither view allows for the probability that the teacher and the black child do not share a communication system in which touching is either achieved in the same flow of events or has the same significance in interpersonal communication. They certainly do not use the same set of cues that lead to physical contact. We cannot, as yet, be explicit about what those cues are in either communication system, but we can see that there is a difference.

The authors believe that part of the problem of racism or prejudice in America and elsewhere is traceable to systematic communication differences in cultural communication systems at this out-of-awareness level. But we do suggest that when communication systems are systematically different, it is difficult if not impossible for the people involved to become communicationally involved *at the level* on which the difference exists. But, as we will see in the last set of observations, there are other available levels on which communication behavior is organized, levels on which the cultural disparity may not be significant.

Observations: The black girl we have observed has looked or glanced at the teacher more often than her white counterpart but with less ensuing interpersonal involvement. She has also moved toward physical contact on several occasions and each time the contract has not been made or it has been fleeting. Near the end of the thirty-three-minute film the same girl went to a corner of the room and pinched her finger slightly playing with a toy shopping cart. She stood quite still in the corner (a contrast to her usual continuous movement), and there was an expression on her face that the teacher eventually saw as "I'm hurt." She walked to the girl, picked her up in her arms, and carried her to a chair. The girl did not wiggle or move away but embraced the teacher around the neck with both arms. The teacher sat down with the girl in her lap and with both arms around her, and the girl smiled visibly and nestled her head in the teacher's bosom.

Comment: Here, at last, was a full, successful interpersonal engagement. It did not, incidentally, begin with a direct initiation of eye contact by the child but it flowed from a situation in which the teacher sought eye contact with the girl, who was then in a situation in which both could predict the outcome. One is, again, at liberty to say either that the teacher or the girl initiated the involvement. But the more important point is that at this level of organization both had learned the classroom procedures for dealing with "injured" children in the same way. No fine, low-level cues involving precise expression and timing were involved.

IV

From this last example of cross-cultural communication conflict, and from this essay as a whole, we can see that communication is a process taking place between or among people; it is not a matter of one person sending messages to another. This most clearly emerges from our observations of the attempts of the white teacher and the black child to get into communication with each other in specific ways. Each of them attempts to initiate communication with the other but their communication behaviors belong to different coding systems. Since they do not share the same cultural codes required for a particular kind of shared communication involvement, the behavior of each is not predictable to the other.

We cannot say that either person causes the communication failure or that either is to be blamed for it, although, if either of the two people looks at the other in terms of her own system, the other is "not doing the right thing." If two people do not speak a common language, we do not blame either one for their failure to communicate through speech, but we do tend to do this when the cross-cultural problem lies out-of-awareness in nonverbal communication. When a person is communicating (nonverbally) according to a different cultural system, it is not possible to correct the behavior by changing only some visible component. No single item such as the eye behavior of the black child can be pulled out and "corrected," for this is only one item in a whole pattern, and the only possible "correction" is in terms of that whole pattern. One cannot play chess, for example, if he does not know how knights move, nor can he begin to play chess by learning the moves of only a few pieces. The whole pattern must be learned.

This is the nature of the confusion in the white teacher–black child communication. The two share the same language with differences that do not seem significant to them, and they certainly share the procedures in the classroom represented by the "a hurt child gets picked up and held" incident. But when we looked closely at deeper or more out-of-awarness levels of communication, we found that the two people seemed to be using a different *grammar* of nonverbal communication.

Margaret Mead has pointed out that in contacts between complex Euro-American societies and primitive societies, our whole pattern has often not been made available to the primitive societies. She offered, as an example, the cotton frocks that may be made available to women but made available without the starch and iron required to maintain them in a Western style sense. When the starch and iron are missing it is possible to laugh at or look down on the way primitive women use cotton dresses. There is a parallel here with the white teacher–black child communication confusion. People with limited access to the whole pattern or system of white American communication cannot learn it, and the only way to learn it is through participation in the whole system.

When two people in communication are finely tuned to each other—i.e., using the same modalities with closely matched codification systems—they both experience a sense of liking or at least feeling good about each other regardless of the content of their communication. This is recognizable in everyday life when people say, "We had a nice time together," or "We enjoyed a nice talk." These are comments on the involvement, the communication, apart from its content. We believe that children are also reflecting this when they like a teacher and find her suitable to learn from or, conversely, when they dislike a teacher and therefore find her difficult to learn from. They are, in reality, reflecting the nature of their participation in communication with the teacher on all levels, and particularly the nonverbal part of that communication. This suggests that the more successful teacher, despite her own possible focus on language presentation, is one who is able to participate with children in far more than language communication alone. Such a teacher enables the children to learn her nonverbal communication coding and thereby *to learn how to learn* the subject matter she is teaching.

This, then, provides a partial answer to the question, Why is it important to learn codes of nonverbal communication? It is important because a child's ability to learn from a teacher depends on the sharing of systems of nonverbal codification. Without this the child cannot be certain he is following the subtle interconnections in any presentation, he cannot account for certain behaviors such as particular tones of voice, and he cannot feel secure in what he has learned or what the significance of the learning is.

It is accepted, now, that all of man's communication behavior and all of his knowledge are organized in such a way that he can learn relatively great amounts of knowledge. If all knowledge were to be learned as separate pieces of information and organized only by immediate association, the learning task would be impossible. Instead, there is ordering in a multilevel, hierarchical system. The organization of the processes of human communication in any culture is the template for the organization of knowledge or information in that culture.

At this stage in our science we do not know how to teach the part of nonverbal communication that is normally out of awareness. We explicitly teach only the part that we recognize as proper social deportment, politeness, manners. But we can observe that children learn their cultural communication systems by participating in them and we can assume that children who have not become competent in a cultural communication system are either organically defective or have had too little opportunity to participate in a single whole culture. In the last illustration, of the white teacher and black children, the problem (if one chooses to consider it a problem) is one of cultural difference. The black child doubtless has command of the communication coding systems of her own culture or subculture but has not had sufficient access to the culture of the white teacher to learn all of its nonverbal components and grammar.

We know a great deal more about the structure of language than we know about the structure of nonverbal communication. We teach language performance throughout the formal education of children, but we do not teach communication competence in the sense that communication is the process of relating to other people. This is probably impossible to do in the sense that we cannot teach a person to be friends or to love another person. This comes about, when it does, *between* two people and is not something that one person learns to perform and which he then performs upon another person. So it is with human communication. It happens *between* people, and the competence required is that gained throughout life by participating in communication with other people.

There are, clearly, cultural rules of communication: rules of language use, of mathematics, of manners, of politeness, and of social deportment in general—even rules that make the institution of marriage work for those who share them and fail for those who do not. The rules cannot be judged by the criteria of right and wrong but rather by the extent to which they enable the participants in a conversation, a marriage, or a whole culture to be predictable to each other and hence able to cooperate.

Whether we are concerned with children, college students, or members of an excluded minority, the extent to which people can be (and see themselves as) members of a group or culture is the extent to which they can participate in the culture. Participation is communication taking place between them. It is *not* the messages that pass from one to the other. The fact of talking together is, itself, more humanly significant than the messages exchanged.

The authors believe that the special less-than-adult behavior that is called *children's behavior* in any society (apart from obvious developmental considerations) is determined by the nature of the adult participation in communication with children in that society. And, of course, the same view can be taken for college "children" or members of an excluded minority.

Learning skilled performances and accumulating knowledge are not substitutes for acquiring competence in managing human relations. When this is applied to the education of children, we believe that the only way nonverbal communication is learned is through the full communication involvement of the adult, the parent or the teacher, with the child. To talk to, to read to, to lecture at— these are not participation. They are not full communication involvement. These are performances by adults for children. In order for a child to acquire competence in the full range of human communication, some adults in his world must "take him seriously" in direct human involvement. Only then can a child begin to imitate adult communication behavior and *learn it through the process of corrective feedback.* Only then can a child discover the meaning and values in the messages and the subject matter he is being taught, and only then can he discover himself in the world of people.

Human encounters are creative involvements in which two people put their personalities together. They can create a unique sharing between them that both can enjoy. If a child does not acquire the competence required for such human involvements, no store of knowledge can have its full human meaning. As Alan Lomax has written in *Folk Song Style and Culture,* "In the end a person's emotional stability is a function of his command of a communication style that binds him to a human community with a history" (1968, p. 5).

Bibliography

Birdwhistell, Ray L. "Communication." In David Sills (ed.), *International Encyclopedia of the Social Sciences.* Vol. 3. New York: Macmillan and The Free Press, 1968.

————. "Kinesics." In David Sills (ed.), *International Encyclopedia of the Social Sciences.* Vol. 8. New York: Macmillan and The Free Press, 1968.

Chapple, Eliot. "Personality Differences as Described by Invariant Properties of Individuals in Interaction." *Proceedings of the National Academy of Sciences* 26 (1940): 10–16.

Chapple, Eliot; and Arensberg, C. M. "Measuring Human Relations: An Introduction to the Study of Interactions of Individuals." *Genetic Psychology Monographs* 22 (1940): 3–147.

Condon, W. C.; and Ogston, W. D. "A Segmentation of Behavior." *Journal of Psychiatric Research* 5 (1967): 221–235.

————. "Speech and Body Motion Synchrony of the Speaker-Hearer." Pittsburgh, Pa.: Western Psychiatric Institute, January 1968.

Hall, Edward T. "A System for the Notation of Proxemic Behavior." *American Anthropologist* 65 (October 1963): 1003–1026.

————. *The Hidden Dimension.* Garden City, N.Y.: Doubleday, 1966.

Kendon, Adam. "Some relationships between body motion and speech: an analysis of an example." In A. Seigman and B. Pope (eds.), *Studies in Dyadic Interaction: A Research Conference.* New York: Pergamon Press, 1970.

Lomax, Alan. *Folk Song Style and Culture.* Washington, D.C.: American Association for the Advancement of Science, Publication No. 88, 1968.

Lomax Alan; and Abdul, Raoul (eds.). *Three Thousand Years of Black Poetry.* New York: Dodd Mead, 1970.

McDavid, Raven I., Jr.; and McDavid, Virginia. "The Relationship of the Speech of American Negroes to the Speech of Whites." *American Speech* 26 (February 1951).

Ruesch, Jurgen; and Bateson, Gregory. *Communication: The Social Matrix of Psychiatry*. New York: Norton, 1951; reprinted 1968.

Whitten, Norman E.; and Szwed, John F. (eds.). *Afro-American Anthropology: Contemporary Perspectives*. New York: Free Press, 1970.

Sign Language Acquisition and the Teaching of Deaf Children

Aaron V. Cicourel
University of California, San Diego
Robert J. Boese
University of British Columbia

Introduction

In this chapter we wish to link a few general ideas about the child's acquisition of language and culture to the education of (1) deaf children born either to deaf or hearing parents, and (2) hearing children born to deaf parents. We shall be concerned with several issues associated with the educational problems of both kinds of children.

First, we assume that the principles governing sign language acquisition and use are natural phenomena of intrinsic interest to the understanding of communicative competence in man.

Next, we assume that treating the acquisition and use of sign language as some kind of pathology, as is often the practice in medicine, education, law, and the larger social community, stems primarily from an ignorance of the nature of sign language. This normative bias of hearing persons vis-à-vis the deaf derives from a failure on the part of hearing persons to understand the com-

We are grateful to Marian Boese for her skillful and generous research assistance. Cicourel wishes to acknowledge the support of the Social Science Research Council, and Boese wishes to acknowledge the support of the Canada Council. Both authors are grateful to Pierre Gorman and Courtney Cazden for helpful comments.

plexity of manual sign language as it is used by the deaf in their everyday experiences.

Finally, in making suggestions on how the education of the deaf child can be better understood and improved, we hope to demonstrate that unless a deaf child is allowed to acquire and then expand his knowledge of sign language, he will be deprived of a natural basis for the acquisition of communicative competence in the deaf community, and find himself to be a pathological curiosity in the hearing world. For a valuable and independent statement that is consistent with our views, the reader should see Herbert Kohl's recent statement (1968), and another helpful comment by James Ridgeway (1969).

Native and Second-Language Signing

In order to understand the problems a deaf child will encounter in the school setting, we must begin with some of the problems that arise naturally in his preschool family setting, how he manages to use some means of communication despite the fact that he may be living in a hearing world because his parents may both hear. But let us begin with the case of the deaf child who is born to deaf parents, where both are on an equal footing.

Our observations in several homes lead us to assume that a deaf child born to deaf parents will automatically begin to use manual signs as a "natural" language (providing the parents have not been raised in a rigid oral tradition), just as a hearing child born to hearing parents will use an oral (and gesturing or quasi-signs) means of communication spontaneously. In both cases the early signing or speaking may not be very intelligible to the adults attending such children. The child who is deaf begins to sign automatically, presumably as a response to his parents' signing in conjunction with specific activities such as eating (placing an object before the child, and motioning to it repeatedly so that the child will watch the parent put the object in his mouth and begin chewing) or pointing to an object and repeatedly displaying a sign the child may imitate a few months later.

The initial signs will have some of the same kinds of defects or missing elements or distortions that a speaker will have who is just learning an oral language. The deaf child leaves out various segments of the sign, in the same sense that a young child will often be unable to pronounce initial, medial, or final consonants or vowels. The parallel that we wish to establish is not accidental. We are assuming that the deaf child is capable of spontaneously acquiring a language through the use of manual signs (even with hearing parents who sign) in the same sense that a hearing child acquires an oral language.

The idea of first- and second-language signing has no comparable analogue in oral language acquisition, though we can say it would be somewhat similar to first learning one oral language and then a second. The first signs learned will depend on the parents' education, that is, the extent to which the parents have incorporated American sign language (for the United States and Canada) into their native signs. Spontaneous signs are learned by uneducated children signing with each other or with adults who use signs developed with other adults independently of their partial link to oral syntax, words, and phrases. American sign language is a use of signs that is linked to words in oral syntax and grammatical relations like tense and inflection. We assume a deaf child learns to sign in a "natural" way because the signs to which he is initially exposed are something like an "imprinting" process.

The child's parents, both hearing and deaf, will overlook certain kinds of distortions or deletions intended by the child, and will fill in the elaborations required to make the child's signing intelligible. This is exactly what is assumed to happen with speaking children when they learn various sound patterns that we like to think represent pieces of sentences that the child may not be capable of generating clearly at an early age. The deaf child, then, acquires his native competence in a language setting that is restrictive, and it is unlikely that strangers, that is, signing strangers, will be able to understand his signs very well unless they manage to interact with him on various occasions. The speaking child may not be understood clearly by strangers and his language will require translation by the parent in order that the stranger understand what the child presumably intends. It is necessary to underscore the notion that it is a "presumed" understanding by the parent, because hearing and deaf parents often complain that they do not understand the child of fifteen months, eighteen months, or even two years. The child's generative semantic ability enables him to combine various signs in the same way that oral speakers combine different words to make up new representations that do not reduce to the features or particulars of the original elements of the new word.

The deaf child imitates adult signs very much the way the speaking child imitates oral terms. The parents "recognize" signs as being the same sign that he or she has used with the child, but must fill in missing elements that are assumed to be characteristic of the child's initial "telegraphic" (Brown and Fraser, 1963; Brown and Bellugi, 1964) attempts at language. This child often insists that his father reveal new signs for various objects and experiences encountered on a particular day. Our research is too incomplete to say that the missing features are comparable to the consonants and vowels that a young child will tend to drop in speech. The deaf child's signs, therefore, will be a truncated version of the adult signs, and as with hearing children, the adult will always fill in more than we, as observers, could attribute to the child's view of what is understood.

Our research with one three-and-one-half-year-old hearing child born to deaf parents reveals that the child invents his own signs, which the parents must learn, in much the same manner as a hearing child often innovates with his own speech. What is not clear is how the child manages to build on his early signs and construct more complex signs when he communicates to other children. The deaf child with deaf parents has no difficulty acquiring sign language immediately. His development of new signs seems to parallel the speech of the hearing-speaking child. For example, between fourteen and eighteen months, a deaf child in a deaf home, or a hearing child in a deaf home, can be observed to use various single or truncated signs to communicate with his parents. A two-year-old deaf child in a deaf home or a hearing child in a deaf home can be seen to sign "sentences" requiring two and three words if spoken. Our observations suggest that the child is capable of generating meanings in particular contexts with ease, but it is difficult to describe the signing systematically because we have no consistent notational system nor a clear idea of native signing. The child's ingenuity with sign language seems to be every bit as productive as oral language, despite the lack of standardized syntax. When signing with an adult, the deaf child will make use of many signs that ostensibly refer to the "same" thing, but will adapt the sign to the particular context. Thus, if looking at a book with an adult, the child may produce the sign for *red* when looking at a red truck. Unless a third signer has access to the book, he would never know what *red* signifies in the particular context observed. The signing is indexical or telegraphic, and, as in the case of hearing children's speech, considerable contextual information is required for the exchange to be understood.

The meaning attributed by the parent is not intended to be the same meaning understood by another child, also deaf but older or the same age, witnessing the same sign. The deaf child must learn native signs in the same way that a hearing child learns lexical items and fragments of what we call sentences, if the deaf child is to communicate with the other deaf children or adults at a later age as a "native" and not merely as a second-language signer. But though we refer to "lexical items" and "sentence" fragments, it should be emphasized that we do not claim that sign language is acquired as is oral language, with the same word order and inflections, for such structures are not found among the deaf (Schlesinger, 1969).

The deaf person must learn to sign initially, as opposed to first learning what we shall call the *oral method* (reading lips, speaking, and then reading and writing syntactically), or he will be cut off from the world into which he would qualify as a native: the world of the deaf. Whereas it may be true that every person must at some time in his life come to grips with the hearing world, it is just as true that the deaf child will probably never be at home in a hearing world, but can be just as comfortable in a deaf world. This problem is especially acute when the deaf child goes to an oral school and is forced to learn how to speak, read lips, and read and write, often with a very pronounced emphasis on the traditional oral method (speech and speech reading) and an almost total suppression of the manual sign method. In order to appreciate this problem, we should digress a moment and spell out a few more details of what we mean by native and second-language signing.

By native signing, we mean that a person has learned to sign as a first language, but that the signs used have no necessary correspondence with signs linked to oral language, unless the parents use these latter signs systematically with the child. We assert that the native signer will develop a sufficiently distinctive style to be recognizable in the same sense as persons who learn a speaking language initially and then are able to recognize immediately that someone else is a native speaker. Deaf users of sign language who have acquired this language as children are easily able to recognize other persons as native signers or second-language signers (the use of signs linked to American oral language syntax). A native signer will be able to recognize subtleties that seldom occur in second-language sign usage.

We are saying that a hearing person who speaks one language as a native will not be able to acquire the same native competency to recognize the subtleties of idiomatic expression, double meanings, and jokes in the second language that he has learned, unless we can call him completely bilingual. The second language may be developed to such an extent that the speaker-hearer acquires many of the details intuitive to the native speaker, but this can only occur after rather intensive use of this second language as well as having lived in the second-language country for some lengthy period of time.

If a second-language signer wants to learn the subtleties of sign language as used by a native, he will have to go and live among the deaf and not rely upon his speaking-hearing ability to appreciate the deaf native's competence. The central point we wish to make, however, is that the deaf person can seldom become a native speaker of an oral language because he cannot monitor his own output.

The rare exceptions to this strong statement, a handful of persons born deaf who read lips quite well and speak moderately well, must always be in a postion to observe the other speaker's lips. This is a problem when several activities occur simultaneously.

One of the biggest problems facing schoolteachers who are attempting to educate deaf children through an oral method is that they are often totally unaware that native signs are important for the child's perception and interpretation of his environment. These native signs are central because they involve the child's emotional mapping of his world. In other words, if the teacher expects to understand how best to communicate with this child, he would want to know something about how this child communicates his feelings about his environment, and how these feelings are closely linked to certain kinds of signs that have been derived from a close attachment to his parents and perhaps to some relatives or friends who are also deaf and native signers.

A brief anecdote might be relevant here. It has been reported, and one of the authors has observed, that two children who are enrolled in schools for the deaf can often be found to be signing to one another in such a way as to tell jokes that the teacher, even if a second-language signer, cannot understand. The teachers of the deaf, therefore, who are using an oral method and do not have a clear conception of what we are trying to describe as native and second-language signing, or may not have any conception of sign language, may not realize that the deaf child is in fact converting everything that is being taught to him in what is presumed to be an oral method into some kind of sign system, as in lipreading or the use of his lips to talk. Even a "compromised" oral method that would include finger spelling would be seen by the child as a sequence of signs.

Preliminary Comments on Sign Language Production

The theoretical basis for talking about native and second-language signing draws upon work on generative-transformational grammar (Chomsky, 1965) and particularly work in sociolinguistics based on the sociology of everyday communication; Cicourel (1964, 1970a, 1970b), Garfinkel (1967), and Schutz (1964).

The notion of a generative syntactic element in the acquisition and use of communicative competence in man has been stressed by linguists who talk about a finite set of rules acquired or innate to the child, and used to generate an infinite string of utterances that can be segmented so as to be seen as well-formed sentences. The idea is that the child learns a few basic rules, and with these rules is able to generate an infinite number of outputs that will be recognized as correct speech by a native hearer.

Our use of the idea of a generative semantics differs somewhat (Cicourel, 1970a, 1970b) from the linguistic conception. Our reference to a generative element means that the native signer is capable of systematically building on a very simple kind of sign-language usage (one that even hearing persons partially tend to rely upon if they are confronted with others who do not speak the same language as they do). The primitive signs include pointing to objects and making some kind of arbitrary movements. Now, the arbitrariness of the sign is not always clear. Many times the sign stems from what appears to be the person's ability to perceive certain kinds of motions that seem natural to the object being described. Thus, a rock may be described by closing the fist or by banging the table or making a somewhat circular motion. A car may described by closing both hands around an imaginary object, which we assume both persons fill in as a wheel, and making motions of turning the wheel to the left and right. A road is signified by moving one arm along a horizonal plane and then going back and forth between two points. Driving a car some distance would mean hands around the imaginary wheel and the right arm alternately describing a plane that would signify a road.

The native signer, in other words, is capable of doing just what the speaker-hearer is capable of doing: developing signs related to objects in the environment. But in contrast to oral language, the signs begin as simulated iconic features and movements and then become more abstract with use. Embellishment of the signs employed occurs by the use of para-language elements that may include the shoulders, the legs, the eyes, the head, the mouth, the nose, or some or all of these in various combinations. Signs, like oral sound patterns, take on distinctive features through intersubjective usage. Particular signs, like words, therefore, index or stand for a larger context or a much broader activity. The broader activity indexed by the sign requires that the participants presuppose unstated meanings called forth by the use of that sign. These meanings are relevant to a typified conception of the occasions when the sign was developed. Thus, a sign used by two persons and embellished while developing their conversation carries more meaning than would be available to a third party who came in later in the conversation and was not exposed to the negotiating the two original signers employed while presuming the creation of some common understanding.

As the two signers begin to build on their development of signs in this "natural" and negotiated way, they begin to rely upon signs that are truncated versions of the activities. The signers' reliance on these truncated sign activities signifies that a much broader horizon of meaning is being filled in by both participants than would be available to someone using the same signs in a different context of usage. A parallel case in oral language is the use of slang or colloquial expressions by two persons who have known each other for a long time, where the use of these expressions becomes embedded in contexts available only to these two persons, and neither available nor retrievable to a newcomer who now happens on the scene. Thus, the newcomer can overhear two parties speaking yet not be able to understand what it is that the two parties are retrieving. So it is with the native signer; he and another native signer can develop rather detailed and involved signs that recover for them elements that a third signer would not be able to understand. This problem becomes compounded when a native signer encounters a nonnative signer. The native signer invariably changes his mode of signing in an effort to allow the nonnative signer to participate in the conversation. This means that the use of standard signs adopted by convention leads to more general but less intimate forms of communication. This standardized delivery is like using formal English syntax instead of colloquial or dialectic expressions (Boese, 1968).

The oral teacher of the deaf may assume that she is teaching the child his native language because he is learning to use his vocal cords, his oral cavity, his tongue, his lips, in order to communicate as "normal" people do. But what the oral teacher of the deaf is actually doing is teaching this deaf child a second language. Even if the deaf child had never been exposed to any kind of signing— that is, the child was removed from a deaf environment or never lived in a deaf environment or never had exposure to other deaf persons using sign language—we would still argue that the use of an oral method would not constitute a deaf child's native language. Our argument is based on the hypothesis that a deaf child, because he does not have access to a monitoring system whereby he has continual feedback from his own output, and therefore can recursively monitor that output in such a way as to make changes in it over the course of a conversation, cannot acquire oral language as a native. The oral language will always be a rather awkward means of communication for the deaf child. Indeed, the oral language must remain a strange phenomenon for the deaf child because nativeness (as in spontaneous oral language acquisition) apparently is lost unless there is some kind of reflexive feedback (Cicourel, 1970a).

Perhaps the best evidence is to be found in those persons who became deaf after the age of approximately ten. Such persons learned to speak, of course, but their speaking ability often deteriorates with each year of age and their delivery becomes more and more difficult to understand by native speakers. But their ability to read and write oral language may not be affected seriously. Deaf persons who have learned the oral method are usually incapable of articulating the oral language in the same way as native speakers, but there are a few people who were born deaf who are capable of speaking with considerable fluency. These latter persons are rather rare, and their use of oral language is a taxing activity—not a free-flowing activity that occurs spontaneously, but a difficult means of communication.

We feel that deaf persons probably experience considerable anxiety when using oral language because they have no way of controlling and grasping the technical and social accuracy of their own output (except by monitoring their own lip movement) or how others react to their output. A speaker-hearer relies not only on the monitoring of his own output, but also on monitoring the output of his speaking partner. If the speaking partner's intonation changes, along with facial gestures, then the deaf person will have great difficulty appreciating this intonation, much less the facial gestures. Deaf persons rely heavily upon facial gestures and body movements, but we suspect that these facial gestures and body movements do not carry the same meaning they have for hearing persons. Thus, the deaf person using the oral method is robbed of the hearing person's richest source of information: monitoring his own output and continually elaborating subtleties of intonation, volume of usage, and hesitation, as well as being able to monitor his partner's delivery, in turn, for intonational subtleties, volume, and so on. Thus, we conclude that the deaf person can never use an oral language as a native speaker-hearer can, and therefore an oral means of communication will never be acquired in the same way that a second oral language can be learned. Not having the same kind of feedback and reflexiveness available to the hearing person robs the deaf person of any natural use of an oral language.

We do claim that the deaf person is able to monitor his own signs and the signs of others, along with his partner's facial expression and intonation, body movements, and the subtleties of the signs themselves, and that he is able to find in those subtle movements analogous kinds of intonational and para-linguistic features that a speaker-hearer finds in the intonational elements of speech. The native signer learns various subtleties of signing early in childhood, and relies upon them for communicating intimacy, emotion, subtlety, double meaning, and the like, which a second-language signer would have very great difficulty acquiring unless he spent a considerable amount of time among the deaf.

Theoretical Foundations

At this point we must be more specific about the theoretical ideas we have tacitly relied upon for our discussion thus far. We begin by noting that a native signer or speaker-hearer of a language must acquire not only linguistic and psychological cognitive abilities, but also a "sense of social structure" or sociological cognitive properties. These sociological cognitive properties are essential presuppositions or "interpretive procedures" (Cicourel, 1970a) necessary for the speaker-hearer (or signer) to make sense of his environment as an emergent temporally constituted scene. Our actor (native signer or speaker-hearer) negotiates his everyday (changing) social environment by utilizing interpretive procedures that cut across particular settings, yet interact with the changing conditions of concrete settings to produce practical solutions to everyday problems. The members of a group or tribe or society do not live by social rules or norms or laws that are self-explicative, but must acquire (psychological and) sociological cognitive properties that generate and provide the basis for interpreting rules as guides to social conduct (Cicourel, 1970b). To understand how a native signer assigns meanings to his everyday world, we must specify some of the key elements making up the interpretive procedures used in practical decision-making.

A critical feature of all communication is the *intentions* of a native signer or speaker-hearer. In transformational grammar the speaker-hearer's competence to generate *and* understand utterances is central for communicating intentions. A key concept for the linguist is the notion of a "deep structure," which the idea of competence presumes. The general idea is that the speaker's intentions are formulated according to some base or phrase structure or rewrite rules. The deep structure can be viewed as a more detailed and basic version of what is actually spoken (and heard by the speaker and hearer). This particular linguistic theory makes reference to transformational rules that operate on the deep structure to delete or rearrange different parts of an utterance to ensure that a surface structure (what we can hear and read) comes out to be grammatically correct. Because of our assumption that all communication systems are "indexical" in the sense that what we hear or read can only reflect an indeterminate part of the intentions and understandings of the speakers and hearers (Garfinkel, 1967; Cicourel, 1970a, 1970b; Garfinkel and Sacks, 1970), sign-language users must also possess the ability to formulate deep and surface structures for signs.

Our sociological concern is with the semantic or meaning component of social interaction or a common scheme or reference (Schutz, 1964) possessed by speaker-hearers for projecting behavior (what Schutz calls an *in-order-to motive*), and reflective acts whereby meaning is assigned to completed and on-going action (or *because motives*). The interpretive procedures (acting as a kind of deep structure) organize and implement the projective and reflexive activities so as to link particular social settings and their features with more abstract or general surface rules or norms. The general idea is that the meaning of a social setting cannot be specified by a participant or an observer by reference to surface norms like the rules of a game or legal rules; these rules are not self-explicative, but presuppose some notion like deep structure or interpretive procedures (Cicourel, 1970a). We will outline a few of the properties making up the interpretive procedures, but will not attempt to discuss all of the features.

First, all signers (or speaker-hearers) rely upon a *reciprocity of perspectives,* whereby participants in communicative acts presume that their mutual experiences in the interaction scene would be the same even if they were to change places. This enables each participant to disregard personal differences in how each assigns meaning to everyday interaction, under the assumption that each attends the present scene in an identical manner, at least for the practical task at hand. Following Schutz (1964), A's question provides a basis (reason) for B's answer, while the possibility of a future answer from B provides a basis (reason) for A's question. A's question intends a more elaborate version (deep structure) than what A actually asks B. A assumes B *fills in* elements A has deleted from his own more elaborate thoughts. We never spell out all of the details that cross our mind before, during, and after an exchange with others—details that would include, for example, our relationships to the speaker or hearer, the relevance of the particular occasion, the topic being discussed, the location of our conversation, and so on—because giving details is cumbersome and tedious, and also might prove embarrassing or incriminating. Both participants must presume that each will generate recognizable statements, mutually intelligible to each, as a necessary condition for the occurrence of the interaction, and each must reconstruct the other's intentions if they are to have meaningful and organized social interaction.

Secondly, when we fill in elements assumed to be deleted from the deep structure yet intended by the other speaker or signer, the idea is that an *et cetera property* (Garfinkel, 1967) is operative: the communicants make use of undisclosed details and presumed larger contexts of meaning. A related temporal property allows the signer to ignore or defer judgment on some sign until additional information is forthcoming. Or tentative meaning is assigned for the moment, and then retrospectively connected to subsequent signs. The speaker or signer also draws upon socially relevant and arranged knowledge (Schutz, 1964) that permits temporary, suspended, or "concrete" linkages among future, present, and past attributions of meaning.

Thirdly, all communication presumes that the speaker's or hearer's socially stored knowledge is organized into *normal form* typifications of objects, motivations, goals, and action patterns (Schutz, 1964), mediated by the language and para-language of the participants. The signers (or speakers) seek to normalize discrepancies between their conceptions of "normal" appearances and presumed deviations, enabling them to reject or recognize particular instances as acceptable representations of a more general normative class of objects. The collapsing, typifying activity of this property occurs within particular social contexts, but the signer (or speaker) can make use of his socially organized memory to recognize specific objects or events as the "same" or "similar" and thus subsume a present situation under more general rules. We all make decisions about things like trees, boats, dogs, or persons as the "same" objects or persons despite considerable differences in the objects' appearances in concrete social settings.

The final property we will present has already been anticipated and has been called *indexical expressions* (Bar-Hillel, 1954; Garfinkel, 1966; Cicourel, 1970a). We noted above that everyday usage requires the participants to presume considerably more meanings than carried by the talk (sign system) itself. The production and comprehension of utterances and/or signs are embedded within a larger horizon of meanings, which can give rise to various potentialities because of the occasion of use of the signs or utterances, social characteristics the participants attribute to each other and their relationship to one another, temporal features experienced by the actors, and the social knowledge the participants invoke as "what anyone knows" in attempting to recover, construct, or imagine the meanings to be considered relevant to the interaction. The descriptive vocabularies used in everyday oral communication cannot be understood by reference to standard dictionaries and the syntactic (and phonological) information the utterances are supposed to signal explicitly, but their comprehension by participants and researcher require they be understood as indexical expressions.

The different features or particulars of a setting that are indexed by various expressions are central to the way meanings are assigned by participants and researchers. The features or particulars of a setting not only index a broader horizon of meanings for speakers and signers, but the participants of an exchange rely on these features over the course of a conversation to communicate reflexively the meanings they intend. The particulars that index a social scene are continually used to document or describe the same scene in which they were introduced originally as indexical features. Thus we introduce certain terms like *hip, scared, crazy,* etc., to stand for many details that we do not spell out, and then use these terms as indexical particulars during the conversation to describe our views as if the terms were clear or communicated obvious meanings. Thus, the very terms that are introduced as indexical, yet are assumed to be obvious or common knowledge, are then used to index the setting itself for the participants.

We assume that both the hearing and the deaf acquire these interpretive procedures in order to negotiate their everyday interaction. The interpretive procedures are central for acquiring the nativeness that makes up the sense of social structure mentioned earlier. This sense of social structure, therefore, is the child's capacity to acquire some knowledge, a basic intuitive knowledge, of his cultural surroundings. This "imprinting" process is something that is difficult to acquire the older a person is when introduced to a different culture or society. We have been implying that the deaf child who moves into a classroom setting where an oral method, or even a formal manual method, is taught, but where neither method recognizes the importance of the deaf person's interpretive procedures for developing an intuitive or native sense of language, will surely misunderstand the nature of sign-language acquisition and the child's ability to adjust in both a deaf and hearing world.

We have attempted to underscore some of the critical theoretical issues teachers of the deaf must understand if they are to appreciate the complexity of the task involved in teaching deaf children a language, be it manual or oral. We have stressed the fact, however, that if the first language that is learned is a manual sign one, then the teacher of the deaf must recognize that a native deaf signer will convert an oral system into something that he can manage with his manual system. Unless this principle is recognized as fundamental to the teaching of the deaf, then maximum use of the oral method cannot be realized. Despite the fact that we have stressed the learning of sign language thus far in this paper, we acknowledge the importance of learning an oral method to enable the deaf persons to communicate in a hearing world he cannot avoid, but we are stressing that if a deaf person is to make maximum use of the oral method, the teacher must recognize that the oral method is being mediated through a natively acquired sign system. Some readers will reason that deaf children born to hearing parents may never be exposed to sign language and hence will not convert the oral method into a sign system. We assume (Cicourel, 1970b) that hearing children all acquire primitive signs and use them even after acquiring oral language. Hence it is possible that even deaf children born to hearing parents make implicit use of signs even while learning the oral method, for reading lips can be seen as a sign-detection system.

The Ethnographic Setting of Deaf Social Interaction

There are a number of important ethnographic features of the deaf that we want to describe in order to locate the kind of environment a deaf child may be dealing with when he is exposed to the oral method in his classroom. Another problem is the deaf child, living in a hearing family, who is exposed to the oral method in his home and classroom.

The deaf person's ethnographic setting is basically a pictorial or iconic kind of environment. New signs are generated by a pictorial representation through gestures and the movement of the body, face, head, arms, hands, and legs. For example, the deaf person's nose might be used to signify negation (to the other person's signing), as his hands and body simultaneously continue to communicate additional information. Deaf persons seem to be much more sensitive to the visual field making up their environment. They are very attentive to the location of physical objects and the general movements that other deaf (or hearing) persons express. No adequate system of notation exists to teach deaf persons native signs in a more systematic way, but there have been several proposed (Stokoe, 1960; Paget, Paget, and Gorman, 1969). The deaf person seems to rely heavily on a moving iconic representation of his visual field through signs that mark events and objects with distinctive yet emergent features.

The world of the deaf, therefore, is like a subset of the larger society, a separate society within the hearing one. Obviously, the two types of social organization articulate at various points, but for social purposes the world of the deaf is completely set apart from the world of the hearing. But since both share the same visual environment, there is presumably some kind of congruence between the understanding both have of various kinds of activities they encounter. We assume that the deaf can mark their visual field in ways that are distinctive from that of the hearing person. We hypothesize that for the deaf person the visual and tactile fields, and the smells that occur therein, take on more meaning because of subtle features of movement and form than is the case for a hearing person whose awareness of para-language particulars is so heavily mediated by the intonation features that accompany talk.

The deaf child in a deaf home will be exposed to other persons who are both deaf and signers, thus providing him with a supportive normative order. In virtually every city in the United States and Canada, deaf persons devote considerable time seeking out and visiting each other, and engage in the same activities as hearing persons—picnics, athletic activities, parties, and the like. Even on vacations, deaf persons will always seek out other deaf persons. They will travel far greater distances than hearing persons in order to visit other deaf persons. The deaf seek each other out continuously because it gives them an opportunity to discuss everyday problems and events with other persons who share a common language.

Arranging social encounters is so important for deaf persons that it is necessary to avoid the kinds of barriers that speaker-hearers often erect for themselves when attempting to get together. Deaf persons always prefer to have direct face-to-face interaction rather than to rely upon any indirect means of communication. They put a high premium on getting together, for that is the focus of their everyday existence.

The deaf child in a hearing world, however, has a much more difficult time trying to find out what is going on around him. The deaf child must communicate almost exclusively through a second language, a language, as stressed earlier, he cannot monitor adequately. The deaf person feels uncomfortable around hearing persons, for he is not always sure of what he is being told despite the fact that he might read lips fairly well, and be capable of producing speech. It is difficult for him to negotiate the meaning of the exchanges in which he participates.

When a new deaf family moves into a community, prior notification almost always precedes their arrival. Formal or informal organizations of the deaf will find some way of communicating with other deaf persons in the area, alerting them to the fact that a new family is about to move into their district. If a deaf person is going to move into a new community, he can usually contact a deaf club and obtain a list of persons who are known to be deaf and living in the community to which he is going. Deaf children who attend a deaf school or a hearing school will develop intimate relationships with one another, and it is very likely that these relationships will continue the rest of their lives.

The deaf person who encounters another native signer in a strange city will find an immediate basis for intimacy despite the fact that the two persons have never met before, for the same reasons that an American speaker-hearer traveling in Japan, with little knowledge of Japanese, will find it easy to engage in lengthy conversation with another native American in Japan. The strain of talking in a foreign language is noticeable to anyone who has done any traveling in a foreign country. A native signer who can manage the oral method—that is, who can speak—will experience the same kind of relief when he moves from extended encounters with speaker-hearers to encounters with other deaf persons, *providing he can use sign language*. A critical consequence of this latter requirement is that two persons raised on the oral method will not be able to communicate in the same detail, that is, generating new signs and thus constructing more and more complicated sign talk, because deaf persons raised in the oral tradition are limited by their inability to monitor what they are saying.

We would not expect deaf persons using an oral method to become close friends. We would expect oralists to utilize this method primarily to communicate with hearing persons. This means that oralists would have to acquire sign language if they are going to have intimate relationships with other deaf persons who use the oral method or rely upon a manual sign method. A person raised exclusively on the oral method will find it more difficult to live among deaf persons and draw upon the advantages of a native in an in-group setting. He will not be able to participate in the oral world on the same basis that native speaker-hearers do—he will simply not have access to the fluency required to carry on detailed and intimate exchanges with other speaker-hearers—nor will he have the ability to carry on detailed, intimate conversation with manual sign users. Thus, the deaf person raised exclusively in the oral method or tradition will be rather isolated, and his marginal relationship to both the hearing and the deaf world will make his everyday life more difficult because of obstacles to establishing intimate relationships.

We make these rather sweeping generalizations despite a lack of studies on persons raised in the oral method, because it is difficult to imagine how a deaf person raised in the oral tradition could possibly fit in with either speaker-hearers or deaf manual sign users. The everyday world of the deaf excludes speaker-hearers, and even second-language signers experience difficulty in becoming intimate with native signers. This is especially true if the second-language signer has not learned many native sign characteristics.

For the native signer, it is particularly important to locate the new signer in terms of his native or second-language acquisition of sign language. The native signer wants to know how the new signer came to use sign language. For the native signer, the second-language signer is something of a problem because second-language signing is somewhat formal, and a shift to native signing is required for more intimate communication. If the native signer is forced to use American sign language (signs in correspondence with American oral language syntax) in a formal way, he finds that many of the expressions that he prefers to use among friends and relatives have to be abandoned. He feels somewhat constrained, in the same way that the speaker-hearer who has received a tenth-grade education feels constrained when he must talk with public officials or persons about whom he knows very little, but senses from appearances and the language used that they have more education than he does.

Thus the nonnative signer is primarily accustomed to using normative or formal speech. It is only if the second language is acquired as a child, or through active use outside the classroom, that a second-language signer can approximate native signing. We also find this problem when teaching a second language to speaker-hearers; they also tend initially to learn a formal language system in the classroom, and only with some difficulty are they able to acquire the subtleties of the native speaker. Thus, the native signers will have to change their mode of delivery in order to speak with the nonnative signer and allow this second-language signer access to their conversation.

The native signer, because he feels he is not very well educated—having usually completed the equivalent of the eighth or ninth grade in America—is not likely to question the second-language signer in detail about the meaning of his different signs. This situation of communicating with a second-language signer becomes compounded when the native signer must resort to a written representation of the oral method in communicating with other persons. For these reasons we stress the importance of studying natural sign language usage and encouraging its development among the deaf to generate intimate social relationships. The acquisition of native sign language must precede American (or second language) sign language and oral methods. The necessity of learning American sign language and oral methods is obvious, but only if the native signing is not ignored or weakened. To ignore natural signing is to cut the deaf off from their native culture.

Among the deaf there are varying degrees of nativeness in the same sense as, for example, there are persons who come to this country from foreign countries at different developmental stages. We are quick to notice that someone who is known to have been born in a foreign country seems to speak American English either with a slight accent or with a heavy or thick accent. Native signers make similar kinds of distinctions among deaf persons. A native signer might feel uncomfortable with a deaf person who became deaf at a later age, say fifteen. The deaf make careful distinctions concerning the age persons became deaf and their ability to use sign language.

Native signers also seem to perceive dialect differences. This can mean that a native signer with little education will find it difficult to communicate more abstract ideas with other native signers who have incorporated their knowledge of American sign language into their native signing. Or the native signer discussing more technical subjects derived from experiences in the hearing world may be forced to use more finger spelling to communicate abstract ideas from the larger society.

One ethnography of the deaf (Boese, 1968) reveals that the deaf live like any other human group except that they rely upon the sign system of communication rather than an oral system of communication. There is no reason to believe that the deaf could not develop by themselves a system of organization that would be entirely self-sufficient. The lack of any self-sufficiency is due not to the inability of the deaf to develop various complex ways of thinking and communicating, but to the fact that they are controlled by speaker-hearers and live in a hearing world, which means that their activities are defined from the point of view of hearers, not deaf persons. Therefore, the only kind of communication that hearers can regard as being normal in deaf persons is the use of the oral method. This bias on the part of speaker-hearers appears to stem from the fact that most speaker-hearers are rather ignorant of many of the spontaneous natural language systems that the deaf have developed over the centuries.

Native Sign Language Acquisition and Classroom Learning and Adjustment

Throughout this chapter we have assumed that a teacher of the deaf must recognize the differences among native signing, second-language signing, and oral methods. Second-language signing is articulated with the use of American English as spoken and written by native Americans. Thus far, we have little knowledge about the syntax of native sign language. We have assumed, however, that the differences between native sign language and oral language are comparable to those between two markedly different foreign languages. Because a child's initial acquisition of language, be it sign language or an oral language, is so crucial to his understanding of his everyday world, we believe that a teacher of the deaf must understand the everyday world of the deaf if he is going to attempt to teach an oral procedure or even American sign language.

The problems that deaf children in hearing homes, and hearing children in deaf homes, face are not always the same but are still central to their experiences in school. In both cases a knowledge of signing, finger spelling, some oral communication ability, and the ability to write are essential, in the order given, if the deaf child or hearing child born to deaf parents is to make a satisfactory adjustment. A deaf child in a hearing environment will always be at a disadvantage in trying to use his sign language as a generative device for building complicated and abstract signs for feelings, emotions, and ideas. The development of more abstract forms of communications such as writing and the reading of complex materials may appear to be exempt from this charge. A deaf person, however, will always have to mediate through his own sign system what he is reading and writing in the oral language, providing his first language was manual signs, a situation very similar to that of any oral second-language learner who invariably relies upon his native language in order to express new ideas in the second language. If the creative powers of a deaf person's native intuition are to be realized, then it is important to link generative semantic devices in sign language to knowledge acquired in the oral system. Thus a bilingual signer depends on his native sign language when making use of American sign language or written English.

An example might clarify this problem. In one family that the authors have been studying, it was observed that when a hearing person passed a written message to the husband, and he wanted to explain its content to his wife, he sometimes would sign to himself while he was reading it, then turn to his wife and sign the message. The rehearsal of this translation is what a bilingual speaker-hearer does when he hears something said in his second language and then wants to translate the meaning to a third person speaking his native language. He may not say it out loud, but he nevertheless goes through the translation to himself before formulating it to the other person.

The teacher conducting a class using the oral method for deaf children will make assumptions about intonation and its relevance for interpreting the visual field in ways that the deaf child simply does not have access to, yet the teacher will find it difficult to suspend her reliance on the implicit information carried by her native-

ness as a speaker-hearer when instructing the deaf child whose nativeness is of a somewhat different order.

The teacher who attempts to teach even finger spelling to the
deaf child must realize that if such a child has been exposed to native sign language, and has acquired it as a first language, finger
spelling itself is likely being mediated by the child's ability to recognize it as an iconic representation both derived from and related to
his sign language. The finger spelling can be learned at an early
age (three years, in the case of one of our subjects), not linked to the
oral alphabet but presumably understood by the child as a sign. If
the finger spelling is done rapidly, each movement blends into the
next and sort of collapses the sequence into one sign instead of three
or five or eight individual letters.

A speaking-hearing child learns that his native language can
be represented through written signs. A hearing child realizes that
whenever he sees the written form of the language, he is capable of
establishing a correspondence between the written form and his oral
expression of that language. The teacher must recognize that if the
deaf child has initially acquired native sign language, his later acquisition of finger spelling and an oral way of speaking will be mediated through this sign language. The deaf child, therefore, may
eventually connect finger spelling to his use of an oral language. The
teacher must help establish the articulation, especially if the link is
achieved by first making use of his native acquisition of sign language. The development of native and American sign language can
then help him acquire the oral method more easily.

If the deaf child lives at home, and home is a deaf world while
school is a hearing environment, it is critical that the teacher understand that this child is now learning the oral method as a foreign
language, not as his first language. A hearing child born to deaf parents who acquired native sign language first is also acquiring an oral
language as a second language. But there is a difference between the
two children: because he can monitor his own speech and the speech
of others, the hearing child born to deaf parents should be capable
of becoming bilingual and passing as a native in both deaf and hearing worlds.

If a deaf child is boarding at a school for the deaf and only the
oral method is taught, then we assume this child will experience

many difficulties. Whenever possible, we would expect this child to try and sign to other students who are native signers, despite the fact he may be punished and observed more closely by school personnel. We do not have evidence for this assertion but only a few anecdotes. One anecdote goes as follows:

In the summer of 1968 one of the authors was observing an oral school for the deaf in Buenos Aires, Argentina. In the youngest class in the school, with children approximately two to four years, the observer noticed that two small children were signing to each other, contradicting the vice-director of the school, who only five minutes earlier had told him that none of the children in the school were capable of signing. These children were learning an oral method but apparently had been exposed to native signing in another context or had developed it between themselves. It is logical that we expect them to sign because it would be several years before they could develop proficiency with lipreading and speaking. We can also add, parenthetically, that children who learn the oral method almost never approximate the speaking voice of the native speaker-hearer.

In September 1969 another oral school for the deaf was observed in Buenos Aires, but in contrast to the first school, manual signing was permitted. The signing was not taught at this school, but learned and promoted by children. Sign language, however, is not taught in Argentina.

Recently one of the authors discovered a deaf family in southern California with four deaf children. Only the two oldest children had just begun to master some of the oral method. The parents had little education, having never attended a school for the deaf nor obtained any kind of formal education and instruction, so neither of them could read nor write, and their signing was at first incomprehensible. The family members, however, had developed their own sign system. After several visits it was possible to negotiate enough signs to establish a basis for conversation, but the task was a slow one. The children are being taught the oral method in a local public school, but without their family sign language system, contact between children and parents would be quite difficult.

Learning the oral method is necessary for daily contact with the oral world and as a basis for an education, but there is no substitute for native sign language and the ability to switch to formal signs in semicorrespondence with standard oral syntax. We are not saying that the oral method should not be encouraged; on the contrary, we are saying that some proficiency in the oral method is obviously necessary for any deaf person because he must negotiate with the hearing world. But the oral method should never be taught at the expense of native and second-language signing.

Hearing persons tend to be ethnocentric about the necessity of speaking and hearing; they attach pathological significance to the fact that a person is deaf. It is difficult for a speaker-hearer to accept the idea that deaf persons are quite capable of living a complex existence quite apart from hearing persons. For the speaker-hearer there is only one "normal" life, and that is through the use of speech and hearing. Yet the number of deaf persons appears to be increasing, and efforts to eliminate a loss of hearing have not been successful. Clearly we need teaching procedures that will coordinate sign-language acquisition with the oral method.

For the teacher who must deal with the deaf child on a day-to-day basis, it is difficult to avoid imposing on this child the teacher's conception of hearing and speaking. It is difficult for the teacher to avoid assumptions that the deaf child is someone who is to be pitied, someone who must be treated as a pathological case. The difficult experiences that an oral teacher of the deaf can have might be minimized if he would observe and study a sign-language environment: deaf children, proficient in native sign language, conversing with one another and playing together.

The teacher of the deaf might modify the oral curriculum for deaf children who have acquired native signs by teaching such a child American sign language. American sign language is like any oral formal grammar, but it tends to be more abstract than the native signs acquired by a native signer because it tends to use categories that are not easy for the native signer to understand. The use of American sign language would enable the deaf child to generalize and deepen his native competence through his natural means of communication, and thus have links to a language that builds on his native system yet has its own organized procedures for generating language outputs. Because American sign language is directly linked to American English syntax, it is easy to teach such a child finger spelling (and thus the alphabet) before he is ever taught to speak. If the deaf student can move from finger spelling to American sign language to writing English, then speaking the language should be acquired more easily.

Learning to finger spell can be independent of syntax, and the teacher should recognize that finger spelling can be incorporated into a native sign system because the movements making up a word have no necessary connection with the oral grammatical properties of the word. The relationship between lexical items in a dictionary and grammatical rules must be linked to finger spelling through classroom instruction. This kind of program is not followed by many schools for the deaf, although schools exist where both sign language and the oral method are taught. The teaching situation is most deficient in public schools, where the oral method usually is the only language to which the child is exposed.

Unless the teacher of the deaf recognizes that the deaf child has acquired a native competence with sign language, he will not be able to make use of this nativeness in teaching the child other languages. We are all accustomed to negotiating our own language output when faced with different interaction settings. This negotiation takes the form of saying things and then recognizing that it does not "quite sound right," and then we begin correcting our output. It is not uncommon to hear speakers correct themselves throughout a dialogue. The deaf child put directly into an oral school, or an oral-method user who does not acquire American sign language first, should make very slow progress learning to use the oral language for negotiating interactional sequences.

Summary and Conclusions

Throughout this chapter we have assumed that the acquisition of any language, be it oral or sign, necessitates a theory that must include some of the properties we have described as interpretive procedures. We claim that these interpretive procedures are basic for the acquisition of communicative competence by the child. A hearing child will develop a competence for hearing and speaking enabling him to generate verbal outputs that will index elements of the experiences and activities such verbal outputs describe. The child acts on those outputs to build up more complex ideas that can transcend the initial and subsequent context-sensitive settings, yet that require particulars of meaning that can be located and made relevant to the occasion of use, the particular participants, their social characteristics, and their relationship to one another. The deaf child's acquisition of sign language follows the same development and can be summarized as follows:

1. The surface appearances of signs presume a wider horizon of meaning (deep structure) for the participants and the recipient by what they presume to see.

2. The child must acquire the ability to develop and remember signs, and remember particulars associated with these signs in such a way that a sign will not only be invoked but the particulars in later contexts will be filled in, leading to the assumption that the recipient of the sign will locate it in a context that both the signer and recipient presumably know, but never state to each other. This means that individual signs or their combination, used in a particular context, recover for the participants a larger horizon of meanings than may be observable by a third party who has not shared the same kind of experiences that the two participants have.

3. The child's use of interpretive procedures is developmental. As he grows older, he acquires more and more complicated forms of expression and meanings so he can approximate adult thinking and use of common-sense rules. This developmental acquisition of meaning, therefore, allows the child to appreciate more and more subtle kinds of activities, such as jokes, double meanings, and ironies.

One way that a teacher of the deaf can better articulate sign-language usage already acquired by the child with the oral method the teacher wishes to teach the child, would be to find out what the child's signs are for different kinds of events and objects. Since these signs and objects are known to the child, the teacher can utilize them in order to motivate the child to practice an oral representation of these same objects. The teacher can make use of the child's native knowledge of sign language to show the child what an object's sign would look like in American sign language, and how that sign can be finger spelled and then directly linked to individual letters making up a word that would be pronounced by the teacher and practiced by the child. The child would be able to utilize his nativeness to make the transition from his knowledge of objects and events to American sign language and finger spelling, and finally the individual letters that the finger spelling represents, and then make up words that can be spoken.

The child who has already acquired native sign language cannot be taught an oral method adequately unless the teacher of the oral method somehow is able to link the oral method with the native signs the child has already acquired. In this way the teacher will ensure that the child's acquisition of interpretive procedures will continue to develop and that he will make use of his knowledge of native signs while learning American signs and the oral language. Unless the teacher makes use of the native's ability to assign meaning to his environment via his use of signs, it will be impossible for this child to move from the deaf world to the hearing world and make maximum use of his native intelligence in a deaf world.

Treating the deaf person's native language as a natural language will enable the teacher to give the child considerable confidence about his own abilities. By showing the child he has already mastered one language, he can be shown that he, unlike other children, is learning two languages at a very early age. If the child's sign lanquage is encouraged and developed by linking it to normative American sign language, and then finger spelling, and then finally the oral representation of what is finger spelled, the deaf child should be able to move between the deaf and the oral world with relative ease as a bilingual, and not feel as marginal to the oral world as he is likely to feel if his first and only language is native sign language.

We have tried to convince the reader that the current conception of the deaf, their use of sign language, and the attempt on the part of most hearing persons to impose an oral system on deaf persons should be reviewed so as to make a place for sign-language usage and its place in the education of deaf children. The deaf person, therefore, must be a bilingual if he is to adjust in a hearing world. This bilingualism will enable him to adapt himself to a deaf world as a native, and then enable him to adapt to a hearing world where he will always be somewhat of a foreigner who has acquired a second language. Unless the school teacher can recognize the fact that the child must live in two worlds, and orient his teaching of the oral and/or American sign language to those two worlds, the child will always be the loser.

At the present time in the United States and Canada there is virtually no agreement as to how deaf children should be instructed. This lack of agreement has led to rival factions, often called the manualists and the oralists. While these two factions struggle at various levels, both economically and politically, to control the teaching of the deaf, it is the deaf child who is suffering because of the fact that he must live in both a deaf and a hearing world, and yet the teachers he must learn from have not paid close attention to the fact that, as a native signer, he has already acquired a language that is every bit as complicated as an oral-written one. Rather than treat the deaf child as some kind of anomaly or pathology, we should instead treat him as a remarkable person capable of very complicated bilingualism. This bilingualism can become a critical basis for our understanding of general communicative competence in all humans.

It is our claim that native sign language is a valuable resource for our understanding of communicative competence in man. As Lenneberg (1969) has stated: "We know there is just one species *Homo sapiens,* and it is therefore reasonable to assume that individuals who speak Turkish, English, or Basque . . . all have the same kind of brain. . . ." The strong implication we draw from Lenneberg is that as every "normal" child learns the language to which he is exposed, so the child born deaf acquires a natural native sign language. If we are to understand the nature of human communication, sign language, particularly native sign language, can become the focal point of any interest in universal properties of language.

Finally, many of these arguments apply to groups other than the deaf. For instance, the language of the blind includes visual elements presupposed by the user that cannot be monitored unless visual experiences are integral to language use and the attribution of meaning by speaker-hearers. The blind are bilingual in the peculiar sense that their use of oral language seems to be quite effective, yet their experience of the everyday world requires kinesthetic, somesthetic, and auditory skills that are not easily stated as linguistic information. To say they are bilingual is to imply that other modalities take on the functions of a "language" that we know little about. Although we have no way of describing touch, movement, and sound as elements of language, they may function as such for the blind. More obviously, the arguments apply to the children of minority groups whose first language or dialect must be recognized and accepted in school.

Bibliography

Bar-Hillel, Y. "Indexical Expressions." *Mind* 63 (1954): 359–379.

Boese, Robert J. "Towards An Ethnography of the Deaf." Master's thesis, Department of Sociology, University of California at Santa Barbara, 1968.

Brown, Roger; and Bellugi, Ursula. "Three Processes in the Child's Acquisition of Syntax." In Eric Lenneberg (ed.), *New Directions in the Study of Language*. Cambridge, Mass.: MIT Press, 1964.

Brown, Roger; and Fraser, C. "The Acquisition of Syntax." In C. N. Cofer and B. S. Musgrave (eds.), *Verbal Behavior and Learning*. New York: McGraw-Hill, 1963.

Chomsky, Noam. *Aspects of the Theory of Syntax*. Cambridge, Mass.: MIT Press, 1965.

Cicourel, Aaron V. *Method and Measurement in Sociology*. New York: The Free Press, 1964.

———. "The Acquisition of Social Structure: Towards a Developmental Sociology of Language and Meaning." In Jack D. Douglas (ed.), *Understanding Everyday Life*. Chicago: Aldine, 1970a. (English version of "L'acquisizione della struttural sociale. Verso una sociologia evolutiva del linguaggio e del significato." *Rassegna Italiana di Sociologia* 9 [April-June 1968]: 211–258.)

———. "Generative Semantics and the Structure of Social Interaction." Paper read at International Days of Sociolinguistics, *Luigi Sturzo Institute*, Rome, September 1969. Published in the proceedings of the conference, 1970b.

———. "Ethnomethodology." In *Current Trends in Linguistics*. Vol. 12. The Hague: Mouton and Co., forthcoming.

Garfinkel, Harold. Lectures, 1966. Mimeographed.

———. *Studies in Ethnomethodology*. Englewood Cliffs, N.J.: Prentice-Hall, 1967.

Garfinkel, H.; and Sacks, H. "On Formal Structures of Practical Actions." In J. C. McKinney and E. Tiryakian (eds.), *Theoretical Sociology: Perspectives and Development*. New York: Appleton-Century-Crofts, 1970.

Gumperz, John J.; and Blom, Jan-Petter. "Some Social Determinants of Verbal Behavior." In J. J. Gumperz and D. Hymes (eds.), *Directions in Sociolinguistics*. New York: Holt, Rinehart and Winston, 1970.

Kohl, H. R. *Language and Education of the Deaf*. New York: The Center for Urban Education, 1966.

Lenneberg, Eric H. "On Explaining Language." *Science* 164 (May 9, 1969): 635–643.

Paget, R.; Paget, G.; and Gorman, P. "A Systematic Sign Language." London, 1969. Mimeographed (4th ed.).

Ridgeway, James. "Dumb Children." *The New Republic,* August 2, 1969: 19–21.

Schlesinger, I. M. "The Grammar of Sign Language: Some Implications for the Theory of Language." Jerusalem, Israel, 1969. Mimeographed.

Schutz, A. *Collected Papers*. Vol. 2 (A. Boderson, ed.). The Hague: Nijoff, 1964.

———. *Collected Papers*. Vol. 3 (I. Schutz, ed.). The Hague: Nijhoff, 1966.

Stokoe, W. C. "Sign Language Structure, an Outline of the Visual Communication Systems of the Deaf." *Studies in Linguistics, Occasional Papers*. No. 8. Buffalo: University of Buffalo Press, 1960.

PART II

Varieties of Language
and Verbal Repertoire

Social Repertoires

What has the Sociology of Language to Say to the Teacher? On Teaching the Standard Variety to Speakers of Dialectal or Sociolectal Varieties

Joshua A. Fishman
Yeshiva University
Erika Lueders-Salmon
Stanford University

Introduction

The major focus of American linguistic and sociolinguistic attentions vis-à-vis the American educational scene has recently gravitated toward the problems of teaching Standard English to speakers of Black English. Whereas the frontier scholars and teachers in this undertaking are engaged in structural and historical studies of Black English and White English, those who are closer to the barricades of daily classroom instruction are largely involved in two other pursuits. On the one hand, instructional materials must be prepared for students of varying ages, abilities, and degrees of distance from Standard English (and teachers and parents must be taught how to use and evaluate these materials). On the other hand, parents, teachers, and administrators, black and white, must be prepared, cognitively and emotionally, to handle the very concepts of "Black English" and "White English" and to consider their implications for our schools and our society.

In the latter connection an aspect of American provincialism that bars our way toward intelligent decision-making is our abysmal ignorance with respect to the sociology of language in general and toward its international and diachronic manifestations in particular. Our problems always strike us as so unparalleled that we rarely grasp their general significance, their general position in human experience, and, as a result, we rarely understand the answers to our problems even when we are fortunate enough to find such.

Cross-National Perspective

Having smugly cut ourselves off from our immigrant origins and from our religious and ethnic roots, the rest of the world has a benighted existence for us, at best, when we are faced with an educational problem that has international significance. Given a moment's thought it is quite apparent that most of the world's schoolchildren (rather than our black children alone) are *not* taught to read and write the *same* language or language variety that they bring with them to school from their homes and neighborhoods. Indeed, if this phenomenon is viewed historically, then the discrepancy between home language and school language increases dramatically the further we go back in time into periods that predate the vernacularization of education and mass education itself. And yet no American educational scholar or planner or leader seems to have shown any curiosity about this at all.

Given our current failure to teach black children to read or write or speak Standard English, is there anything to be learned from the German experience of teaching standard German to speakers of regional German varieties? Is there anything to be learned from similar experiences with nonstandard speakers—many of them obviously socially and culturally disadvantaged—that *typify* Italian education, Spanish education, Chinese education, Soviet education, etc.? Whereas *we* have only discovered our speakers of Black English a few years ago—when their needs could no longer be ignored and their anger no longer contained—other countries have been aware of their regionally/socially different students for generations.

Is there nothing that we can learn from their experiences? Let us briefly examine one such case, the German, and see.

For a German who grew up in the 1950's, speaking a dialect, it would sound strange to note several aspects of the discussion of Black English that has been carried on so heatedly during the past several years by language scholars and language teachers in the United States. Even though the complaints against the German school system were and are at least as manifold as are the complaints against the American school system in the United States, the category "complaint about dialect-only speaking graduates" is and was almost entirely absent in Germany. This might lead to the impression that all or most German youngsters, after eight or nine years of schooling can speak an acceptable High German, i.e., at least High German with no more than a minor local accent. If this is really the case, the comparison to black ghetto youth who after ten years of schooling cannot speak Standard English would justifiably prompt the question: "Why do we accomplish so much less with *our* dialect speakers here in the United States?"

We first ask whether all or most German students can in fact speak High German with "no more than a minor local accent" by the time they complete the nine years of compulsory schooling.

The Schwaben Region and the Schwäbisch Varieties

We will mainly consider the area around Stuttgart called Schwaben, where the Swabian dialect is spoken. If we are to compare black ghetto students with the Swabian students around Stuttgart with any degree of validity we must, of course, attempt to hold constant various variables that pertain to language-learning, e.g., social class and overall scholastic achievement. If we look for a comparable sample in Schwaben, we find it most easily in the small rural villages. Narrowing our comparison down to this subsample of students, one quickly becomes uncertain about the general impression reported above, that most German students who have completed compulsory schooling speak an acceptable High German.

What is the criterion for "acceptable"? Even today we still meet a small percentage of young people in the Swabian villages who can speak their local dialect only and who become mute and embarrassed if they are requested to speak High German. If it is *absolutely* required, their speech becomes slow and very artificial, with much functional and structural hypercorrection. If this population is examined as carefully as the black ghetto youngster has been in the United States, it is very doubtful that the German school system is more successful in teaching High German to disadvantaged speakers of regional German than the United States system is in teaching standard English to its disadvantaged pupils.

Nevertheless, the vast majority of Swabian dialect-speaking children—even those in rural villages—are eventually able to express themselves in a higher dialect (H) than the one that they originally learned at home from family and friends. However, only a small minority of Schwäbisch speaking people ever reach the point where they can hide their Swabian background. This statement (based upon our own observations) is in direct contrast to Leopold, who claims that "now it is often difficult or impossible to detect which region an educated speaker comes from" (1968, p. 362). Leopold may have been unduly influenced by dislocated German speakers or by German speakers stemming from northern rather than southern regions. Rahn, on the other hand, does not hesitate to write: "It can be stated that no Swabian who has not benefited from an unusually thorough language education is in a position to pronounce words such as *Undank, Anbetung, ausreiten,* etc. . . . in such a way that his Swabian origins are not immediately recognized" (1962, p. 28).[1] Indeed, we find in Schwaben a *continuum* of different varieties of Schwäbisch, whereas there seems to be much more of a break between, for example, the Black English spoken in the Oakland ghetto and the English of native white Californians in the same city.

As do most others, Rahn (1962) distinguishes five varieties of Schwäbisch, namely:

1. Grundschicht: Bauernsprache (Rural language; p. 86).
2. Obere Grundschicht: Provinzielle Umgangssprache (Provincial vernacular; p. 12).

[1] *Man wird behaupten können, dass kein Schwabe, der nicht eine gründliche Spracherziehung genossen hat, in de Lage ist, Wörter wie "Undank; Anbetung, ausreiten" . . . so zu sprechen, dass man nicht sogleich den Schwaben in ihm erkennt* (1962, p. 28).

3. Mittlere städtische Sprachschicht: Württembergische Umgangssprache (Regional vernacular; p. 21).

4. Obere städtische Sprachschicht: Honoratiorenschwäbisch (Dignified Swabian; p. 18).

5. Einheitssprache: Schwäbisch getöntes Hoch- oder Schriftdeutsch (Swabian-accented High or written German), which is quite close to Hochsprache: Mundartfreie Bühnensprache (High language: nondialectal-stage language, p. 8).

With these five varieties (examples of which have been reproduced in the appendix at the end of our paper), it is easier to indicate what one means by "poor High German" or "acceptable High German."

Somewhat in accord with Leopold's observations is our own that variety 1 seems to be dying out slowly. But varieties 2 to 5 are still very much alive. Nor should these be viewed as merely minor departures from standard German. For example, a visitor from North Germany would not be able to understand when the Swabians talk variety 2 or 3 to each other; as the appendix examples of the different varieties demonstrate clearly enough their pronunciation is very different from that of standard German; in addition, there are many lexical and grammatical differences that must confuse every outsider. A little poem expresses this last point nicely:

Wer ist das?
Er hat keine Beine, bloss Füsse.
Wenn er geht, dann läuft er.
Wenn er läuft, dann springt er.
Wenn er springst, dann hüpft er.
Und wenn er rennt, dann, saust er . . . (Rahn, 1962, p. 29).[2]

How are the more formal varieties of Schwäbisch acquired?
How is standard German acquired? There is among the Swabians a very small minority of highly educated and peripatetic individuals (by no means a speech community) who can, if they want to, dis-

---

[2] "This riddle-poem, meaningless in translation, pokes fun at the many lexical and semantic differences between Swabians and other Germans. 'Who is it,' the poem asks, 'who has no legs, only feet (i.e., who lacks the word *Beine*, "legs," used by other Germans and instead only has the word *Füsse*, which means "feet" to other Germans)? Who uses the word that means "run" (in other parts of Germany) when he means "walk"? Who uses the word that means "jump" when he means "run"?' etc., etc. The answer to the riddle-poem, of course, is 'The Swabian.' " Rahn, 1962, p. 29.

guise in their speech their Swabian background. A much larger group are those in business, education, administration, and so forth who can easily speak variety 5, a Schwäbisch getöntes Hoch- oder Schriftdeutsch. However, these people usually fall back to variety 4 when they are among friends or at home. Honoratiorenschwäbisch is also the variety that most people, who *usually* speak variety 1, 2, or 3, *can* speak if they are in a sufficiently demanding, formal situation. And then we have, especially in the rural area, a small minority who cannot speak anything but the local variety 1 or 2 of Schwäbisch. Generally speaking, there is little overt educational concern about these limited-repertoire speakers.

This leaves us with two questions to raise if we compare the Swabian situation to that in the United States.

1. Why is there almost no concern over the minority group that cannot switch into any higher variety of Schwäbisch?

2. How are the majority of Swabian children (who come from variety 1, 2, or 3 homes and communities) taught to speak the higher varieties of Schwäbisch and standard German as well?

Question 1 is fairly easy to answer. Most of the students who are *not* able to speak Honoratiorenschwäbisch are to be found in the small villages. These students are the most likely to learn a simple trade or go into farming and to stay in the general area in which they were born. In this way they are perfectly capable of supporting themselves and, later on, of supporting a family. Their dialect is no social barrier since it is the local dialect, generally used and respected by all. The situation for the ghetto boy is quite different. Since there are not enough jobs in the ghetto he has to go outside in order to be self-supporting—and, thus, is immediately outside his home dialect. The dialect speaker in Germany, on the other hand, finds himself as one of a large *Gemeinschaft* of people who all speak the dialect to each other in at least some contexts. The sophistication of a speaker is indicated not by whether he speaks dialect but by the *ease* and the completeness with which he switches to a higher variety in appropriate contexts. The speaker of Black English, however, speaks an outcast's variety as soon as he steps across the boundary of the ghetto. Since many black students are aware of the fact that their dialect is not accepted in the white community, one can in turn understand their growing hostility toward

Standard English and their growing ideological defense of Black English.

In Schwaben it is considered very desirable to be able to speak High German. Students know that they need to be able to read and write High German in order to get a good job. They also know that the more honored people in the community don't speak variety 1 Schwäbisch—but at the same time these honored people still speak Schwäbisch rather than standard German! It is only recently that Black English has obtained this same recognition from more successful sectors of the black community and, indeed, has begun to be acknowledged for general instructional purposes in some ghetto schools. All in all, however, Black English is still often a sign of rebellion or of identity manifestation, whereas Schwäbisch is a much more ordinary aspect of everyday school life.

Regional German and Standard German in the Classroom: The Theory

Being in front of a class of Schwäbisch-speaking children, interspersed here and there with a foreign child and with a few children speaking other dialects, what does the teacher do to make the children comfortable in speaking Honoratiorenschwäbisch? A pattern is followed that does not at all involve a stagewise progression from regional Schwäbisch material to standard texts (one suggestion currently espoused by some American students of Black English) but, rather, that involves the recognition of diglottism and of the functional dfferences between regional and standard German. This may be illustrated by quoting from a teacher-training text that is a century old and has a chapter entitled *Das Hochdeutsch sollte gelehrt werden im Anschluss an die Volkssprache oder Haussprache* (High German should be taught in connection with the vernacular or the language of the home). In this chapter the author compares High German to Latin as follows:

. . . To a village schoolmaster High German is his Latin, and his feeling of superiority toward the German spoken by his youngsters is the same as that formerly held by the Latin teacher toward his elementary school pupils. . . .

. . . High German must not be taught as the opposite of the vernacular, but, rather, the pupil must be brought to feel that it grows forth out of the vernacular; High German must not appear as a substitute for and a displacement of the vernacular but as a refined form of it, like one's Sunday clothes alongside one's work clothes (Hildebrand, 1903, p. 68).[3]

Hildebrand's four principles of teaching German are still taught to teachers today:

1. Language instruction must fully, briskly, and warmly capture the content of language and its life-values together with the language itself. 2. The teacher of German should not teach things that pupils can find out by themselves but, rather, should enable them to find out everything under his guidance. 3. Main stress should be put on the spoken and heard language and not on the written and seen. 4. High German, the goal of instruction, should not be taught in isolation, as if it were another kind of Latin, but in the closest possible connection with the vernacular or the home language of the class (Rutt, 1963, p. 222).[4]

Long before Hildebrand the demand was made clear by various German educators, especially by Lorenz Kellner, that German should only be taught in connection with the spoken language. Indeed, after the influence of Hildebrand the formal teaching of German was abolished completely for a while by Gansberg and Scharrelmann, who cared about content only. The formal teaching of German recovered quickly, however, with Seidemann, who prepared the first complete methods series on teaching standard German for grades

---

[3] *Einem Dorfschullehrer ist das Hochdeutsch sein Latein und er steht damit dem Deutsch, das seine Buben reden, in demselben überlegenen Hochgefühl gegenüber wie der Lateinlehrer früher seinen Elementarschülern. . . .*
    . . . das Hochdeutsch darf nicht als ein Gegensatz zur Volkssprache gelehrt werden, sondern man muss es dem Schüler aus dieser hervorwachsen lassen; das Hochdeutsch darf nicht als verdrängender Ersatz der Volkssprache auftreten, sondern als eine veredelte Gestalt davon, gleichsam als Sonntagskleid neben dem Werktagskleid.

[4] *1. Der Sprachunterricht soll mit der Sprache zugleich den Inhalt der Sprache, ihren Lebensgehalt voll und frisch und warm erfassen. 2. Der Lehrer des Deutschen soll nichts lehren, was die Schüler selbst aus sich finden können, sondern alles das sie unter seiner Leitung finden lassen. 3. Das Hauptgewicht soll auf die gesprochene und gehörte Sprache gelegt werden, nicht auf die geschriebene und gesehene. 4. Das Hochdeutsch als Ziel des Unterrichts soll nicht als etwas für sich gelehrt werden, wie ein anderes Latein, sondern im engsten Anschluss an die in der Klasse vorfindliche Volkssprache oder Haussprache.*

one to ten. However, he ignored the dialects almost completely. The only times *Mundart* (dialect) is mentioned in his book is where he says: "Everyone masters a different segment of the general mother tongue and has, according to his age, degree of education, and regional attachment, his particular 'dialect' " (Seidemann, 1963, p. 36)[5] and "Language instruction must free the child from his original language, which supplies him with [his] vocabulary" (p. 37).[6]

The idea that the child had to be freed *from* the language so that he would be the master *of* the language has been carried on by Weisgerber. He states several times that the teacher must guard against producing a student ". . . who, by and large, passively permits himself to be molded by his mother tongue" (Weisgerber, 1950, p. 92).[7] He warns with strong words against any forcing of the child, as far as his language is concerned. Mastery of the language cannot be forced. He demands of the school:

Obviously the task of language instruction is as follows: to provide the child with the vocabulary that is necessary and useful in its language development in accord both with the world-view of its mother tongue and the psychological development of the child itself; to foster these verbal skills in the child in such a way that it adopts them for its own use on a genuinely intuitive basis; to clarify and complete verbal growth at the proper time so that these verbal skills really become the child's own possession (Weisgerber, 1950, p. 31).[8]

Weisgerber doesn't give concrete examples, but based on his principles one can justify dialect in the classroom, since this is where the

---

[5] *Jeder beherrscht einen andern Abschnitt aus der gemeinsamen Muttersprache, hat je nach Altersstufe, Bildungsgrad und landschaftlicher Zugehörigkeit seine besondere "Mundart."*

[6] *Der Sprachunterricht muss das Kind frei machen von der Sprache des Herkommens, die ihm gleichwohl seinen Wortschatz liefert.*

[7] *. . . der sichvvorwiegend passiv von der Muttersprache prägen lässt.*

[8] *Was der Sprachunterricht dabei soll, ist dem Grundsatz nach ganz offensichtlich: aus der doppelten Einsicht in den Aufbau des muttersprachlichen Weltbildes und in die geistige Entwicklung des Kindes die Sprachmittel bereitstellen, die dem Kinde zu seinem sprachlichen Wachstum jeweils notwending und förderlich sind; sie dem Kinde so nahe bringen, dass es sie in einem echten Nachaffen sich aneignet; das Ergebnis des natürlichen Sprachwachsens an der rechten Stelle so klären und ergänzen, dass diese Sprachmittel nun wirklicher Besitz sind.*

child is. From here, largely through fun and games, the vocabulary is to be slowly enlarged and the child guided to the standard variety. Thus the emphasis on the spoken word over reading and writing has been a constant in German education for at least the past century.

Regional German and Standard German in the Classroom: From Theory into Practice

Even the strictest teachers in Schwaben never push students to speak High German in class discussion. However, there are quite a few drills in speaking High German through many recitations of proverbs, songs, and poems. In such a literary context standard German does not sound "phony" to the child but "in place." Young children also play at "being building blocks for a story." Here each child is responsible for adding one sentence to a story in High German. In this way the child learns to *use* High German—but doesn't have to employ it in *spontaneous speech*.

High German is also constantly taught when the child learns how to read, since none of the German primers is in dialect. Actually it is quite hard for any German to read little stories written in dialect. The naturally spoken language just isn't the written one. The junior author of this paper learned most of her best High German pronunciation when she started to sing in a choir. Again, here the participants had fun pronouncing the words correctly, since to their own ears a choir singing in dialect just didn't sound right. Low-ability students caught on to this very quickly, too. It was usually enough to sing once demonstratively: "... *es druckten ihn die Sorga schwär, är suchte neies Land em Mär*" to have them all unified in correct "... *es drückten ihn die Sorgen schwer, er suchte neues Land im Meer.*"

It does not seem necessary for a teacher in Schwaben to speak the dialect herself but, rather, merely to accept the children's spontaneous speech for the above result to obtain. Of course, it does not *harm* the quality of her students' speech if she speaks Honoratioren-schwäbish most of the time. However, she should also be able to speak variety 5 (Schwaben accented high or written German)—and do so from time to time as appropriate—so that the students have a proper model to follow in their repertoire acquisition.

Repertoire Expansion and Repertoire Retention

Most Swabian students who do not go to the Gymnasium (and fewer than half do) never experience any conflict between regional and standard German. They are well accepted with no higher variety than Honoratiorenschwäbisch. The only ones that *do* experience any such conflict are the better-educated students. Most of them finally manage variety 5, but they rarely feel fully comfortable in it. They usually fall back into Honoratiorenschwäbisch when they are among friends. Thus it is not the ordinary student who faces a problem but, rather, the more accomplished one. However, he is also more able to handle this problem, if it really becomes serious, via special courses, travel, etc. Finally, it should be clear that the regional varieties remain both strong as well as functionally differentiated themselves. Varieties 2 and 3 particularly are surrounded by emotional and primary experiences and relationships that none would forego. Certainly the black ghetto child should not have to forego his verbal links to spontaneity and familiarity. If other Americans can learn to accept him as he is linguistically and socioculturally, there is no reason why he should not be able to learn other varieties of English as well for particular functions and relationships. The learning gap is on *both* sides of the ghetto wall, rather than merely on one or the other.

Verbal Repertoire and Functional Differentiation

Clearly, one of the central notions that is required in order to ponder the foregoing discussion of regional German–standard German experience is that of verbal repertoire. In the broader Swabian area a five- or six-variety repertoire exists, and all of the varieties in this repertoire are considered "okay" by the larger speech community, provided each is kept by and large in its own place. American teachers are still largely innocent of this elementary fact of the sociology of language, namely, that speech communities characteristically exhibit verbal repertoires and that the varieties in these repertoires are functionally differentiated—rather than merely linguistically so—in accord with societally established and reinforced norms of communicative appropriateness. Indeed, American teachers (and parents and administrators) are by and large still mesmerized by the fiction that there is only one proper kind of English for all purposes and that it alone should be allowed to cross the threshold of the classroom. American teachers still insist that they themselves only talk *one* kind of English, the *right* kind, and that this is the only kind to which their charges should be exposed.

Written Language—Spoken Language

The distinction between the written language and the spoken language is obviously easier to grasp in a context such as the German (where the varieties involved are so different from each other) than in the white American. Nevertheless, that alone does not explain the German willingness to *accept* the spoken language for most school discussion purposes, nor does it explain the widespread American insistence on the written language as the proper model for communications to and from the teacher. Of course, both these matters can be explained as a result of particular sociohistorical experiences, but that is not our task here. It should be sufficient here to say that the German regional approach not only reveals more sociolinguistic sensitivity and toleration on the part of teachers but that it seems to foster such as well. The child and the adult deserve to have and to hold their home speech. The home and regional speech can be used for many purposes in school as well. The standard language has serious functions, but it can be enjoyably learned and unashamedly restricted to its prescribed prerogatives.

Regional is Neither Wrong nor Funny

Not only is regional or nonstandard "schoolworthy," but it has several varieties itself. Thus, the distinction is not between two straw men, an exaggeratedly pure or correct standard on the one hand and an impossibly gross and barbarous nonstandard on the other. Indeed, regional speech can boast varieties that are more frequently associated with local formal events, ceremonies, and interactions than can the standard. The mayor, the priest, the doctor, and the teacher utilize the highest forms of the regional speech in their *formal capacities* and in their official roles, thereby placing the regional repertoire within the pale of sanctity rather than reserving that role for the standard alone. Indeed, more opprobrium would be attached to a would-be local dignitary who could not command variety 4 or 5 than would be to one who could not control High German in speech. Thus, the respect attached to varieties of regional speech makes it *easier* to avoid pressures to necessarily read and write the regional varieties—or to start with primers in these varieties—in order to defend regional dignity or to recognize the child as he is or to making learning easier.

Contextual Markers vs. Demographic Stereotypes

In white eyes, Black English not only stamps one as black but as lower-class black. It is taken to be a demographic marker of basically one-variety speakers. It does not occur to the teacher that the speakers of Black English may really control other varieties of English as well, or that Black English itself is subdivisible into several varieties. Thus Black English is a stereotype that represents a certain kind of person, all of him, all of the time. Regional German, on the other hand, is not a demographic stereotype at all, certainly not within the area of its use. Rather, it is a contextual marker standing for a particular kind of situation or metaphorical content, depending on the particular regional variety being employed from one speech act or event to another. Whites in general and white teachers in particular are not accustomed to viewing speakers of Black English in anywhere near such subtle, contextual terms.

Speech Community

Contextual shifting from one variety to another within a verbal repertoire and the correct and effortless interpretation of the communicative significance of such switching is the undeniable sign of the existence and the functional operation of a speech community. Teachers and pupils in regional Germany are usually co-members of the same speech community. They accept and implement common norms of communicative appropriateness, whether these pertain to the use of regional variety 3, regional variety 4, or standard

German itself. Teachers and pupils in our black ghetto schools are most often *not* members of the same speech community. They do not share common norms of communicative appropriateness. They do not engage in or even fully recognize each other's verbal repertoires. They do not have common norms vis-à-vis the use of standard English on the one hand or of Black English on the other. What is a contextual marker for the one is a demographic stereotype for the other, and vice versa. One imposes communications upon the other rather than engage in joint contextual shifting.

Should Black Children be Taught to Read and Write Black English?

If the parallel question were asked in regional Germany the answer would be no. Regional German is not for reading and writing, as far as the indigenous diglottic system is concerned. Over a period of years a variety of German that no one uses conversationally is slowly and enjoyably learned so that *it* can be used for reading and writing (and certain signing and reciting), and those who go higher in society learn this variety better than do others. During elementary school in particular, more attention is given to educating children and to encouraging them to express themselves clearly, forcefully, and effectively than to standard German reading and writing or formal language skills as a whole. Seemingly, "getting educated" and "learning standard German" are not considered to be one and the same.

Would such an approach to standard and non-standard language varieties work in our ghetto schools? Perhaps so, if teachers and students and parents and administrators more frequently constituted a single speech community, and, furthermore, if substantial role relationships and networks involving standard English were really available to ghetto adolescents and adults, either within their *own* speech communities or in *neighboring* ones. Under such circumstances it would obviously be disfunctional to teach reading and writing of Black English. Instead of sharing a variety with the white world, and instead of using this variety for some of the same functions as it has in the white world, the black and the white verbal repertoires would become even more discontinuous, linguistically and functionally, than they are today. The interacting relationship between language and social behavior being what it is, such discontinuity would not only reflect the social distance between blacks and whites but it would further reinforce and extend this distance as well. Perhaps this is the ultimate lesson that we must derive from the cross-national examination of sociolinguistic processes: if we are to foster a broader speech community we must safeguard not only the internal vitality and legitimacy of its smaller subcommunities but also their links with each other (Fishman, 1971 and forthcoming).

Appendix: Examples of Varieties of Schwäbisch[9]

I (p. 86):

(Bauer und Bäuerin unterhalten sich über die Werbung des Jungbauern Karl um ihre Tochter)

Bauer: Om s Kathrele hot er gfroget, der Karl.

Bäuerin: I hao s no ghairt. — Om s Kathrele! — Dussa stohts ond heulet, — so graoss es isch.

Bauer: Brachscht e Weib, Karl — s ischt wohr. Brauchscht naitech e Weib. — Aber wa soll mer sa: — zwenga ka' mer s et.

II (p. 12):

(Becka ond Becka)

Wo em Becka Schlumberger sei' Denschtmädle gmerkt hot, dass ihr Bauch jeden Tag a bissle dicker wird, hot se dr Schlumberger an dr Hand gnomma ond hot so tröschtet: "Butz dei' Na's, Luisle! Du brauchsch koi Angscht hau'. I zahl älles. Bloss muesscht mr versprecha, dass de koim Mensche saisch, wer dr Vatter isch."

Ond wie s no ghoissa hot, dass s Luisle en Buebe kriegt häb, isch dr Beck en d Fraueklinik nuff ond hot se bsuecht. Aber glei zairscht hot er se gfrogt, ob se au gwiiss neamer gsait häb . . . se wiss scho' was. Aber s Luisle hot bloss gschluchzt: "O Moischtr, uf Ehr ond Seligkeit, i hau's koim Menscha gsait, aber di Herra wisset halt älles. Die sehets de Kender von ausse-n-a', wer dr Vatter isch."

"Domms Zeug," sait dr Beck, "bild dr no'nex ei'. Woher sollet s au die Herra wissa, wenn du nex gsait hosch!" "Doch, se wisset s! I hau' s selber ghairt. Wo dr Professer zu Visitt komme-n-isch, hot

ehn dr Oberazt: glei an der Tür zu mir gwiesa ond hot gsait: Do henta leit des Mädle mit dem kloina Becka. Ond no haun-es au namme verleugna kenna."

III (p. 21):
(Schiffsschaukel)

Meire' Lebtag han-e d Tante in keire' so Aufregung gsehe'
   Wia an sellem Mittag, an eme' Johrmarkt isch gwä: Alles hot zitteret an re' bis nauf zu der Feder am Hüatle,
   Ond noch Luft hot se gschnappt wia e' heniger Fisch.
"Jesesmariaondjosef! was ist denn passiert ond was fehlt dr?"
   "I ka' nemme, i muass zersta' verschnaufe' e' Weil . . .
Wisseter, wer in der Stadt ist: der Fritz! Mit eigene Auge'
   Han-e se gsehe' dia Schand, drausse' beim Turnhalleplatz:
Mittle' onter de Bude'—ond Karre'leut hot r sei' Schaukel
   Ond auf em Schild an der Kass ausgschemmt de' Name debei!"

IV (p. 18):
(Der Traum)

D Frau Pfarrer hat emal Bsuch kriegt von dr Bachbäure. Die hat sich ebe immer so scheniert bei de bessere Leut. Aber d Pfarrfrau hat ihr a Gläsle Wei hi'gstellt und hat so e recht freundlich s Gespräch mit ihr a'gfanga:

   "Heut nacht hat mr s übrigens von Ihne träumt, denket Se nur!"

   "Oms Himmels Wille, Frau Pfarrer! Dees wär aber doch mei *Plicht ond Schuligkeit gwä . . .!"*

Bibliography

Fishman, Joshua A. "The Sociology of Language." In J. A. Fishman (ed.), *Advances in the Sociology of Language.* The Hague: Mouton and Co., 1971. Pp. 217–404.

Fishman, Joshua A. "The Sociology of Language." In *Current Trends in Linguistics.* Vol. 12. The Hague: Mouton and Co., forthcoming.

Hildebrand, Rudolf. *Vom deutschen Sprachunterricht in der Schule,* 8th rev. ed. Leipzig: Verlag von Julius Klinkhardt, 1903.

Leopold, Werner. "The Decline of German Dialects." In J. A. Fishman (ed.), *Readings in the Sociology of Language*. The Hague: Mouton and Co., 1968. Originally published in *Word* 15 (1959): 130–153.

Rahn, Fritz. *Der schwäbische Mensch and seine Mundart*. Stuttgart: Hans E. Günther Verlag, 1962.

Rutt, Theodor. *Didaktik der Muttersprache*. Frankfurt, Berlin, Bonn: Verlag Moritz Diesterweg, 1963.

Seidemann, Walther. *Der Deutschunterricht als innere Sprachbildung*, 6th ed. Heidelberg: Quelle und Meyer, 1963.

Weisgerber, Leo. *Das Tor zur Muttersprache*. Düsseldorf: Pädagogischer Verlag Schwann, 1950.

Weisgerber, Leo. *Das Menschheitsgesetz der Sprache*, 2d rev. ed. Heidelberg: Quelle und Meyer, 1964.

Bilingualism, Bidialectalism, and Classroom Interaction

John J. Gumperz
Eduardo Hernández-Chavez
University of California, Berkeley

I

Recent systematic research in the inner city has successfully disproved the notions of those who characterize the language of low-income populations as degenerate and structurally underdeveloped. There is overwhelming evidence to show that when both middle-class and nonmiddle-class children, no matter what their native language, dialect, or ethnic background, come to school at the age of five or six, they have control of a fully formed grammatical system. The mere fact that their system is distinct from that of their teacher does not mean that their speech is not rule governed. Speech features that strike the teacher as different do not indicate failure to adjust to some universally accepted English norm; rather, they are

An earlier version of this paper, prepared by John J. Gumperz alone, appeared in Monograph Series on Languages and Linguistics No. 23, ed. James E. Alatis. Washington, D.C.: Georgetown University Press, 1970.

Research reported on in this paper has been supported by grants from the Urban Crisis Program and the Institute of International Studies, University of California, Berkeley. We are grateful to Louisa Lewis for assistance in field work and analysis.

The point of view expressed in this paper leans heavily on the work of Claudia Mitchell-Kernan (1969).

the output of dialect or language-specific syntactic rules every bit as complex as those of Standard English (Labov, 1969).

It is clear furthermore that the above linguistic differences also reflect far-reaching and systematic cultural differences. Like the plural societies of Asia and Africa, American urban society is characterized by the coexistence of a variety of distinct cultures. Each major ethnic group has its own heritage, its own body of traditions, values, and views about what is right and proper. These traditions are passed on from generation to generation as part of the informal family or peer-group socialization process and are encoded in folk art and literature, oral or written.

To understand this complex system, it is first of all necessary to identify and describe its constituent elements. Grammatical analysis must be, and has to some extent been, supplemented by ethnographic description, ethnohistory, and the study of folk art (Hannerz, 1969; Stewart, 1968; Abrahams, 1964; Kochman, 1969). But mere description of component subsystems is not enough if we are to learn how the plurality of cultures operates in everyday interaction and how it affects the quality of individual lives. Minority groups in urbanized societies are never completely isolated from the dominant majority. To study their life ways without reference to surrounding populations is to distort the realities of their everyday lives. All residents of modern industrial cities are subject to the same laws and are exposed to the same system of public education and mass communication. Minority group members, in fact, spend much of their day in settings where dominant norms prevail. Although there are significant individual differences in the degree of assimilation, almost all minority group members, even those whose behavior on the surface may seem quite deviant, have at least a passive knowledge of the dominant culture. What sets them off from others is not simply the fact that they are distinct, but the juxtaposition of their own private language and life styles with those of the public at large.

This juxtaposition, which is symbolized by constant alternation between in-group and out-group modes of acting and expression, has a pervasive effect on everyday behavior. Successful political leaders, such as Bobby Seale and the late Martin Luther King, rely on it for much of their rhetorical effect. C. Mitchell-Kernan, in her recent ethnographic study of verbal communication in an Afro-

American community (1969), reports that her informants' everyday conversation reveals an overriding concern—be it positive or negative—with majority culture.

Majority group members who have not experienced a similar disjuncture between private and public behavior frequently fail to appreciate its effect. They tend merely to perceive minority group members as different, without realizing the effect that this difference may have on everyday communication. This ignorance of minority styles of behavior seems to have contributed to the often discussed notion of "linguistic deprivation." No one familiar with the writings of Afro-American novelists of the last decade and with the recent writings on black folklore can maintain that low-income blacks are nonverbal. An exceptionally rich and varied terminological system, including such folk concepts as *sounding, signifying, rapping, running it down, chucking, jiving, marking,* etc., all referring to verbal strategies (i.e., different modes of achieving particular communicative ends), testifies to the importance Afro-American culture assigns to verbal art (Kochman, 1969; Mitchell-Kernan, 1969). Yet, inner-city black children are often described as nonverbal, simply because they fail to respond to the school situation. It is true that lower-class children frequently show difficulty in performing adequately in formal interviews and psychological tests. But these tests are frequently administered under conditions that seem unfamiliar and, at times, threatening to minority-group children. When elicitation conditions are changed, there is often a radical improvement in response (Labov, 1969; Mehan, 1970).

The fact that bilingualism and biculturalism have come to be accepted as major goals in inner-city schools is an important advance. But if we are to achieve this goal we require at least some understanding of the nature of code alternation and its meaning in everyday interaction. Bilingualism is, after all, primarily a linguistic term, referring to the fact that linguists have discovered significant alternations in phonology, morphology, and syntax in studying the verbal behavior of a particular population. Although bilingual phenomena have certain linguistic features in common, these features may have quite different social significance.

Furthermore, to the extent that social conditions affect verbal behavior, findings based on research in one type of bilingual situation may not necessarily be applicable to another socially different one.

Sociolinguistic studies of bilingualism for the most part focus on the linguistic aspects of the problem. Having discovered that speakers alternate between what, from a linguistic point of view, constitute grammatically distinct systems, investigators then proceed to study where and under what conditions alternants are employed, either through surveys in which speakers are asked to report their own language usage (Fishman, 1965) or by counting the occurrence of relevant forms in samples of elicited speech. The assumption is that the presence or absence of particular linguistic alternates directly reflects significant information about such matters as group membership, values, relative prestige, power relationships, etc.

There is no doubt that such one-to-one relationships between language and social phenomena do exist in most societies. Where speakers control and regularly employ two or more speech varieties and continue to do so over long periods of time, it is most likely that each of the two varieties will be associated with certain activities or social characteristics of speakers. This is especially the case in formal or ceremonial situations, such as religious or magical rites, court proceedings, stereotyped introductions, greetings, or leave-takings. Here language, as well as gestures and other aspects of demeanor, may be so rigidly specified as to form part of the defining characteristics of the setting—so much so that a change in language may change the setting.

There are, however, many other cases where such correlations break down. Consider the following sentences cited in a recent study of bilingualism in Texas:

(1) Te digo que este dedo (*I tell you that this finger*) has been bothering me so much.
Se me hace que (*it seems that*) I have to respect her porque 'ta . . . (*because she is*).
But this arthritis deal, boy you get to hurting so bad you can't hardly even . . . "cer masa pa" tortillas (*make dough for tortillas*). [Lance, 1969, pp. 75–76]

Similar examples come from a recently recorded discussion between two educated Mexican-Americans.

(2a) WOMAN: Well, I'm glad that I met you. Okay?

M——: Andale, pues *(okay, swell)* and do come again, mmm?

(b) M——: Con ellos dos *(with the two of them)*. With each other. La señora trabaja en la canería orita, you know? *(The mother works in the cannery right now)*. She was . . . con Francine jugaba . . . *(she used to play with Francine . . .)* with my little girl.

(c) M——: There's no children in the neighborhood. Well . . . sí hay criaturas *(there are children)*.

(d) M——: . . . those friends are friends from Mexico que tienen chamaquitos *(who have little children)*.

(e) M——: . . . that has nothing to do con que le hagan esta . . . *(with their doing this)*.

(f) M——: But the person . . . de . . . de grande *(as an adult)* is gotta have something in his mouth.

(g) M——: An' my uncle Sam es el mas agabachado *(is the most Americanized)*.

It would be futile to predict the occurrence of either English or Spanish in the above utterances by attempting to isolate social variables that correlate with linguistic form. Topic, speaker, setting are common in each. Yet the code changes sometimes in the middle of a sentence.

Language mixing of this type is by no means a rarity. Linguists specializing in bilingualism cite it to provide examples of extreme instances of interference (Mackey, 1965). Some native speakers in ethnically diverse communities are reluctant to admit its existence. It forms the subject of many humorous treatises, and in Texas it tends to be referred to by pejorative terms, such as Tex-Mex. Yet in spite of the fact that such extreme code switching is held in disrepute, it is very persistent wherever minority language groups come in close contact with majority language groups under conditions of rapid social change.

One might, by way of an explanation, simply state that both codes are equally admissible in some contexts and that code switching is merely a matter of the individual's momentary inclination. Yet the alternation does carry meaning. Let us compare the following passage from a recent analysis of Russian pronominal usage with an excerpt from a conversation.

(3) An arrogant aristocratic lieutenant and a grizzled, older captain find themselves thrust together as the only officers on an isolated outpost

in the Caucasus. Reciprocal formality at first seems appropriate to both. But while the latter is sitting on the young lieutenant's bed and discussing a confidential matter he switches to *ty* (tu). When the lieutenant appears to suggest insubordination, however, the captain reverts to *vy* (vous) as he issues a peremptory demand. . . . [Friedrich, 1966, p. 240]

(4) M——: I don't think I ever have any conversations in my dreams. I just dream. Ha. I don't hear people talking: I jus' see pictures.

E——: Oh. They're old-fashioned, then. They're not talkies yet, huh?

M——: They're old-fashioned. No. They're not talkies, yet. No. I'm trying to think. Yeah, there too have been talkies. Different. In Spanish and English both. An' I wouldn't be too surprised if I even had some in Chinese. *(Laughter)*. Yeah, E——. Deveras *(really)*. (M—— *offers* E—— *a cigarette, which is refused.*) Tú no fumas, ¿verdad? Yo tampoco. Dejé de fumar.

The two societies, the social context, and the topics discussed differ, yet the shift from English to Spanish has connotations similar to the alternation between the formal (second person pronoun) *vy* (vous) and the informal *ty* (tu). Both signal a change in interpersonal relationship in the direction of greater informality or personal warmth. Although the linguistic signs differ, they reflect similar social strategies. What the linguist identifies as code switching may convey important social information. The present paper is an attempt (1) to elucidate the relationship among linguistic form, interactional strategies, and social meaning on the basis of a detailed study of a natural conversation, and (2) to suggest implications for understanding language use in the culturally diverse classroom.

The conversation cited in items 2 and 4 was recorded in an institution specializing in English instruction for small Mexican immigrant children. The staff, ranging in age from recent high school graduates to persons in their middle fifties, includes a large number of people of Mexican or Mexican-American descent as well as some English-speaking Americans. Of the latter group, several speak Spanish well. The recording was made by a linguist (E——), a native American of Mexican ancestry who is employed as an adviser for the program. His interlocutor (M——) is a community counselor employed in the program. She is a woman without higher education who has been trained to assist the staff in dealing with the local community. She has had some experience in public affairs. In spite of the difference in education and salary, both participants regard each other as colleagues within the context of the program. When speaking Spanish they address each other by the reciprocal *tú*. The program director or a Spanish-speaking outsider visitor would receive the respectful *usted*. Conversations within the office are normally carried on in English, although, as will be seen later, there are marked stylistic differences that distinguish interaction among Mexican-Americans from interaction across ethnic boundaries.

For analysis the taped transcript was roughly divided into episodes, each centering around a single main topic. Episodes were then subdivided into "turns of speaking" (i.e., one or more sentences reflecting a speaker's response to another's comment). The author and the interviewer cooperated in the analysis of social meaning.

Two types of information were utilized. Turns containing a code switch were first examined as to their place within the structure of the total conversation in terms of such questions as, What were the relevant antecedents of the turn and what followed? or, What was the turn in response to, either in the same or preceding episodes? The purpose here was to get as detailed as possible an estimation of the speaker's intent. In the second stage a phrase from the other language would be substituted for the switched phrase in somewhat the same way that a linguistic interviewer uses the method of variation within a frame in order to estimate the structural significance of a particluar item. By this method it was possible to get an idea of what the code switch contributed to the meaning of the whole passage.

Before discussing the social aspects of code switching, some discussion of what it is that is being switched is necessary. Not all instances of Spanish words in the text are necessarily instances of code switching. Expressions like *ándale pues* (item 2a) or *dice* (he says) are normally part of the bilingual's style of English. Speakers use such expressions when speaking to others of the same ethnic background in somewhat the same way that Yiddish expressions like *nebbish, oi gewalt,* or interjections like *du hoerst* characterize the in-group English style of some American Jews. They serve as stylistic ethnic identity markers and are frequently used by speakers who no longer have effective control of both languages. The function of such forms as an ethnic identity marker becomes particularly clear in the following sequence, already cited in item 2b, between M——and a woman visitor in her office.

(5) WOMAN: Well, I'm glad that I met you. Okay?
M——: Andale, pues *(Okay, swell)* and do come again, mmm?

The speakers, both Mexican-Americans, are strangers who have met for the first time. The *ándale pues* is given in response to the woman's *okay*, as if to say, "Although we are strangers we have the same background and should get to know each other better."

Aside from loan word nouns such as *Chicano, gabacho,* or *pocho,* the ethnic identity markers consist largely of exclamations and sentence connectors. For example:

(6) M——: I say, Lupe no hombre *(why no),* don't believe that.
(7) M——: Sí *(yes)* but it doesn't.
(8) M——: That baby is . . . pues *(then).*

Mexican-Spanish is similarly marked by English interjections. Note, for example, the *you know* in the sentence:

(9) M——: Pero como, you know . . . la Estela . . .

The English form here seems a regular part of the Spanish text, and this is signaled phonetically by the fact that the pronunciation of the vowel *o* is relatively undipthongized and thus differs from other instances of *o* in English passages. Similarly, words like ice cream have Spanish-like pronunciations when they occur within Spanish texts, and English-like pronunciations in the English text.

The greater part of the instances of true code switching consist of entire sentences inserted into the other language text. There are, however, also some examples of change within single sentences, which require special comment. In the items below, the syntactic connection is such that both parts can be interpreted as independent sentences.

(10) M——: We've got all these kids here right now, los que están ya criados aquí *(those that have been raised here).*

This is not the case with the noun qualifier phrase in item 2d and the verb complement in item 2e. Other examples of this latter type are:

(11) M——: But the person . . . de . . . de grande *(as an adult)* is gotta have something in his mouth.

(12) M——: ¿Será que quiero la tetera? para pacify myself? *(It must be that I want the baby bottle to . . .)*

(13) M——: The type of work he did cuando trabajaba *(when he worked)* he . . . what . . . that I remember, era regador *(he was an irrigator)* at one time.

(14) M——: An' my uncle Sam es el mas agabachado *(is the most Americanized)*.

Noun qualifiers (2d), verb complements (2e), parts of a noun phrase (13), the predicate portion of an equational sentence (14), all can be switched. This does not mean, however, that there are no linguistic constraints on the co-occurrence of Spanish and English forms. The exact specification of these constraints will, however, require further detailed investigation. Clearly, aside from single loan words, entire sentences are most easily borrowed. Sentence modifiers or phrases are borrowed less frequently. And this borrowing does seem to be subject to some selection constraints (Blom and Gumperz, 1970). But some tentative statements can be made. Constructions like *que have chamaquitos (who have boys)* or *he era regador (he was an irrigator)* seem impossible.

When asked why they use Spanish in an English sentence or vice versa, speakers frequently come up with explanations like the following taken from our conversation:

(15) If there's a word that I can't find, it keeps comin' out in Spanish.

(16) I know what word I want and finally when I . . . well, bring it out in Spanish, I know the person understands me.

Difficulty in finding the right word clearly seems to account for examples like *para pacify myself* (item 12). In other instances, some items of experience, some referents or topics are more readily recalled in one language than in another, as in:

(17) M——: I got to thinking vacilando el punto este *(mulling over this point)*.

(18) M——: They only use English when they have to . . . like for cuando van de compras *(when they go shopping)*.

Linguistically motivated switches into English occur when the discussion calls for psychological terminology or expressions, e.g., *pacify, relax, I am a biter.* Such expressions or modes of talking seem rarely used in typically Mexican-American settings. On the other hand, ideas and experiences associated with the speaker's Spanish-speaking past such as items 20 and 21 below trigger off a switch into Spanish.

In many other instances, however, there seems to be no linguistic reason for the switch. *Sí hay criaturas* (item 2c) is directly translated without hesitation pause in the following sentence. Many other Spanish expressions have English equivalents elsewhere in the text. Furthermore, there are several pages of more general, abstract discussion that contain no Spanish at all.

One might hypothesize that codes are shifted in response to E——'s suggestion and that M—— answers him in whatever language he speaks. This is clearly not the case. Several questions asked in English elicit Spanish responses and vice versa.

In discussing the social aspects of switching, it is important to note that while the overt topic discussed is the use of English and Spanish, much of the conversation is dominated by a concern with Mexican versus non-Mexican, i.e., common middle-class values or group membership. Spanish occurs most in episodes dealing with typically Mexican-American experiences. In several places fears are expressed that Mexican-American children are losing their language and thus, by implication, denying their proper cultural heritage. To some extent the juxtaposition of English and Spanish symbolizes the duality of value systems evidenced in the discussion.

At the start of the conversation several exchanges dealing with the mechanics of tape-recorder operation are entirely in English. Code shifts begin with a sequence where M—— asks E—— why he is recording their talk and E—— responds:

(19) E——: I want to use it as a . . . as an example of how Chicanos can shift back and forth from one language to another.
(20) M——: Ooo. Como andábamos platicando *(Oh. Like we were saying).*

M——'s switch to Spanish here is a direct response to his, E——'s, use of the word *Chicanos.* Her statement refers to previous conversations they have had on related subjects and suggests that she is willing to treat the present talk as a friendly chat among fellow Chicanos rather than as a formal interview.

Codes alternate only as long as all participants are Chicanos and while their conversation revolves around personal experiences. Toward the end of the recording session, when a new participant enters, talk goes on. The newcomer is an American of English-speaking background who, having lived in Latin America, speaks Spanish fluently. Yet in this context she was addressed only in English and did not use her Spanish. Furthermore, in the earlier part of the session, when E—— and M—— were alone, there was one long episode where M—— spoke only English even when responding to E——'s Spanish questions. This passage deals with M——'s visit to San Quentin prison, to see an inmate, and with prison conditions. The inmate was referred to only in English and the conversation contained no overt reference to his ethnic background. Further inquiries made while analysis was in progress revealed that he was a non-Chicano. It is evident from the first example that it is social identity and not language per se that is determinant in code selection. The second example indicates that, when conversations have no reference to speakers or their subjects' status as Chicanos, and when as in the present case a subject is treated in a generally detached manner without signs of personal involvement, code switching seems to be inappropriate.

On the whole, one has the impression that, except for a few episodes dealing with recollections of family affairs, the entire conversation is basically in English. English serves to introduce most new information, while Spanish provides stylistic embroidering to amplify the speaker's intent. Spanish sentences frequently take the form of precoded, stereotyped, or idiomatic phrases.

While ethnic identity is important as the underlying theme, the actual contextual meanings of code alternation are more complex.

Turning to a more detailed analysis, many of the Spanish passages reflect direct quotes or reports of what M—— has said in Spanish or of what other Mexican-Americans have told her, for example:

(21) Because I was speakin' to my baby ... my ex-baby-sitter, and we were talkin' about the kids you know, an' I was tellin' her ... uh, "Pero,

como, you know . . . uh . . . la Estela y la Sandi . . . relistas en el telefón.
Ya hablan mucho inglés." Dice, "Pos . . . sí. Mira tú," dice, "Pos . . .
el . . . las palabras del televisión. Ya que me dice . . . ya me pide dinero
pa'l ayscrín y . . ." You know? "Ya lue . . . y eso no es nada, espérate
los chicharrones, you know, when they start school . . ." *(But, how, you
know . . . uh . . . "Estella and Sandi are very precocious on the telephone.
They already speak a lot of English." She says, "Well, yes, just imagine,"
she says, "well, the words on television, and she already asks me for
money for ice cream and" . . . You know? "And then . . . and that isn't
anything, wait for the kids, you know, when they start school . . .")*

Throughout the conversation Spanish is used in quoting statements by individuals whose Chicano identity is emphasized. However, the following passage in which Lola, who is of Mexican origin,
is quoted in English seemed at first to contradict this generalization.

(22) An' Lola says, "Dixie has some, Dixie" . . . So Dixie gave me a
cigarette.

Lola, however, is in her late teens; and members of her age group,
although they know Spanish, tend to prefer English even in informal
interaction. Later on, however, if they marry within the Chicano
community, they are quite likely to revert to the predominant usage
pattern. The use of English in her case reflects the fact that for the
present, at least, Lola identifies with the majority group of English
monolinguals with respect to language-usage norms.

The pattern of quoting Chicanos in Spanish and talking about
them in English is reversed in the following passage, in which
M—— reports on the way she talks to her children:

(23) Yeah. Uh-huh. She'll get . . . "Linda, you don' do that, mija . . .
(daughter). La vas . . . *(you are going to . . .)* you're going to get her . . .
give her . . . a bad habit." Le pone el dedo pa' que se lo muerda *(she gives
her her finger to bite),* you know, "Iiya, she'll bite the heck out of you."
"Ow!" La otra grita *(the other one yells).* So, una es sadist y la otra es
masochist *(so, one is a sadist and the other is a masochist). (Laughter.)*

Further enquiry again reveals that in M——'s family children are
ordinarily addressed in English.

Aside from direct quotes, Spanish occurs in several modifying
phrases or sentences, such as *friends from Mexico que tienen chamaquitos* (item 2d). The effect here is to emphasize the ethnic iden-

tity of the referent. The use of *sí hay criaturas* (item 2c) is particularly interesting in this respect. It is preceded by the following exchange:

(24) M——: There's no children. The Black Panthers next door. You know what I mean.
E——: Do they have kids?
M——: Just the two little girls.
E——: No. no. I mean, do some of the other people in the neighborhood have kids?
M——: They don't associate with no children . . . There's no children in the neighborhood. Well . . . sí hay criaturas *(there are children)*.

M—— goes on to talk about the one other Mexican family in the building. The *sí hay criaturas* here serves to single out Mexican children from others and in a sense modifies the *there's no children* several sentences above. The implication is that only the other Chicano children are suitable playmates.

In the next group of examples the switch to Spanish signals the relative confidentiality or privateness of the message. The first example, cited in item 2b above, is a case in point:

(25) With each other. La señora trabaja en la canería orita, you know? *(The mother works in the cannery right now).*

Here M——'s voice is lowered, the loudness decreasing in somewhat the same way that confidentiality is signaled in English monolingual speech. Next, consider the following:

(26) E——: An' how . . . about how about now?
M——: Estos . . . me los hallé . . . estos Pall Malls me los hallaron *(These . . . I found . . . these Pall Malls . . . they were found for me . . .)* No, I mean . . .

M—— has been talking about the fact that she smokes very little, and E—— discovers some cigarettes on her desk. Her Spanish, punctuated by an unusually large number of hesitation pauses, lends to the statement an air of private confession. She is obviously slightly embarrassed.

Note the almost regular alternation between Spanish and English in the next passage:

(27) Mm-huh. Yeah. An' . . . an' they tell me, "How did you quit, Mary?" I di'n' quit. I . . . I just stopped. I mean it wasn' an effort I

made que voy a dejar de fumar porque me hace daño o *(that I'm going to stop smoking because it's harmful to me, or . . .)* this or that, uh-uh. It just . . . that . . . eh . . . I used to pull butts out of the . . . the . . . the wastepaper basket. Yeah. *(Laughter.)* I used to go look in the *(unclear)* se me acababan los cigarros en la noche *(my cigarettes would run out at night)*. I'd get desperate, y ahi voy al basurero a buscar, a sacar, you know? *(and there I go to the wastebasket to look for some, to get some)*. *(Laughter.)*

The juxtaposition of the two codes here is used to great stylistic effect in depicting the speaker's attitudes. The Spanish phrases, partly by being associated with content like "it is harmful to me" or with references to events like "cigarettes running out at night" and through intonational and other suprasegmental clues, convey a sense of personal feeling. The English phrases are more neutral by contrast. The resulting effect of alternate personal involvement and clinical detachment vividly reflects M——'s ambiguity about her smoking.

A further example derives from a discussion session recorded in Richmond, California, by a black community worker. Participants include his wife and several teen-age boys. Here we find alternation between speech features that are quite close to standard English and such typically black English features as lack of postvocalic "r," double negation, and copula deletion.

(28) You can tell me how your mother worked twenty hours a day and I can sit here and cry. I mean I can cry and I can feel for you. But as long as I don't get up and make certain that I and my children don't go through the same, *I ain't did nothin' for you,* brother. That's what I'm talking about.

(29) Now Michael is making a point, where that everything that happens in that house affects all the kids. It does. And Michael and *you makin' a point, too. Kids suppose' to learn how to avoid these things.* But let me tell you. We're all in here. *We talkin' but you see . . .*

Note the italicized phrase in item 28, with the typically Black English phrase *ain't did nothin'* embedded in what is otherwise a normal standard English sequence. On our tape the shift is not preceded by a pause or marked off by special stress or intonation contours. The speaker is therefore not quoting from another code; his choice of form here lends emphasis to what he is saying. Item 29 begins with a general statement addressed to the group as a whole. The speaker then turns to one person, Michael, and signals this change in focus by dropping the copula "is" and shifting to black phonology.

It seems clear that, in all these cases, what the linguist sees merely as alternation between two systems serves definite and clearly understandable communicative ends. The speakers do not merely switch from one variety to another, but they build on the coexistence of alternate forms to convey information.

It can be argued that language choice reflects the speaker's minority status within the English-speaking majority, and that selection of forms in particular cases is related to such factors as ethnic identity, age, sex, degree of solidarity or confidentiality, etc. But the relationship of such social factors to speech form is quite different from what the sociologist means by correlation among variables. One could not take a rating of, for instance, ethnicity or degree of solidarity, as measured by the usual questionnaire techniques or other scaling devices, and expect this rating to predict the occurrence of Spanish or black dialect and Standard English in a text. Such ratings may determine the likelihood of a switch, but they do not tell *when a switch will occur, nor do they predict its meaning.* What seems to be involved here, rather, is a symbolic process akin to that by which words convey semantic information. Code switching, in other words, is meaningful in much the same way that lexical choice is meaningful.

To be sure, not all instances of code alternation convey meaning. Our tapes contain several instances where the shift into Black English or the use of a Spanish word in an English sentence can only be interpreted as a slip of the tongue, frequently corrected in the next sentence, or where its use must be regarded merely as a sign of the speaker's lack of familiarity with the style he is employing. But, even though such errors do occur, it is nevertheless true that code switching is also a communicative skill, which speakers use as a verbal strategy in much the same way that skillful writers switch styles in a short story.

How and by what devices does the speaker's selection of alternate forms communicate information? The process is a metaphoric process somewhat similar to what linguists interested in literary style have called *foregrounding* (Garvin, 1964). Foregrounding, in the most general sense of the term, relies on the fact that words are more than just names for things. Words also carry a host of culturally specific associations, attitudes, and values. These cultural values derive from the context in which words are usually used and from the activities with which they are associated. When a word is used in other than normal context, these associations become highlighted or foregrounded. Thus, to take an example made famous by Leonard Bloomfield (1936), the word *fox* when it refers to a man, as in "He is a fox," communicates the notions of slyness and craftiness that our culture associates with the activities of foxes.

We assume that what holds true for individual lexical items also holds true for phonological or syntactic alternates. Whenever a speech variety is associated with a particular social category of speakers or with certain activities, this variety comes to symbolize the cultural values associated with these features of the nonlinguistic environment. In other words, speech varieties, like words, are potentially meaningful, and in both cases this is brought out by reinterpreting meanings in relation to context. As long as the variety in question is used in its normal environment, only its basic referential sense is communicated. But when it is used in a new context, it becomes socially marked, and the values associated with the original context are mapped onto the new message.

In any particular instance of code switching, speakers deduce what is meant by an information-processing procedure that takes account of the speaker, the addressee, the social categories to which they can be assigned in the context, the topic, etc. (Blom and Gumperz, 1970). Depending on the nature of the above factors, a wide variety of contextual meanings derives from the basic meaning inclusion (we) versus exclusion (they). This underlying meaning is then reinterpreted in the light of the co-occurring contextual factors to indicate such things as degree of involvement (5), anger, emphasis (7), change in focus (8), etc., the numbers in parentheses referring to the items on page 91.

We have chosen our examples from a number of languages to highlight the fact that the meanings conveyed by code switching are independent of the phonological shape or historical origin of the alternates in question. The association between forms and meaning is quite arbitrary. Any two alternates having the same referential meaning can become carriers of social meaning.

The ability to interpret a message is a direct function of the listener's home background, his peer group experiences, and his education. Differences in background can lead to misinterpretation of messages. The sentence "He is a Sikh" has little or no meaning for an American audience, but to anyone familiar with speech behavior in northern India it conveys a whole host of meanings, since Sikhs are stereotypically known as bumblers. Similarly, the statement "He is a fox," cited above, which conveys slyness to middle-class whites, may be interpreted as a synonym for "He is handsome" by blacks. Communication thus requires both shared grammar and shared rules of language usage. Two speakers may speak closely related and, on the surface, mutually intelligible varieties of the same language, but they may nevertheless misunderstand each other because of differences in usage rules resulting from differences in background. We must know the speakers' normal usage pattern, i.e., which styles are associated as unmarked forms with which activities and relationships, as well as what alternates are possible in what context, and what cultural associations these carry.

Note that the view of culture that emerges from this type of analysis is quite different from the conventional one. Linguists attempting to incorporate cultural information into their descriptions tend to regard culture as a set of beliefs and attitudes that can be measured apart from communication. Even the recent work that utilizes actual speech samples by eliciting "subjective reactions" to these forms or evaluations, going considerably beyond earlier work, does not completely depart from this tradition, since it continues to rely on overt or conscious judgment. Our own material suggests that culture plays a role in communication that is somewhat similar to the role of syntactic knowledge in the decoding of referential meanings. Cultural differences, in other words, affect judgment both above and below the level of consciousness. A person may have every intention of avoiding cultural bias, yet, by subconsciously superimposing his own interpretation on the verbal performance of others, he may nevertheless bias his judgment of their general ability, efficiency, etc.

Communication problems are compounded by the fact that we know very little about the distribution of usage rules in particular populations. For example, there seems to be no simple correlation with ethnic identity, nor is it always possible to predict usage rules on the basis of socioeconomic indexes. While the majority of the speakers in a Puerto Rican block in Jersey City used Spanish in normal in-group communication and switched to English to indicate special affect, there are others residing among them, however, whose patterns differ significantly. A Puerto Rican college student took a tape recorder home and recorded informal family conversation over a period of several days. It is evident from his recording, and he himself confirms this in interviews, that in his family English is the normal medium of informal conversation while Spanish is socially marked and serves to convey special connotations of intimacy and anger.

It follows that, while the usual sociological measures of ethnic background, social class, educational achievements, etc., have some correlation with usage rules, they cannot be regarded as accurate predictors of performance in particular instances. On the contrary, social findings based on incomplete data, or on populations different from those for which they were intended, may themselves contribute to cultural misunderstanding. The use of responses to formal tests and interviews to judge the verbal ability of lower-class bilinguals is a case in point. Rosenthal (1968) has shown that teachers' expectations have a significant effect on learning, and psychological experiments by Williams (1969) and Henrie (1969) point to the role that dialect plays in generating these expectations. *When expectations created by dialect stereotypes are further reinforced by misapplied or inaccurate social science findings, education suffers.*

Imagine a child in a classroom situation who in a moment of special excitement shifts to black speech. The teacher may have learned that black speech is systematic and normal for communication in Afro-American homes. Nevertheless, intent as she is upon helping the child to become fully bilingual, she may comment on the child's speech by saying, "We don't speak this way in the classroom," or she may ask the child to rephrase the sentence in standard English. No matter how the teacher expresses herself, the fact that she focuses on the form means that the teacher is not responding to the real meaning of the child's message. The child is most likely to interpret her remark as a rebuff and may feel frustrated in his attempt at establishing a more personal relationship with the teacher. In other words, by imposing her own monostylistic communicative norms, the teacher may thwart her students' ability to express themselves fully. An incident from a tape-recorded classroom session in Black Language Arts will illustrate the point.

STUDENT (*reading from an autobiographical essay*): This lady didn't have no sense.
TEACHER: What would be a standard English alternate for this sentence?
STUDENT: She didn't have any sense. But not this lady: *she didn't have no sense.*

Note the difference in focus between teacher and student. The former, in her concern with Standard English, focuses on the deviant double negatives, while the student is concerned with creating the proper narrative effect.

II

If the teacher were able to interpret the social meaning conveyed by the child's use of particular linguistic forms, her teaching would be enhanced. All too often, however, his use of forms other than Standard English has a negative effect—not because linguistic differences per se would prevent the child from learning to read but because they affect how the teacher behaves toward him.

Classroom observation of first-grade reading sessions in a racially integrated California school district illustrates some of the problems involved. Classes in the district include about 60 percent white and 40 percent Chicano, black, and Oriental children. College student observers find that most reading classes have a tracking system such that children are assigned to fast or slow reading groups, and that these groups are taught by different methods and otherwise receive different treatment.

Even in first-grade reading periods, where presumably all children are beginners, the slow reading groups tend to consist of 90 percent blacks and Chicanos. Does this situation reflect real learning difficulties, or is it simply a function of our inability to diagnose reading aptitude in culturally different children? Furthermore, given the need for some kind of ability grouping, how effective and how well adapted to cultural needs are the classroom devices that are actually used to bridge the reading gap?

One reading class was divided into a slow reading group of three children, and a second group of seven fast readers. The teacher worked with one group at a time, keeping the others busy with individual assignments. With the slow readers she concentrated on the alphabet, on the spelling of individual words, and on supposedly basic grammatical concepts such as the distinctions between questions and statements. She addressed the children in what white listeners would identify as pedagogical style. Her enunciation was deliberate and slow. Each word was clearly articulated, with even stress and pitch, as if to avoid any verbal sign of emotion, approval, or disapproval. Children were expected to speak only when called upon, and the teacher would insist that each question be answered before responding to further ideas. Unsolicited remarks were ignored even if they referred to the problem at hand. Pronunciation errors were corrected whenever they occurred, even if the reading task had to be interrupted. The children seemed distracted and inattentive. They were guessing at answers, "psyching out" the teacher in the manner described by Holt (1965) rather than following her reasoning process. The following sequence symbolizes the artificiality of the situation:

TEACHER: Do you know what a question is? James, ask William a question.
JAMES: William, do you have a coat on?
WILLIAM: No, I do not have a coat on.

James asks his question and William answers in a style that approaches in artificiality that of the teacher, characterized by citation form pronunciation of [ey] rather than [ə] of the indefinite article, lack of contraction of *do not,* stress on the *have,* staccato enunciation as if to symbolize what they perceive to be the artificiality and incomprehensibility of the teacher's behavior.

With the advanced group, on the other hand, reading became much more of a group activity and the atmosphere was more relaxed. Words were treated in context, as part of a story. Children

were allowed to volunteer answers. There was no correction of pronunciation, although some deviant forms were also heard. The children actually enjoyed competing with each other in reading, and
the teacher responded by dropping her pedagogical monotone in
favor of more animated natural speech. The activities around the
reading table were not lost on the slow readers, who were sitting
at their desks with instructions to practice reading on their own.
They kept looking at the group, neglecting their own books, obviously wishing they could participate. After a while one boy picked
up a spelling game from a nearby table. He started to work at it
with the other boy, and they began to argue in a style normal for
black children. When their voices became raised, the teachers
turned and asked them to go back to reading.

In private conversation, the teacher (who is very conscientious
and seemingly concerned with all her children's progress) justified
her ability grouping on the grounds that children in the slow group
lacked books in their homes and "did not speak proper English."
She stated they needed practice in grammar, abstract thinking,
and pronunciation and suggested that, given this type of training,
they would eventually be able to catch up with the advanced group.
We wonder how well she will succeed. Although clearly she has the
best motives and would probably be appalled if one were to suggest
that her ability grouping and her emphasis on the technical aspects
of reading and spelling with culturally different children is culturally
biased, her efforts are not so understood by the children themselves.
Our data indicate that the pedagogical style used with slow readers
carries different associations for low-middle-class and low-income
groups. While whites identify it as normal teaching behavior, blacks
associate it with the questioning style of welfare investigators and
automatically react by not cooperating. In any case, attuned as they
are to see meaning in stylistic choice, the black children in the slow
reading group cannot fail to notice that they are being treated quite
differently from and with less understanding than the advanced
readers.

What are the implications of this type of situation for our understanding of the role of dialect differences in classroom learning?
There is no question that the grammatical features of black dialects
discovered by urban dialectologists in recent years are of consider-

able importance for the historical study of the origin of these dialects and for linguistic theory in general, but this does not necessarily mean that they constitute an impediment to learning. Information on black dialect is often made known to educators in the form of simple lists of deviant features with the suggestion that these features might interfere with reading. There is little if any experimental evidence, for example, that the pronunciations characteristic of urban Black English actually interfere with the reading process.

Yet the teacher in our classroom spent considerable time attempting to teach her slow readers the distinction between *pin* and *pen.* Lack of vowel distinction in these two words is widespread among blacks, but also quite common among whites in northern California. In any case, there is no reason why homophony in this case should present more difficulty than homophony in such words as *sea* and *see* or *know* and *no* or that created by the midwestern dialect speaker's inability to distinguish *Mary, marry,* and *merry.*

The problem of contextual relevance is not confined to contact with speakers of Black English. It also applies, for example, to the teaching of both English and Spanish in bilingual schools. When interviewed about their school experiences, Puerto Rican high school students in New York as well as Texas and California Chicano students uniformly complain about their lack of success in Spanish instruction. They resent the fact that their Spanish teachers single out their own native usages as substandard and inadmissible both in classroom speech and writing.

On the contrary, a recent study, using testing procedures specifically adapted to black school children, shows that children who fail to distinguish orally between such word pairs as *jar* and *jaw, toe* and *tore, six* and *sick* are nevertheless able to distinguish among them when presented with the written forms.

It is not enough simply to present the educator with the descriptive linguistic evidence on language or dialect differences. What we need is properly controlled work on reading as such, work that does not deal with grammar alone. Our data suggest that urban language differences, while they may or may not interfere with reading, *do have a significant influence on a teacher's expectation, and hence on the learning environment.* In other words, regardless of overtly expressed attitudes, the teachers are quite likely to be influenced by what they perceive as deviant speech and failure to respond to questions and will act accordingly, thus potentially inhibiting the students' desire to learn. Since bilinguals and bidialectals rely heavily on code switching as a verbal strategy, they are especially sensitive to the relationship between language and context. It would seem that they learn best under conditions of maximal contextual reinforcement. Sole concentration on the technical aspects of reading, grammar, and spelling may so adversely affect the learning environment as to outweigh any advantages to be gained.

Experience with a summer program in language arts for minority group members — mostly of Chicano origin — suggests a method of dealing with this problem (Waterhouse, 1969). Course attendance in this program was voluntary, and it soon became evident through group discussion that if the course were to be continued it could not start with the usual grammar and instruction. Several weeks of discussion were therefore devoted to achieving some agreement on the kind of communicative goals that would be relevant to students and that would require standard English. Once this agreement had been achieved, students then set out to enact such interaction sequences in the classroom, using a role-play technique. Texts then produced in this way were discussed in relation to their communicative effectiveness, and in the course of this discussion students soon began to correct their own and fellow students' grammar. The teacher's role was reduced to that of a discussion moderator, an arbiter of effectiveness, with the result that student motivation increased tremendously and learning improved dramatically.

It seems clear that progress in urban language instruction is not simply a matter of better teaching aids and improved textbooks. Middle class adults have to learn to appreciate differences in communicative strategies of the type discussed here. Teachers themselves must be given instruction in both the linguistic and ethnographic aspects of speech behavior. They must become acquainted with code selection rules in formal and informal settings as well as with those themes of folk literature and folk art that form the input to these rules, so that they can diagnose their own communication problems and adapt methods to their children's background.

Bibliography

Abrahams, Roger D. *Deep Down in the Jungle*. Hatboro, Pa.: Folklore Associates, 1964.

Blom, Jan Petter; and Gumperz, John J. "Social Meaning in Linguistic Structures." In John J. Gumperz and Dell Hymes (eds.), *Directions in Sociolinguistics*. New York: Holt, Rinehart and Winston, 1970.

Bloomfield, Leonard. *Language*. New York: Holt, Rinehart, 1936.

Fishman, Joshua. "Who Speaks What Language to Whom and When." *La Linguistique* 2:67–88.

Friedrich, Paul. "Structural Implications of Russian Pronomial Usage." In William Bright (ed.), *Sociolinguistics*. The Hague: Mouton and Co., 1967.

Garvin, Paul (ed.). *A Prague School Reader*. Washington, D.C.: Georgetown University Press, 1969.

Gumperz, John J.; and Hernández, Eduardo. "Cognitive Aspects of Bilingual Communication." Working Paper No. 28, Language Behavior Research Laboratory, University of California at Berkeley, December 1969.

Hannerz, Ulf. *Soulside*. New York: Columbia University Press, 1968.

Henrie, Samuel N., Jr. "A Study of Verb Phrases Used by Five Year Old Non-standard Negro English Speaking Children." Doctoral dissertation, University of California at Berkeley, 1969.

Holt, John Caldwell. *How Children Fail*. New York: Pitman, 1964.

Kochman, Thomas. " 'Rapping' in the Black Ghetto." *Transaction*, February 1969: 26–34.

Labov, William. "The Logic of Non-Standard Negro English." In James E. Alatis (ed.), *Linguistics and the Teaching of Standard English*. Monograph Series on Languages and Linguistics, No. 22. Washington, D.C.: Georgetown University Press, 1969.

Lance, Donald M. "A Brief Study of Spanish-English Bilingualism." Research report, Texas A. and M. University, 1969.

Mehan, B. Unpublished lecture on testing and bilingualism in the Chicano community, delivered to the Kroeber Anthropological Society Meetings, April 25, 1970.

Melmed, Paul, J. "Black English Phonology: The Question of Reading Interference." Ph.D. dissertation (Language Behavior Research Laboratory, Monograph I), University of California at Berkeley, 1970.

Mitchell-Kernan, Claudia. "Language Behavior in a Black Urban Community." Doctoral dissertation (Working Paper No. 23, Language Behavior Research Laboratory), University of California at Berkeley, 1969.

Rosenthal, Robert; and Jacobson, Lenore. *Pygmalion in the Classroom.* New York: Holt, Rinehart and Winston, 1968.

Sacks, Harvey. "On the Analyzability of Stories by Children." In John J. Gumperz and Dell Hymes (eds.), *Directions in Sociolinguistics.* New York: Holt, Rinehart and Winston, 1970.

Schegloff, Emanuel. "Sequencing in Conversational Openings." In John J. Gumperz and Dell Hymes (eds.), *Directions in Sociolinguistics.* New York: Holt, Rinehart and Winston, 1970.

Shuy, Roger W. *Social Dialects and Language Learning.* Proceedings of the Bloomington, Indiana, Conference, 1964. N.C.T.E. Cooperative Research Project No. OE5-10-148.

Stewart, W. "Continuity and Change in American Negro Dialects." *The Florida FL Reporter,* Spring 1968.

Troike, Rudolph C. "Receptive Competence, Productive Competence and Performance." In James E. Alatis (ed.), *Linquistics and the Teaching of Standard English.* Monograph Series on Languages and Linguistics, No. 22. Washington, D.C.: Georgetown University Press, 1969.

Waterhouse, John. Final report, Comparative Literature 1A (Section 4) and Comparative Literature 1B (Section 5), English for Foreign Students Program, University of California at Berkeley, 1969. Typescript.

Williams, Frederick. "Psychological Correlates of Speech Characteristics: on Sounding 'Disadvantaged.' " Institute for Research on Poverty, University of Wisconsin, March 1969.

Cognitive Repertoires

Abstract Versus Concrete Speech: A False Dichotomy

Eleanor Burke Leacock
Polytechnic Institute of Brooklyn

A little learning can be a dangerous thing. The sciences abound with instances in which tentative formulations and working hypotheses, or partial leads and discoveries, have either become translated into definitive findings when reinterpreted for the public, or have been lifted out of context and oversimplified to the point of hopeless distortion. Presently we are only at the threshold of understanding the nature of language and of thought and their interrelation. Nonetheless it is commonly assumed, and often stated, that characteristic speech patterns of lower-class children have been demonstrated to be linguistically deficient, laying the basis for cognitive disabilities that, in turn, lead to poor school performance.

According to one set of inferences, language dialects or speech styles can be distinguished as either "abstract" or "concrete"; a presumably more "abstract" style is of a higher order than a "concrete" one, and lays a superior basis for thought; and the "abstract" style characterizes the speech patterns of middle-class speakers of English as compared with the "concrete" style of lower-class speakers. My aim in this paper is to question all three assumptions and reveal how discussions of linguistic and cognitive abilities (or disabilities) ascribed to working-class children, particularly those who are black, are often distorted, stereotyped, and pernicious.

Premature Assumptions About Language and Thought

Systematic cross-cultural research into the childhood process of language learning is quite new, and cross-cultural studies of per-

111

ception, categorization, and the like are still hindered by inadequate methodologies.[1] Nonetheless, so widespread is the notion that a linguistic basis for presumed cognitive deficiencies among lower-class children has been clearly defined, that even so careful and sensitive an observer as Edgar Friedenberg can write blandly, without qualification or explanation, that there are "systematic differences in cognitive ability" (between children of different classes), and that they follow from "differences in the way symbols are used in the homes of the very poor and of the middle class [which] are so great as to be perhaps ineradicable" (1969, p. 57). In a text for teacher education, Grace Graham has stated that "working men . . . tend to think in the concrete rather than the abstract and they find little meaning in verbal symbols" (1963, pp. 317–18). In his book *Intelligence and Cultural Environment,* Philip Vernon speaks of the "mother-tongue" of black children as an ineffective "medium for advanced education, communication and thinking" (1969, p. 231).

Generally speaking, three social and intellectual influences have formed the background against which such statements are made. These are: (1) the inappropriate extrapolation from the type of research into language and thought associated primarily with the name of Benjamin Lee Whorf; (2) the ethnocentric habit of seeking differences between "civilized" and "primitive" man in terms of quantitatively conceived and evaluated polar opposites, and the transfer of this practice to discussions of differences between middle- and lower-class attitudes and life styles; and (3) the

[1] In a recent paper, the psychologist Joseph Glick (1969) discussed the need to broaden both cross-cultural tools and concepts in the study of culture and cognition. Among the Kpelle of Liberia he found, in keeping with most previous studies of the type, that a first level sorting of random objects by his subjects was "functional" (with the knife put with the orange it cuts, for example), rather than "logical" in the Western sense (with foods in one category and utensils in another). However, when Glick asked for alternative groupings, he found that his subjects would define the "logical" categories, even recognizing them as Western. Thus findings based on incomplete testing according to the usual methods can lead to serious distortions.

As an interesting example of training in perception, consider how readily we decode the highly stylized illustrations in advertising posters that would be unintelligible to anyone unfamiliar with them.

reaction in educational circles to the social functions of "Standard English" as one attribute of status, and the significance of this function in the unequal education that has been accorded to black children.

The Whorfian Hypothesis

During the 1930s, the anthropological linquist Edward Sapir, and after him Benjamin Lee Whorf and others, raised the question of whether the categories set up by a given language, and the relationships implied by its structure, might not have a profound influence on the habits of perception and the assumptions about causal relations made by its speakers. At a simple level, terminological distinctions presumably help a person define and order otherwise random perceptions. For example, the highly elaborated technical vocabulary of English makes it an efficient tool for ordering an inquiry into many technological problems. Yet there are circumstances where English would be deficient. For example, the Eskimo use a variety of words for *snow*. In traditional Eskimo life it was essential to recognize snow lying on shifting ice and hence unsafe, or snow suitable for house-building, or snow tainted by salt water, hence not to be melted for drinking, and so forth. Presumably, the refined terminology for *snow* expedites the process of sensitizing a young Eskimo's perception of such variations.

Whorf, however, was interested in the more complex question of what influence the morphological features of a language might have on thought, in relation to concepts such as space, time, matter, severality, and causality. Whorf wrote that each uniquely and intricately patterned language "ordains the forms and categories by which the personality not only communicates, but also analyzes nature, notices or neglects types of relationships and phenomena, channels his reasoning and builds the house of his consciousness" (1956, p. 252). The extremity of Whorf's position is generally argued. It has been pointed out that he ignored the fact that people with similar cultures may speak widely divergent languages, or, conversely, people with divergent cultures may speak closely related languages; that he overemphasized the cognitive aspects of language at the expense of its communicative functions; and that he did not take sufficient account of nonlinguistic cognition. Nonetheless, some relation between language and thought along the lines of Whorf's argument is generally considered to exist.

In any case, through his analysis of the ways in which different ideas can be embedded in linguistic structures, Whorf demonstrated the naïveté of any assumption that English was more sophisticated than other languages in its facility for handling causal relationships. He wrote that in many languages spoken by American Indians and by Africans, there were "finely wrought, beautifully logical discriminations about causation, action, result, dynamic or energic quality, directness of experience, etc., all matters of the function of thinking, indeed the quintessence of the rational" (1956, p. 80). An example of Whorfian analysis pertains to the English conjunction *that,* and its limitations when compared with the Hopi Indian language of the American Southwest. Two different forms of reasoning are involved when English speakers say, "I see that it is red," and "I see that it is new," but we do not discriminate between them grammatically. Indeed, so habituated are we to these usages that we do not easily recognize any difference. Hopi speakers, on the other hand, use one form for the first case, where seeing "presents a sensation of redness," and another for the second, where it presents "unspecified evidence from which is drawn the inference of newness." To carry the matter further, in English we say, "I hear that it is new," whereas in Hopi this calls for another relator, since "the significant presentation to the consciousness is that of a verbal report, and neither a sensation per se nor inferential evidence." In such instances, Whorf pointed out, "English compared to Hopi is like a bludgeon compared to a rapier" (p. 65).

Ethnocentric Views of Cross-cultural Differences in Thought

Unfortunately, despite Whorf's clear statement to the contrary, his hypothesis about the influence of language upon thought has at times become tied in with the tradition, all too common in the West, of viewing the heretofore "primitive" peoples of the world as functioning at a conceptually cruder level than the "civilized" peoples. According to this line of thought, which has now been extended to comparisons between middle- and lower-class groups within Western society, white middle-class members of

Western culture are seen as abstract, rational, and logical in their patterns of thought, as opposed to members of simpler societies and lower-class people, who are said to be concrete, nonrational, and nonlogical.[2]

Two important spokesmen for this position with regard to so-called primitive society have been Lucien Lévy-Bruhl and Heinz Werner. Lévy-Bruhl wrote extensively on the subject of primitive thought, elaborating on the assertion that "the entire mental habit which rules out abstract thought and reasoning" constituted "a characteristic and essential trait of primitive mentality" (1923, p. 29). To Lévy-Bruhl, primitive thought was characterized by "direct intuition, immediate apprehension, rapid and almost instantaneous interpretation of what has been perceived," and had nothing in common with intellectual processes as Western man knows them (1923, p. 443). Even the technical skills of primitive society Lévy-Bruhl saw as arising from a "sort of intuition" rather than deliberate reasoning and analysis.

In his *Comparative Psychology of Mental Development,* Werner described the thought of primitive peoples, children, brain-damaged persons, and the mentally ill as being "concrete," or "dominated by personal reference, sensory-motor qualities and a functional organization of events." He wrote:

Typical European reflection is universal in nature, abstract; it functions more or less independently of the immediate concrete reality and is governed by an awareness of general laws. The thought of primitive man is pinned down to the reality of the thing-like world and is therefore pragmatic, concrete and individual (1961, p. 299).

It is true that a great potential for understanding is made possible by the enormous accumulation of knowledge in Western culture. Although it is hardly taken full advantage of, it is far beyond the limits imposed by smaller social units with less elaborate technologies. There are also obvious differences between technologically advanced societies and technologically and economically simpler societies (now, of course, rapidly becoming a thing of the past), that relate to the sociology of knowledge, and the specialization of "thinking" itself as a pursuit of scientists and philosophers. With

[2]For a detailed discussion of this tradition, cf. Drucker (1971).

"civilization" there has been the development, not only of highly organized and concentrated bodies of theory and knowledge in different areas, but also an emphasis on thinking about the nature of thought itself.

To say this, however, is quite different from saying that there is a qualitative difference in thought processes among the members of advanced societies as a whole, when compared with members of simpler societies. Franz Boas pointed out long ago that the advance of civilization means traditional knowledge has become more rigorously subjected to logical analysis, but that this does not mean the ordinary individual in a complex society necessarily thinks more logically (1919). Neither does it mean, as the reactions to today's social issues constantly evidence, that the force of nonlogical emotional associations is any the less for so-called civilized man.

Anthropologists have typically found among the peoples of other (and heretofore "primitive") cultures they have come to know, the same things that researchers are now finding among working-class people once they stop making premature judgments and start asking serious questions. Anthropologists have found, first, that there is a compartmentalization of the areas in which "abstract" notions of "lawfulness" are consciously applied, and areas in which they are not, both on a cultural and an individual level. The application of rigorous rules for analysis and decision-making in certain aspects of one's work does not mean they need be extended to the rest of one's activities. The stereotype of the absent-minded professor, who relies on his wife and secretary to manage his daily affairs, is an implicit comment on this fact.

Second, anthropologists have noted great variability in the degree to which individuals in any group indulge in "abstract" speculation. Most people in any society are not philosophers or scientists. The anthropologist Paul Radin developed this point explicitly, and contrasted the "man of action" with the "thinker" as psychological types found in all cultures. Everywhere the man of action predominates, the person who, "broadly characterized, is oriented toward the object," and who "is interested primarily in practical results and indifferent to the claims and stirrings of his inner self" (1953, p. 38). But in all societies, Radin wrote, one can see the influence of the thinker. Although the thinker is also "definitely desirous of practical results," he is "nevertheless impelled by his whole nature to spend a considerable time in analyzing his subjective states" (p. 38), and he has "a temperament[al] craving for a logical coordination and integration of events" (p. 43).

Radin's distinction was brought home forcefully to me in my own field work among the Naskapi Indians, hunters, fishermen, and trappers of the Labrador peninsula. At first I was surprised by the eminently rational and practical tenor of daily activities among the Indians, and I realized how deeply ingrained had been an ethnocentric and stereotypical image of "primitive" man as governed by magic and ritual. My further surprise at the variety of personal styles I found in a band of but a few score people exposed another stereotype not eradicated by all the reading I had done—that of the conforming primitive man, slave to tradition. The man with whom I worked most closely, since he knew some English, was definitely a "man of action." One day he expressed his impatience with my endless questions by carving a small model of a fish spear and salmon while we talked. At the end of our session he handed it to me, commenting, with satisfaction, that today he had done some *work.* I learned to break my questions to him down into parts that could be answered with a yes or no or a direct description of some incident. In sharp contrast were two men constantly to be heard talking as they worked around the camp. They told me some traditional stories with the aid of an interpreter, and explained parts of them to me with interest. They were "thinkers" who loved discussing, probing, evaluating.

In his books Paul Radin (1927, 1953) presents many examples of speculative poetry and mythology collected by anthropologists from societies around the world. An interesting example of philosophical speculation I came across in my own reading is taken from a richly documented record by George Dorsey of the Sun Dance ceremony as practiced by the Arapaho Indians around the turn of this century (cf. Dorsey, 1903; Leacock, 1946). Like the other Indians of the Great Plains, the Arapaho had an elaborate symbolism accompanying their rituals that was known to and passed down by certain revered clan elders. Ceremonially, the color red symbolized a cluster of associated ideas: mankind, the female form, the earth, fire, life, blood. However, in the Sun Dance, when it was paired with black as one of the "two most important colors," representing "a division for the bad and good," red was "bad." Black was "good," since it was associated with night, the moon, the north, and the left or "harmless" side, thus meaning peace, goodwill, and brotherly love among the people. Red was "bad," because as day it was also the right side, and the right hand, responsible for war and bloodshed, was used in doing wrong. Traditionally, black was worn after cessation of hostilities, when it symbolized victory over human enemies as well as over hunger and disease. However, the Arapaho told Dorsey that some years earlier a great priest by the name of Fire Wood said that, since the right hand was the protective element leading to victory, black, the color for victory, should be on the right and the south. Therefore black came to have the contradictory association in some rituals with the right side, the south, summer, and day, while red was the reverse.

Thinkers such as Fire Wood, concerned with rationalizing a body of belief, are rare in any culture. Yet primitive poetry, philosophy, and ritual show the impress of such men. And, Lévy-Bruhl to the contrary, primitive technology bears the imprint of the scientist who consciously applies "abstract" principles in the solution of a problem he has posed to himself. For example, consider the use of a special woven device to squeeze the poisonous juice out of manioc and make it edible; the use of various substances such as fish oils and animal brains in the working of leather; the use of torsion and leverage in the making of often very complicated traps with elaborate triggering mechanisms; the invention of the bow and arrow; the use of various substances as temper, to keep potting clay from cracking when fired; and so on in hundreds of other cases.

This is not to say that "intuition" probably did not play some role in such inventions, just as it does in the work of any scientist. In fact, as the literature on the nature of invention attests, we use the word "intuition" to indicate some part of the discovery process that we do not understand. Suffice it to say for the present that invention and discovery involve moving back and forth between a consideration of "general laws" and specific cases or from the abstract to the concrete. It makes no sense to speak of abstract speculation as capable of being divorced for long from "concrete" and "individual" cases—a consideration to which we shall return below.

The Role of Standard English in the Conflicts Around the Schools

Before turning to theoretical aspects of the abstract-concrete polarity, it is important to outline the social background against which discussions of language and thought styles among lower-class and especially black children are being conducted, and which has been conducive to the application of the spurious primitive-civilized dichotomy to middle class–lower class comparisons.

In the United States, "Standard English" is one index of assured status. A primary function of schooling has been in the recent past to teach the children of immigrants to speak and read Standard English with, as their reward, the opening of occupational channels for upward mobility. Memorization and rote-teaching were common; these methods seem to be related, in the history of nations, to the initial period of building literacy in a common language.[3] They make schooling easier for the non-English speaker than does the contemporary emphasis on individual participation in discussion, an emphasis that places him at a sharp disadvantage.

The dialectic variant of English spoken by black Americans went more or less unnoted as long as segregated schooling with lower performance levels for black schools was taken for granted. However, the determination of black America to win equal opportunities for social and occupational advancement that followed World War II meant, among other things, achieving a vastly improved education for black children. This posed a challenge to a deeply entrenched system of differential status and privilege. It has left no major school system untouched, and has been characterized by anger, bitterness, and confusion that need no documentation here.

In the flurry of research, writing, and programming that has accompanied the school conflict, there has been a search for simple formulas that either promise (unrealistically) to rectify inequalities with the introduction of relatively superficial changes, or, by their failure, supposedly demonstrate that it is an assumed inferior ability of black children that is really at fault. In this context, preliminary research on the "linguistic competence" of middle- as com-

---

[3] As can be observed today in schools for farmers and working-class urbanites in Africa and Latin America.

pared with lower-class children, and white as compared with black children, has been seized on as one explanation for the low performance of the black and the poor. Speech patterns of black students that teachers either do not understand, or, since they are a mark of lower status, most teachers are unwilling to accept, have long been a bone of contention in the classroom. Baratz and Baratz write:

The schools tend to regard Standard English as "right" and any dialects as "wrong." Therefore, instead of recognizing that the ghetto child is speaking a well-developed language, and then using that language to teach him Standard English (something that he must acquire if he wishes to compete in the middle-class world), the teacher defines her goal in regard to the Negro ghetto child as that of stamping out his "bad" language (which relates to his culture and his basic Negro identity) and replacing the child's language with standard middle-class English (1969, p. 402).

Now this supposedly inadequate language could be referred to as the basis for the children's presumed cognitive deficiencies and their lower level of school performance.

Ironically, however, just when such "findings" were making their way into teacher-training texts, the rapidly maturing movement of black people to win some control over their own lives was producing leaders who used the idiom of their people with a new pride and assertiveness. Students of language, struck by the rich speech they heard from black America, began to replace testing methods geared to the particular training of middle-class children with the recording of black children's actual speech. By comparison with the truncated language used in formal testing or other institutionalized settings where the low-status child is placed in a restricting and threatening situation, the language of the ghetto was revealed to the social scientist in its own "natural" fullness. As a result, alongside books and articles that supposedly inform the confused teacher about the inadequacy of the black idiom, works are appearing that explain that the language patterns of black children are different from, but not inferior to, Standard English and that they represent a well-ordered, highly structured variant of English with which teachers should familiarize themselves as part of their teaching technology.

Concepts of "Abstract" and "Concrete"

Various strategies of speech have been subjected to analysis, particularly in the "street-corner society" of the ghetto, and consciously elaborated and constantly proliferating terminologies for social situations, personality types, and psychological states have been defined that are no less "abstract" than the scientific or academic terminologies utilized (part of the time) by various sections of the white middle-class world. Furthermore, the marked use of metaphor as a form of analytic description, which has been noted among working-class people in general and black people in particular, involves a high order of abstraction. In order to explicate this point, it is first necessary to examine the terms "abstract" and "concrete" and their spurious designation as apposing forms of speech or thought, one said to be "higher," one "lower."

Our intellectual tradition that "abstract" thought is separable from and superior to thinking about "concrete" things and situations stems, of course, from Plato's statement of the ideal "form" as the ultimately true, good, and beautiful. Over the centuries the tradition has been reinforced by the generally superior position of the educated man to the manual laborer, and the strong emphasis of education upon philosophy. Yet it was none other than G. W. F. Hegel, one of the more abstruse among nineteenth-century philosophers, who some hundred years ago poked fun at the touting of the "abstract."

In a short article entitled "Who Thinks Abstractly," Hegel spoke of the prejudice for abstract thinking, and wrote:

That everybody present should know what thinking is and what is abstract is presupposed in good society, and we certainly are in good society. The question is merely *who* thinks abstractly? (1966, p. 115).

Not the educated, he answered, but the uneducated, and he continued, "Good society does not think abstractly because it is too easy, because it is too lowly . . ." (p. 116). To illustrate his point, Hegel describes a murderer being led to execution. Ladies may comment that he looks strong, handsome, and interesting; and an insightful person may wonder about the source of the crime in the individual's life history. The populace is horrified. "How can one think so wickedly and call a murderer handsome?"—or how can one want to excuse him for his crime? Hegel points out:

This is abstract thinking: to see nothing in the murderer except the abstract fact that he is a murderer, and to annul all other human essence in him with this simple quality (pp. 116–117).

If one is driven to argue that such abstraction is not worthy of the name, that it is a mere low-level "stereotype," one has changed the terms of the discussion, from the relative presence or absence in different groups of abstracting behavior, to a concern with the form and purpose of the abstraction. One must then ask, as Hegel of course intended, what *is* an abstraction, or, conversely, what is it to be "concrete?"

According to Webster, who as might be expected is not altogether unambiguous on the matter, there seem to be four main notions involved in the term "abstract": intangibility, generality, separation, and essence. To form a general idea about some intangible but essential quality separated from any context is the epitome of abstraction. To abstract is "to think of [a quality] apart from any particular instance or material object that has it; form [a general idea] from particular instances." Interestingly enough, in its etymological meaning, "to draw from" or "separate," it has also meant "to take dishonestly," "to purloin."

As long as "concrete" refers to some immediately experienced specific event or tangible object, it appears to be altogether different from "abstract." But the matter is not so simple, and elements of intangibility, generality, separation, and essence all creep in at some point. The etymological meaning of concrete is "to unite or coalesce into a mass," and a term that designates not only a thing but "a class of things" may still be concrete if these are things that "can be perceived by the senses, as opposed to naming a quality or attribute." One can have a "concrete idea." According to Webster, "man" is a concrete term, "human" is abstract.

It would be concrete, then, according to Webster, to have an idea of "tables," but abstract to have an idea of "tableness." The question is, is the first possible without the second? The linguist Eric Lenneberg suggests that it is not. He writes:

In all languages of the world *words label a set of relational principles* instead of being labels of specific objects. Knowing a word is never a simple association between an object and an acoustic pattern, but the successful operation of those principles, or application of those rules, that lead to using the word "table" or "house" for objects never before encountered (1969, p. 641; italics added).

Thus the simplest act of naming involves abstracting certain features of an object (both formal and functional—where precisely do tables, desks, and bureaus begin and end?), generalizing on the basis of these features, and referring to the object by a series of stylized sounds. This is "symboling," or the act that differentiates human from animal behavior.[4] To say as Graham does that any group of people does not find meaning in "verbal symbols," is utter nonsense. In a criticism of Vernon's work cited above, the socio-linguist Joshua Fishman writes that when such a person, "himself not a specialist in language theory, language data, or language analysis," relies on studies by others "who also lack adequate sophistication in these respects":

it is quite predictable that he will regress to crude Whorfianisms . . . which describe entire languages or language varieties—and, therefore, their speakers—as characterized by "necessary" deficiencies in abstractness, flexibility, and so on (1969, p. 1108).

One might also question how far one can take such elegant and widely accepted "abstractions" as beauty, truth, honesty, piety, and so on, without some notion of specific contexts within which they apply. Not far, if one really *thinks* about them, instead of merely parroting them with appropriate remarks or definitions, as happens all too often in our classrooms. Thinking about such notions, "taken dishonestly" from their contexts, necessarily involves moving back and forth between them and various of their "concretions." It involves uniting the "abstract" and the "concrete." Ironically, the failure to do this in scientific research, and the uncritical use of "abstract" terms, results in their inappropriate concretization; they become implicitly translated into entities that obscure operational thinking about social and natural processes. For instance, in his

---

[4] Cf. White (1949), Chapter II, "The Symbol: the Origin and Basis of Human Behavior"; also Kenneth Burke (1963–1964).

book *Ethology of Mammals,* R. F. Ewer writes, "Behavior is something which an animal has got in the same way as it may have horns, teeth, claws, or other structural features" (Klopfer, 1969). In a critical review of Ewer's book, Peter Klopfer takes issue with his statement and the way in which lumping various acts together under a too-general word leads to the drawing of inappropriate analogies between the actions of humans and those of animals. Klopfer writes:

The notion that behavior is a "noun," a palpable entity, has been responsible for much of the nonsense that ethologists have uttered. We read of "aggression" accumulating and needing discharge, as if it were a fluid liable to seep through cracks in the cranium. I believe we "contain" aggression about as much as a radio "contains" the music we hear issuing from it (1969, p. 887).

Unfortunately, operational definitions are accorded a lower status in the classroom than knowing the right name, and naming is all too often confused with knowing or understanding. In psychological testing, children who give operational definitions instead of names for a series of objects are considered not to be "abstracting," and a child's response "Animal" to a set of animal pictures is ranked higher than a response such as "They all have four legs." However, the first response may be simply knowing the proper word to say—one would not know what the child's actual concept of "animal" was until one asked—whereas "they all have four legs" *abstracts* a common characteristic on the basis of individual thought. It is closer to the operational type of definition so important in scientific endeavor.

A humorous example of how language can be manipulated in a purely "abstract" fashion, with no reference to meaning, is quoted by Ogden and Richards in their classic work, *The Meaning of Meaning:*

Suppose someone to assert: *The gostak distims the doshes.* You do not know what this means; nor do I. But, if we assume that it is English, we know that *the doshes are distimmed by the gostak.* We know too that *one distimmer of doshes is a gostak.* If, moreover, the *doshes* are *galloons,* we know that some *galloons are distimmed by the gostak.* And so we may go on, and so we often do go on (1946, p. 46).

A great deal of teaching amounts in essence to going "on and on" in this manner, and while it is comfortable for the child habituated to playing the game, it can lead to total confusion for the child who is ill at ease with Standard English and who probably suffers more often from the illusion that participation in classroom discussion necessarily involves real *understanding.* I am sometimes saddened as a college teacher when marking a paper that parrots back my words with reasonable accuracy, although I know the student has barely scraped the surface of understanding. More regrettable, however, is the student who searches for meaning but lacks skill in the use of language, the student who is clumsy about expression according to the formalities of "educated" discourse. While I will reward the effort with a good mark, I know such a student is slated for failure in terms of higher education, while the successful "bull artist" is headed for success.

All of this is not the fault of teachers as such, of course, but relates to requirements for professional roles in a society where such roles are rapidly proliferating in what are essentially parasitic and mediating arenas; the enormous expansion of the mass media themselves affords the best example. In addition to the old saw, "It ain't what you know but who that counts," must be added, "It ain't what you say but how you say it." The behaviorial sciences deserve stringent criticism in this respect. Sigmund Koch, editor of *Psychology: A Study of a Science,* a book that embodies the results of a survey conducted for the American Psychological Association, discusses the shortcomings of the social sciences in terms relevant to the present discussion. He speaks of the extent to which an emphasis on formal rules for discovery has resulted in "ameaningful thought or inquiry" and a "fictionalistic, conventionalistic" conception of knowledge, so that thousands of studies, such as on the process of learning, for example, can be conducted without improving our actual insight into the learning process. Koch describes "meaningful thinking" as necessarily wedded to its object. His view brings us full circle—some of what Lévy-Bruhl saw as "primitive" and deficient he sees, also using the word "primitive," as wholly desirable:

Meaningful thinking involves a *direct perception* of unveiled relations that seem to spring from the quiddities, particularities of the objects of thought, the problem situations that form the occasions for thought.

There is an organic determination of the form and substance of thought by the properties of the object, the terms of the problem. And these are real in the fullest, most vivid, electric, undeniable way. The mind caresses, flows joyously into, over, around, the relational matrix defined by the problem, the object. There is a merging of person and object or problem. It is a fair descriptive generalization to say that meaningful thinking is ontological in some primitive, accepting, artless, unselfconscious sense (1969, pp. 14, 64).

Before proceeding further, it would be helpful to sum up the above points in relation to the three assumptions stated to be false at the outset of this article:

First, all meaningful speech (that is, true speech, not the experimental babbling of the infant or confused utterances of the mentally ill) involves a high and specifically human order of abstraction. Strictly speaking, there is no such thing as "concrete" speech or language.

Second, like language, thought cannot be separated into the "abstract" and the "concrete." Speculative thought is little understood,[5] but almost by definition it involves moving back and forth between the level of specific phenomena—whether events, objects, or situations—and the level of generalization about properties they may have in common. Even formal logic, the most abstract of all fields, is not devoid of "concrete" loci of reference.

Third, one can say, however, that some people think more than others, or some more profoundly than others. Having said this, one can then argue that group differences in levels of thought would follow from the fact that "thinking" behavior is professionalized as a major activity for a sizable group in technologically advanced societies. The difficulty with this position is, according to the viewpoint represented by Koch, that the professionalization of thought

---

[5] The psychologist J. P. Guilford and his associates (1968), building primarily on the work of Thurstone, have been testing a one hundred and twenty-cell cubical model as representing presently identified or identifiable dimensions of intellectual ability. The model supposes five types of mental "operations," working with four types of information or "contents," to yield six types of information or "product." "Operations" are: evaluation, convergent production, divergent production, memory, cognition. "Contents" may be figural, symbolic, semantic, or behavioral. "Products" are either units, classes, relations, systems, transformations, or implications.

(and, we would add, speech[6]) can as readily lead to its stultification as to its enrichment. As an example, Koch writes:

Consider the problem of "learning" . . . . Consider the hundreds of theoretical formulations, rational equations, mathematical models of the learning process that have accrued; the thousands of research studies.... Consider also that after all this scientist effort our actual *insight* into the learning process—reflected in every humanly important context in which learning is relevant—has not improved one jot (1969, p. 66).

Our enormous advances in the physical sciences are a product of a vast technological machine, coupled with the creative thinking of a very few. And now, when faced with the need for an understanding of the complex interrelations of phenomena, in the face of the threat to man's existence on this earth we have created, we are stymied.

Group differences in styles of speech (and thought), as we presently know them in our society, involve not more or less "abstracting" behavior, but differences in the areas wherein conceptualization is more consciously developed, and in the ways in which concepts are expressed or elaborated upon. It is to this point that I now turn, in a consideration of metaphorical usage, since it is conceded to be common in the idiom of the black community.

Metaphor, Abstraction, and the Social Contexts of Speech

The elaboration of the metaphor is only one of the characteristics that have been noted for black speech style. Others are the constant innovation of new terms for "in-group" interchange; the refinement of terminologies for dealing with social situations and social-psychological types; and the marked concern with linguistic strategies for manipulation, competition, or sheer entertainment; all of which evidence a degree of interest in language that stands in marked contrast to the muted behavior of black children and youth when in formal and threatening situations with teachers, testers, and

[6] This subject is discussed by the philosopher Herbert Marcuse in Chapter 4, "The Closing of the Universe of Discourse," of his *One-Dimensional Man* (1964). Marcuse describes the manipulation of language by the mass media and the devices that are used to block the awareness of social and political realities, with the result that the language of the media itself becomes stunted and restricted.

other such authority figures (cf. Kochman, 1969; Abrahams, 1970).
However, such linguistic concerns, when noted at all in educational
circles, are characteristically considered more a matter of "expressiveness" than of intellectual ability. "Playing" with language
is not often credited as involving conscious and creative thought, or
as evidence of intellectual abilities that can be put to use in the arena
of traditional education. It also goes unnoted that metaphorical
usages may involve a high level of abstraction.

A metaphor is, according to Webster, the "use of a word or
phrase literally denoting one kind of object or idea in place of another
by way of suggesting a likeness or analogy between them." As
examples Webster gives "the ship *plows* the sea," and "a *volley* of
oaths." Metaphors are usually seen as belonging to the world of
literature and poetry—as vivid ways of bringing to mind visual
images or emotional states. Consider, however, the strictly *intellectual* content of the metaphor. At a symposium on metaphor and
symbol, D. G. James stated that a metaphor is one form of symbol.
The metaphor "is the imagination of one thing in the form of another; it is the mode in which the nature, the *being,* the imagined
extra-sensual essence of a thing, is represented by the identification
with the apparently different . . ." (1960, p. 100). Metaphor depends on the abstraction of qualities perceived as similar from
dissimilar phenomena. Howard Nemerov writes in an article on the
metaphor, "Metaphor works on a relation of resemblances; one
resemblance draws another, or others, after it" (1969, p. 628).

A classroom teacher asks for the difference between two pieces
on the same subject that she has read aloud, one a prose selection,
the other a poem; the first one, a black eight-year-old proffers,
"thumped out," the second, the poem, "silked out."[7] All too often
such a response, if noted at all, would be considered a nice example
of the "expressiveness" somehow "natural" to black children. In
fact, however, it is the result of an intellectual process whereby the
child has searched his vocabulary to find the words whose qualities
most succinctly express his perception. To give another instance
from the same classroom, the teacher urges a group of boys not to
exclude another child from their activities. The boys argue that
the child is not actively isolated by them, but in part isolates himself. To clinch the point, a metaphor is employed: the child is for-

[7] I am indebted for these examples to Wendy Lehrman.

gotten as a marble that has rolled away from the center of the game is forgotten. Through metaphorical usage, the salient points of the situation are abstracted and presented as sharply as possible for the teacher's consideration.

Some further examples of metaphorical perspective are taken from the discussion of black workers on the effects of discrimination in employment and how to organize to combat it. There are the enormous odds against which black people must work: "They clip your wings and tell you to fly"; "You take the starch out of a shirt and it doesn't iron too good"; indeed, "You have to learn to step between the raindrops." There is the need for leaders, but they must have a following, a "base": "An airplane can't get along without an airfield." There is the behavior of union leaders, "wheels": "Wheels run over you." And the black worker who has been given the security of a staff job with his union: "He's found his hook, and he's put his coat on it." Mistaken tactics in relation to two union leaders are evaluated: "We didn't appraise this situation. There were two dogs at each other's throats bleeding each other to death. We should have played it cool and let them fight with each other." One was defeated: "His fangs are pulled . . . ." As for a particularly lurid bit of demagogy from a union official: "It's not even good rubber for a balloon."

Through the metaphor, the relevant characteristics of a situation are abstracted and stated in the form of an analogy that clearly divests it of extraneous features. Metaphors employ great linguistic economy; there is no need for the overload of explanatory and qualifying terms that are typically employed in exposition. Unfortunately, however, such terms are themselves often considered the hallmark of scientific thought, so the cognitive aspects of metaphorical usages are generally overlooked. Yet, as Kenneth Burke pointed out in *Permanence and Change,* scientific inquiry itself proceeds metaphorically, through the processes of oversimplification, abstraction, and analogical extension (1937, pp. 97–124). It is only in its expositions or "proofs" that science reverses the process of inquiry and proceeds "logically."

Through the use of "analogical extension," metaphors express, in active form, the process whereby abstract terms commonly arise. Owen Barfield writes that the "tens of thousands of abstract nouns which daily fill the columns of our newspapers, the debating chambers of our legislatures, the consulting rooms of our psychiatrists" once referred to "the concrete world of sensuous experience" (1960, pp. 52–53). As an amusing example, he offers *scruple,* a word derived from the Latin *scrupulus,* which "originally meant a small, sharp stone—the kind that gets into your shoe and worries you" (p. 50). Thus words for being moved, for going ahead, for drifting, for holding in, for answering, become concepts of motivation, progress, tendency, inhibition, responsibility. For this reason, Burke alludes to abstractions as "dead metaphors" (1937, p. 73), and Barfield speaks of language itself as "an unconscionable tissue of dead, or petrified, metaphors" (Nemerov, 1969). (Clichés like "leave no stone unturned" are "completely *fossilized metaphor(s)"* [Barfield, 1960, p. 48; italics in the original].)

Herein lies a problem, however, for as Nemerov indicates, "these metaphors may be not dead but merely sleeping"; they "may arise from the grave and walk in our sentences . . . something that has troubled everyone who has ever tried to write plain expository prose wherein purely mental relations have to be discussed as though they were physical ones" (1969, p. 627). Abstract terminologies, whether scientific or humanistic, are far from the precise and neutral tools they are sometimes considered to be. We are somewhat aware of the semantic load carried by terms such as the various "isms" that incorporate the weight of far-reaching conflicts in their connotations. We are also somewhat aware of stylistic changes in speech in keeping with different situations (such as when we shift gear in style as well as tone of discourse if a family quarrel is interrupted by a telephone call from, say, a department chairman). We are far from aware, however, of a further social dimension incorporated into our terminologies, the one that arises from the fact that words are the end points (or midpoints) in complex sequences of events; they are "compressed fables, or histories" (Nemerov, 1969, p. 635).[8]

It is largely through the process of "analogical extension" that scientific terminologies become developed. Burke writes:

Indeed, as the documents of science pile up, are we not coming to see that whole works of scientific research, even entire *schools,* are hardly

[8] Cf. also the chapter, "What Are the Signs of What?" in Burke (1966).

more than the patient repetition, in all its ramifications, of a fertile metaphor? Thus we have, at different eras in history, considered man as the son of God, as an animal, as a political or economic brick, as a machine, each such metaphor, and a hundred others, serving as the cue for an unending line of data and generalizations (1965, p. 95; italics in the original). [9]

And the choice of metaphor, the direction of analogical extension, is governed largely by one's viewpoint, or bias, or, in Burke's terms, one's *interest*. The world is like a pie that can be sliced, terminologically, any number of ways, "and the course of analogical extension is determined by the particular kind of interest uppermost at the time. . . . The poet may be interested in the sea's anger, the chemist in its iodine . . ." (p. 104).

As terminologies become established, they become a mark of common sense, of good taste: "Good taste is manifested through our adherence to the kinds of relationships already indicated by the terminology of common sense" (Burke, 1965, p. 103). All of which makes it easy for the language—and thought—of those low in status to be misinterpreted, sloughed off. In an extraordinarily candid article, Linda Scheffler, a young counselor working with black and Puerto Rican students in a City College of New York SEEK program, writes of them as at first "literal-minded, deficient in handling abstract concepts and unable to make appropriate generalizations" (Scheffler, 1969, p. 114). After working with them closely and consistently, she finds they grow rapidly in "functional intellectual capacity," and expresses surprise, since this contradicts accepted psychological theory. Scheffler is clear about the steps whereby her own increased self-awareness and ability to deal honestly and informally with the students' problems have enabled her to find points of identification with them. However, she is not aware of the extent to which her original distance from them was affecting her perception of their intellectual abilities, and of the changes in her that followed a mutual moving toward a common basis for identification and communication. For she herself indicates that language style was more of a problem than intellectual ability for the students. She writes:

Some students who barely passed introductory courses in the basic skills

[9] Cf. also Burke (1945).

blossomed and succeeded when they got to regular college courses whose content answered some of the many questions they had about the world around them (p. 116).

In conclusion, then, the rapidly growing study of language in its full social context reveals it to be a highly ambiguous and flexible tool for handling strategies of action and interaction, and renders meaningless the stereotyped views about class differences in language style stated at the outset of this article. A final example of linguistic strategy is germane to the significance these conclusions hold for educators. A quatrain of Edwin Markham's, "Outwitted," illustrates—in metaphor—how a terminological shift in the delineation of the "we" and the "they," the "ingroup" and the "outgroup" —a different slicing of the social pie—redefines as friendly what are originally hostile expectations for attitudes and actions:

He drew a circle that shut me out—
Heretic, rebel, a thing to flout.
But love and I had the wit to win:
We drew a circle that took him in!

Bibliography

Abrahams, Roger D. *Positively Black*. Englewood Cliffs, N.J.: Prentice-Hall, 1970.

Baratz, Stephen S., and Baratz, Joan C. "Negro Ghetto Children and Urban Education: A Cultural Solution." *Social Education* 33 (April 1969): 401–405.

Barfield, Owen. "The Meaning of the Word 'Literal'." In L. C. Knights and Basil Cottle (eds.), *Metaphor and Symbol*. London: Butterworths, 1960.

Boas, Franz. *The Mind of Primitive Man*. New York: Macmillan 1938.

Burke, Kenneth. *Attitudes Towards History*. Vol. 2. New York: New Republic, 1937.

————. *A Grammar of Motives*. Englewood Cliffs, N.J.: Prentice-Hall, 1945.

————. "Definition of Man." *The Hudson Review* 16 (Winter 1963–1964).

————. *Permanence and Change.* New York: Bobbs-Merrill Co., 1965.

————. *Language As Symbolic Action.* Berkeley: University of California Press, 1966.

Dorsey, George A. *The Arapaho Sun Dance.* Field Columbian Museum Publication No. 75, Anthropological Series, vol. 4 (1903).

Drucker, Ernest. "Cognitive Styles and Class Stereotypes." In Eleanor Burke Leacock (ed.), *The Culture of Poverty: A Critique.* New York: Simon and Schuster, 1971.

Fishman, Joshua A. Review of Vernon, *Intelligence and Cultural Environment,* and Baratz and Shuy (eds.), *Teaching Black Children to Read.* In *Science* 165 (September 12, 1969): 1108–1109.

Freidenberg, Edgar Z. "What Are Our Schools Trying to Do?" *The New York Times Book Review* (Special Educational Supplement), September 4, 1969.

Graham, Grace. *The Public School in the American Community.* New York: Harper & Row, 1963.

Glick, Joseph. "Thinking About Thinking, Aspects of Conceptual Organization among the Kpele of Liberia." Paper given at the meeting of the American Anthropological Association, November 1969.

Guilford, J. P. "Intelligence Has Three Facets." *Science* 164 (May 10, 1968): 615–620.

Hegel, G. W. F. In Walter Kaufman (ed. and trans.), *Hegel: Texts and Commentary.* Garden City, N.Y.: Doubleday, 1966.

James, D. G. "Metaphor and Symbol." In L. C. Knights and Basil Cottle, (eds.), *Metaphor and Symbol.* London: Butterworths, 1960.

Klopfer, Peter H. Review of Ewer, *Ethology of Mammals.* In *Science,* 165 (August 29, 1969), 887.

Koch, Sigmund. "Psychology Cannot Be a Coherent Science." *Psychology Today* 3 (September 1969).

Kochman, Thomas. " 'Rapping' in the Black Ghetto." *Trans-action* 6 (February 1969).

Leacock, Eleanor. "Some Aspects of the Philosophy of the Cheyenne and Arapaho Indians." Master's Thesis, Columbia University, 1946.

Lenneberg, Eric H. "On Explaining Language." *Science,* 164 (May 9, 1969), 635-643.

Lévy-Bruhl, Lucien. *Primitive Mentality*. 1923. Reprint. Boston: Beacon, 1966.

Marcuse, Herbert. *One-Dimensional Man*. Boston: Beacon, 1964.

Nemerov, Howard. "On Metaphor." *The Virginia Quarterly Review* 45 (Autumn 1969).

Ogden, C. K., and Richards, I. A. *The Meaning of Meaning*. New York: Harcourt, Brace, 1946.

Radin, Paul. *Primitive Man as Philosopher*. New York: D. Appleton and Company, 1927.

————. *The World of Primitive Man*. New York: Henry Schuman, 1953.

Scheffler, Linda Weingarten. "What SEEK Kids Taught Their Counselor." *The New York Times Magazine* (November 16, 1969).

Vernon, Philip E. *Intelligence and Cultural Environment*. London: Methuen, 1969.

Werner, Heinz. *Comparative Psychology of Mental Development*. New York: Science Editions, 1961.

White, Leslie A. *The Science of Culture*. New York: Farrar, Straus, 1949.

Whorf, Benjamin Lee. *Language, Thought, and Reality*. Cambridge, Mass.: MIT Press, 1956.

A Critique
of the Concept
# of Compensatory Education

Basil B. Bernstein
University of London Institute of Education

Since the late 1950's there has been a steady outpouring of papers and books in the United States concerned with the education of children of low social class whose *material* circumstances are inadequate, or with the education of black children of low social class whose *material* circumstances are chronically inadequate. An enormous research and educational bureaucracy developed in the United States, financed by funds obtained from federal, state, or private foundations. New educational categories were developed—culturally deprived, liguistically deprived, socially disadvantaged—and the notion of compensatory education was introduced as a means of changing the status of those children in the above categories. Compensatory education appeared in several forms: massive preschool introductory programs, large-scale research programs such as those of Deutsch (1964) in the early 1960's, and a plethora of small scale "intervention" or "enrichment" programs for preschool children or children in the first years of compulsory education. Very few sociologists were involved in these studies, as until now education was a low-status area. On the whole, they were carried out by psychologists.

The focus of these studies was on the child in the family and on the local classroom relationships between teacher and child. In the last two years, however, one can detect a change in this focus. As

This paper, in a slightly different form, was prepared for inclusion in *Opening Opportunities for Disadvantaged Learners,* edited by A. Harry Passow (New York: Teachers College Press, 1972).

a result of the movements towards integration and the opposed movement towards community control (the latter a response to the wishes of the various Black Power groups) more studies are being made in the United States of the *school*. Work in England has been almost limited to the effects of streaming. Rosenthal and Jacobson's (1968) study *Pygmalion in the Classroom* drew attention to the critical importance of the teacher's expectations of the child. In this country we have been aware of the educational problem since the writings of Sir Cyril Burt before the war. His book *The Backward Child* (1937) is probably still the best descriptive study we have. After the war a series of sociological surveys and public inquiries into education brought this educational problem into the arena of national debate, and so of social policy. Now in Wales there is a large research unit, financed by the Schools Council, concerned with compensatory education, and important research of a most significant kind is taking place in the University of Birmingham into the problems of the education of Commonwealth children. The Social Science Research Council and the Department of Education and Science have given £175,000 in part for the development of special preschool programs to introduce children to compensatory education.

Colleges of education offer special courses in compensatory education, and one university department of education offers an advanced diploma in this area. It might be worth a few lines to consider the assumptions underlying this work and the concepts which describe it, particularly as my own writings have sometimes been used (and more often abused) to highlight aspects of the general problems and dilemmas.

To begin with, I find the term *compensatory education* a curious one for a number of reasons. I do not understand how we can talk about offering compensatory education to children who, in the first place, have not as yet been offered an adequate educational environment. The Newsom report showed that 79 percent of all secondary-modern schools in slum and problem areas were materially grossly inadequate, and that the holding power of these schools over the teachers was horrifyingly low. The same report also showed very clearly how the depression in the reading scores of these children compared with the reading scores of children who were at school in areas that were neither problem nor slum. This does not conflict with the findings that on average for the country as a whole there has been an improvement in children's reading ability.

The Plowden report was rather more coy about all the above points, but we have little reason to believe that the situation is very much better for primary schools in similar areas. Thus we offer a large number of children, both at the primary and secondary level, materially inadequate schools and unstable teaching staff, and we further expect a small group of dedicated teachers to cope. The strain on these teachers inevitably produces fatigue and illness, and it is not uncommon to find, in any week, teachers having to deal with doubled-up classes of eighty children. And we wonder why the children display very early in their educational life a range of learning difficulties. At the same time, the organization of schools creates delicate overt and covert streaming arrangements which neatly lower the expectations and motivations of teachers and taught, setting up a vicious spiral with all too determinate outcome. It would seem then that we have as yet failed to provide on the scale required an *initial* satisfactory educational environment.

The concept of compensatory education serves to direct attention away from the internal organization and the educational context of the school, and focuses it instead upon the families and children. It also implies that something is lacking in the family, and so in the child. As a result the children are unable to benefit from schools. It follows then that the school has to "compensate" for the something which is missing in the family, and the children become little deficit systems. If only the parents were interested in the goodies we offer; if only they were like middle-class parents, then we could do our job. Once the problem is seen even implicitly in this way, then it becomes appropriate to coin the terms *cultural deprivation, linguistic deprivation,* etc. And then these labels do their own sad work.

If children are labeled *culturally deprived,* then it follows that the parents are inadequate, and that the spontaneous realization of their culture, its images and symbolic representations, are of reduced value and significance. Teachers will have lower expectations of the children, which the children will undoubtedly fulfill. All that informs the child, that gives meaning and purpose to him outside of the school, ceases to be valid and accorded significance and opportunity for enhancement within the school. He has to orient toward a different structure of meaning, whether it is in the form of reading books *(Janet and John),* in the form of language use and dialect, or in the patterns of social relationships. Alternatively, the meaning structure of the school is explained to the parents and imposed upon, rather than integrated within, the form and content of their world. A wedge is progressively driven between the child as a member of a family and community, and the child as a member of a school. Either way the child is expected, and his parents as well, to drop his social identity, his way of life and its symbolic representation, at the school gate. For, by definition, their culture is deprived, the parents inadequate in both the moral and skill orders they transmit. I do not mean by this that no satisfactory home-school relations can take place or do not take place. I mean rather that the parents must be brought *within* the educational experience of the school-child by doing what they *can* do, and can do with *confidence.* There are many ways in which parents can help the child in his learning that are within the parents' sphere of competence. If this happens, then the parents can feel adequate and confident both in relation to the child *and* the school. This may mean that the contents of the learning in school should be drawn much more from the child's experience in his family and community.

So far, then, I have criticized the use of the concept of compensatory education because it distracts attention from the deficiencies in the school itself and focuses upon deficiencies within the community, family, and child. We can add to these criticisms a third. The concept of compensatory education points to the overwhelming significance of the early years of the child's life in the shaping of his later development. Clearly, there is much evidence to support this view and its implication that we should create an extensive nursery school system. However, it would be foolhardy indeed to write off the post-seven-years-of-age educational experience as having little influence. Minimally, what is required initially is to consider the whole age period up to the conclusion of the primary stages as a unity. This would require considering our approach at any *one* age in the context of the *whole* of the primary stage. This implies a systematic, rather than a piecemeal, approach. I am arguing here for taking as the unit, *not* a particular period in the life of the child (for example, three to five years, or five to seven years), but a *stage of education,* the primary stage. We should see all we do in terms of the sequencing of learning, the development of sensitivities within the context of the primary stage. In order to accomplish this the present social and educational division between infant and junior stages must be weakened, as well as the insulation between primary and secondary stages, otherwise gains at any one age in the child may well be vitiated by losses at a later age.

I suggest that we should stop thinking in terms of compensatory education but consider instead, most seriously and systematically, the conditions and contexts of the educational environment.

The very form our research takes tends to confirm the beliefs underlying the organization, transmission, and evaluation of knowledge by the school. The research proceeds by assessing criteria of attainment that schools hold and then measures the competence of different social groups in reaching these criteria. We take one group of children whom we know beforehand possess attributes favorable to school achievement, and a second group of children whom we know beforehand lack these attributes. Then we evaluate one group in terms of what it lacks when compared with another. In this way research, unwittingly, underscores the notion of *deficit* and confirms the status quo of a given organization, transmission, and, in particular, *evaluation* of knowledge. Research very rarely challenges or exposes the social assumptions underlying what counts as valid knowledge, or what counts as a valid realization of that knowledge. There are exceptions in the area of curriculum development, but even here the work often has no built-in attempt to evaluate the changes. This holds particularly for the EPA "feasibility" projects.

Finally, we do not face up to the basic question: *What is the potential for change within educational institutions as they are presently constituted?* A lot of activity does not necessarily mean *action.*

I have taken so much space discussing the new educational concepts and categories because, in a small way, the work I have been doing has inadvertently contributed toward their formulation. It might be, and has been said, that my research, through focusing upon the subculture and forms of familial socialization, has also distracted attention from the conditions and contexts of learning in school. The focus upon usage of language sometimes led people to divorce the use of language from the substratum of cultural meanings which are initially responsible for the language use. The concept *restricted code* has been equated with linguistic deprivation, or even with the nonverbal child.

I want first to start with the notions of elaborated and restricted speech variants. A variant can be considered as the contextual constraints upon grammatical-lexical choices. Sapir, Malinowski, Firth, Vygotsky, and Luria have all pointed out from different points of view that the closer the identifications of speakers and the greater the range of shared interests, the more probable that the speech will take a specific form.

For instance, imagine that a husband and wife have just come out of a movie theater and are talking about the film.

"What do you think?"

"It had a lot to say."

"Yes, I thought so, too. Let's go to the Millers—there may be something going on there."

They arrive at the Millers, who ask about the film. An hour is spent on the complex, moral, political, aesthetic subtleties of the film and its place in the contemporary scene. Here we have an elaborated variant: the meanings now have to be made public to others who have not seen the film. The speech shows careful editing, at both the grammatical and lexical levels; it is no longer context tied. The meanings are explicit, elaborated, and individualized. While expressive channels are clearly relevant, the burden of meaning inheres predominantly in the verbal channel. The experience of the listeners cannot be taken for granted. Thus each member of the group is on his own as he offers his interpretation. Elaborated variants of this kind involve the speakers in particular role relationships, and *if you cannot manage the role, you cannot produce the appropriate speech.* For as the speaker proceeds to individualize his meanings, he is differentiated from others like a figure from its ground. The roles receive less support from each other. There is a measure of isolation. *Difference* lies at the basis of the social relationship in this context, and is made verbally active, whereas in the other context it is *consensus.* The insides of the speaker have become psychologically active through the verbal aspect of the communication. Various defensive strategies may be used to decrease potential vulnerability of self and to increase the vulnerability of others. The verbal aspect of the communication becomes a vehicle for the transmission of individuated symbols. The "I" stands over the "we." Meanings which are discrete to the speaker must be offered so that they are intelligible to the listener. Communalized roles have given way to individualized roles, condensed symbols to articulated symbols. Elaborated speech variants of this type realize universalistic meanings in the sense that they are less context tied. Thus individualized roles are realized through elaborated speech variants which involve complex editing at the grammatical and lexical levels and which point to universalistic meanings.

Let me give another example. Consider the following two stories, which Peter Hawkins, associate research officer in the Sociological Research Unit, constructed as a result of his analysis of the speech of middle-class and working-class five-year-old children. The children were given a series of four pictures which told a story, and were then invited to tell the story. The first picture showed some boys playing football, in the second the ball goes through the window of a house, the third shows a woman looking out of the window and a man making an ominous gesture, and in the fourth the children are moving away.

Here are the two stories, (1) middle class and (2) working class:

1. Three boys are playing football and one boy kicks the ball and it goes through the window   the ball breaks the window and the boys are looking at it   and a man comes out and shouts at them   because they've broken the window   so they run away   and then that lady looks out of her window   and she tells the boys off.
2. They're playing football   and he kicks it and it goes through there   it breaks the window and they're looking at it   and he comes out   and shouts at them   because they've broken it   so they run away   and then she looks out   and she tells them off.

With the first story the reader does not need the four pictures which were used as the basis for the story, whereas in the case of the second story the reader would require the initial pictures in order to make sense of the story. The first story is free of the context which generated it, whereas the second story is much more closely tied to its context. As a result the meanings of the second story are implicit, whereas the meanings of the first story are explicit. It is not that the working-class children do not have in their passive vocabulary the vocabulary used by the middle-class children. Nor is it the case that the children differ in their tacit understanding of the linguistic rule system. Rather, what we have here are differences in the use of language arising out of a specific context.

One child makes explicit the meanings which he is realizing through language for the person he is telling the story to, whereas the second child does not, to the same extent. The first child takes very little for granted, whereas the second child takes a great deal for granted. Thus for the first child the task was seen as a context in which his meanings were required to be made explicit, whereas the task for the second child was not seen as a task which required such explication of meaning. It would not be difficult to imagine a context in which the first child would produce speech rather like the second. What we are dealing with here are differences between the children in the way they realize in language use what is apparently the same context. We could say that the speech of the first child generated universalistic meanings in the sense that the meanings are freed from the context and so understandable by all. The speech of the second child, on the other hand, generated particularistic meanings, in the sense that the meanings are closely tied to the context and would only be fully understood by others if they had access to the context which originally generated the speech. Thus universalistic meanings are less bound to a given context, whereas particularistic meanings are severely context bound.

It is again important to stress that the second child has access to a more differentiated noun phrase, but there is a restriction on its *use*. Geoffrey Turner, linguist in the Sociological Research Unit, shows that five-year-old working-class children in the same contexts examined by Hawkins use fewer linguistic expressions of uncertainty when compared with the middle-class children. This does not mean that working-class children do not have access to such expressions, but that the eliciting speech context did not provoke them. Telling a story from pictures, talking about scenes on cards, *formally framed* contexts, does not encourage working-class children to consider the possibilities of alternate meanings, and so there is a reduction in the linguistic expressions of uncertainty. Again, working-class children have access to a wide range of syntactic choices which involve the use of logical operators: "because," "but," "either," "or," "only." The constraints exist on the conditions for their *use*. Formally framed contexts used for eliciting context-independent universalistic meanings may evoke in the working-class child, relative to the middle-class child, restricted speech variants, because the working-class child has difficulty in managing the role relationships such contexts require. This problem is further complicated when such contexts carry meanings very much removed from the child's cultural experience.

In the same way we can show that there are constraints upon the middle-class child's use of language. Turner found that when middle-class children were asked to role play in the picture story series, a higher percentage of these children, when compared with working-class children, initially refused. When the middle-class children were asked, "What is the man saying?" or linguistically equivalent questions, a relatively higher percentage said, "I don't know." When this question was followed by the hypothetical question, "What do you think the man might be saying?", they offered their interpretations. The working-class children role played without difficulty. It seems then that middle-class children at five need to have a very precise instruction to *hypothesize in that particular context*. This may be because they are more concerned here with getting their answers right or correct. When the children were invited to tell a story about some doll-like figures (a little boy, a little girl, a sailor, and a dog) the working-class children's stories were freer, longer, more imaginative than the stories of the middle-class children. The latter children's stories were tighter, constrained within a strong narrative frame. It was as if these children were dominated by what they took to be the *form* of a narrative, and the content was secondary. This is an example of the concern of the middle-class child with the structure of the contextual frame.

It may be worthwhile to amplify this further. A number of studies have shown that when working-class black children are asked to associate to a series of words, their responses show considerable diversity, both from the meaning and form class of the stimulus word. In the analysis offered in the text, this may be because the children, for the following reasons, are less constrained. The form class of the stimulus word may have reduced associative significance, and so constrains the selection of potential words or phrases less. With such a weakening of the grammatical frame a greater range of alternatives are possible candidates for selection. Further, the closely controlled middle-class linguistic socialization of the young child may point the child toward both the grammatical significance of the stimulus word and a tight logical ordering of semantic space. Middle-class children may well have access to deep interpretive rules which regulate their linguistic responses in certain formalized contexts. The consequences may limit their imagination through the tightness of the frame these interpretive rules create. It may even be that the five-year-old middle-class child will innovate *more* with the arrangements of objects (i.e., bricks) than in his linguistic usage. His linguistic usage is under close supervision by adults; he has more autonomy in his play.

Let us take another example. One mother when she controls her child places a great emphasis upon language because she wishes to make explicit, and to elaborate for the child, certain rules and the reasons for the rules, and their consequences. In this way the child has access through language to the relationships between the particular act of his which evoked the mother's control and certain general principles and reasons and consequences which serve to universalize the particular act. Another mother places less emphasis upon language when she controls her child, dealing only with the particular act and not relating to general principles and their reasoned basis and consequences. Both children learn that there is something they are supposed or not supposed to do, but the first child has learned rather more than this. The grounds of the first mother's acts have been made explicit and elaborated, whereas the grounds of the second mother's acts are implicit, they are unspoken. Our research shows just this, that the social classes differ in terms of the *contexts* which evoke certain linguistic realizations. Mothers in the middle class (and it is important to add not all), relative to the working class (and again it is important to add not all, by any means), place greater emphasis upon the use of language in socializing the child into the moral order, in disciplining the child, and in the communication and recognition of feeling. Here again we can say that the first child is oriented toward universalistic meanings which transcend a given context, whereas the second child is oriented toward particularistic meanings which are closely tied to a given context and so do not transcend it. This does not mean that working-class mothers are nonverbal, only that they differ from the middle-class mothers in the *contexts* which evoke universalistic meanings. They are *not* linguistically deprived, neither are their children.

We can generalize from these examples and say that certain groups of children, through the forms of their socialization, are oriented toward receiving and offering universalistic meanings in certain contexts, whereas other groups of children are oriented toward particularistic meanings. The linguistic realization of universalistic orders of meaning is very different from the linguistic realization of particularistic orders of meaning, and so are the forms of the social relations (e.g., between mother and child) which generate these. We can say then that what is made available for learning, how it is made available, and the patterns of social relations are also very different.

Now, when we consider the children in school we can see that there is likely to be difficulty. For the school is necessarily concerned with the transmission and development of universalistic orders of meaning. The school is concerned with making explicit, and elaborating through language, principles and operations as these apply to objects (science subjects) and persons (arts subjects). One child, through his socialization, is already sensitive to the symbolic orders of the school, whereas the second child is much less sensitive to the universalistic orders of the school. The second child is oriented toward particularistic orders of meaning which are context bound, in which principles and operations are implicit, and toward a form of language use through which such meanings are realized. The school is necessarily trying to develop in the child orders of relevance and relation as these apply to persons and objects, which are not initially the ones he moves toward spontaneously. The problem of educability at one level, whether it is in Europe, the United

States, or newly developing societies, can be understood in terms of a confrontation between the universalistic orders of meaning and the social relationships which generate them, of the school, and the particularistic orders of meanings and the social relationships which generate them, which the child brings with him to the school. *Orientations toward meta-languages of control and innovation are not made available to these children as part of their initial socialization.*

I have stressed that the school is attempting to transmit uncommonsense knowledge, that is, public knowledge realized through various meta-languages. Such knowledge I have called universalistic. However, it is also the case that the school, both implicitly and explicitly, is transmitting values, and morality attendent to them, which affect both the contents and contexts of education. They do this by establishing criteria for acceptable pupil and staff conduct. Further, these values and morals affect the *content* of educational knowledge through the selection of books, texts, and films, and through examples and analogies used to assist access to public knowledge (universalistic meanings). Thus the working-class child may be placed at a considerable disadvantage in relation to the *total* culture of the school. It is not made for him; he may not answer to it.

Now I have suggested that the forms of an elaborated code give access to universalistic orders of meaning in the sense that the principles and operations controlling object and person relationships are made explicit through the use of language, whereas restricted codes give access to particularistic orders of meaning in which the principles and operations controlling object and person relationships are rendered implicit through the use of language (Bernstein, 1962). I have also tried to explain the cultural origins of these codes and their change (the most developed version is in Bernstein and Henderson, 1969). If we now go back to our earlier formulation, we can say that elaborated codes give access to universalistic orders of meaning, which are less context bound, whereas restricted codes give access to particularistic orders of meaning, which are far more context bound, that is, tied to a particular context.

Because a code is restricted is does not mean that a child is nonverbal, nor is he in the technical sense linguistically deprived, for he possesses the same tacit understanding of the linguistic rule system as any child. It simply means that there is a restriction on the *contexts* and on the *conditions* which will orient the child to universalistic orders of meaning, and to making those linguistic choices through which such meanings are realized and so made public. It does not mean that the children cannot produce at any time elaborated speech in particular contexts.

It is critically important here to distinguish between speech variants and a restricted code. A speech variant is a pattern of linguistic choices specific to a particular context—for example, an adult talking to children, a policeman giving evidence in court, a person talking to friends when one knows well the rituals of cocktail parties or of train encounters. Because a code is restricted it does not mean that a speaker will not in *some* contexts, and under *specific* conditions, not use a range of modifiers or subordinations, etc., but it does mean that where such choices are made they will be *highly context specific*. Also, because a code is elaborated it does not mean that in some contexts, under specific conditions, a speaker will not use a limited range of modifiers, subordinations, etc., but it does mean that such choices will be *highly context specific*. For example, if an individual has to produce a summary (consider a précis), then it is likely that this will affect his linguistic choices.

The concept code refers to the transmission of the deep meaning structure of a culture or subculture—the core meaning structure.

Codes on this view make substantive the culture or subculture through their control over the linguistic realizations of contexts *critical* to the process of socialization. Building on the work of Professor Michael Halliday (1969), we can distinguish analytically four critical contexts:

1. *The regulative contexts.* These are the authority relations, in which the child is made aware of the moral order and its various backings.

2. *The instructional contexts.* Here the child learns about the objective nature of objects and acquires various skills.

3. *The imaginative or innovating contexts.* Here the child is encouraged to experiment and re-create his world on his own terms and in his own way.

4. *The interpersonal contexts.* Here the child is made aware of affective states—his own and others.

In practice these are interdependent, but the emphasis and contents will vary from one group to another. I am suggesting that the critical orderings of a culture or subculture are made substantive, are made palpable through the form of the linguistic realizations of these four contexts, initially in the family. If these four contexts are realized through the predominant use of restricted speech variants pointing to particularistic—that is, relatively context-tied— meanings, then I infer that the deep structure of the communication is controlled by a restricted code. If these four contexts are realized predominantly through elaborated speech variants, which point toward relatively context-independent—that is, universalistic— meanings, then I infer that the deep structure of the communication is controlled by an elaborated code. Because the code is restricted it does not mean that the users do not realize, at any time, elaborated speech variants, *only that such variants will be used infrequently in the process of the socialization of the child in his family.*

The concept code involves a distinction similar to the distinction which linguists make between surface and deep structure of the grammar. Thus sentences which look different superficially can be shown to be generated from the same rules. In the same way, although the linguistic choices involved in a summary will be markedly different from the linguistic choices involved in a self-conscious poem, which in turn will be markedly different from the linguistic choices involved in an analysis of physical or moral principles, or different again from the linguistic realization of forms of control, they may all, under certain conditions, point to the underlying regulation of restricted or elaborated codes.

Now, because the subculture or culture through its forms of social integration generates a restricted code, it does not mean that the resultant speech and meaning system is linguistically or culturally deprived, that the children have nothing to offer the school, that their imaginings are not significant. Nor does it mean that we have to teach the children formal grammar. Nor does it mean that we have to interfere with their dialect. There is nothing, but nothing, in the dialect as such which prevents a child from internalizing and learning to use universalistic meanings. But if the contents of learning, the examples, the reading books are not contexts which will trigger the child's imaginings, will not trigger the child's curiosity and explorations in his family and community, then the child is not at home in the educational world. If the teacher has to say continuously, "Say it again, darling, I didn't understand you," then in the end the child may say nothing. If the culture of the teacher is to become part of the consciousness of the child, then the culture of the child must first be in the consciousness of the teacher. This may mean that the teacher must be able to understand the child's dialect, rather than deliberately attempt to change it. Since many of the contexts of our schools are unwittingly drawn from aspects of the symbolic world of the middle class, when the child steps into school he is stepping into a symbolic system which does not provide for him a linkage with his life outside.

It is an accepted educational principle that we should work with what the child can offer. Why, then, don't we practice it? The introduction of the child to the universalistic meanings of public forms of thought is not compensatory education—*it is education.* It is in itself not making children middle class, but how it is done, through the implicit values underlying the form and context of the educational environment, might do so. We need to distinguish between the principles and operations, which we as teachers must transmit to and develop in the children, and the contexts we create in order to do this. We should start knowing that the social experience the child already possesses is valid and significant, and that this social experience should be reflected back to him as being valid and significant. It can only be reflected back to him if it is a part of the texture of the learning experience we create. If we spent as much time thinking through the implications of this as we do thinking about the implications of the Piaget developmental sequences, then possibly schools might become exciting and challenging environments for parents, children, and teachers.

Over and beyond the issues raised so far stand much larger questions: the question of what counts as having knowledge, the question of what counts as a valid realization of that knowledge, the question of the organizational contexts we create for educational purposes. And for each of these questions we can add, "In relation to what age?" I have deliberately avoided extending these questions to include "In relation to what ability group?" because even if such a question at some point becomes relevant, the answer to it depends upon the answers to the earlier questions.

We need to examine the social assumptions underlying the organization, distribution, and evaluation of knowledge, for it is not the case that there is one and only one answer to the above questions. The power relationships created outside the school penetrate the organization, distribution, and evaluation of knowledge through the social context of their transmission. The definition of educability is itself at any one time an attenuated consequence of these power relationships. To ask these questions is not to eschew the past, is not to foreshorten one's perspective to the strictly contemporary, but is rather to invite us to consider R. Lynd's (1939) question: knowledge for what?

Finally, we do not know what a child is capable of, as we have as yet no theory which enables us to create sets of optimal learning environments, and even if such a theory existed, it is most unlikely that resources would be made available to make it substantive on the scale required.

Bibliography

Bernstein, B. "Linguistic Codes, Hesitation Phenomena and Intelligence." *Language and Speech* 5 (1962): 31.

———. "A Socio-Linguistic Approach to Social Learning." In J. Gould (ed.), *Social Science Survey*. Baltimore: Penguin Books, 1965.

———. "A Socio-Linguistic Approach to Socialisation: With some reference to educability." In J. J. Gumperz and D. Hymes (eds.), *Directions in Sociolinguistics*. New York: Holt, Rinehart and Winston, 1972.

Bernstein, B.; and Henderson, D. "Social Class Differences in the Relevance of Language to Socialisation." *Sociology* 3, No. 1 (January 1969).

Burt, Sir Cyril. *The Backward Child*. London: University of London Press, 1937.

Deutsch, M. "Facilitating Development in the Pre-School Child: Social and Psychological Perspectives." *Merrill-Palmer Quarterly of Behavior and Development* 10, No. 3 (July 1964): 249–263.

Halliday, M. A. K. "Relevant Models of Language." *Educational Review* 22, No. 1 (November 1969): 26–37.

Hawkins, P. R. "Social Class, the Nominal Group and Reference." *Language and Speech* 12, Part II (April–June 1969): 125–135.

Lynd, R. *Knowledge for What?* Princeton, N.J.: Princeton University Press, 1939.

Rosenthal, Robert; and Jacobson, Lenore. *Pygmalion in the Classroom.* New York: Holt, Rinehart and Winston, 1968.

Black Uses of English

John and Mary: A Pilot Study in Linguistic Ecology

Vivian M. Horner
Yeshiva University

Joan D. Gussow
Teachers College, Columbia University

Some time ago two three-year-old lower-class Negro children were "bugged" in their homes in an attempt to find out just how such children talked and were talked to when no outside observer was physically present. We shall be discussing here some of what was found.[1] Before we do so, however, we should like to consider why such a study seemed worthwhile.

At the time this adventure was undertaken there were no linguistic studies available of the spontaneous verbal interactions of lower-class Negro preschoolers—indeed, there were no linguistic studies available on the speech of young Negro children, period. Yet on the basis of some teacher observations, some partial speech samples elicited usually from school-age children, and much speculation about what their speech learning environment *must* be like, the language of lower-class children was widely assumed to constitute a major barrier to their classroom success.

The origins of this assumption are well enough known that they need be merely outlined here. Beginning with the belated acknowledgment that large numbers of poor and/or minority group children were failing to profit from the educational system, and that their relative learning disadvantage was evident early—at least by the time they left the first grade (Coleman, *et al.,* 1966)—a

---

[1] The research discussed here is based on the first author's doctoral dissertation, "The Verbal World of the Lower-Class Three-Year-Old: A Pilot Study in Linguistic Ecology," University of Rochester, 1968.

number of investigators had come to the conclusion that many of the characteristics that seemed to foredoom certain children to failure in the existing educational system were built into these children before they ever entered school. Children exposed to what Strodtbeck (1964) called the "hidden curriculum" of the middle-class home were apparently programmed for success in the traditional—largely middle-class—classroom, while the hidden curriculum of the lower-class home conferred no such benefits.

Given the fact of differential characteristics among children from different kinds of homes, it remained to determine which of these differences were educationally significant. One area that *seemed* to be so was language. Lower-class children quite obviously "talked different" than middle-class children. Frequently characterized by their teachers as nonverbal, they were judged to be producing substandard speech even when they *were* verbal. The high visibility of talking behavior (as opposed to other variables like motivation, nutrition, or perception, which might also influence achievement) virtually guarantees that these characteristics should be noted early and that, once noted, they should be frequently cited thereafter as evidence of the "handicap" of disadvantaged children.

Lending support to this impression was a widely held hypothesis linking language and cognitive development, as well as a respectably large and growing body of literature documenting the fact that measurable social class differences in speech performance did indeed exist. In 1966 Cazden, reviewing a series of studies that had, over the years, counted everything from vocabulary size to transformations, concluded that "on all measures, in all the studies, children of upper socio-economic status, however defined, are more advanced than the lower socio-economic children" (p. 191).

Linguists, the scientists of language, were not responsible for this growing conviction that the language of lower-class children was a major obstacle to their intellectual progress. Indeed, their involvement in the problem was virtually mandated after the relevance of language to school failure had already been decided upon. By the time they entered the lists, it was to lend a kind of scientific tone to an issue whose general outlines were already mapped. Psychologists and educators were engaged in counting words, parts of speech, and sentences. To this crude endeavor the science of language contributed a dazzlingly technical analytic methodology, making possible a much more sophisticated documentation of the fact that poor children, especially nonwhite poor children, "talk different."

Almost without exception, existing studies of the language of lower-class children have ignored questions of how language functions for children and have focused on the forms of speech—on descriptions of dialect features, on analysis of structural differences between Negro dialect and Standard English, or at best on an examination of the status significance of certain formal features of the dialect. This focus on purely formal concerns has grown naturally out of the fact that of all the features of language, formal aspects are the most visible, the most easily described, and the most readily classifiable. Moreover, formal analysis is an activity for which classical linguistics has provided a model. The traditional role of linguistics, that of rationalizing a bewildering array of languages, has been admirably served by just these formal tools. But while a focus on formal features can produce a perfectly valid description, it has proved a questionable basis for prescription where questions of developing verbal competence are concerned.

The formal orientation has tended to imply that a detailed and accurate description of a language or a nonstandard dialect will uncover the "trouble spots" in each, suggest an approach to their elimination or modification, and ultimately result in an individual with an enhanced ability to learn. Where the language differences of lower-class children are concerned, such an assumption is at best open to question. It is likely that if we could take what we now think of as a middle-class child and magically substitute for his middle-class phonological and grammatical forms a lower-class phonology and grammar, he would still perform in school more like a middle-class than a lower-class child. There is simply no evidence that certain formal characteristics interfere with the learning of anything except other formal characteristics. We may argue that a child's teacher will like him better or that he will be more comfortable if he speaks a standard dialect, but we have no empirical foundation for assuming that differences in the way children sound are in any way central to the problem of whether or not they can learn in a classroom.

Indeed, other than the fact that the speech of children who fail in school often differs from that of those who do not, we have only one logical reason for even suspecting that there is any association between children's language and their school success. That is the apparent existence of a relationship between language and certain aspects of cognition. This is a topic not pertinent to our immediate concern, for it remains to be demonstrated that certain kinds of "thinking" require certain formal structures for mediation. The fact that children "sound different" from one another is equally irrelevant, since neither have we demonstrated that their phonology has anything to do with what they have, in the vernacular, "upstairs."

Thus, because of its almost exclusive focus on structure, the science of linguistics has to date added little that was useful to the arsenal of those attacking the problem of educational disadvantage. This is said more in comment than in criticism. In any field of knowledge, familiarity does not so often breed contempt as commitment and affection, and the greater one's investment in the techniques of a discipline, the more troubling becomes the recognition that they may not be useful in the solving of certain problems—most particularly those to which they seem as if they ought to apply. Given the assumption that the language of poor children is one source of their academic problems, it has been difficult for linguists to admit that the very elegant language-problem-solving tools and techniques their science has produced may be quite inapplicable to either the analysis or the resolution of these problems. To say so much is not to argue that linguists should return chastened to what is their proper endeavor, the pursuit of knowledge, and leave the field of social concern once more to those less knowledgeable about language. It is to argue, rather, as it has been argued by some for decades, that language includes a good deal more than has been dealt with in linguistics. If the linguists are to enjoy "the prestige of dealing with something fundamental to human life," as Hymes (1966, p. 3) has put it, they must—in the phrase of another noted linguist—"look beyond the pretty patterns of their subject matter," and "whether they like it or not . . . become increasingly concerned with the many anthropological, sociological and psychological problems which invade the field of language" (Sapir, 1929, p. 214).

What kinds of language studies can we do that might be more

relevant to the problems of poor children? The question relates to both how we ought to look at our data and what kinds of data we ought to look at. We have already looked at language as a set of sounds, produced according to certain rules and hung together according to certain other rules, and we have concluded that poor children are not as good at making these sounds, nor as skilled at putting them together as are middle-class children. Let us begin instead with the time-honored dictum that all languages are adequate to meet the needs of the linguistic communities that speak them. Given such a point of view one can then deal with the problem created by social class differences as a "languages-in-contact" phenomenon growing out of two linguistic communities whose *uses* of what is presumably the same language do not overlap precisely. From this point of view the task is not that of describing how the formal attributes of any dialect, whether "impoverished" or "of lower status," differ from those of a more prestigeful one, but rather of specifying the degree to which the "uses" of language differ, reflecting differential needs for and expectations about language in the two subcultures. In other words, language must be viewed from a functional standpoint—in terms of what it does and not what it consists of. A view of language that places it firmly in its social matrix is especially critical to any understanding of language learning in children. For the prevailing view in linguistics is that a child's increasing mastery of formal language features results from the natural unfolding of innate capacities (Chomsky, 1965). If this is so, and if at the same time there are evident differences in children's use of language even at an early age, then we must either postulate different genetic structures for language acquisition or accept the notion that language learning involves the acquiring of a great deal more than formal features.

Language as Verbal Behavior

A most suggestive approach as to how we might begin to look at language function has been put forward by the psychologist B. F. Skinner (1957). He has advanced the notion that language behavior can be dealt with like other behaviors, according to the paradigm stimulus-response-reinforcement. His point of view is based on a totally different conception of the domain the study of language ought to encompass. When any of us speaks of language, we all at least begin from a set of observations about something that people do, and do very frequently. They talk, they listen—to others and themselves. They also write and read and think—processes which we presume to be related to talking and listening. In looking at these interrelated phenomena, we must agree upon the set of defining characteristics; that is, we must all see the domain to be investigated as a cohesive whole. The domain called "language" has traditionally been defined as a subject for study by virtue of its patterned internal consistency and of certain similarities in the manner in which it is produced. This is what Skinner refers to when he states that the traditional formulation of "language" as a domain has rested upon a central concern with response *topography*.

Concern with the topography of a phenomenon inevitably results in the setting up of classes whose characteristics and interrelationships are defined by their formal attributes. Skinner's conception involves not an extension of these traditional approaches to language, but rather a reformulation of the domain of inquiry. As a consequence he understandably shuns the term *language* because of its history of association with formal concerns and offers instead the term *verbal behavior*. The term acknowledges the existence of a set of events displaying the topographical similarity that has served for centuries as the defining characteristic of language; yet it places that set of events among the many phenomena to be investigated in the analysis of behavior. This definition requires that the phenomena topographically defined as "verbal" be studied in the same manner as other behavioral events—that is, in interaction with their environments. In an experimental analysis different classes of behavior emerge from an examination of the differential effects of behavioral events upon the environment. Thus a class of verbal behaviors, just as any other behaviors, is defined by a characteristic relationship among controlling stimuli, responses, and their consequences. The examination of the relationships between a behavioral event and its controlling environment is what Skinner calls *functional* analysis. He has written:

In all verbal behavior under stimulus control, there are three important events to be taken into account; a stimulus, a response, and a reinforcement. They are contingent upon each other . . . in the following way: the stimulus, acting prior to the emission of the response, sets the occasion upon which the response is likely to be reinforced. . . . The terms comprising the contingency statement—stimulus, response, and reinforcement—are not descriptive; they are functional. Three events contiguous in time come to be identified in this relationship to one another because changes in one of them will produce predictable changes in the others (1957, p. 81).

Evidence supporting this assertion of interrelationships must, of course, be derived from manipulation of various of these interrelated events to produce predictable consequences in an experimental situation.

In the linguistic literature, one finds that only Sapon has considered Skinner seriously and extended in a linguistically sophisticated manner the hypothesis put forward in *Verbal Behavior*. Utilizing Skinner's notion of a verbal "repertoire" for all those behaviors (vocal, kinesic, paralinguistic, etc.) through which communication takes place between the individual and his people-mediated environment, Sapon has pointed out that it is just such a repertoire that a child must learn in acquiring what we call language. "We must not look upon the acquisition of spoken language as a simple transition, part of a genetically programmed course of development," Sapon has written, "but rather as the acquisition of a complex repertoire of learned behaviors. The question is, 'how do children acquire these new behaviors?' " (1965b, p. 5).

Sapon goes on:

When we talk about [language] learning, what we generally mean is that we have established in the environment certain contingencies for reinforcement, and we can then leave the organism alone to "find out for himself" which behaviors are reinforced, which punished and which seem to have no consequences at all. When we say that a child has "learned to be polite," we are saying that the child has "found out for himself" that requests preceded by "please" are more likely to be granted than those that begin with "gimme." . . . To say that children who are raised in an environment where language is used eventually "learn" to understand the language is another way of saying that somehow the child has "found out by himself" what are the relevant aspects of his environment. It is this agglomeration of "eventually," "somehow" and "found out" that accounts for much of the wide range of achievement in children of the same chronological age (1966, p. 171).

Yet, as Sapon points out, language learning does take place in what are clearly haphazard learning environments (1966, p. 158). That this is the case is an indication of the extent to which a child's *survival* depends upon his learning to respond in a culturally appropriate manner to verbal situations. Sapon believes that the key word is *control*. The child survives by coming under the control of the verbal behavior of others while at almost the same time he learns to control increasingly complex environments through his own verbal behavior (as cited in Bailey and Gussow, 1966). Thus a verbal repertoire, viewed functionally, is not one but two sets of behavior, verbally *controlled* behavior and verbally *controlling* behavior. An organism's receptive repertoire consists of those behaviors in which the individual serves as audience or "understander"; his expressive repertoire consists of those behaviors in which he functions as speaker. (Such a notion is, of course, impossible within a formal framework, since these two behaviors are assumed to be but two sides of the same coin.) The essentially different character of the organism as speaker and understander is related, as was noted earlier, to the dimension of control. "An individual can be said to understand when his behavior can be shown to be under the control of another's (his own) verbal output," Sapon has written. On the other hand, "speaking can be looked upon as evidence of an individual's attempts to control his environment through his own verbal output" (as quoted in Bailey and Gussow, 1966, pp. 2–3).

Where language learning is concerned:

We start with the point of view that language is a vital piece of operant behavior for a human being. It is defined as a means by which an organism controls his physical and social environment with his talking apparatus rather than with his feet, and we would include body gestures and body communications in the same general pattern. Now if a child shows signs of acquiring any kind of verbal behavior, it obviously has to be in some kind of a home environment (regardless of how enriched or impoverished that might be) and it obviously does have some at-the-moment-unspecified operant function (Bailey and Gussow, 1966, p. 89).

Sapon believes that it is the child's expanding ability to "move the world around" by means of his own language that reinforces most powerfully the expansion of his own verbal repertoire.

Such a formulation requires us, if we wish to look at language learning in children, to examine the ways in which their language behavior affects and is affected by the environment. This in turn requires us to consider the second part of the question we raised earlier, namely what kinds of data ought we to be looking at in studying language? Obviously the most sensitive analysis can produce nothing of worth if it is based on inadequate or inappropriate data. To understand a living process we must at least begin with something vital.

Two linguists with a social-anthropological bent, Hymes and Gumperz (e.g., Hymes, 1962, 1964, 1967; Gumperz, 1958, 1964, 1965), have focused attention on the fact that since the language and other behaviors of any individual are under the control of the environment, different environments produce different behaviors. Since this is the case, we need more than speech samples elicited in artificial settings if we wish to assess a child's verbal repertoire; we will have to sample language behavior in a variety of interactions that are typical for that child and for the group to which he belongs.

Yet almost without exception, studies dealing with lower-class children's language have been based on speech samples elicited in school or in school-like settings. To assess a lower-class child in such a situation may be somewhat equivalent to taking a fish from water, putting it on the table to examine it, and observing that it seems to have no means of locomotion. We are seeing the language of the lower-class child in a situation of our own making, a situation we call "normal" but which may be highly "abnormal" for the lower-class child. Labov (1967) has noted that generalizations based on responses in the classroom have resulted in Negro children's being labeled nonverbal, even though the children can be shown to have a wide range of verbal skills in other settings. More recently Houston (1969) observed two quite distinct manners of speech among black children in rural Florida. Formal recording sessions elicited from the children what she called a School Register. Utterances in School Register were shorter, slower, differently pitched and stressed, and more emotionless than the Nonschool Register, a form of speech the children used in informal situations.

Thus a speech sample elicited through an interview or a test, or even in the most informal classroom situation, cannot be considered to be representative of anything other than a set of responses to that particular environment. When the performance of lower-class minority children is compared with that of middle-class children in this particular kind of setting, the comparison may be especially invidious, since the ordinary classroom situation may be, indeed surely is, much more familiar and comfortable to a middle-class than to a lower-class child.

If we are looking at preschool children—youngsters whose language behaviors are in the process of being formed—it is clear that any setting outside the home or neighborhood may well be unfamiliar enough to eliminate a large portion of the "repertoire" available to such a child in his natural environment. To learn something about the language of young children one would have to listen to them in their homes and—especially in the case of poor young children—in the street where most of their spontaneous language behavior takes place. Yet the solution is not merely to invade the homes of these children and to assume that what we will then hear is "typical" speech. There are few middle-class parents who would wish the intelligence and loquacity of their three-year-old judged on the basis of his unyielding muteness in the presence of Great Aunt Minnie or some other unfamiliar visiting adult. How much more distorting to his normal behavior must be the presence of an observer of a different class, and often of a different race, in the home of a lower-class child.

Moreover, such a presence would affect not only the child, but the adults with whom he interacts, for all social behavior is highly sensitive to intrusion by alien elements in the environment. In any social class the home is a private domain—no stranger to the household is ever witness to the full range of events that occur there when he is not present—the claims of *Life* photographers to the contrary notwithstanding. And when the social distance between the stranger and the members of the household is as great as it is in the case of a white, middle-class investigator attempting to study a poor Negro family, the effect of that stranger on the behavior, verbal and otherwise, of those in the home is apt to be quite marked. Thus the problem of how to overhear the language behaviors of a young child without profoundly distorting them in the process long appeared insoluble.

A possible approach to the naturalistic study of language, however, was suggested several years ago by the pioneering study of Soskin and John (1963), who monitored the conversations of two graduate student couples vacationing at a lake resort. In this study the subjects' speech was picked up by compact radio transmitters that they wore strapped to their backs for sixteen hours a day. Though the cumbersomeness of such equipment limited its usefulness, miniaturization has subsequently brought the weight and size of a functional transmitter down to a point where such equipment can reasonably be sewed into a child's clothing. A child can carry around such a transmitter all day without (after a brief period of adaptation) being too aware of its presence.

Such equipment made possible an approach to the language of lower-class Negro children that, as we hope has by now been made evident, seemed highly desirable from a conceptual standpoint. The study to be discussed here, then, is a very small—and, to date, isolated—attempt to get a piece of natural verbal behavior from two Negro children of language-learning age—and to analyze it in functional terms.

The Study

The data for this study were gathered, as we have said, by "bugging" two children in their homes with sophisticated electronic equipment. Given the problems encountered in accomplishing this —in locating families willing to participate who had children of appropriate age, and in finding equipment that would both provide intelligible tapes and resist demolition by small hands—no claim for typicality is made for these children or their families. They are poor Negro families, next-door neighbors who each occupy one floor of almost identical duplex houses in a ghetto area of a small city in upstate New York. The data analyzed covered two days' worth of the audible events surrounding a single three-year-old in each of the families.

Mary Davis's family lived on the second floor of a one-up-one-down duplex with a railed porch overlooking a shabby slum street. An only child, Mary was part of a household consisting of a mother, an attractive fortyish grandmother, two adolescent uncles, and a married aunt and her husband. Johnny Cooper (Boo-Boo) lived

Figure 1. Sample transcription

Context	Child	Person Interacting with Child	Background Talk
9:41 A.M.			
Mary on porch, playing. Clink of toy tin dishes. Mary sneezes. Child on street, crying. Mary alone on porch.	Clean up. Hey Reggie!		
		REGGIE: What?	
	Hey, Reggie!		
		REGGIE: Huh?	
	Come here and play with me. Hey, Reg! ——. Reg coming up. Yup.		
People talking in street	Um.		BOY: Oh, shut up!
	Hey, Reggie. Come here.		
		REGGIE: Where you at?	
	Come up here and play with me.		
		REGGIE: Call Boo-Boo.	
Water pouring.	Boo-Boo! Come up here and play with me.		
		BOO-BOO: X	
	Huh? Come up here and play with me.		

Figure 1. Sample transcription (continued)

Context	Child	Person Interacting with Child	Background Talk
		Boo-Boo: I be up there in a minute.	
	Okay.		
		Boo-Boo: —— say I can come up.	
	Oo-Oo. Come on, Boo-Boo. Hey, Boo! Come on, Boo-Boo.		

in a similar apartment on the first floor of the house next door with his mother and father, a six-year-old brother, a ten-year-old sister, and a grandfather.

To obtain the tapes, each child was provided early on the first morning with an appropriate garment into which was sewed a miniature wireless transmitter with an internal microphone. A small radio receiver set to pick up the microphone signal and plugged into a tape recorder was housed in a suitcase put out of sight and out of reach behind a couch. Each child was monitored from the time the "bugged" garment was delivered in the morning until about 9 P.M., when the garment was picked up for laundering and the day's tapes retrieved. The pattern was repeated on the following day. For each child the two-day recording period included a weekday and a weekend day.

At the conclusion of the monitoring the tapes were professionally mastered and all derivable acoustic information was transcribed, including background noises, unintelligible speech, TV, music, and so on. Figure 1 presents a sample of the transcription and is relatively self-explanatory. Unintelligible speech is rendered as an *X*— or several *X*'s, if there is an indication on the tape that several utterances occurred. An underlined blank indicates an unintelligible portion of an otherwise intelligible utterance.

It was possible to make some generalizations about both households on the basis of simple observation and the overall pattern of activities that emerged from the tapes. The first was that these people talked to each other a lot. So pervasive has been the notion of the "nonverbal poor" that the universal first reaction to the tapes was that middle-class families had been accidentally selected. Such a fear proved groundless—characterized as to income, occupation, education, housing, and even life style, the families were unquestionably poor, and unquestionably "lower class."

Overall these were intensely active, indeed somewhat hectic, households where many people—family, friends, and neighbors—were in and out, where privacy was difficult to come by, and where the experiences of one member thus tended to be those of all members. On the whole the environments could be described as busy and rather noisy, but no more so than would seem reasonable in circumstances where many people came and went, conversations were frequent, and children played together. Television sets were turned on most of the time in both houses, but TV appeared to occupy a lesser role than its omnipresence would suggest. The children, at least at this age, did not seem to attend to TV with great frequency, or for any extended period, usually sitting to watch for only a minute or two at a time. Generally neither child watched it alone. TV was thus more of a ripple than a current in the stream of behavior for these children. However, themes from television (and television commercials) were apparent in the children's games —monsters, war, hillbillies, Batman and Robin— and it was in this role, as a catalyst for play, that television appeared to have its greatest influence.

Routines in both houses were somewhat more ordered and predictable on the weekday than on the weekend day. Mary's mother worked full time and Mary was usually looked after by her aunt and occasionally by her grandmother or one of her teen-age uncles. The weekday activities were thus dictated by the mother's work schedule. The morning was a hurried time for getting the child up, giving her some cereal and milk, rushing her through a bath, getting her dressed, and sending her to play. When her mother had left for work, the theme of the day for Mary was play on the outdoor porch with her dolls and toy dishes, an activity punctuated by excursions into the house for attention or to be with Mama when she came by at noon to give Mary lunch. Then Mary had a short walk with her aunt, a nap, and more doll play. During this period, unless she could coax one of the other children in the neighborhood up to play with her, Mary had no playmates; when her mother was not home she was not allowed outside, except under close adult supervision. With her mother home from work Mary went outside for play with other children, coming in to grab a bite when she was hungry and then going back outside until bedtime. On warm summer evenings everyone was outside, the children playing, the grownups chatting as they sat around on the porches or stood in the driveways.

The weekend was more relaxed. Mary, up early, tried and failed to get the others up and then played alone in the kitchen or on the porch until her mother finally got up and dressed her. Mary watched some TV with her uncle, had breakfast, and then John came over from next door with his brother and sister and the four played together, Mary frequently turning to her mother for attention. In the early afternoon Mary's mother cleaned her up—repeatedly—and sent her off for the afternoon to a neighborhood birthday party. When she returned home she played outdoors until bedtime.

Though John's daily pattern was markedly different from Mary's, there was the same contrast between the weekday and the weekend. His weekday pattern was dominated by outdoor play, and adult-child interactions generally centered around such necessities as getting dressed, eating, going to the bathroom, being comforted when hurt, etc. The weekend, on the other hand, was a time for family interaction, and, as in Mary's household, the atmosphere was more relaxed. It provided John with an opportunity to be with his mother and to join in family activities—going shopping, engaging in a friendly argument over the pronunciation of "Czechoslovakia," participating in a family tussle in which Mother and the children gang up on Daddy.

These, of course, are the most general impressions. Before we go beyond them, however, to more quantitative statements, it is important to point out that the raw data obtained are subject to a number of technical limitations. To begin with, and most critically perhaps in terms of *our* view of what ought to be included in a consideration of "verbal behavior," is the fact that the study produced only acoustic data. Of necessity the investigator's observations took place outside of the recorded periods, so that one can surmise but not see what is happening during specific verbal interchanges. A second difficulty is that the microphone picked up only sounds within its own range, so that some of the background acoustic signals were missed; and a third problem arose from the fact that when the child moved out of range of the receiver (which included most of the outdoor time), neither his own speech nor that of those around him was recorded. The best of the recorded data therefore represents only a portion of the environmental events for a portion of each day. The majority of each of John's days was spent out of doors; in Mary's case just over one-fifth of the weekday time and more than half of the weekend day was spent out of doors. Had the data been gathered in the winter rather than in the summer, both children might have been indoors more. Thus in every sense the data are both fragmentary and selectively distorted. Keeping in mind all these limitations, we should like to summarize in the broadest terms the kinds of things that emerged from the data and the kinds of analyses applied to them, after which we will propose some implications of both for future research and action.

The Concept of the "Verbal Event"

The first question to be decided in relation to this body of data was what to count. As the previous discussion has made clear, analyses based on formal units have not proved effective in "getting at" the functional aspects of language. We have therefore adopted for quantification a different kind of unit, a "verbal event," here defined as a piece of verbal behavior emitted by one person addressing another. The concept is derived from Skinner's notion that the principal controlling stimulus for verbal behavior is the presence of an audience, but since purely acoustic data make determination of the "audience" for an utterance difficult, we have used instead the term "addressee," indicating essentially that the person being addressed is physically present.

Individual verbal events are separated from one another by: (1) a shift in addressee—such as that which occurs when speakers "take turns talking," or when an individual carries on a conversation with two people at once and shifts from talking to one to talking to another; or (2) a substantial period of silence on either end of an utterance—such as that which occurs when a speaker calls out to someone and not being answered calls out again, or when an individual talks to an imaginary audience and is, of course, not responded to.

The first quantitative question asked of the data was who talks to whom and how often. To answer this question a modified sociogram technique like that suggested by Bloomfield (as cited by Gumperz, 1958) was used. "Imagine a huge chart with a dot for every speaker . . . and imagine that every time any speaker uttered a sentence an arrow were drawn into the chart pointing from his dot to the dot representing each of his hearers. At the end of a given period of time . . . that chart would show us the density of communication . . ." (Bloomfield, 1933, p. 46). One such chart is shown for one ninety-minute period from the point of view of the child as speaker (Figure 2). Similar diagrams were made from two other points of view, that of the child as addressee and that of the child as present but not participating (background talk). The circle in which the arrow originates represents the speaker and the number in the arrowhead indicates the frequency of verbal events in that direction for a specified time period.

From such diagrams tabulations were made of the frequency of verbal events from the three points of view for all recorded periods. The mean number of verbal events per hour were then calculated for each child during each of the two days and across both days, and similar calculations were made for other persons in the environment. On the basis of such calculations, certain quantitative statements can be made.

Over the recorded period as a whole both children talked to friends and family somewhat more than they were talked to; and their level of talk remained relatively constant for the two days. However, the total amount of talk in their environments increased somewhat over the weekend when Mary, especially, was more likely to be *talked to*. Though Mary talked and was talked to more than

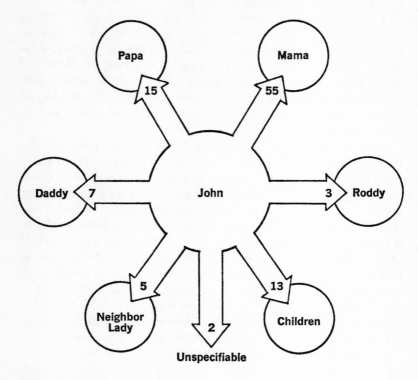

Figure 2. Network of verbal interaction and frequency of verbal events, with John as speaker, 90 minutes, weekend morning

John, John's total verbal environment was somewhat denser than Mary's—that is, there was more talk in John's vicinity but less of it involved him directly. Mary's personal share of all the talk around her was very high (85 percent).[2]

During the period as a whole, both children interacted most with the adults in their environment. About 60 percent of the total verbal interaction involving the children directly was with adults.[3]

[2] The difference may be underestimated by the data, since John spent so much time out of doors.

[3] Keeping in mind, once again, that this is time spent indoors.

Since it has been widely assumed (e.g., Milner, 1951; John and Goldstein, 1964) that the quality and quantity of a child's interaction with adults is a critical variable in the language-learning process, it is perhaps worth noting that there was at least one adult present (and therefore at least potentially available to the child) in each household during virtually the entire recorded period. In neither case was this the child's mother during the weekday—Mary had an aunt home full time, John a grandfather. But on the weekend day John's mother was present 89 percent of the recorded time and Mary's mother 100 percent. However, these relative availabilities are only partially reflected in the interaction pattern. The single most frequent interlocutor for both children for both days was the mother, even though she was clearly not always the most available adult. Overall the children interacted verbally about three times as often with their mothers as with the next most frequent interlocutor, and when the mother was more available on the weekends, there was twice as much talk with her. This "centrality" of the mother in the lives of the children was reflected in the total pattern of verbal interaction with adults; given the presence of the mother, very little interaction took place between other adults and the three-year-olds. John, for example, had his father and his grandfather frequently available, yet verbal interaction with them was slight at all times and virtually nonexistent when the mother was available. Mary's pattern was more extreme. When her mother was present she simply did not talk to other adults at all, but when her mother was away at work she sometimes engaged in verbal interchanges with whatever adult was around.

Interactions with small children—largely playmates up to about the age of eight—were second in frequency for both children. When the data were divided by day Mary proved to maintain a high level of verbal interaction with adults on both weekday and weekend day, but doubled her verbal interactions with small children over the weekend when her mother was home and allowed her to play with less supervision. John, on the other hand, actually had more interaction with small children than with adults on the weekday when his mother was at work (and more interaction with adults than small children on the weekend when she was home). His six-year-old brother Roddy was John's second most frequent interlocutor, and accounted for a good deal of John's time both indoors and out. The two boys, who were close in age, played together, ate together, washed and brushed their teeth together. Altogether there was a strong peer influence in John's verbal behavior, much of which could not be directly observed in the proctocols, since it occurred when John was out of doors playing with other children.

Both subject children interacted least of all with children in the age group from about ten to fifteen, to whom they represented neither playmates nor, except on occasion, responsibilities.

These data on the frequency of verbal events are interesting, but in themselves only marginally useful. They enable us to quantify several general observations: that these poor Negro children are not nonverbal, at least in their own homes, but rather talk and are talked to extensively; that patterns of verbal interaction may vary markedly for individual children of the same "social class" according to their particular family constellation; and that poor children, like all children, talk a lot with adults—at least indoors—especially with their mothers. We still do not know anything about the conditions under which children's verbal responses occur in these environments or the "functions" that language comes to serve for these children.

Somewhat more provocative patterns emerged when the days' actvities were laid out sequentially, with the child's cumulative verbal behavior charted in the context of the activities that surrounded it. The sequential description of events was necessarily a judgment from recorded material and thus more "interpretive" than the other data. When such an analysis was done it became clear that verbal behavior in the child's environment, particularly that in which he actively engaged, tended to occur in two particular types of settings: those in which "transactions" (Blom and Gumperz, 1966, p. 21) were being completed, i.e., those in which speech centered around getting something done; and those which were "emotionally charged." With children transactional speech occurred in the context of organizing for games like Batman or war with the Germans, obtaining toys and food, taking turns at an activity, and the like. With adults such transactions were likely to include getting the child dressed or to the bathroom, giving him a meal or a bath. The second type of setting was characterized by one or more of the participants' responding emotionally, such as when the child had hurt himself or been struck by another child and ran to the mother for attention or consolation, or when the child himself overstepped the acceptable bounds in talk or action and incurred the mother's wrath.

As a consequence of time pressures on the mother, many transactional situations in which she was engaged with the child were also emotionally charged; that is, the mother, fearful of being late for work, would be trying desperately to get the child's cooperation in getting himself dressed or fed. The very highest rates of verbal interaction recorded occurred under such circumstances as these, and it thus emerged that the mother was the child's most frequent interlocutor, not because she was present most, which she was not, but at least partly as a consequence of a very high rate of verbal interaction between her and her child during rather brief, intense periods of contact.

An observation such as this, of course, while it implies causation, cannot verify it, which brings up a second limitation of these data. To *demonstrate* cause-effect relationships requires an experimental setting in which environmental modifications can be introduced and their effect on behavior precisely measured. Unfortunately, existing laboratory studies of verbal behavior have provided us with few generalizations useful in the real world. In any experimental situation it is necessary to eliminate many of the factors that influence behaviors in nature so that they will not interfere with the controlled conditions of the experiment. An investigator assumes, however, that by later taking these eliminated factors into account he can usefully apply in a natural setting the generalizations experimentally arrived at. But in the case of verbal behavior, our knowledge of the controlling factors is so rudimentary that we do not really know what critical factors we are leaving out in laboratory situations. Consequently we do not know what to put back in later. Under the circumstances it has seemed to us that it would be a productive first step to learn something about verbal behavior in the real world. In the technique described above one begins by constructing laboratory-type records for behavior just as it occurs (though after the fact, to be sure), in all its complexity, in the natural environment. On the basis of these records, displayed with all the additional information that can be presumed to be of relevance, one can construct working hypotheses that can then be tested under controlled experimental conditions. Such a technique provides a means of dealing with verbal data from natural settings without so structuring it that the information is irrelevant to controlled research. Laboratory studies deriving from such a give-and-take relationship with investigations in the natural environment should result in generalization of far wider utility. In the meantime it may be more useful to have observations that are tentative and pertinent than those which are exactly replicable but irrelevant to real-life behavior.

The Functional Analysis

It is perfectly clear that this same tentativeness must apply to our attempt at a Skinnerian functional analysis of the data reported here. In an experimental setting the functional relationships between the terms of Skinner's three-term-contingency statement would be demonstrable. The manipulation of one event to produce changes in another could provide powerful evidence supporting the general formulation. In a setting such as the one in which these children have been observed, however, the stimulus-response-reinforcement statement can only be utilized as a model for analysis, and the stated relationships must be viewed as essentially descriptive—i.e., audience and other variables of context are assumed to provide conditions of prior stimulation, the verbal events identified are considered responses, and subsequent events are assumed to constitute reinforcements or consequences of these responses.

It is critical to keep in mind that responses fall into particular classes not because of their form, but because the relationships among stimuli, responses, and reinforcements vary in characteristic ways. Among the classes of verbal behavior identified by Skinner (1957) are four that are of particular interest for investigating the verbal behavior of a very young, preliterate subject: mands, tacts, and echoic and intraverbal responses. We shall merely define these here; they will be more fully discussed in the context of the study data.

The mand—its essence most effectively captured in certain of its etymological predecessors such as com*mand* and de*mand*—is verbal behavior that works primarily for the benefit of the speaker. Technically it is a verbal operant which is under the functional control of various states of relative deprivation or aversive stimulation and thus specifies its reinforcer—e.g., "Gimme a cookie," "Leave me alone." A mand usually sounds like a request that something be done, but it is defined by its consequences—i.e., by what happens after it is uttered, not by its form.

The essence of the tact is also best conveyed by its etymological relatives, such as *tact*ile and con*tact*. Essentially it is a verbal event in which the speaker "talks about" something—e.g., "My, that's pretty!"—hence it acts to benefit the listener because it extends his contact with the environment. In technical terms, the tact is a verbal operant in which the controlling stimulus is any one of the whole world of things and events a speaker may "talk about" and the reinforcer is varied or general—essentially the fact that in a given verbal community such statements are characteristically responded to.

An echoic response is just what it sounds like—a verbal response that has a point-to-point correspondence with the topography of the verbal controlling stimulus. In Skinner's view it is established in the child by such deliberate reinforcers on the part of the parents and teachers as "Right!" or "Good boy!" contingent upon a "correct" mimic response from the child.

And finally there is a second verbal operant, which is under the control of specific verbal stimuli, the intraverbal response. Intraverbal behavior may best be thought of as a chain, each link of which is dependent on the previous link, such as in the chain "one . . . two . . . three . . . four, etc.," with each response controlling the next in predictable fashion.

These classifications of Skinner's are useful as a first attempt at ordering verbal behavior on a functional basis, but, more importantly, they are useful because they derive from the same empirical framework upon which the experimental analysis of behavior is based. Thus they permit us to bring to bear upon the study of verbal behavior the knowledge accumulated with regard to behavior in general.

Since our concern is with language learning, we shall first

examine the children's verbal environment—looking at the kinds of functional classes that characterize the language around them— before turning to an examination of the functional classes in the children's own language.

John and Mary: The Receptive Repertoire

In the light of our earlier discovery about the circumstances (i.e., transactional) under which verbal behavior is most likely to occur in these children's environments, it is not surprising, perhaps, to find that mands—verbal events reinforced by a specified behavior on the part of the person addressed—are particularly prevalent, representing a greater proportion of all the verbal behavior addressed to the child than any other class of response. Mands represent two-thirds of all the verbal behavior the children's mothers direct at them and almost three-fourths of the verbal behavior directed at the two children by their next most frequent interlocutors, namely other small children.

As Table 1 shows, when mands were broken down into seven subclasses in terms of the manner in which they were characteristically reinforced (i.e., by movement, information, attention, confirmation, permission, repetition, or continuation), the pattern of mands addressed to the children by their mothers and others in their environment showed a fairly consistent distribution. By far the greatest proportion of mands were those that exactly specified the action by which they would be reinforced, labeled "movement." These included such statements as "Go and get me the telephone book," "Don't do that!", and even direct commands that did not, strictly speaking, call for movement, e.g., "Say 'thank you'." Over half of the mands directed toward John by his mother were of this type; as were an even larger proportion, over two-thirds, of those that Mary's mother addressed to her. The physical size of the child, of course, means that all those bigger and stronger than he is can exercise the authority implicit in direct commands, but beyond that, such behavior on the part of the mother is sanctioned by a society that dictates that mothers control their children, shaping and strengthening behaviors important to their physical and social survival. In this environment, protecting the child from harm, keeping

TABLE 1

Total Mands and Tacts of Major Interlocutors by Functional Subclass, John and Mary as Addressees

	By Mother		By Other Small Children	
	John	*Mary*	*John*	*Mary*
Mands				
Movement	52.6%	63.1%	36.0%	43.9%
Attention	3.8	4.5	20.3	14.6
Information	26.6	18.9	42.2	19.9
Permission	0.0	0.0	0.0	7.8
Repetition	.6	6.3	0.0	3.5
Confirmation	9.2	7.2	0.0	8.4
Continuation	7.1	0.0	1.6	1.7
Tacts				
Simple	67.6	67.4	95.7	100.0
Elaborating a Mand	32.4	32.6	4.3	0.0

Note: The columns may not add to 100% because of rounding.

him out of the grown-ups' hair, calling attention to inappropriate behavior, are often accomplished by means of direct commands.

Manding for movement was also strong among the small children who addressed John and Mary, and once again it was Mary who of the two was "moved around" more. The strength of this behavior is perhaps best accounted for by the fact that these children are usually engaged in active play. Accomplishing the ends of games such as building a hut with a blanket and sticks, fighting a war with twenty Germans, catching a butterfly, or fishing in a hole with a homemade pole, of necessity involves the solicitation of cooperation, the specifying of allegiances, and a considerable amount of instruction on the part of the participants.

The next most frequent subclass of mands directed to the children by their interlocutors were mands for information, comprising one-fourth of the total. These mands usually took the form of questions, and in John's case they were sometimes "honest" requests for information, e.g., "Where's Roddy?", reinforced by, "He's next door playing with Eddy." However, the principal effect (i.e., function) of such mands addressed to the child appeared to be that of engaging the child's attention and holding it, even though the audible pattern approximated the question-answer sequence so characteristic of adult speech. John was manded proportionately more for information by his mother and by other children than was Mary. Indeed, mands for information constituted about two-fifths of all mands directed toward John by other children. This may have been in part an artifact of the investigation. John was manded for information a number of times because of the children's curiosity about his transmitting equipment—his "radio." The fact that he rather than Mary was asked about it, however, suggests in addition that John was treated by the other children as a peer and not, like Mary, as a "little kid."

Direct mands for attention—e.g., "Hey, Boo-Boo"—constituted between 15 and 20 percent of all the mands directed toward the children by other small children. Yet for both mothers such mands to the children represented well under 5 percent of the total. Mands for attention are probably important in a busy, noisy environment such as this one—that is, the necessity to specify the intended audience may well be critical. There are a number of possible reasons why such mands are proportionately less frequent in the mothers' speech; for example, the mothers may simply get more mileage—i.e., produce more verbal events from any given mand for attention—than do the small children. John and Mary may attend to their mothers when they are present without being manded to do so, or the mothers may use physical means such as taking hold of the child, to get his attention.

Mands for confirmation, usually tag questions following tacts —e.g., "That's real cute, ain't it?" or "You don't like gum, do you?" —represented about 10 percent of the total mands addressed to the children. Except for the fact that John had no mands for confirmation addressed to him at all by small children, the proportion represented by these mands remained relatively constant for the various interlocutors.

Not unexpectedly, no mands for permission were directed toward these small children by their mothers or other adults, nor toward John by other small children. Mary, however, though she was one of the smallest children in the neighborhood, was sometimes manded for permission by other children. This finding seems to reflect the fact that Mary has, and regularly receives, more "things" than the other children. She had toys and a bike and there always seemed to be a store of bubble gum in her house. If the children wanted to play with her toys or ride her bike or take some of her gum, they had to ask her permission. While in these protocols she always said no, she apparently has said yes often enough in the past to maintain the behavior in the other children.

For the five subclasses of mands already discussed, the distribution was roughly similar for the two children where their mothers were their interlocutors. There were two classes, however, in which they differed markedly. John was almost never manded to repeat, but mands for repetition—i.e., "Huh?" or "I didn't hear you"— represented 6.3 percent of the total mands addressed to Mary by her mother. Mary was also sometimes manded to repeat by small children (3.5 percent); John never was. Undoubtedly this pattern is explained by the low intelligibility of Mary's speech, which is made evident by a perusal of the protocols. Mary's verbal contributions are studded with blanks indicating that the transcriber could not understand what was said. But while Mary was often manded to repeat, she was never manded to continue. Mands for continuation—"Huh?" or "Yes, what is it?" invariably following a mand for attention by the child—are typically reinforced by a continuation of the verbal exchange and are thus indicators of an attentive audience. Such mands constituted 7.1 percent of the total mands that John's mother addressed to him but none of those which Mary's mother addressed to her.

Tacts, which Skinner has called the most important of verbal operants, comprised a considerably smaller portion of all the recorded verbal behavior than did mands. Thirty-seven percent of the verbal events in which John was addressee and 29 percent of the verbal events in which Mary was addressee were tacts. In the analysis, all tacts were classified as "simple" except for one subclass, which was singled out for attention. Since the data were purely auditory and the discriminative stimuli for different subclasses of tacts are objects or events in the environment, most subclasses of tacts were not readily identifiable from these purely acoustic data. However, the subclass dealt with separately, "tacts elaborating a mand," was so identifiable. There is reason to think that this is a subclass especially important in the training of children. One assumes that part of the reason why young children are manded frequently is that they have not yet learned to attend and respond to their world in ways that are acceptable to the adult community. Thus the parents mand the child's behavior to protect him from danger and from social disapproval as well as to assist him in learning the relevant cues in the environment and how he should respond to them. Functionally, however, it is by means of the tact, not the mand, that the listener's contact with the environment is extended. Thus, while certain behaviors may be established at strength in the child's repertoire through manding, the aspects of the natural environment which must eventually come to control these behaviors will be more rapidly, and probably more efficiently, learned if the child is "trained" to attend to relevant cues as the behavior is strengthened. Presumably this is most effectively done through tacting such cues until such time as the child demonstrates socially appropriate responses to them without the parent's verbal assistance.

The pattern of tacts addressed to the children by their mothers was similar—about a third of them were tacts elaborating a mand, a not surprising finding, perhaps, in light of the "instructional" role suggested for such tacts. But the overall pattern of tacts for all interlocutors was quite different for the two children. Tacts elaborating a mand represented 23.9 percent of all tacts addressed to John and only 8.9 percent of all tacts addressed to Mary, a reflection of the fact that almost no one except Mary's mother ever pointed out or "explained" things to her.

Taken as a whole, then, the verbal environment around John and Mary was one in which there was a heavy dominance of manding—especially manding to get the other person to do something specific. Much of the time people, including the two children, were simply being "moved around." While both John and Mary were moved around a great deal by everyone, the differences between them were marked. Mary was moved around more by everyone; she was asked for information much less than John but was asked to repeat herself much more often; and in two days of speech she was never asked by anyone to continue an utterance she had begun. Yet, as we have seen, her share of the verbal behavior in her immediate vicinity was 85 percent. What sorts of language behaviors will the experiencing of such a verbal environment provoke in a child? Clearly Mary talks more. One might hypothesize that her own speech would function somewhat differently for Mary than his does for John, reflecting the fact that she is differently controlled by the speech of others. One would also anticipate that both children would mand others heavily, as they are themselves manded.

John and Mary: The Expressive Repertoire

In fact, both children mand somewhat less, proportionately, than do those who address them, especially when their interlocutors are their mothers. While the proportion of mands to tacts in the mothers' speech to their children is about 2:1, the proportion in the children's speech to their mothers is closer to 1:1. Where small children are concerned, however, all of them except John show intensive manding of one another—the proportion of mands to tacts is about 3:1. John mands other children only slightly more than he does his mother. The fact that both children mand their mothers less than they are manded by their mothers suggests that they have already learned one socially appropriate pattern of adult-child interaction. This hypothesis, that an audience-specific rather than a simply imitative pattern has developed, is supported by the manner in which the mands are distributed into subclasses.

Eighty-five percent of all manding by the children consists of mands for movement, attention, or information. But the relative strength of these three and their distribution indicates that the children have apparently learned appropriate manners of manipulating different audiences. As Table 2 shows, both children mand other children for *movement* much more heavily than they do their mothers, indicating, perhaps, the relative equality of peer relationships. But they mand their mothers for *attention* much more heavily than they do other children. The strength of this behavior suggests that manding the mother's attention is a permissible way (i.e., one that is likely to be reinforced) of competing for her attention with other children and even with adults.

While the children's verbal repertoires thus appear to be equally audience-specific, mands for attention and movement are very

TABLE 2
Total Mands and Tacts of John and Mary by Functional Subclass, Mothers and Small Children as Addressees

	Total		To Mother		To Other Small Children	
	John	Mary	John	Mary	John	Mary
Mands						
Movements	42.2%	28.3%	25.1%	20.6%	51.7%	36.7%
Attention	24.1	41.1	34.2	56.9	23.3	30.0
Information	21.0	12.1	32.2	4.9	17.2	9.1
Permission	4.8	6.3	6.3	8.1	5.2	9.1
Repetition	6.0	10.6	0.0	6.5	.9	12.9
Confirmation	1.0	.9	1.4	2.4	.9	.9
Continuation	1.0	.4	.7	0.0	.9	.5
Tacts						
Simple	93.5	95.2	95.9	96.2	90.4	92.2
Elaborating a Mand	6.5	4.8	4.1	3.8	9.6	7.8

Note: The columns may not add to 100% because of rounding.

differently distributed in their verbal behavior. Mary mands for attention more than John; John mands for movement much more than Mary. Indeed, for John the ratio of mands for movement to mands for attention is about 8:5, while for Mary the ratio is almost reversed, 5:8. An even more marked difference appears in regard to mands for information. Proportionately John mands both children and adults for information almost twice as much as Mary does. About one-third of all John's mands to his mother, and about 17.2 percent of those to other children, are for information. The questions are not ritual—rather, John pursues information actively, asking for the names or locations of objects, how things work, etc.

Mary mands her mother's permission only a little more than John, and both children mand the permission of other children about as much as they do their mothers', a reflection probably of the fact that they are among the youngest children in their play group.

John almost never mands his mother or other children to repeat. Interestingly enough, however, Mary, whose own speech is often unintelligible, mands repetition from her mother proportionately as much as her mother mands it from her, and her mands to other small children for repetition are proportionately twice as frequent.

Tacts, as we have seen, represent a greater proportion of the children's verbal behavior than of the verbal behavior addressed to them. Almost half of John's speech consisted of tacts and over 38 percent of Mary's. However, neither John nor Mary nor any of the other children made much use of the subclass of "tacts elaborating a mand." Both of them addressed such tacts to other children proportionately over twice as much as they did to their mothers.

Of the four functional classes earlier defined, we have thus far discussed only mands and tacts. The fact is that both echoic responses and intraverbal chains were not present in the data in sufficient numbers to deal with quantitatively. Where intraverbal chains are concerned, their virtual absence from the data may be partially a factor of the observer's unfamiliarity with the group—their verbal routines may be unrecognizable to an outsider.

Of more significance, perhaps, is the fact that there were strikingly few instances of echoic behavior, a form widely thought to be of great importance in developing the language skill of young children. In fact there were no instances of echoic behavior in the protocols in which the behavior was not specifically manded; e.g.:

MOTHER: Say "thank you."
CHILD: Thank you.

Since there is no information on middle-class children with which to compare this, we cannot judge whether the children at three are beyond such behavior, or whether it simply is not reinforced in this environment.

We have already noted certain dissimilarities between John and Mary in terms both of the speech classes they hear and those which characterize their own expressive repertoires. These differences are quite obvious when overall patterns of interaction are compared. John's pattern of manding and tacting in interaction with small children, for example, appears to be quite similar to theirs with him, suggesting that in child-child verbal interactions, his verbal behavior is fully appropriate. There is also a striking similarity between much of John's manding behavior and that of the older persons with whom he interacts; so that altogether his behavior as a speaker is not greatly different from that of his interlocutors, suggesting a fairly mature level of verbal behavior.

Mary, on the other hand, has a speaking behavior quite different from that of her interlocutors. Mands for attention are five times as frequent in her utterances as in utterances addressed to her (John's by contrast are 2:1), a fact which is perhaps best explained by illustrating another characteristic of her language behavior. We have already called attention to the low intelligibility of Mary's speech and the fact that, apparently as a result of an imitative pattern, she has learned to mand for repetition when she speaks, just as she is manded by others. What we have not pointed out is the perseverative repetitious quality of Mary's speech (notable even in the monologues and imaginary conversations involved in doll play). A brief sample will illustrate:

M: Come up here and play with me.
Boo: X
M: Huh? Come up here and play with me.
Boo: I be up there in a minute.
M: Okay.
Boo: ——— say I can come up.
M: Oo-Oo. Come on, Boo-Boo. Hey, Boo! Come on, Boo-Boo.
Boo: Wait till your mama change her clothes.
M: Huh?
Boo: ——— come down.
M: Hey, Boo-Boo. Come on. Boo-Boo, come on.
M: Hey, Boo-Boo. Hey, Boo-Boo. Come here and play with me.
Boo: Wait till your mama put your clothes on.
M: Hey, Boo-Boo. Boo, come on. Come on up. Come on up.
M: Boo come on up. Boo come up. Hey, Boo-Boo, come on.

The density of attentional mands in the brief fragment quoted goes far toward explaining why that class accounts for 41 percent of Mary's total manding behavior. But what, in the first place, has produced Mary's repetitious verbal behavior? Obviously, in certain circumstances, her own unintelligibility. Sometimes, that is, Mary is manded to repeat. But even more significant may be the inattentiveness of the environment that surrounds her. Skinner has noted with regard to repetitious verbal behavior that it tends to occur "when it is not clear that a single response has had the desired effect. ... Unseen audiences, ... inattentive listeners ... atypical audiences such as small babies, dogs, dolls, and so on ... show no signs of an effect and thus verbal behavior is characteristically repetitious" (1957, p. 221).

This assessment seems to be particularly applicable to Mary's circumstances. We have noted earlier that Mary was never manded to continue when she had begun an utterance or addressed someone by name, and that such mands tend to indicate the presence of a ready and attentive audience. Mary does not have such audiences. Another of our earlier observations was that Mary never talked to an adult other than her mother when her mother was around. In fact the protocols show that there was not much interaction between Mary and the other adults in her environment at any time and that the other adults and Mary shared a kind of mutual disregard. This relationship was reinforced by the fact that when interactions did occur they were—and doubtless had also been so in the past— unpleasant. Thus inattentive and unsatisfactory real audiences who tend to respond punishingly or randomly have produced a repetitious quality in Mary's speech, a quality further reinforced by patterns of solitary play in which imaginary audiences (e.g., dolls) play a major role—and similarly do not respond to the child's speech.

Now in general the effectiveness of a verbal operant may be gauged by the number of times it must be repeated to achieve the desired effect. By this criterion we must observe that although Mary's verbal behavior is strong and plentiful, it is apparently quite ineffective. Given the apparent ineffectiveness of her ordinary attempts at gaining control of some part of her world by means of positive approaches, it is not surprising that Mary had developed a whole set of aversive verbal controls.

The quantitative material presented earlier has only hinted at certain qualitative differences between these children that are quite evident in the protocols. On a subjective basis what all these differences added up to was that John was perceived by all those who dealt with the protocols as a quiet, pleasant little boy, while Mary was perceived as a brat. Several observations provide an empirical basis for this perception. To begin with, Mary utilizes a broad variety of aversive verbal techniques to control the individuals in her environment. She whines frequently, she mands attention constantly—the exchange with John could be duplicated throughout the protocols—often interrupting conversations or pulling people from other activities to attend her; and she screams and cries frequently. In addition, in her play with other young children she refuses to cooperate, she will not share her toys or food, she calls the other children names and, in a playful physical exchange, will inevitably scream for her mother. Mary is a child whose environment has apparently taught her that individuals can be controlled largely by aversive means. To see the family in this light is to realize that the household is not so much "child-centered"—as might be suggested by the finding that Mary takes part in 85 percent of all the verbal interactions recorded—but rather child-dominated, to what would appear to be no one's benefit.

The fact that Mary mands her mother's attention constantly when the mother is available may well account, at least in part, for the fact that Mary is out of doors mostly on weekends and in the evenings, at the very times when her mother is home and could be interacting with her. Mary's presence is aversive—sending her out to play provides the mother with an escape. Since Mary does not behave toward other adults in this manner—sharing with them, as we have noted, a kind of mutual disregard—there is no need for such behavior on their part, so she is kept indoors. Interactions with small children may also be limited not only by circumstance—i.e., the fact that Mary is indoors during the week—but also by Mary's temperament. Other children may be reluctant to play with her since she is really very difficult.

Verbal Behavior and the School

On a very specific level these observations about how two slum children operate in their worlds seem to us to raise some questions of educational significance. John and Mary are both from poor Negro families, living in relatively small and noisy slum apartments. (In a relative sense John's family may be poorer because there are more children to provide for.) In both families the mother works so that the children are subject to the authority of a number of different adults; and neither child interacts very much with these "other" adults. All these qualities have been associated from time to time with the "language problems" of disadvantaged children.

Yet, as we have seen, the families are actually very different from each other and have produced—in John and Mary—children who are quite unalike and who have strikingly different sets of verbal techniques for dealing with life. John is a quiet and verbally efficient child. What he wants to know he asks about; what he needs to get he asks for; and to a reasonable extent his world seems to respond in such a way as to encourage this behavior. Mary is shrill, highly talkative, and verbally inefficient. She seldom asks for information and is seldom given any voluntarily. She appears to have learned to wrest what she needs from the adults around her. It is hardly startling news that children are different, and we mention it only because the fact that poor children, like middle-class children, are individuals with discrete sets of language behaviors appears to have been obscured for many by the observation that poor children sound alike.

John and Mary also sound alike. Yet we have seen from the functional analysis that their verbal skills are quite different. One must now raise the question of how these skills will interact with the demands of school to produce a learning or nonlearning child. One would have to predict that John, who is quiet, information-seeking, and not excessively "talkative," would succeed better than Mary, who talks continuously, demands a good deal of attention, and has no history of information-seeking. Yet if we look functionally at the behaviors that the school demands, we are forced to ask whether indeed John, who "ought" to succeed in school, will do so. For John's style would seem to be, at least in part, a product of the success of his behavior in "moving the world around." John is able to act effectively on his environment and the adults in it to achieve what he needs: e.g., his mother's attention, a sense of himself, and a degree of control over the events that affect him. There is almost no opportunity to "move the world around" in the usual school setting. The self-reinforcing quality of such behavior given out largely for sitting still, and for keeping still unless manded is replaced, or displaced, by teacher-administered reinforcement—to speak.

Such observations are highly speculative, of course. This has been a study of two children, and its limitations are obvious. There are ambiguities that cannot be resolved by these data; there are relationships that can only, without full information on related events, be suggested. Yet there are some less individual and less speculative observations to be derived from this study, and they have to do with schools and children and how behaviors are learned.

If we are to carry out programs of educational intervention, we must know into what we are intervening. If there are to be any lasting effects, at least positive lasting effects, we must either structure our interventions so that the life patterns of the individuals for whom they are designed support the structure, or we must concentrate our efforts on changing the life patterns so that the two do not work at odds with one another, as is at present the case. Current research has emphasized the necessity for tying any behavior modification to supports present in the real world. Yet, practically speaking, the behaviors presently being shaped by the schools are not supported by the realities of the world in which these children spend their lives. Labov (1969) has pointed out that the pattern of giving monosyllabic answers, a pattern actively discouraged in the classroom, has real survival value for the slum child. Interlocutors on the street may be anyone from welfare workers to policemen—in relation to all of whom the shortest answer is the safest. Thus behaviors appropriate at school might actually prove dangerous to the child sufficiently naïve to substitute them for the already learned behaviors with which he currently copes with slum life.

For this reason all educational endeavors must be designed to shape and strengthen behaviors that are not only compatible with society's goals but will also find support in the everyday world. The task of designing such educational programs will be made much easier if we have a precise behavioral specification of the response repertoires, the controlling stimuli, the contingencies for reinforcement, and the reinforcers present and operating in the "outside" world. This study suggests what some of these may be. As we have already observed, manding is a dominant functional class in this environment. It is a cardinal principle among operant conditioners to search for strong reinforcers where you find strong behavior. In view of the fact, then, that manding is a strong behavior among these children, it follows that the consequences that shape and maintain manding are particularly strong. From the point of view of the child, "moving the world around" is, as we have suggested, that critical consequence. There is not too much that a small child can do to affect his world; manipulating the individuals in his environment with his verbal behavior appears to be one of the most powerful reinforcers available to the young child, physically small and as yet unskilled in more directly affecting his world.

The strength of manding behavior among these children suggests a functional behavior little capitalized upon in the school setting. An educational program that permits, indeed encourages, the child to "move the world around" with his verbal behavior would be assured of vitality and a self-motivating reinforcer. By the same token, the heavy reliance on direct manding on the part of the adults to shape and maintain behavior has an impact on the child's manner of responding. "Roughly speaking," Skinner has written, "the mand permits the listener to infer something about the condition of the speaker regardless of external circumstances, while the tact permits him to infer something about the circumstances regardless of the condition of the speaker" (1957, p. 83). Logically, then, a pattern of heavy manding would lead to the development of interpersonal sensitivity, a focus on personal variables. The individual would learn to attend to factors like tone of voice as indications of warmth or threat of punishment, for example, rather than to characteristics of the nonpersonal environment, objects and properties of objects. While it is impossible to be certain from these data whether attention to interpersonal variables is stronger than attention to the physical stimuli in the environment, the literature on children of poverty certainly suggests that this might be the case.

Since these children are obviously moved around by a lot of people in their homes, the school would need to structure its programs in such a way as to gradually transfer the control of the children's behavior to features of the environment rather than simply to a new set of adults. In this way certain behaviors can be "built in" to the child, who can then become independent of the need for direct personal supervision to maintain appropriate behaviors.

The "centrality" of the mother noted in almost every aspect of the data suggests that her attention is another powerful reinforcer in the child's world. The mother appears to function not only as an agent of reinforcement, but as a shaper of behavior. There were several instances in the protocols of directly instructional behavior on the part of the mother, who either manded information from the child on the names of objects or their properties, "corrected" some incorrect or inappropriate speech behavior on the child's part, or volunteered new information. Though the pedagogy is usually shaky, the intention of the mother to teach her child is certainly evident. If the "centrality" of the mother is a widespread phenomenon among lower-class children, it may well be that efforts that focus on modifying the behavior of the mother as she interacts with her child could provide not only the most rapid but, in the long run, the most fruitful approach to early intervention. Such an approach, while permitting the directed development of the child's skills, would also ensure that continuity between home and school which appears to be so critical to education.

With all its limitations, this study is useful in helping to define the nature of the "language problem" of disadvantaged children as it relates to education. It seems perfectly clear that these children have learned the verbal behavior required to cope with the situations in which they are growing up. This is what language-learning theory tells us should be the case. It seems equally clear that although these children may well come to school with distinctive speech patterns, these may have little or nothing to do with what the children are able or unable to learn. Educational intervention in the case of verbal behavior must be more than the replacement of one set of forms with another. If we concentrate our educational efforts on "correcting" their phonology and their grammar (hopefully without simultaneously eliminating verbal behavior altogether), we may end up with children who speak in well-enunciated, "grammatical" sentences but who have nothing to say.

Bibliography

Bailey, Beryl L.; and Gussow, Joan D. (eds.). *Proceedings of the Research Planning Conference on Language Development in the Disadvantaged.* New York: Yeshiva University, Department of Educational Psychology and Guidance, 1966.

Blom, J. P.; and Gumperz, J. J. "Some Social Determinants of Verbal Behavior." Berkeley: University of California, 1966.

Bloomfield, L. *Language.* New York: Holt, 1933.

Cazden, Courtney B. "Subcultural Differences in Child Languages: An Interdisciplinary Review." *Merrill-Palmer Quarterly* 12 (1966): 185–219.

Chomsky, N. *Aspects of the Theory of Syntax.* Cambridge, Mass.: MIT Press, 1965.

Coleman, J. S., *et al. Equality of Educational Opportunity.* Washington, D.C.: U.S. Office of Education, 1966.

Gumperz, J. J. "Dialect Differences and Social Stratification in a North Indian Village." *American Anthropologist* 60 (1958): 668–682.

——— . "Linguistic and Social Interaction in Two Communities." In J. J. Gumperz and D. H. Hymes (eds.), "The Ethnography of Communication." *American Anthropologist* 66 (1964): 137–153.

——— . "Linguistic Repertories, Grammars, and Second Language Instruction." In Charles W. Kreidler (ed.), *Report of the Sixteenth Annual Round Table Meeting on Linguistics and Language Studies.* Monograph Series on Languages and Linguistics, No. 18. Washington, D.C.: Georgetown University Press, 1965.

Houston, Susan. "A Sociolinguistic Consideration of the Black English of Children in Northern Florida." *Language* 45 (1969): 599–607.

Hymes, D. H. "The Ethnography of Speaking." In T. Gladwin and W. Sturtevant (eds.), *Anthropology and Human Behavior.* Washington, D.C.: Anthropological Society of Washington, 1962.

——— . "Introduction: Toward Ethnographies of Communication." In J. J. Gumperz and D. H. Hymes (eds.), "The Ethnography of Communication." *American Anthropologist* 66 (1964): 1–34.

——— . "On Communicative Competence." In Beryl L. Bailey and Joan D. Gussow (eds.), *Proceedings of the Research Planning Conference on Language Development in the Disadvantaged.* New

York: Yeshiva University, Department of Educational Psychology and Guidance, 1966.

————. "Models of the Interaction of Language and Social Setting." *Journal of Social Issues* 23 (1967): 8–28.

John, Vera P.; and Goldstein, L. S. "The Social Context of Language Acquisition." *Merrill-Palmer Quarterly* 10 (1964): 265–275.

Labov, W. "The Non-Standard Vernacular of the Negro Community: Some Practical Suggestions." Paper presented at the Seminar in English and Language Arts, Temple University, May 1967.

————. "The Logic of Non-Standard English." In James E. Alatis (ed.), *Linguistics and the Teaching of Standard English.* Monograph Series on Languages and Linguistics, No. 22. Washington, D.C.: Georgetown University Press, 1969.

Milner, Esther. "A Study of the Relationship between Reading Readiness in Grade One School Children and Patterns of Parent-Child Interaction." *Child Development* 22 (1951): 95–112.

Sapir, E. "The Status of Linguistics as a Science." *Language* 5 (1929): 207–214.

Sapon, S. M. " 'Receptive' and 'Expressive' Language." Paper presented at the Annual Meetings of the American Psychological Association, September 1965a.

————. "Micro-Analysis of Second-Language Learning Behavior." *International Review of Applied Linguistics* 3 (1965b): 131–136.

————. "Shaping Productive Verbal Behavior in a Non-Speaking Child: A Case Report." In Francis P. Drinneen, S. J. (ed.), *Report of the Seventeenth Annual Round Table Meeting on Linguistics and Language Studies.* Monograph Series on Languages and Linguistics, No. 19. Washington, D.C.: Georgetown University Press, 1966.

Skinner, B. F. *Verbal Behavior.* New York: Appleton-Century-Crofts, 1957.

Soskin, W. F.; and John, Vera P. "A Study of Spontaneous Talk." In R. Barker (ed.), *Stream of Behavior.* New York: Appleton-Century-Crofts, 1963.

Strodtbeck, F. L. "The Hidden Curriculum of the Middle-Class Home." In E. W. Hunnicutt (ed.), *Urban Education and Cultural Deprivation.* Syracuse, N.Y.: Syracuse University Press, 1964.

On the Status of Black English for Native Speakers: An Assessment of Attitudes and Values

Claudia Mitchell-Kernan
Harvard University

Introduction

In much of the literature, Black English or Nonstandard Negro English is described with reference to phonological, grammatical, and syntactic features exhibited in the speech of blacks that contrast systematically with Standard English referential equivalents. It is these differences which tend to define the category Black English for the linguist. Native speakers, however, do not employ the same parameters in differentiating the speech of blacks from that of nonblacks. In this paper we shall explore Black English as it is conceptualized by native speakers and the basis of these native speaker concepts.

The data that form the basis for this paper were drawn from a black urban community in a large West Coast city and were col-

I gratefully acknowledge the financial support of the following institutions: The Anthropology Department, University of California at Berkeley, which provided support for pilot work conducted during the summer of 1965; The Social Science Research Council, which made possible the extended period of research; The Ford Foundation, which provided support for follow-up research. I am indebted also to Brent Berlin, Ben Blount, Lilyan Brudner, Jan Brukman, Susan Ervin-Tripp, John Gumperz, Eduardo Hernández, Paul Kay, Dan Slobin, Brian Stross, and my husband, Keith Kernan, all of whom provided helpful comments for earlier versions of this paper.

lected over a span of years, from 1965 to 1969, in several short periods and a period of a year's duration.

Metalinguistic Terms of Evaluation

Attention to verbal art is an elaborated theme in black American culture. This concern has given rise to indigenous metalinguistic terms for commenting about language. The problem of interpreting with precision the referents of these terms is not easy, since they have not been subjected to the constraints imposed on the terms of analysis in a formal analytic system. There appears to be no labeled folk category that is isomorphic to the linguist's analytic category labeled Black English or Nonstandard Negro English. There are, however, descriptive terms in currency that correspond in some ways to those labels. Some of the variants that are labeled *Black English* by the linguist are referred to as *flat, country,* and *bad English* by native speakers. The antonyms for these terms are *proper* and *good English.*

When called upon to describe *country-flat* speech, informants attributed to it the features of mispronouncing words, not speaking distinctly, and putting words in the wrong places. Requests for examples usually elicited short inventories of country-flat forms, such as: yestiddy (yesterday); nae'n (none); they is (they are); his'n (his).

A term such as *flat* groups together a set of phenomena that would require differentiation in a linguistic analysis. When a native speaker applies the label *flat* to an utterance such as, "Wouldn' nobody a'knowed she de olest if she hadn'a tol it," it must be determined whether the basis of the judgment has reference to all or some combination of phonological, morphophonemic, and syntactic features. Moreover, the terms often require distinctions between linguistic and sociolinguistic phenomena. When an individual labels "Miz Mary" *country,* he may be referring in his assessment to inappropriate selection rules for terms of address rather than phonology.

Early in the field study a number of informants were asked, in a rather formal interview situation, if some people were better speakers than others. This query brought unanimous affirmative responses. Good speakers were distinguished by their pronunciation, which was said to be clear and distinct, and their ability to put words in the right places. It was deviation in these same areas that was underlined in characterizing country-flat as bad English.

While abstract characterizations of good speech exhibit a fair amount of uniformity, they are not at all revealing of how native speakers might apply the folk labels to given samples of speech. Attempts to elicit models of bad and good speech (Name someone you think is a good/poor speaker) brought responses ranging from naming a personal acquaintance, some known and others unknown to the investigator, to naming a well-known public figure. When Martin Luther King emerged as an example of a good speaker, the researcher attempted to pursue this for a number of reasons. First of all, informants had probably been exposed to the same samples of his speech as the researchers, and it seemed relevant to determine if, in fact, native speakers would exhibit uniformity in assigning the status "good speaker" to a given individual. The two women whose views are represented below are roughly the same age, and both are high school graduates. One is northern born, and the other is from the South, having moved North in early childhood. They are also rather good friends.

QUESTIONER: Do you think he's (M.L.K.) a good speaker?
INFORMANT: Yes. I really like to hear him talk. I don't always agree with what he's saying, though.
Q.: What makes him a better speaker than other people?
I.: Oh, I don't know. For one thing, he has a very nice-sounding voice. He speaks clearly and correctly. He doesn't mispronounce his words and he doesn't use bad grammar.

QUESTIONER: Do you think he's a good speaker?
INFORMANT: No!
Q.: Why not?
I.: I don't know how to explain it, but there's something about his speech that sounds too much like a country preacher to me. Oh, I guess you might call him a good speaker. He's not one of those "dis, dat, and I is" kind of people. He expresses himself well, you really got to give him that. But there's something about the way he sounds that I just don't like. Do you like the way he talks?
Q.: I think he's a pretty good speaker.
I.: I guess it's a matter of opinion and I just don't go for all that "down home stuff."
Q.: If you just heard his voice and didn't know him, could you tell that he was a Negro?

I. (in a tone of voice that implies that *anyone could*): Couldn't you? Some people can fool you with that, but he sure isn't one of them.

If the remote possibility that the views of these two informants were formed on the basis of vastly different speech samples is dismissed, we are faced with intracultural variation in assigning speech to shared folk categories that is almost polar. The first informant considers Martin Luther King a good speaker; the second considers his speech country.

While it is not possible to discriminate the factors that underlie these two judgments, the second informant seemed to devalue what she considered ethnically marked speech and to regard the ability to disguise such an "accent" as a skill. *Down home* is a term often used to distinguish cultural types, meaning southern black. It is not always used in a denigrative sense, however, as it was above. Although the first informant was never asked if she considered Martin Luther King's speech ethnically marked, she was often rather insistent about her own ability to detect ethnic accent. She never appeared to make invidious distinctions on this basis, as her friend did.

Country-flat-bad English is differentiated from proper-good English primarily along the dimensions of phonology, grammar, and lexicon. Syntactic, intonational, and sociolinguistic features also seem to enter into judgments for some informants. The country-flat values along these dimensions are conceptualized as mistakes. A particular usage that an individual labels *country* or *flat* is considered stigmatized. Such usages are felt to have "correct" values, which would be considered proper or good English.

The country-proper contrast rests, in part, on native-speaker awareness of norms of prescriptive grammar. It emerges in response to the recognition that a variant has a referential equivalent and that one of the variants is incorrect, in the prescriptive sense, in reference to the other. Correctness from an individual perspective is based on beliefs that a particular variant conforms to prescriptive norms that form the theoretical model of proper speech.

Many native speakers use the terms *country, flat,* and *bad English* interchangeably in describing usages that deviate from prescriptive norms. The term *country,* however, has a rather strong connotation of southern "backwoods," and is sometimes applied to usages that are felt to be regionalisms rather than mistakes. When a regionalism is labeled *country,* it is considered a stigmatized usage. The stigmatization of some variants is thus not always related to deviation from prescriptive norms, and may stem, as well, from the variant being considered southern. This is one source of noncongruence between the folk and analytic categories.

In order to apply the label *country* or *proper* to a given utterance, an individual must recognize it as a stigmatized usage in the former case, and, in the case of applying the label *proper,* he must make a judgment about the utterance on the basis of what he believes to be the prescriptive norm. The native speaker reacts to the variants:

He handsome.
He gon wash the dishes.
Don't nobody know.
I ain't had it.
It's some books on the table.

in much the same way that speakers in other communities react to:

Neither John nor Bill are bringing records.
Between you and I, he's a dishonest salesman.
There's some books on the table.
He don't have it.

He either edits the utterances or fails to notice anything peculiar about them. The editing process appears to involve the assignment of some variants to a category of mistakes. In one sense the label *country* might be considered a nominal head for a category of mistakes. It is not a label for variants that have grammatical status in another system. The intracultural view of grammaticality, interpreted in the prescriptive sense, serves as a basis for categorizing variants according to their conformance to a single set of prescriptive norms.

Co-occurrence Restrictions in Speech

Although there exists within the community an ideological basis for discriminating between speech that conforms to prescriptive norms from that which does not, actual speech data reveal that co-occurrence restrictions between nonstandard and standard variants are far from rigid. Much speech exhibits a characteristic variation between nonstandard and standard referential equivalents (cf. Labov, Cohen, and Robbins, 1968). Some examples will illustrate this point:

Informal context *(female 30 years):*	*In writing* *(female 17 years):*
. . . these are men with families that are there that are goin on the G.I., and they trying to make it, and they have to put so much studying in it. These the people who are really suffering, you know.	He know how to read because he goes to school. He said he don't but he does all the time.

If we examine data that exhibit other characteristic features of Black English we find the following kinds of variations. The examples below were taken from the data of a twenty-four-year-old female informant.

Nonstandard	*Standard*
. . . because Billy come home and be singing it. He spend most of his time over there. . . . he come right back and tell me.	Suann thinks its something to write on. He makes me mad. Barbara, now she comes practically everyday.

Well, see, Billy *spends* (S) most of his weekends over his great aunt but he *think* (NS) that's his granmother.

. . . out of all the kids he have.	Well, he has a name tab. . . .

She *has* (S) a morning class and a afternoon class and she *have* (NS) their name taped down on a piece of cardboard.

She do things that . . .	She does that right now.
You was mentioning . . .	. . . when we were coming up.
When you was in a dormitory . . .	You still weren't gon tell me.
We was gon take them.	We were gonna get married.

Such variability in a single speaker is not an unusual idiolectual situation. Young children exhibit similar kinds of variation. We find the following in the data of a three-and-a-half-year-old subject:

Nonstandard	Standard
This a A.	This is a circle.
What you doing?	What are you laughing at?
My daddy work at the outside.	He lives by us.
They was on the tree.	They were playing with the ball.

They *seen* (NS) the bird, *saw* (S) the ducks.

He have a umbrella.	He has a red jacket on.

The variable nature of these variants may be seen in sentence imitations elicited from the same child on different occasions.

Model	Brigitte
There isn't any more.	There isn't no more.
	It isn't any more.
He's not going to the party.	He's not going to the party!
	He not going to the party.
She does the shopping and cooking and baking.	She do the shopping and cooking.
(Natural conversation)	Why does the king have this much money?

Paralleling this variability are norms of appropriateness that do not require separation between many Black English–Standard English contrasts in everyday speech.

Norms of Appropriateness

Parents universally express the desire that their children speak "good" English. Just as they make judgments about others on the basis of their speech, evaluating them favorably or unflatteringly, they feel that speech is an important identity carrier vis-à-vis the wider community. They do not predict bright futures for those who fail to learn good English. The benefits of mastery of good English are frequently expressed in terms of employment possibilities and upward mobility. Good English manages impressions favorably, in that people will tend to view one as educated and intelligent, whereas using bad English tends to give the impression that one is uneducated and to some degree unintelligent. It is possible to observe this value in operation in the following examples of censure of on-going speech.

MOTHER: Give your brother some of those cookies.
NINE-YEAR-OLD SON: I ain' got no mo.
M.: For goodness sakes, can't you do any better than that?
S.: I don't have any more.

SIX-YEAR-OLD SON *(whining):* She done ate up all of my potato chips.
MOTHER: Done ate! She has . . . have ate up all of my potato chips.

While it is usually the positive valuation of good English that is articulated directly, it is not uncommon to hear "proper" speech appraised unfavorably. One way of commenting indirectly about another's speech is by *marking* that individual. Marking is a style of quotation in which remarks are repeated accompanied by paralinguistic mimicry. Marking is often highly stylized. One informant marked one of her neighbors in commenting upon the latter's inappropriate use of "proper" speech. She considered this an affectation and described her neighbor as a phony. The following exchange between two nine-year-old girls illustrates conflict between abstract valuation of good English and norms of appropriateness.

CAROL: Don't aks me for none of my crayons. You wouldn't give me none of yours.
BETTY: The word is *ask!* You should say, Don't ask me for any of my crayons.
CAROL *(jeeringly):* Aw, you always trying to talk so proper.

While the ability to speak "good" English is a valued skill, behavioral observations point to a more complex set of values regarding speech. These values might best be discussed in terms of situational norms of appropriateness. In support of this view, informants report that they attempt to speak as correctly as possible in more formal situations and when they make mistakes they are embarrassed and feel foolish.

Despite the respect many speakers of Black English have for adherence to the perceived prescriptive norms of the Standard English code, the prestige of such adherence is neutralized in much everyday linguistic interaction between blacks.

Although there were a few individuals who were singled out as "proper talking" and "country talking," this form of censure usually occurred where implicit norms of appropriateness were violated. It was somewhat of a faux pas to give the impression of "talking proper" when the situation was defined by others as informal. On the other side, one informant found the speech of her younger brother a source of irritation because he mispronounced words and used bad grammar. She mentioned this after he had participated in a skit in a church Easter program. She said, "Everytime he opened his mouth, I just cringed. He kept saying 'yo' and if that wasn't bad enough, he said 'mines'." Insisting that he could do much better, she attributed his poor performance to obstinacy. An *r*-less *your* is very common in the community, and would go unnoticed except in circumstances where the expectation is that one should be on his best linguistic behavior.

There are a number of circumstances that lead people in the community to make efforts to avoid what they consider making mistakes in speaking. An unfamiliar interlocutor is one such stimulus. A socially distant interlocutor, because he occupies an official status, may also serve as a stimulus for *switching*. I have heard this occur, for example, when an informant was talking to a white insurance broker. When an unfamiliar interlocutor stimulates someone to switch in the presence of others, this may be the subject of teasing and joking when the stranger leaves.

To say that someone is "talking proper" seems to involve the judgment that they have switched from their normal position on Black English–Standard English contrasts. Because of the idiolectal variation present in the community, this involves some rather subtle distinctions. On occasion the Standard English pronunciation of some lexical item or idiom may signal "talking proper." Because some words and phrases almost always co-occur with Black English phonology, the use of Standard English phonology has a rather jarring effect where such items are involved. The idiom "I'm not stud'n him" is one such phrase. *Studying* would sound ludicrous, whereas a shift from *runnin* to *running* would not. On other occasions, judgments are made on the basis of linguistic and paralinguistic cues that seem to go hand in hand with switching. They include disturbances in speech rate and fluency that accompany efforts to use a code one does not ordinarily use, as well as hypercorrections.

While such things as changes in topic may cause unconscious shifts where Black English–Standard English contrasts are present, it seems to be the expectation that people should not switch in the direction of Standard English in everyday social interaction among friends. Such switching may leave the impression that one was being unfriendly or distant. To do this consistently may earn one the pejorative labels of proper talking and phony. On the other hand, to evidence an inability or unwillingness to switch to Standard English when the occasion demands it may put one in the class of country-talking people.

The kind of shifting discussed above will be called *monitoring* because monitoring expresses the idiolectal variety characteristic of such shifting. There is also a kind of monitoring which involves the deliberate use of Black English marked variants. An individual will sometimes use Black English variants that are not his normal position. For example, a person will say "over yonder" rather than "over there," as he usually does, or "his'n" rather than "his." One source of such choices are variants that may, for example, be in currency for an older generation of Black English speakers but that are considered taboo by the younger generation. Individuals will also use forms that are almost never heard but that play on areas of contrast between Standard English and Black English. Such a variant might be "I is." I have referred to this elsewhere as *hyper-Black English* (cf. Mitchell-Kernan, 1971). The Black English phonological component is typically exaggerated, and it is clear to the hearer that this is not an ordinary choice for the speaker.

Gumperz has emphasized in a number of places (1964, 1965, 1967) that choice among referential equivalents in a speech community is frequently dictated by social norms, which select for a particular alternant. These social norms relate to the culturally meaningful ways in which social categories may be realized linguistically. The deliberate use of Black English variants seems to signal solidarity because it emphasizes the use of a code that marks a shared social identity. The same might be said of the maintenance of normal position, but in this instance the effect of creating a consciousness of kind is more subtle.

Black English–Standard English contrasts are used to signal social meaning. Depending on the community of interests a speaker desires to arouse, he may monitor in one direction or another. A socially distant interlocutor according to the criterion of race, for example, may be included in the defined in-group by choosing Black

English variants. The deliberate use of Black English variants may also signal separatist ends. Just as speakers use Black English variants and communicative style to activate solidarity with blacks, when motivated by a similar objective toward a nonblack, a black speaker may attempt to monitor in the direction of Standard English by deleting linguistic markers that would serve to underline their different social identities. The available resources, do not, however, comprise a systematic code that is drawn upon uniformly from speaker to speaker. Black English–Standard English boundaries shift from speaker to speaker and from generation to generation.

When informants say that they value the ability to speak good English, I do not think they are paying mere lip service to majority norms. To conclude, however, that Standard English is positively valued and Black English negatively valued would be an oversimplification of a rather complex set of norms about speech. Many of these norms are implicit and rarely articulated. Their presence becomes salient ordinarily only when they are violated.

While serving as a consultant to a school district near the area where this research was conducted, I was discussing school problems with four students who were enrolled in a course designed to teach Standard English. These students, seventeen- and eighteen-year-olds, were not convinced that learning Standard English was going to bring them any benefits, but were ambivalent enough about the matter to have been participating in this class on a volunteer basis.

One of the young men began discoursing at length on problems he felt the students created. He used a very careful "proper" style, marked not so much by hypercorrection as by isolated word pronunciation, accompanied by exaggerated lip movements. The other students were immediately in stitches and began hooting and shouting at the speaker. One of the girls remarked, "Aw, he trying to talk so proper." The incident serves to illustrate one kind of social response likely to occur when Standard English usage is felt to be inappropriate.

Many Black English variants have come to be thought of as illiterate and uneducated speech. The low prestige these variants enjoy is strikingly evident when individuals are marked using exaggerated country-flat speech. The intent is clearly to communicate that they are uneducated and often not very bright. The view of variants as country *qua* southern contributes to their devaluation among some members of the community, particularly the generation born in the urban North. Country also has nonlinguistic behavioral parallels, such as *country acting* and *country dressing.* Failure to adjust to the Northern urban behavioral patterns is considered nonhip and *lame.*

The researcher has witnessed reference to the South creating such vivid images for children that the statement "Joan was born in Mississippi" was whispered as though it were "Joan was born with two heads," evoking uncontrollable giggling. Southern expressions noted by children are often used to taunt other children who use them. Individuals who move North during their formative years are pressured to conform in these matters. As a nine-year-old informant put it, in criticizing the speech of a classmate: ". . . it's just not fit for up here." For many northern blacks, the least prestigeful speech of all is speech that is defined as being southern.

Native Speaker Concepts of Black English

Native speakers tend to interpret questions about Black English or Negro English within two basic frames of reference. The first of these seems to be that of prescriptive grammar. Terms such as *Black English* and *Negro English* bring to mind usages that deviate from prescriptive norms. In this event, informants characteristically point out that there is no speech common to all black people. It is not unusual for them to add that within their circle of friends there is great variation in command of "good" English. Such allusions to "good" English strongly suggest that the frame of reference is indeed prescriptive grammar.

The second frame of reference involves aspects of usage, rarely included in grammars, which are felt to set the black community apart from other speech communities. These features include speech events such as verbal dueling, known by the regional variants of *woofing, joning,* and *playing the dozens;* message forms such as *signifying;* and metaphors and idioms that originate in the Black community. In addition, the term *Black English* brings to mind many stylistic features that lack convenient labels in common usage. Examples include narrative styles that make use of gesture and mimicry as expressive devices. The manner in which blacks use their eyes in nonverbal communication, referred to as *rolling* or *cutting* the eyes, was also pointed to as a feature of black communicative style.

Informant reactions suggest that a distinction between code and communicative style is a useful one for purposes of generalization. Although verbal dueling may be prized by young teen-age boys and disapproved of by their parents, aspects of Black English as a communicative style seem to be more appreciated than aspects of Black English as a code.

Informants seem to agree that there is something distinctive about the speech of black people. What these distinctive features are is conjectural, however. The processing of ethnic identity via speech cues is not at all uncommon in this community. One afternoon, during a visit with an informant, she received a telephone call. Her eight-year-old daughter answered the phone, and, when asked who was calling, replied, "Some white lady." Yet isolating precisely which features of an utterance determine such identification is not easy for the researcher. Informants found it difficult to be explicit about the nature of the cues they employed in assessing the ethnic identity of a speaker. They most often reported that they were able to identify speakers as black because "They just sound different" or "They talked country."

Native speaker concepts of Black English cover a range of phenomena. Discussions of code features do not exhaust differences in language use between the black community and other communities. The language of the community has evolved its own idiomatic usages, metaphors, special styles, and speech events, as well as other language uses that are deeply embedded in the shared experience and cultural heritage of black people. The code features that linguistic grammars tend to be concerned with may have little to do with the sense of appreciation evidenced by an informant's quotation of a phrase felt to have a Black English flair. The intracommunity view of Black English relates as well to knowledge of black culture demonstrated through conformance to rules of usage. A native speaker is recognized not only by the code or subcode of the language he uses in communication but also by the topics he chooses to comment upon and the channels and body language he employs in conveying expressive information. Structural features such as consonant-cluster simplification, copula deletion, etc., are only incidentally tied to the welter of other factors that serve as distinctive features of black speech. Control of the many facets of black speech serves to create a consciousness of kind and rapport with other blacks. Adeptness in this matter seems to be predicated on background knowledge and skills derivable only from participation in black culture. In this respect, the language of the community serves to promote unity among blacks and to underline a shared community of interests.

Summary

The subject of Black English is surrounded by a great deal of cultural sensitivity. In the context of teaching a course on Standard English to high school students, I used the strategy of having them tape-record samples of their peers' speech for classroom analysis. More than once when the tape recorder was present, fellow students showed clear resentment. They demanded to know why anyone wanted to tape their speech, as if the very gesture intimated something was wrong with it. This sensitivity stemmed from their own knowledge of standards they felt they did not meet. While their linguistic insecurity no doubt served as the stimulus for joining this course, they showed acute self-consciousness and ambivalence regarding attempts to emulate outside standards. By this age many black youngsters are so fed up with demands for conformance that they are not easily approached with new ones. They are, moreover, becoming increasingly politicized in their views toward such demands.

Socialization for many black Americans is a process during which an individual, while acquiring his culture, is also enculturated to its disadvantaged and negatively valued status as defined by the wider culture of which he is also a part. To the extent that an aspect of black culture is different from some corresponding aspect of standard average American culture, even when it enjoys normative status intraculturally, it may become stigmatized for some individuals because of their identification and desire to participate in the wider culture.

The bicultural status of Black Americans makes the socialization process a time when each individual attempts to find some viable personal reconciliation to cultural patterns, values, and attitudes that do not cohere or intersect in any consistent fashion. Some solutions find individuals essentially submerged in things black, rejecting outside standards and valuations across the board. Others look outward toward the wider culture, and still others straddle the two, selecting from both as the needs of the moment require. Language is an important reflector of these various positions.

Black English–Standard English contrasts play a functional role in the communication system of the black community. Some Black English code variants are devalued and stigmatized. It would appear that the prevailing intracultural pressure is in the direction of eliminating some code differences between Standard English and Black English. In more recent years, Black English has come to have a more explicit symbolic value. Differences in language use are seen as adaptations to the circumstances of pariah status. They are also viewed as reflecting a culture history linked to Africa as well as Western Europe. This view tends to be articulated where cultural nationalism has made inroads and among educated blacks. The use of Black English is beginning to symbolize a spirit of liberation in the black community, and the separatist function of Black English has become more explicit. If my experience in working with teenagers is at all indicative of new trends, it would appear that a desire for distinctness will probably serve in the future as an ideological basis for the maintenance of some differences between the language of blacks and the language of the wider culture. But the negative valuations toward many Black English code variants as incorrect, southern, and illiterate, which remain pervasive, seem to point out that the new distinctness of black speech will be different from the old.

Bibliography

Gumperz, John J. "Linguistic and Social Interaction in Two Communities." In J. J. Gumperz and D. Hymes (eds.), "The Ethnography of Communication." *American Anthropologist* 66, No. 6 (part 2) (1964): 137–153.

————. "Linguistic Repertoires, Grammars, and Second Language Instruction." In Charles W. Kreiler (ed.), *Report of the Sixteenth Annual Round Table Meeting on Linguistics and Language Studies.* Monograph Series on Languages and Linguistics, No. 18. Washington, D.C.: Georgetown University Press, 1965.

————. "On the Linguistic Markers of Bilingual Communication." In J. Macnamara (ed.), "Problems of Bilingualism." *Journal of Social Issues* 23, No. 2 (1967): 48-57.

Labov, William; Cohen, Paul; and Robbins, Clarence. *A Study of the Non-Standard English of Negro and Puerto Rican Speakers.* Final Report, New York City Cooperative Research Project No. 3288, vols. 1 and 2. Washington, D.C.: Office of Education, 1968.

Mitchell-Kernan, Claudia. "Language Behavior in a Black Urban Community." Monographs of the Language-Behavior Research Laboratory, No. 2. University of California at Berkeley, February 1971.

Black American Speech Events and a Language Program for the Classroom

Thomas Kochman
University of Illinois at Chicago Circle

Introduction

This essay is divided into four sections. Section II attempts to reveal how language functions for the black child in his own cultural environment from an analysis of speech events that typically occur there; the third and fourth sections discuss possible ways in which speaker skills and situational features associated with black *indigenous* use of language might become part, or even form the basis, of a language-development program for black children, *in the classroom*. Section I, of less practical assistance to the teacher than the other three, attempts to sketch briefly both the traditional sociocultural context on which educational goals and methods have generally been based, and out of which perspective the curriculum for English and speech teaching has been defined, and the *changing* sociocultural framework that makes traditional methods and practices inappropriate and that compels us to find additional resources from which education and, specifically in this article, language-development programs, can benefit.

I. The Goal of Education in the United States— General and Specific

It has been axiomatic to say that the goal of education is the successful socialization of the individual. What this means is that generally education is the medium that molds and adapts the individual to a role regarded by society as desirable or acceptable. In the United States, it is the Anglo middle class whose culture is dominant and who determines what the social goals of the nation are. The goal of this dominant group has been and generally continues to be assimilationist, which can simply be defined as behaving in accordance with the norms of the dominant culture.

The national attitude underlying this goal is expressed in a statement by Theodore Roosevelt in 1919, recorded recently in *El Grito,* a journal of contemporary Mexican-American thought (1968, p. 1):

> Our principle in this matter should be absolutely simple. If the immigrant who comes here in good faith becomes an American and assimilates himself to us he shall be treated on an exact equality with everyone else. . . .
>
> But this is predicated on the man's becoming in very fact an American and nothing but an American. . . .
>
> There can be no divided allegiance here. Any man who says he is an American, but something else also, isn't an American at all. We have room for but one flag the American flag. . . .
>
> We have room for but one language here, and that is the English language, for we intend to see that the crucible turns our people out as Americans, of American nationality, and not as dwellers in a polyglot boarding house. . . .

As socializing agent of the dominant culture, the teacher has defined her task as molding the child into a form that will be acceptable to that culture. As a result, she has judged behavior and performance that accord with the dominant aesthetic as *good* (acceptable) and that not in accordance with it as *bad* (unacceptable).

The attitude of English and speech teachers was almost unanimously prescriptive and doctrinaire in matters concerning language usage. Rules governing language use, more often based upon myth than reality and generally reflecting an ignorance of historical processes and development, were applied to every utterance the pupil spoke.

The inflexibility of these performance rules repeatedly clashed with the dynamism inherent in actual language use, which is another way of saying that it became increasingly obvious that the rules influencing what people *actually* said were clearly at odds with those rules that stipulated what people *ought* to have said.

It also became apparent that the aesthetic that defined acceptable language performance was far too narrow to account for the obvious success speakers and writers were having with their audiences with language performances that were in obvious violation of what the old guard regarded as correct.

As a consequence, it became necessary to enlarge the aesthetic, which entailed widening the area of what was considered acceptable language performance. The term used to designate this new approach to language was *descriptive,* a term that was to apply to an ostensibly more permissive attitude regarding language performance. As a point of departure from the prescriptive approach toward language use, which felt that *rules* should determine *usage,* the descriptive approach generally established that *usage* should determine *rules,* that just as norms for dress change over a period of time, so do the norms for language use. The point, however, that indicated that while the aesthetic had broadened it still remained restrictive was that the usage that determined the rules was in fact that of your "educated" writers and speakers. In terms of social penetration, moving from the prescriptive to the descriptive actually widened the aesthetic to the point of including only more of the dominant culture (i.e., the educated), but still remaining closed to the mass of less educated. The aesthetic tyranny exercised by the few educated over the many educated has diminished, but the aesthetic tyranny exercised by the educated over the uneducated remains. As far as the rules were concerned, it meant that it became acceptable in speech, for example, to end sentences with prepositions (because educated people did it), but it was still unacceptable to use the emphatic double negative (because educated people did not).

This is not to say that the descriptive approach did not add a measure of tolerance to the English classroom that must have seemed to many like a welcome breath of fresh air compared to its predecessor. It even went to the point of acknowledging the existence of nonstandard dialects and respecting the right of those speakers to use them (although only in *native* contexts). The nonstandard dialect achieved the distinction of legitimacy, the right to exist, but not the distinction of *acceptability,* the right to move with self-respect.

Confronted with the prospect of having to widen the aesthetic still further to accept *all* people of our society as they are—i.e., as individual organisms who are part of cultural organisms with independent life styles (the part of the "pot" that didn't "melt")—the alternative has been rather to process people into acceptability, an approach that was consistent with the assimilationist perspective.

There have been efforts made to change methodology when attempting to educate the culturally different while still operating out of the assimilationist perspective. This was the point of view advocated by Miles V. Zintz, for example, in his important book *Education Across Cultures* (1963), which concerned itself with the teaching problems facing the Anglo teacher in her efforts to acculturate Pueblos, Navajos, and Spanish Americans of New Mexico into the mainstream culture as a result of differing and conflicting world views and value systems. Zintz essentially advocated that the teacher learn the students' respective cultures for the reason that cultural differences constituted a barrier or obstacle in achievement according to mainstream norms, and that knowledge of the "other" culture would be an invaluable aid to the teacher in easing the transition toward such achievement. This is an appropriate first step in moving from the position outlined in the first part of this section. It is the present position of a small group of educators, linguists, and anthropologists—for example, those interested both in teaching standard English to speakers of other dialects without tampering with the native dialect and in getting the teachers to recognize the *legitimacy* of the language and behavior patterns of the culturally different child.

Acknowledging the legitimacy of a child's native dialect and culture is a big concession to exact from the ethnocentric Anglo teacher, as anyone can tell you whose job has been teaching teachers, but legitimacy, as has been mentioned, is only the first step on the road to social acceptability (equality), which is the ultimate cultural pluralistic goal. Learning about the child's language and culture is step two. Here the teacher needs to ask herself these questions: If formal education were not to reach this child, what would his culture teach him? What skills and abilities are developed by the child as he functions within his native environment? What are the motivational forces that operate in his culture, those prestige norms that influence the child to behave in one way as opposed to another? What values, attitudes, and life style does *he* hold and regard favorably, i.e., are part of his aesthetic? Both step one and step two can be taken by the teacher even if she does *not* relinquish her assimilationist ethos. However, both steps involve a substantial and significant shift in her attitude. It is absolutely essential that every teacher presently teaching culturally different children take these initial steps, which are designed to establish a meeting ground between the culturally different child and the school curriculum and soften somewhat the present antagnonism that exists between the school, the teacher, and the culturally different child.

This third step in this period of transition deals with changes in the school curriculum itself, as decentralization occurs and the goals of cultural pluralism emerge to replace the goals of assimilation.

II. Culture and Education

The general need for incorporating indigenous culture into the educational process has long been overdue, and judging from trends toward local community control of the schools and emerging cultural pluralism, accompanied by demands to make the school curriculum more relevant to the culturally different (black, Puerto Rican, Mexican-American, Appalachian, etc.), this need will become increasingly urgent.

One of the many important questions educators operating out of pluralistic perspective must concern themselves with is the role that indigenous culture is to play in the educational process for the culturally different. How much of what part of the culture should be used in the classroom? What rationale determines what is included and what is excluded? Such weighty considerations cannot be embarked upon here, since it is obvious that the educational policy and objectives of each cultural group will be determined and defined by community leaders and educators from *within* each respective group and by decentralized boards of education that represent the broad interests of that group in the overall society. What *is* clear at this time, however, is that before one can begin to make such determinations, one must possess descriptive cultural data of the kind that ethnography can provide with suggestions as to ways in which these cultural data *might* be useful, e.g., in developing a language problem for black children *in the classroom*. For this reason, as well as others, the following section on black American speech behavior and its implications for education is important.

A Brief Ethnography of Black American Speech Events (Chicago)[1]

What follows is a brief description of black speech events that typically occur in the black community of Chicago and have been found to occur in all major black communities in the United States. The names for these speech events vary and sometimes identify different aspects, but the basic characteristics of the speech event are the same. For example, what is known as *signifying* in Chicago is known as *sounding* in New York City, *screaming* in Harrisburg, *joning* in Washington, D.C., *ranking* in Philadelphia, etc. *Sounding* is also known in Chicago but designates only the initial thrust of the verbal contest (to *sound* out a prospective opponent to see if he will play the game). The names for the verbal insults that follow also subdivide differently. What my informants in Chicago labeled *sigging* (signifying), Labov's informants from New York labeled *louding* and *rifting,* and so on.[2] The significant point here is that these terms refer basically to the same type of speech, viz., verbal insult, known generally as *playing the dozens*. Abrahams has also found speech events in the West Indies and Africa analogous to those occurring here, so it appears we are dealing with a widely observed Afro-American practice (see, for example Abrahams, 1968). In any event, by focusing on the microcosm of the black community in Chicago and describing and analyzing those black speech events that occur there, teachers in other black inner-city areas can be reasonably assured that the same kind of events occur there.

In addition to *sounding* and *signifying,* other terms in the black idiom designating other kinds of speech events are *rapping, shucking and jiving, running it down, gripping,* and *copping a plea*.[3] In the description that follows, we would hope to distinguish those features of form, style, and function that differentiate one type of speech event

---

[1] For the most complete account, see Kochman (1970).
[2] From personal correspondence. However, see Labov (forthcoming).
[3] For an analysis of *gripping* and *copping a plea,* see Kochman (1970).

from the other and show how the variable threads of the communication situation—speaker, setting, and audience—function within the social context of the black community.

Rapping, while also used to refer to ordinary conversation, distinctively refers to a fluent and lively way of talking, generally characterized by a high degree of personal style, through which the speaker intends to draw the audience's attention to himself or some feature of himself that he feels is attractive or prestigious with his audience. To one's peer group, rapping may be descriptive of an interesting narration, a colorful rundown of some past event. A recorded example of this type of rap (rapping 1) follows, an answer from a Chicago gang member to a youth worker who asked how his group became organized.

Now I'm goin tell you how the jive really started. I'm goin tell you how the club got this big. 'Bout 1956 there used to be a time when the Jackson Park show was open and the Stony show was open. Sixty-six street, Jeff, Gene, all of 'em, little bitty dudes, little bitty . . . Gene wasn't with 'em then. Gene was cribbin [living] over here. Jeff, all of 'em, real little bitty dudes, you dig? All of us were little.

Sixty-six [the gang on sixty-sixth street], they wouldn't allow us in the Jackson Park show. That was when the parky [?] was headin it. Everybody say, if we want to go to the show, we go! One day, who was it? Carl Robinson. He went up to the show . . . and Jeff fired on him. He came back and all this was swelled up 'bout yay big, you know. He come back over to the hood [neighborhood]. He told [name unclear] and them dudes went up there. That was when mostly all the main sixty-six boys was over here like Bett Riley. All of 'em was over here. People that quit gang-bangin [fighting, especially as a group], Marvell Gates, people like that.

They went on up there, John, Roy and Skeeter went in there. And they start humbuggin [fighting] in there. That's how it all started. Sixty-six found out they couldn't beat us, at *that* time. They couldn't *whup* seven-o [70]. Am I right Leroy? You was cribbin over here then. Am I right? We were dynamite! Used to be a time, you ain't have a passport, Man, you couldn't walk through here. And if didn't nobody know you it was worse than that . . . .

The rap here is designed to establish the status of the speaker and draw attention to those qualities—strength, intelligence, courage, and leadership—his group regards as prestigious by referring to a role that he played in the formation of the group. But the aesthetic of the rap was designed to focus attention not only on *what* was said (content) but the *way* it was said (expression). This is essentially the difference between *running it down* and *rapping;* running it down draws attention to the content of what was said while rapping focuses the attention of the audience as much (or more) on the way it is said.

This is especially true of rapping when the audience is a girl or woman, in which the speaker draws attention to that aspect of himself which he feels will be most attractive to her (his looks, sexual ability, affluent appearance, etc.). The role of the female here is to respond verbally to the overture of the male. If she rejects his invitation she does so by insulting him, either by impugning the *content* of what was said or the *way* it was said, the man's originality (or lack of it) and delivery.

The competitive aspect of the event is keen, leading frequently to a lively repartee between male and female as each attempts to outperform the other in verbal insult, with the woman becoming as verbally adept as the man. The term *capping*—i.e., to put a cap on something someone else has said, outperform a person by improving on his verbal insult in your retort ("one-upmanship")—is often applied to this exchange.

The third form of rapping is often called *whupping a game* (also *running a game*), and is the means through which the speaker tries to obtain goods or services from someone, a "trick" or "lame" who looks like he can be swindled. Rapping here would be descriptive of the highly stylized (and carefully planned) verbal part of the maneuver. Examples of this, the mark of the adept hustler, may be read in Iceberg Slim's book *Pimp: The Story of my Life* (1967). The ability to use words in this manipulative way is a valuable asset to a person growing up in a community in which one is likely to be threatened and exploited by outsiders and where the competition for the limited amount of goods and services available is keen. Therefore this ability is prized and highly regarded by one's peers.

The aesthetic of rapping, i.e., that which the speaker gets credit for from his group or audience, consists of the expressive and directive features of his speech behavior. In all of the forms of rapping discussed, the *way* the speaker projected his personality was noticed and evaluated, with credit given for originality and style. In addition, when rapping to a woman (rapping 2) or to a lame (rapping 3), credit is extended for the ability to use language in a directive way, i.e., the ability to manipulate and control people for the purpose of getting them to give up or do something that will benefit the speaker. The relatively high status of the pimp and hustler is attributable to his success in manipulating people. The high status symbols—beautiful women, stylish clothing, and an expensive car, as evidence of this ability—are appropriately flaunted.

Chucking, shucking it, shucking and jiving, S-ing and J-ing, or just *jiving,* are terms used by blacks to refer to one form of speech behavior practiced by the black man when interacting with authority figures, and to another form of speech behavior practiced by blacks when interacting with each other on the peer-group level. When referring to the black's dealings with the white man and the power structure, the above terms are descriptive of his talk and accompanying physical movements that are appropriate to some momentary guise, posture, or façade.

Originally, in the South and later in the North, the black man learned that American society had assigned to him a restrictive role and status. Among whites his behavior had to conform to this imposed station, and he was constantly reminded to "keep his place." He learned that before white people it was not acceptable to show feelings of indignation, frustration, discontent, pride, ambition, or desire; that real feelings had to be concealed behind a mask of innocence, ignorance, childishness, obedience, humility, and deference. The terms used by the black to describe the role he played before white folks in the South were *tomming* or *jeffing.* Failure to accommodate the white southerner in this respect was almost certain to invite psychological and often physical brutality.

In the northern cities the black man encountered authority figures equivalent to the southern "crackers": policemen, judges, probation officers, truant officers, teachers, and "Mr. Charlies" (bosses), and soon learned that the way to get by and avoid difficulty was to *shuck.* Thus, he learned to accommodate "the Man," to use the total orchestration of speech, intonation, gesture, and facial expression for the purpose of producing whatever appearance would be acceptable. It was a technique and ability that was developed from fear, a respect for power, and a will to survive. This type of accommodation is exemplified by the "Yes sir, Mr. Charlie," or "Anything you say, Mr. Charlie," "Uncle Tom" type "Negro" of the North. The language and behavior of accommodation became the prototype out of which other slightly modified forms of shucking evolved.

Through accommodation, many blacks became adept at concealing and controlling their emotions and at assuming a variety of postures. They became competent actors in the process. Many developed a keen perception as to what affected, motivated, appeased, or satisfied the authority figures with whom they came into contact. What became an accomplished and effective coping mechanism for many blacks to "stay out of trouble," became for others a useful artifice for avoiding arrest or "getting out of trouble" when apprehended.

Some field illustrations of shucking to get out of trouble after having been caught come from some seventh-grade children from an inner-city school in Chicago. The children were asked to "talk their way out of" a troublesome situation. Examples of the situation and their impromptu responses follow:

Situation:
You're cursing at this old man and your mother comes walking down the stairs. She hears you.

Response (to "talk your way out of this"):
"I'd tell her that I was studying a scene in school for a play."

Situation:
What if you were in a store and were stealing something and the manager caught you?

Responses:
"I would tell him that I was used to putting things in my pocket and then going to pay for them and show the cashier."
"I'd tell him that some of my friends was outside and they wanted some candy so I was goin to put it in my pocket to see if it would fit before I bought it."
"I would start stuttering. Then I would say 'Oh, oh, I forgot. Here the money is'."

Situation:
You're at the beach and they've got signs posted all over the beach and

floating on the water and you go past the swimming mark and the sign says "Don't go past the mark." How do you talk your way out of this to the lifeguard?

Responses:
"I'd tell him that I was having so much fun in the water that I didn't pay attention to the sign."
"I'd say that I was swimming under water and when I came back up I was behind the sign."

The function of shucking and jiving as it refers to transactions evolving out of confrontations between Negroes and "the Man" is both expressive and directive. It is speech behavior designed to work on the mind and emotions of the authority figure for the purpose of getting him to feel a certain way or give up something that will be to the other's advantage. When viewed in its entirety, shucking must be regarded as a performance. Words and gestures become the instruments for promoting a certain image, or posture. In the absence of words, shucking would be descriptive of the actions that constitute the deception, as in the example above where the seventh-grade boy recognized the value of stuttering before saying, "Oh, oh, I forgot. Here the money is," knowing that stuttering would be an invaluable aid in presenting a picture of innocent intent.

Significantly, the first form of shucking that I described above, which developed out of accommodation, is becoming less frequently used today by many blacks, as a result of a new-found self-assertiveness and pride, which has begun to challenge the system. The willingness on the part of many blacks to accept the psychological and physical brutality and general social consequences of not "keeping one's place" is indicative of the changing self-concept of the black. Ironically, the shocked reaction of the white power structure to the present militancy of the black is partly due to the fact that the black had been so successful at "putting whitey on" via shucking in the past, i.e., compelling belief in whatever posture he chose to assume.

Shucking, jiving, shucking and jiving, or *S-ing and J-ing,* when referring to language behavior practiced by blacks when interacting with each other on the peer-group level, are descriptive of the talk and gestures that are appropriate to "putting someone on" by creating a false impression, conveying false information, etc. The terms seem to cover a range from simply telling a lie, to bullshitting, to

subtly playing with someone's mind. An important difference between this form of shucking and that described earlier is that the
same talk and gestures that are deceptive to "the Man" are often
transparent to those members of one's own group who are able
practitioners at shucking themselves. Also, S-ing and J-ing within the
group often has play overtones in which the person being "put on"
is aware of the attempts being made and goes along with it for the
enjoyment of it or in appreciation of the style involved. As with rapping, the aesthetic of shucking and jiving incorporates both expressive and directive features of the speech event. When speaker and
audience are from the same group, attention is focused on the expressive features displayed—the verbal art of the speaker; when
speaker and audience are from different groups with the latter generally representing an authority figure, credit is given, in addition,
for the manipulative aspect of the speech event. It should be mentioned that credit is not being given now as it was before for being
manipulative in those situations where it is felt one ought to have
been assertive (as in shucking). Blacks who are nonassertive in
these situations, especially when accommodating the establishment,
are called *Toms*.

Running it (on) down is the term used, as mentioned earlier, to
refer to the speech event where the focus for both speaker and audience is on content: giving information, advice, etc. For example,
the information component in the field example cited under rapping
1 would constitute the "rundown."

Signifying is the term used to describe the language behavior
that, as Abrahams (1964) has defined it, attempts to "imply, goad,
beg, boast, by indirect verbal or gestural means." In Chicago it is
also used as a synonym to describe a form of language behavior that
is more generally known as "sounding" elsewhere and will be discussed under the latter heading below.

Some excellent examples of signifying as well as of other forms
of language behavior discussed above come from the well-known
"toast" (narrative form) "The Signifying Monkey and the Lion,"
which was collected by Abrahams from black street-corner bards in
Philadelphia. In the following toast the monkey is trying to get the
lion involved in a fight with the elephant:

Now the lion came through the jungle one peaceful day,

When the signifying monkey stopped him, and that is what he started
to say:
He said, "Mr. Lion," he said, "a bad-assed motherfucker down your
way,"
He said, "Yeah! The way he talks about your folks is a certain shame.
I even heard him curse when he mentioned your grandmother's name."
The lion's tail shot back like a forty-four
When he went down that jungle in all uproar.

Thus the monkey has goaded the lion into a fight with the elephant by *signifying,* i.e., indicating that the elephant has been *sounding on* (insulting) the lion. When the lion comes back, thoroughly
beaten up, the monkey again signifies by making fun of the lion:

. . . lion came back through the jungle more dead than alive,
When the monkey started some more of that signifying jive.
He said, "Damn, Mr. Lion, you went through here yesterday, the jungle
rung.
Now you come back today, damn near hung."

The monkey, of course, has been delivering this taunt from a
safe distance away on the limb of a tree, when suddenly his foot slips
and he falls to the ground, at which point

Like a bolt of lightning, a stripe of white heat,
The lion was on the monkey with all four feet.

In desperation the monkey quickly resorts to *copping a plea* (shucking?!):

The monkey looked up with a tear in his eyes,
He said, "Please, Mr. Lion, I apologize."

His "plea," however, fails to move the lion to show any pity or
mercy, so the monkey tries another verbal ruse, shucking:

He said, "You lemme get my head out of the sand
Ass out the grass, I'll fight you like a natural man."

In this he is more successful, as

The lion jumped back and squared for a fight.
The motherfucking monkey jumped clear out of sight.

A safe distance away again, the monkey returns to signifying:

He said, "Yeah, you had me down, you had me at last,
But you left me free, now you can still kiss my ass" (Abrahams, 1964,
pp. 150 ff.).

The above example illustrates the methods of provocation,
goading, and taunting as artfully practiced by the signifier. Interestingly, when the *function* of signifying is *directive,* the tactic employed
is one of *indirection,* i.e., the signifier reports or repeats what someone else has said about the listener; the "report" is couched in plausible language designed to compel belief and arouse feelings of anger
and hostility. There is also the implication that if the listener fails
to do anything about it—what has to be "done" is usually quite
clear—his status will be seriously compromised. Thus the lion is
compelled to vindicate the honor of his family by fighting or else
leave the impression that he is afraid, and that he is not "king" of
the jungle. When used for the purpose of directing action, signifying is like shucking in also being deceptive and subtle in approach
and depending for success on the naïveté or gullibility of the person
being "put on."

When the function of signifying is only expressive— i.e., to
arouse feelings of embarrassment, shame, frustration, or futility for
the purpose of diminishing someone's status, but without directive
implication—the tactic employed is in the form of a taunt, as in the
part in the above example where the monkey makes fun of the lion.
Signifying frequently occurs when things are dull and someone
wishes to generate some excitement and interest within the group.
This is shown in another version of the above toast:

There hadn't been no disturbin in the jungle for quite a bit,
For up jumped the monkey in the tree one day and laughed, "I guess
I'll start some shit" (Abrahams, 1964, pp. 149–150).

Sounding is the term that is today most widely known for the
game of verbal insult known in the past as *playing the dozens, the
dirty dozens,* or just *the dozens.* Other current names as indicated
above for the game have regional distribution. In Chicago, as mentioned earlier, the term *sounding* would be descriptive of the initial
remarks designed to "sound" out the other person to see whether he
will play the game. The verbal insult is also subdivided, the term
signifying applying to insults hurled directly at the person and the

term *dozens* applying to insults hurled at your opponent's family, especially the mother.

Sounding is often catalyzed by such "signifying" remarks as "Are you going to let him say that about your mama?" for the purpose of spurring on an exchange between two (or more) other members of the group. It is begun on a relatively low key and built up by means of verbal exchanges.

Abrahams describes the "game":

One insults a member of another's family; others in the group make disapproving sounds to spur on the coming exchange. The one who has been insulted feels at this point that he must reply with a slur on the protagonist's family which is clever enough to defend his honor (and therefore that of his family). This, of course, leads the other (once again, more due to pressure from the crowd than actual insult) to make further jabs. This can proceed until everyone is bored with the whole affair, until one hits the other (fairly rare), or until some other subject comes up that interrupts the proceedings (1962b, pp. 209–210).

An example of the "game" collected by one of my students goes as follows:

Frank looked up and saw Leroy enter the Outpost. Leroy walked past the room where Quinton, "Nap," "Pretty Black," "Cunny," Richard, Haywood, "Bull" and Reese sat playing cards. As Leroy neared the T.V. room, Frank shouted to him.

(Frank) "Hey Leroy, your mama—calling you man."

Leroy turned and walked toward the room where the sound came from. He stood in the door and looked at Frank.

(Leroy) "Look motherfuckers, I don't play that shit."

(Frank [signifying]) "Man, I told you cats 'bout that mama jive" (as if he were concrerned about how Leroy felt).

(Leroy) "That's all right Frank; you don't have to tell these funky motherfuckers nothing; I'll fuck me up somebody yet."

Frank's face lit up as if he were ready to burst his side laughing. "Cunny" become pissed at Leroy.

("Cunny") "Leroy, you stupid bastard, you let Frank make a fool of you. *He* said that 'bout your mama."

("Pretty Black") "Aw, fat ass head 'Cunny' shut up."

("Cunny") "Ain't that some shit. This black slick head motor flicker got nerve 'nough to call somebody 'fathead'. Boy, you so black, you sweat Super Permalube Oil."

This eased the tension of the group as they burst into loud laughter.

("Pretty Black") "What 'chu laughing 'bout 'Nap', with your funky mouth smelling like dog shit?"

Even Leroy laughed at this.

("Nap") "Your mama motherfucker."

("Pretty Black") "Your funky mama too."

("Nap" [strongly]) "It takes twelve barrels of water to make a steamboat run; it takes an elephant's dick to make your Grandmammy come; she been elephant fucked, camel fucked and hit side the head with your Grandpappy's nuts."

(Reese) "Goddor damn; go on and rap motherfucker."

Reese began slapping each boy in his hand, giving his position approval of "Nap's" comment. "Pretty Black" in an effort not to be outdone, but directing his verbal play elsewhere, stated:

("Pretty Black") "Reese, what you laughing 'bout? You so square, you shit bricked shit."

(Frank) "Whoooowee!"

(Reese [sounded back]) "Square huh, what about your nappy ass hair before it was stewed; that shit was so bad till, when you went to bed at night, it would leave your head and go on the corner and meddle."

The boys slapped each other on the hand and cracked up.

("Pretty Black") "On the streets meddling, but Dinky didn't offer me no pussy and I turned it down."

(Frank) "Reese scared of pussy."

("Pretty Black") "Hell yeah; the greasy mother rather fuck old ugly, funky cock Sue Willie than get a piece of ass from a decent broad."

(Frank) "Godorr-damn! Not Sue Willie."

("Pretty Black") "Yeah ol meat beating Reese rather screw that cross-eyed, clapsy bitch, who when she cry, tears drip down her ass."

(Haywood) "Don't be so mean, Black."

(Reese) "Aw shut up, you half-white bastard."

(Frank) "Wait man, Haywood ain't gonna hear much more of that half-white shit; he's a brother too."

(Reese) "Brother, my black ass; that white ass landlord gotta be this motherfucker's paw."

("Cunny") "Man, you better stop foolin with Haywood; he's turning red."

(Haywood) "Fuck yall" (as he withdrew from the "sig" game).

(Frank) "Yeah, fuck yall; let's go to the stick hall."

The group left enroute to the billiard hall (Maryland, 1967).

The above example of sounding is an excellent illustration of the "game" as played by fifteen-, sixteen-, and seventeen-year-old black boys, some of whom have already acquired the verbal skill that for them is often the basis for having a high "rep." Abrahams observed that ". . . ability with words is as highly valued as physical strength" (Abrahams, 1964, p. 62). In the sense that the status of one of the participants in the game is diminished if he has to resort to fighting to answer a verbal attack, verbal ability may be even more highly regarded than physical ability. However, age within the peer group may be a factor in determining the relative value placed on verbal vis-à-vis physical ability.

Nevertheless, the relatively high value placed on verbal ability must be clear to most black boys at an early age in their cognitive development. Abrahams (1964, p. 53) is probably correct in linking sounding to the taunt that is learned and practiced as a child and is part of signifying, which has its origins in childlike behavior. The taunts of the "signifying monkey," illustrated above, are good examples of this.

The function of the "dozens" or sounding is invariably self-assertive. The speaker borrows status from his opponent through an exercise of verbal power. The opponent feels compelled to regain his status by sounding back on the speaker or some other member of the group whom he regards as more vulnerable. The social interactions of the group at the Outpost, for example, demonstrated less an extended verbal barrage between two people than a "pecking order." Frank sounds on Leroy; Cunny signifies on Leroy; Pretty Black sounds on Cunny; Cunny sounds back on Pretty Black, who (losing) turns on Nap; Nap sounds (winning) back on Pretty Black; Pretty Black finally borrows back his status by sounding on Reese. Reese sounds back on Pretty Black but gets the worse of the exchange, and so borrows back his status from Haywood. Cunny also sounds on Haywood. Haywood defaults. Perhaps by being "half white," Haywood feels himself to be the most vulnerable.

The presence of a group seems to be especially important in controlling the game. First of all, one does not "play" with just anyone, since the subject matter is concerned with things that in reality one is quite sensitive about. It is precisely *because* Pretty Black has a "black slick head" that makes him vulnerable to Cunny's barb, especially now when the Afro-American "natural" hair style is in vogue. It is precisely *because* Reese's girl friend *is* ugly that makes him vulnerable to Pretty Black's jibe that Reese can't get a "piece of ass from a decent broad." It is *because* the living conditions are so poor and intolerable that they can be used as subject matter for sounding. Without the control of the group, sounding will frequently lead to a fight. This was illustrated by a tragic epilogue concerning Haywood; when Haywood was being sounded on in the presence of two girls by his best friend (other members of the group were absent), he refused to tolerate it. He went home, got a rifle, came back, and shot and killed his friend. In the classroom, from about the fourth grade on, fights among black boys invariably are caused by someone sounding on the others person's mother.

Summary Analysis

A summary analysis of the different forms of language behavior, which have been discussed above, permits the following generalizations:

The prestige norms influencing speech behavior are those which, when operating in *intra*group contexts, have been successful in gaining recognition from one's peers and generally adding to one's "rep" (status). Here the speaker knows that the focus of his group is on expression, specifically verbal art. In *inter*group contexts, the prestige norms influencing speech behavior include, in addition, those which have been successful in manipulating and controlling people and situations. The function of all of the forms of speech behavior discussed above, with the exception of *running it down,* which focused on content, was either expressive or expressive-directive. Specifically, this means that language was used to project personality, assert oneself, or arouse emotion, frequently with the additional purpose of getting the person to give up or do something that will be of some benefit to the speaker.

The purpose for which language in intergroup contexts is used suggests that the speaker views those social situations as essentially agonistic, by which I mean that he sees his environment as consisting of a series of transactions requiring that he be continually ready to take advantage of a person or defend himself against being victimized. He has absorbed what John Horton has called *street rationality.* As one of Horton's respondents put it: "The good hustler . . .

conditions his mind and must never put his guard too far down, to relax, or he'll be taken" (1967, p. 8).

I have carefully avoided, throughout this essay, limiting the group within the black community of whom the speech behavior and perspective of their environment is characteristic. While I have no doubt that it is true of those who are generally called "street people," I am not certain of the extent to which it is also true of a much larger portion of the black community, especially the male segment. My informants consisted of street people, high school students, and blacks who by their occupation as community and youth workers possess what has been described as a "sharp sense of the streets." Yet it is difficult to find a black male in the community who has not witnessed or participated in the dozens or heard of signifying or rapping or shucking and jiving at some time during his growing up. It would be equally difficult to imagine a high school student in a Chicago inner-city school not being touched by what is generally regarded as "street culture" in some way.

III. Developing a Language Program: Basic Goals and Assumptions

I indicated elsewhere (Kochman, 1969b) that an oral language program that attempts to replace nonstandard forms with socially preferred forms does not develop the child's ability to use language beyond what he is already capable of doing. This is also true of attempts to teach standard dialect as a second dialect, which attempts to augment, rather than replace, his nonstandard forms with standard forms, attempting to create a "new set of language habits." I argued there that the efficiency quotient (input vs. output) of such a program is extremely low, and that, vis-à-vis language performance, it also does not attempt to develop the ability to use language in the second dialect beyond what the child is already capable of doing in his native dialect. It is concerned with *how* the child says something rather than *how well* he says it.

An oral language program ought to aim at an ability to use language well, which I can further define as performance capability in a variety of social contexts on a variety of subject matter. This does not necessarily mean accommodating the audience as far as shifting dialect is concerned. We don't, for example, demand that an educated southerner or south midlander accommodate a Chicago audience by modifying his dialect pattern, even though it is a social liability in Chicago and elsewhere. Educated south midlanders experience much the same difficulty as uneducated ones in getting housing in Chicago. Clearly, the speaker from these areas has a right to expect the audience to accommodate him in this respect, and so does a speaker of nonstandard dialect. And the audience will, provided that he handle the other aspects of a speech event well; such aspects might be listed tentatively as the ability to project personality, style, self-assurance, authoritativeness, and native coloring in a fluent manner. Conversely, speaking the prestige dialect will not save a person from his audience who fails to accommodate them in these other, more important respects.

The notion that "dialect" is a liability rather than an asset is an arbitrary determination. The BBC of London has recently found that news broadcasted on the scene by reporters in local dialect added a touch of "realism" to the presentation (Mouckley, 1969). Black social workers, news reporters, and others find that knowledge of black dialect is an invaluable asset in communicating with indigenous community people, a factor that puts white workers in these and other professions at a clear disadvantage. Who accommodates whom and under what circumstances is part of the task the ethnographer of communication tries to determine.

An oral language program in an inner-city school with a 100-percent black student body or in a suburban school with any percentage of black enrollment should have the same goal as a language development program in an all-white neighborhood with a 100-percent white middle-class student body or in that suburban school with a mixed enrollment, namely, the growth and development of the speech ability of the child *in his native dialect*. I envision such development evolving through the creation of "low contexts" that focus on vocabulary enrichment and sentence expansion, with vocabulary items embodying conceptualizing elements and sentence expansions involving the learning of such operations as embedding and conjoining as well as developing such cognitive processes as the perception and expression of relationships. There is no reason why this cannot be done using the native dialect the student possesses, as will be enlarged upon further below. It ought to be obvious that what is being discussed here with respect to black dialect has application to Appalachian or other nonstandard dialects as well.

Essential to the rationale of using the native dialect is that vocabulary items are not integral features of a dialect, even though they may be ethnically, occupationally, or geographically correlated.[4] It is perhaps unfortunate that introductory books on dialects often begin by using vocabulary to highlight "dialect differences," leaving the impression that it is partly vocabulary that *underlies* dialect differences. This is misleading, because teachers and the public already believe, a belief these books reinforce, that educated or noneducated vocabulary items determine whether a person is speaking standard dialect or not, when it is grammar that differentiates dialects, use of more or less educated vocabulary generally reflecting differences in education and/or style, the latter responsive to topical and situational criteria and not caused by the dialect one is using. For example, the greater or fewer number of words of Latin or French origin in an utterance does not affect the fact that it is "English" that is being spoken.

Vocabulary is a resource available to all dialects of English and not an intrinsic feature of any one. One can use *any* vocabulary item in a grammatically nonstandard utterance. This is important to note because teachers have been known to say, "There are things you can't say in nonstandard dialect," implying that somehow the nonstandard dialect is deficient in vocabulary (as well as logic, beauty, etc.) and that there is some causal relationship existing between vocabulary and the system a person is using to express himself in, the erroneous conclusion being that you have to teach standard dialect *before* you can get a person to use educated vocabulary items, which is nonsense.

That this confusion is so entrenched in the minds of teachers and educators has prompted William Labov to write about "The Logic of Non-Standard English" (1970), in which he correctly points out, among other things, that logic, like the use of educated vocabulary items, is not a consequence of the language system (dialect) a person uses to express himself in. Therefore, it is incorrect to talk about a "standard" and "nonstandard" vocabulary, as if conjunctions like *although, because, nevertheless* were part of a sys-

---

[4] William Stewart (1969, p. 200) also makes this point.

tem, rather than a resource available to all systems (dialects) of English.

Similarly, sentence expansion, which utilizes such conjunctions in the performance of various syntactic operations like embedding and conjoining, is as possible in nonstandard black dialect as in standard. Whether the rules of sentence expansion operate differently in black dialect than in standard has yet to be shown. However, one should not doubt the capacity of black dialect to expand. For example, one can observe such expansions in Gullah, a black American Creole, even though the conjunctions used are different from the standard. What follows is an example from a record from the Library of Congress folklore collection *Animal Tales Told in the Gullah Dialect,* narrated by A. H. Stoddard, specifically, "Buh Rabbit Fools B'Olifaum [Elephant] and Buh Whale":

Buh Rabbit: "Buh whale, little as I is and big as you is I bet I could pull you out dat river."

Buh Whale: "Go along Buh Rabbit. What kind of talk are you to talk. You couldn't move me in de river scusin for pullin me out."

Buh Rabbit: "Buh Whale, if I deday [stand by] on the river shore for see your bigness when you de comin out de water for your bigness for scared me I couldn't pull you out de river for true. But if you let me tie a rope to you so I can back on the hill where I couldn't see f'when you de comin out de water for your bigness for scared me, I betcha hundred dollar I can pull you out dat river.'

The teacher is invited to underline connectives in the above passage.

The illustration from Gullah is not meant to suggest that sentence expansion in black dialect operates the same way but rather to show that any dialect has the capacity for creating sentences that show causal relationships, contrary to fact relationships, etc. The confusion, existing among many educators and teachers, that equated educated vocabulary and Standard English dialect, mentioned earlier, is compounded again by the erroneous equation that elaborated style or use of language is also an integral feature of the system (standard dialect), and that in order to develop an elaborated style in language one first has to acquire the system in which elaborated style has been demonstrated. Here again *associative* criteria have been erroneously interpreted to be *causal.*

This confusion exists on the one hand because of a notion still lingering from the prescriptive tradition that tended to equate Standard English with formal written English, i.e., "good" English, and on the other hand from the impact of Basil Bernstein's concepts of elaborated code and restrictive code and the oversimplified application of these terms to the language situation here. Bernstein's choice of the term *code* is particularly unfortunate because it *is* used by sociolinguists to refer to system (grammar, dialect) as *opposed* to speech behavior.[5] The term *code* therefore reinforces the confusion that equates a *system* with a *use* of language. On the other hand, if one is to attach any credibility to Bernstein's concepts, one has to interpret his *code* to mean, in fact, *message,* and assume that he is referring to a habituated use of language, an elaborated or restrictive *output,* as opposed to *input,* which he then links to social class. This is, in fact, Bernstein's most recent view (1970), in which he equates his concept of code with Chomsky's concept of performance, as opposed to competence.

Needless to add, the importance of correct interpretation is crucial here, because if one says that it is the *input* that is elaborated or restrictive as has been the prevalent interpretation of Bernstein, then one is "justified" in promoting language intervention, substituting one system (standard dialect) for another one that is deficient (nonstandard black dialect). On the other hand, if it is the *output* that is elaborated or restrictive, then one is operating with a *use* of language that is not a consequence of a system, except as that system generates grammatical utterances, but a consequence of educational level and of context (situation and topic), for which varying styles of speech are appropriate. This means that a restrictive utterance is not a product of grammatical constraints but rather of social (situational, topical) constraints, that potentially, at least, the rules of black dialect permit the same type of elaborated utterances that the rules of standard dialect permit. The notion that more elaborated utterances would seem to occur in standard dialect than in black dialect is merely a statement that reflects the habits of both white speakers and those black speakers who are bidialectal to use standard dialect in those formal situations where a more elaborated style of speaking is appropriate.

In an effort to show, however, that elaborated utterances often

---

[5] See the dichotomy expressed by Joshua Fishman in his review of Joyce Hertzler's *The Sociology of Language* (1967, p. 590).

occur in the speech of monodialectal speakers of Black English, Carolyn Nygren, for her master's thesis (1969), searched for and found, in a random selection of tapes of speakers of only black dialect from Job Corps training programs, most of the qualitative criteria that Basil Bernstein cited as being characteristic of "elaborated code" in his article "Aspects of Language and Learning in the Genesis of the Social Process" (1964, p. 253). There was every indication that had more tapes been selected and analyzed, after first ascertaining that the dialect was black, more "elaborated" criteria would have been found. The intent of the paper was to show as false the correlation that equated nonstandard black dialect with a "restrictive code."

There is an important feature operating here to which I feel Bernstein's ideas can be applied, and that is where, as a result of habit a particular mode of speech dominates to the veritable exclusion of other modes, the facility to produce other modes cannot be assumed. Whether it actually inhibits the production of other modes is unclear. In fact, it says that if a person is habituated to an informal mode of speech, characteristic of a range of styles (*intimate* to *consultative,* using Joos's terms [1969]), this does not prepare for the ready utilization of language in a *formal* or *frozen* style. This should in no way prejudice the potential of the speaker for using language in a formal or frozen way; it's just that the occasion for cultivating those styles in the speaker never occurred, much as a person who plays the piano well enough for the style of performance suitable for parties might have to practice a great deal to develop the style and proficiency of performance required for a concert. Needless to add, the piano is hardly to blame for the ability of the player. So the standard or nonstandard dialect is hardly at fault for the ability of its speakers. What we are dealing with here is essentially an orientation toward a mode (style) of speech, which facility is developed more so than other modes, because of the higher frequency of occurrence of those contexts for which that mode is felt to be appropriate.

This last statement applies not only to those whose customary range of styles is intimate-casual-consultative, but to those, most of them teachers, whose customary modes cover the range, according to Joos, consultative-formal-frozen. This is not meant to be facetious. Many teachers who are single rarely have occasion to use the mode intimate-casual, and are frequently thought to be pretentious in using a formal-consultative mode in a situation where the casual mode would be most appropriate. One gets the impression that they never leave the classroom. This habituated use of language can be socially handicapping—persons like that are frequently accused of being unable to "get down"—much as failing to develop the formal and frozen style for students, the mode in which books and papers are written, is academically handicapping. In the latter case, however, the failure is more public and the penalty more severe.

Implications for the Classroom

For those unfamiliar with Martin Joos's essay *The Five Clocks,* already cited, I list his five styles of speech and some of their characteristics as I intend to use them in my discussion. Joos's five styles are *intimate, casual, consultative, formal,* and *frozen.* The consultative style is indicative of conversation between persons who have a limited shared background. Features identifying consultative style would be free and easy participation of both speaker and listener. Sentences are complete; background information is supplied. Formal style is characterized again by complete sentences that reflect logical development of thought and careful planning; background information is provided; speech is extemporaneous as opposed to impromptu (which is characteristic of styles intimate, casual, and consultative). A key feature distinguishing formal from consultative style is that in the former the listener's active participation drops out. All styles are responsive to group size. For example, a speaker using consultative style might find himself shifting to formal when his audience increased beyond seven.

Frozen style is more characteristic of writing than speech, reserved for the most formal occasions when spoken, and then frequently read. The writing reflects the efforts of revision. It is here that such items as logical development of thought, careful planning, attention to stylistic features, word appropriateness, rules of usage, etc., come into full play.

Casual style, Joos says, pays the listener the compliment of assuming a shared background. Sentences are not necessarily complete; there is free and easy participation of both speaker and listener; unconventional English such as slang and profanity mark this style.

Intimate style reflects the use of language that operates under the speaker's and listener's skins. This style is characterized by an economy of words, with a high incidence of significant nonverbal communication: gesture, facial expression, etc. It would be characteristic of persons who knew each other quite well.

If we attempted to apply Bernstein's terms *restrictive* and *elaborated* to the range of styles as Joos has defined them, we might arrive at something that looks like this:

restrictive ⟵—————⟶ elaborated

intimate—casual—consultative—formal—frozen

Focusing on context rather than on behavior, E. T. Hall and Frederick Erickson, as reported by the latter in his doctoral thesis (1969a), have introduced the terms *high context* and *low context,* where a high context evokes a kind of behavior that suggests a high degree of familiarity with the situation and the people in it, and a low context elicits behavior that suggests an unfamiliarity with a situation and the people in it. The range of restrictive use of language (intimate-casual, moving into consultative) is characteristic of a high to a diminishing high context; the range of elaborated use of language (frozen-formal, moving into consultative) is characteristic of a low to a diminishing low context. The home, playground, and street corner would constitute a high context. An employment office would constitute a low context.

Developing Elaborated Style

The range of familiarity with which a child views his environment and the people in it would tend to promote the development of those styles which are operative in a high to a diminishing high context, viz., intimate, casual, and consultative. It remains for education to teach the mode of language used in reading and writing, which, by and large, reflects the more elaborated style. As stated earlier, this essentially involves the use of complex sentences, the providing of background information, logical development of thought, and those features characteristic of Joos's formal and frozen styles.

Since style, like vocabulary, is not an integral feature of a dialect but one that is responsive to social context (situation, topic), it is important to create low contexts that make the greatest demands on the verbal resources of the child. The important point to emphasize here is that this can be done using the native dialect of the child. As a consequence of the confusion that equated Standard English with elaborated style, educators felt they had to teach Standard English in order to produce elaborated style. They failed to consider the alternative, which is operative, for example, among black bidialectals, namely, that style determines which dialect is used and that context determines which style is employed. Black bidialectals, in an intra-ethnic context, where typically black dialect is used, find that they switch to standard dialect when a topic comes up of sufficient intellectual quality to require a more elaborated style.

Bilingual and diglossic studies have revealed a tendency to switch automatically, as a result of conditioning, from one language to another or from one dialect to another, depending not only on audience and setting (situational criteria), but on what was being discussed (topical criteria). For example, Rona's study (1966) on the use of Guarani vis-à-vis Spanish in Paraguay clearly shows a progression of ability to use Guarani, i.e., some speakers used Guarani better than others to express technical notions, while others resorted to Spanish. Eventually they all had to, but at different levels and at different times. Clearly, what was limiting was not the language, Guarani, but the respective ability or disability of the speakers to use that language. In order to discuss a particular subject they shifted to the stylistic level appropriate to the topic being discussed. I am using the term *style* here to include levels of vocabulary and degrees of syntactic complexity pertinent to the discussion. The important point here is that it was the topic that was the stimulus that challenged the speaker to evaluate his verbal resources and choose the system in which his stylistic level was sufficiently developed to be useful to him.

Low Contexts

Low contexts, which make the greatest demands on the verbal resources of the child, offer the greatest possibility for developing elaborate style. It would be useful here to distinguish between low-context situations and low-context topics. A low-context situation is one in which the speaker cannot rely on nonverbal features (a mark of intimate-casual style), has little or no shared background with his audience, is in an unfamiliar setting, and is speaking to a group consisting of more than seven persons. Low-context topics are those that require logical development of thought, extensive pre-planning, exposition, and vocabulary acquisition. In drawing upon the verbal resources of the child it is important to consider not only the quantity of an utterance (volume of words) but the quality of it. Therefore, much attention should be given here to vocabulary enrichment and the development of syntactic complexity. The focus here is to develop an ability with language generally characterized as formal and frozen, which is the style used in writing and therefore the style confronted when reading, the mastery of which is necessary for academic achievement.

An important point for the teacher to consider is that as restrictive use of language as well as elaborated are consequents of situational and topical stimuli, the teacher should not arbitrarily assume that restrictive use of language suffers by comparison, which is like saying that formal style is *better* than casual. Teachers, being more verbal, have the tendency to believe that what can be said with more words (or more "educated" words) is better than what can be said with fewer words. The assumption that information becomes more precise commensurate with the increase in number of words is not borne out by observation. The reverse is often the case. What teachers have often interpreted as limited ability to use language was in fact precise information conveyed through an economy of means as a result of a high shared background. Teachers attempting to do their own ethnography in the classroom must be careful to assess correctly the context in which language occurs.

IV. Some Implications of Black Speech Events for a Black English Curriculum

Culture as Teacher

In perhaps the most important respect, educators must show deference to culture, and that is in the effectiveness of the latter's role as teacher—if by effectiveness is meant the efficiency of what is learned from what is taught. Whatever learning difficulties present themselves for the black student in the classroom, all such difficulties are resolved when he hits the street. Educators must ask, Why is learning on the street so efficient? Why has learning in the classroom been so inefficient? How can education as a process benefit by observing how children learn outside the classroom?

A Comparison of Some Black and White Mainstream Cultural Communication Patterns

The Channel of Communication. The prestige norms within the culture of the black inner-city child place a high premium on the ability to use words. The channel through which this ability is promoted and developed and through which recognition is given is oral-aural. Expertise via this channel is more highly regarded and developed in black culture than in white middle-class culture. On the other hand, expertise via the written channel, by virtue of the cultural aesthetic that motivates achievement through this channel, is more highly regarded and more extensively developed in white middle-class culture than in black culture.

The prestige attached to men of words—preachers, story-tellers, tellers of toasts and jokes, signifiers, "dozens" players—within the black community is unrivaled. A rich and colorful oral tradition is an integral part of the black cultural aesthetic.

The prestige attached to the oral channel vis-à-vis the written goes back to Africa. As an African colleague of mine said, a person reading a speech to an African audience rather than delivering it extemporaneously would provoke the response, "Well, he's not very intelligent!"

White mainstream culture also attaches prestige to the ability to speak well, although this recognition seems confined to the public arena and for that reason to an oral facility that is restrictive more or less to a formal style. Since public speaking style is often quite similar to the style used in writing, the early orientation of the middle-class child to the written word makes for an easy transition to the style used in public speaking, debates, etc. The prestige differential of the spoken word over the written seems greatest in politics, where no credit is given at all to the person who *writes* the speech, just to the person who *delivers* it. In other socioeconomic contexts, oral ability would seem to be more highly valued than writing ability, although this may vary according to occupation. A survey as to which of the two types of ability is utilized more and which is more highly regarded (rewarded!) would be quite revealing. It would indicate whether the written channel is entitled to the reputation it has in the academic arena, to the extent that scholastic achievement is singularly recognized through the written channel by means of tests and papers with little or no scholastic recognition given for oral expertise. That there is some inconsistency between the value oral expertise holds outside the scholastic arena and the credit given for such expertise within the arena there can be no doubt. For example, it is inconceivable to me that an intelligent black student who can write and recite poetry, speak in front of a large audience, perform in drama groups, engage in debates, argue logically and persuasively, and demonstrate the entire range of oral skills should not pass the introductory course in college English.[6]

If scholarly recognition can be given in areas that the cultural norms of the middle-class child promote, i.e., in which the child is already oriented toward expertise, there should be no reason why scholastic recognition cannot be extended to include those areas where the black child is oriented toward expertise, especially when the selection and emphasis on certain areas of curriculum is arbitrary, i.e., cannot be defended on the basis of its need or usefulness outside the scholastic arena.

That scholastic recognition is given in areas that the norms of the culture of the middle-class child promote is evidenced by the fact that familiarity with the formal style is promoted by the early orientation toward the written word (reading), which facilitates learning throughout the scholastic context where such style is utilized.

A curriculum designed to fit the needs of the black or Puerto Rican child in a pluralistic framework would take into account the respective cultural aesthetic that orients a child toward the development of one skill as opposed to another, such as the orientation with-

---

[6] It is significant that poetry in the Black community is written to be *heard,* as in Ukrainian culture and Slavic culture in general—ch. the nineteenth century Ukrainian national poet Schevchenko and the recent tour of Yevtushenko in the United States. By contrast, poetry in the white community here is written to be *read!*

in black culture toward achievement via the oral channel, just as the present curriculum, designed from an assimilationist perspective, favors the middle-class child in measuring achievement in those areas in which the middle-class child is already oriented by his cultural aesthetic toward expertise.

Mechanism of Communication. It is perfectly proper and acceptable in black culture for a black man to approach a black woman whom he does not know and talk to her. This is because there is a mechanism in black culture that permits him to do this. The mechanism is called *rapping,* and both male and female roles are clearly defined within the framework of this initial transaction, as has been described above. Other cultures, such as the Italian, also provide for this kind of initial interaction, much to the chagrin of white American girls who go to Italy.

White mainstream culture does not generally have this mechanism except under controlled circumstances, i.e., a "situation" has to be created, such as a party or a cruise, and even then intermediaries are often needed to introduce people to each other. Females in white mainstream culture generally screen potential male friends *before* the talking stage. The mechanism of rapping forces the black woman to screen potential black male friends *by means of* talking. It also motivates the black man to develop his verbal ability in order to improve his chances of success with women. The meeting ground between the man and the woman in white mainstream culture does not compel either the man or the woman to develop the art of verbal play. Black culture is much like Elizabethan culture in the promotion of this art (cf. Romeo and Juliet). It should therefore not be surprising that blacks as a group surpass whites in this ability. To quote a black woman colleague, "The black man sure knows how to rap."

Correlation of Manipulative Ability with Words and Status. Status on the street is not inherited or conferred but has to be earned. Acquiring status is a prime motivation for the black street youngster. Verbal ability, like the ability to dance, fight, sing, or run, is highly prized in the black community because such ability helps to establish one's "rep." At the same time life on the streets is full of hazards, and control over events is desirable. While one is often secure within one's group, intergroup transactions are often filled with uncertainties. Verbal ability helps the black child maximize control in those contexts, especially expert development of the directive function that permits him to establish control over people through the art of persuasion, manipulation, deception, and a developed sensitivity as to what motivates others. Since status is often achieved by this directive use of words, there is generally a high correlation in black street culture between high status and this kind of ability.

In white mainstream culture, except in certain occupations, the ability to use language manipulatively is often inversely correlated with status because we rely on status to get things done rather than on persuasion. The salesman, who has no status vis-à-vis the customer from which he can direct the latter to buy something, relies more heavily on the art of persuasion than does a supervisor with his employees. Women, as a group in our culture, use language manipulatively more frequently and artfully than do men, because their status does not permit them to use language assertively.

Blacks, by virtue of their cultural aesthetic, which promotes this kind of verbal ability, would have a special aptitude for the occupations of salesman, businessman, or politician, among others. On the psychological level, Peter Haraty sees no difference between the hustler and the business man:

The insidious aspect of Black Capitalism is that it exploits the basic psychological drives that have been built into the personalities of all citizens and subjects of America. This explains the phenomenon of the hustler, whose goals are the same as the white middle-class businessman or professional—money for self-expression. The means used are radically different, and the life-styles even more so, but stripped of these externals, the psychologies of the middle-level executive for IBM and the Harlem pimp are the same. Both are profit-motivated, self-centered, and enjoy manipulating people especially against their own best interests and desires (Haraty, 1969, p. 8).

The Communication Network (Sociogram of the Street). Peer-group influence on the inner-city child, white or black, occurs earlier and is far more extensive than peer-group influence on the middle-class child.

Consideration should therefore be given to include in the classroom an alternative network of communication (pupil-pupil) to that of the present dyad (teacher-pupil). The stimulus for most verbal play is clearly the presence of the peer group. For example, parents and teachers might elicit shucking, gripping, and copping a plea, which occur in *inter*group contexts, but are hardly likely to elicit rapping, signifying, or sounding, which, like joke telling, occur almost exclusively in *intra*group contexts. Taped examples from teachers who have attempted to elicit signifying remarks from their students in their presence are generally stilted, full of hesitations and nervous laughter, generally reflecting the student's feeling about the lack of appropriateness of the context for those types of speech events. It is important to note however, that it was the teacher (audience) rather than the classroom (setting) that was the constraining factor in the situation. This was shown when the teacher left the room. The boys relaxed and showed none of the discomfort they displayed earlier. The teacher should be aware of the positive value of the peer group stimulus, as well as the importance of correctly assessing the constraining variables of the context that influence behavior.

Setting. The classroom constitutes a low context for the teacher and the middle-class child. There are indications, however, that the classroom in an inner-city school constitutes a high context for the black child. Factors that lead me to believe that the classroom as well as the school as a setting exert a different kind of constraint on the black inner-city child vis-à-vis the middle-class child are based on reports by many teachers, my own observation, and my analysis of the influence of setting on speech behavior from my ethnography of black speech events in Chicago. Nevertheless, I offer such findings as tentative, subject to amendment and confirmation by a more exhaustive study. For example, the use of profanity in the classroom and in the hallway by black children to each other reflects a difference in the evaluation of the school as a constraining setting.[7] Middle-class students and teachers tend to regard the entire school build-

[7] The assumption here is that profanity begins to be used at about the same respective *casual* level of speech for both middle-class and black inner-city students.

ing as a place where a more formal behavior is appropriate. Middle-class use of profanity generally begins outside the building. The school setting acts as a greater constraining influence on the middle-class child, less so on the black inner-city child. It should be clear here that we are dealing with a cross-cultural aesthetic difference regarding the influence of setting on behavior, and that what is considered appropriate in one cultural setting is considered inappropriate in another. The church, for example, is conceived of typically in middle-class services as appropriate for whispering; shouting would not be tolerated. In black (and some white) Baptist and other denominational services, shouting (call and response) is continuous and screaming frequent. Both are encouraged and are part of the aesthetic of the church service.

In the typology of speech events I have discussed, setting remained throughout an indeterminate variable, the form of speech behavior exhibited by the speaker being rather person (audience) determined.

The significance of this is that the teacher should not expect the school or classroom as a setting to influence the black inner-city child toward a more formal mode of speech. Her presence may be of sufficient import to influence a more formal manner in the child when talking to *her*, but it does not seem to influence the child to behave in a formal manner when talking to his peers. Compare siblings talking to parents and then to each other in an informal setting.

Audience Dynamics. Black speech events such as rapping to a peer group frequently involve active audience participation. For example, the "call and response" pattern and accompanying rhythms, which may also include handclapping, nodding, and swaying, and which derive from the black church service and the role the audience plays in that event, are often extended to secular speech events such as the first form of rapping, discussed above.

The traditional notion of a passive-receptive audience for the classroom is modeled after the white prototype. As indicated above, black audiences are active-participative. Restlessness in a white audience would be a cue to the speaker that he was losing them. Restlessness in a black audience would have exactly the opposite meaning (Powell, 1969).

The present school structure and the rules that govern "acceptable" behavior are in general harmony with the white middle-class cultural aesthetic. Actually, I could argue that the "passive-receptive-obedient" ethos that the schools and its teachers promulgate, especially on the elementary level, which is dominated by women, is comfortable only for middle-class girls. In any event, it is clearly discordant with the greater audience expressiveness of black inner-city children, which is sanctioned by the black cultural aesthetic. Perhaps even more generally significant, the "passive-receptive-obedient" ethos is promoted, not because it is the most efficient formula for learning, but because it makes it easier for the teacher to teach, again demonstrating the misplaced focus and concern of much of our present educational policy.

Performance Style. Because of the esteem with which blacks regard the expressive function of language within the contexts of their own culture, as the above typology illustrates, and which involves clearly delineated aesthetic criteria concerning form and style, the teacher should be aware that her admonitions with respect to performance style, which are based upon different aesthetic criteria, may be in direct conflict with the strongly felt aesthetic notions of her black students.

In addition, traditional notions governing classroom performance style, which have tended to promote a repetitious and uniform expressiveness, are in direct contrast to the individualistic notions of performance expressiveness generally held by blacks. For example, the types of speech events described above, while suggesting a uniform cultural focus and generic context, are invariably marked by a distinctive and highly personal performance style. Motivation within any language program would therefore be enhanced by allowing for the expression of individual style as well as for the incorporation of general features associated with cultural speech events.

For instance, if the teacher wanted to develop elaborated style through low contexts, there is no reason why the low context could not be developed within an expressive-manipulative frame. For example, the situations listed above in the typology under *shucking,* labeled *talk your way out of this,* could be made more complex and challenging so as to necessitate a more elaborated response. The

thread that ties this exercise into the culture and supplies the motivation for it is the cultural aesthetic that makes manipulative use of
language both functional and prestigious.

Also, the teacher can also expect a better than average skill on
the part of the black student (as compared with students who are
products of mainstream culture) in the expressive-manipulative use
of language because the culture-as-teacher has already oriented and
developed him toward accomplishment in this area.

World View and Inquiry Style. In his doctoral dissertation, previously cited, Erickson (1969a) compared the inquiry style of black
inner-city youth with that of suburban youth and latched on to a possible difference that I mention here to stimulate further observation
and analysis by the teacher-ethnographer in the classroom. Erickson
and a team of analysts, after listening to taped discussions by inner-
city and suburban youth, suggested that black inner-city youth in
their discussion tended to use the inductive approach, i.e., they made
concrete statements that implied rather than stated fundamental assumptions, as opposed to the suburban youth, who used the deductive approach, working on stated propositions and speculating about
behavior (concrete examples).[8] The questions such a discovery
raises are significant.

For instance, is one kind of style more appropriate for handling
one type of communication process than another? For example, the
attainment of formal and frozen style is considered to be a necessary
prerequisite to academic achievement. Bernstein and others have
cited the importance of impersonalizing utterances, generalizing
about events, especially the ability to disassociate oneself from an
event in which one was involved to talk about it in general terms,
more commonly called *intellectualizing*. Does the development of
the elaborated style compel the user to start thinking differently, a
kind of linguistic determinism, and is this the reason the elaborated
style should be developed? And following that, is the ability to in-

---

[8] For example, inner-city youth said in talking about city hall indifference to
the problems of the inner city, "Yeah, they never pick up the garbage
around here," which implied the underlying proposition "If the politicians
at City Hall weren't so corrupt . . ." etc.

tellectualize necessary for academic success or do educators think so because so many of them do it?

If one decides that Erickson's discovery is so, what to make of it? For what kind of problem, idea, situation, is one type of inquiry style "better" than the other? It has been suggested earlier that habituated use of a particular mode of speech does not of itself prepare the verbal resources for the ready utilization of other modes. Applying this to inquiry style, can we ask, with respect to the inductive approach, if assumptions are left unsaid and examples are given that imply underlying propositions, can the speakers state these propositions if called upon to do so, and can they do so as readily as a person accustomed to stating fundamental premises? Also, are these assumptions obvious to the speaker?

Conversely, with respect to the deductive approach, if a speaker is habituated to the speculative style of inquiry, does that diminish the ready ability to provide concrete examples when they are needed? Finally, is it not possible that the inquiry style difference here was rooted less to an absolute difference in world view but rather as that cultural outlook related to the topical context? For example, Erickson and his team analyzed discussion behavior that partly focused on life in the inner city, e.g., the meaning of Lou Rawls's song "Tobacco Road." Could not one interpret the use of the deductive approach by the suburban youth as a response to this topic as a result of a deficiency in experience? Likewise, isn't it possible that black inner-city youth felt the concrete (inductive) approach most appropriate in discussing life in the inner city, i.e., rejecting alternatives out of hand by virtue of their negative truth value (nothing experientially would support an alternative statement)? One way to determine the influence of world view on discussion behavior is to see if inner-city youth would have used the inductive approach in discussing life in the suburbs or some other place with which they were unfamiliar. If so, would this suggest an inability to step outside of one's skin? For example, is it more difficult for a black man to speculate about not being black than it is for a white man to speculate about not being white by virtue of living in a society and community in which he is continually reminded that he *is* black? If so, life in the suburbs is the same if you're black as it is in the inner city, and events are seen as confirming already internalized basic hypotheses and assumptions (Erickson's "self-sealing system"). More significantly, might not this cultural world view act as an obstacle in getting black inner-city children to perceive a context as low—i.e., outside the purview of their experience, which would require a different frame of reference—much as the world view of the suburban white youth interfered with their perception of the inner-city—i.e., seeing it as a low context whereas the inner-city youth saw it as a high context?

Much more needs to be said about comparative communication patterns than can be said here. For example, it may very well be that the sound volume generated by an all-black group is higher than that generated by an all-white group. The decibel tolerance of the younger generation as a whole seems to be distinctively higher than that of the older. Blacks, when interacting with each other, touch each other more than whites do. When blacks dance, the utilization of space is vertical, all parts of the body "gyrating" and feet fairly stationary (*Rapsodi in Black,* 1968, p. 2). When whites dance, except when they are imitating blacks, the utilization of space is horizontal, the upper part of the body is stiff, with only the legs and feet moving across the floor.[9]

The purpose of this section has been to provide information with regard to some black cultural communication patterns as distinct from mainstream communication patterns and to suggest ways in which the former may be incorporated into a Black English curriculum. It ought to have become clear to the reader that each culture has produced a different world view and life style with different sets of norms. These sets of norms are what I have referred to

[9] Any program promoting intercultural communication must deal with cultural differences and the impact such differences make on the attitude of each respective group. For example, as a consequence of differences in the handling of space and touch, blacks tend to regard white group behavior as cold, uninvolved. Whites tend to regard black group behavior as too loose and unrestrained. Statements of this kind invite invidious comparisons, are ethnocentrically rooted and mutually denigrating. The devastating impact of these attitudes, which constitute a tyranny when held by members of a majority group toward members of a minority group, were greatly responsible for the alienation of minority groups in American society, as discussed in section I of this essay. Further discussion in this section will deal briefly with other assumptions contributing to cross-cultural interference in communication, especially arising out of respective cultural distinctiveness in the use of language. Any such discussion, however, must be considered as preliminary and heuristic at this time.

throughout this paper as the *cultural aesthetic*. The motivation within each group to achieve according to the standards of the group plus the pressures of the group to reinforce their own aesthetic are what make culture such a good teacher and make learning so efficient. Educators should not only envy but reconstruct the teaching-learning process of culture.

Cross-Cultural Interference

The term *interference* refers to those deviations or distortions that are produced as a result of conflicting norms. For example, a linguist would explain a "foreign accent" as being caused by a speaker's perceiving the sounds of a nonnative language in terms of his own sound system. His reproduction of nonnative sounds is distorted because he "hears" the nonnative sounds through his own perceptual grid rather than through the perceptual grid of the native speaker. In order to perform "accent free," the nonnative speaker must acquire the perceptual grid of the native speaker. Thus the American speaker must learn that he cannot reproduce the French *u* sound with his own *u* sound, but must in fact realize an entirely different set of phonetic parameters in speaking French from those he uses in speaking English. On a semantic level, moving from one cultural system into another, the Amercan speaker must learn that his word *friend* is *not* culturally equivalent to German *Freund* or Mexican Spanish *amigo,* that the terms, as used in each of the respective languages, signify a different level of intimacy. The norms, or semantic parameters, for each term overlap, but are not equal.

It should be apparent that the term interference has appropriate application to cultural as well as linguistic systems. The comparisons between black and white mainstream culture illustrated herein point up consistent differences in the nature of their respective patterns of communication, perhaps more as a result of differences in emphasis than in substance, yet sufficient to cause interference in contexts in which members of one group are communicating with the other. What follows are some selective areas that are likely to be the cause of interference between the teacher and student in the inner-city classroom as a consequence of the teacher's and student's operating out of different cultural and linguistic systems. The teacher, in her role as ethnographer, should be alert for others.

Interference: World Outlook and Inquiry Style

If the teacher uses her formal mode of expression in the classroom, which operates for her as a low context, does interference develop between her and the black children as a consequence of the latter's viewing the classroom as a high context and appropriate to a casual mode of expression? Is this compounded by differences in approach—deductive versus inductive—leading to a general conflict of world views and styles? Could the teacher, by adopting a more casual mode, and where applicable an inductive approach, improve communication until the children learn to develop a more elaborated style of their own?

Sociocultural Interference. Much has been said about this already in section I. It is clearly the most prevalent and important factor interfering with communication. Essentially, here the teacher "turns off" or "tunes out" the child the minute he begins to express himself in his native dialect or demonstrate "other" culturally sanctioned behavior. What interferes here are the teacher's own arrogant attitudes toward cultural differences. All kinds of deficiencies are imputed to the native dialect and its speakers to justify her attitude and intervention. Mutual rejection ensues, nourished and intensified by other cultural and aesthetic differences already mentioned.

Phonological Interference. I quote from Stewart here: "I don't know where they live," can become in black dialect, "Ah'own know wey 'ey lib" (1967). Phonological representation in Black English tends to simplify consonant clusters and lose final consonants, more so than in standard dialect. The teacher's phonological representation to the black child on the other hand may be viewed as "over-articulated." The following example was reported to me by a teacher who was attempting to correct the pronunciation of a black child who said *axe* for *ask.* The teacher tried to get the child to say *ask,* which the child heard as *ass* since final *-sk* reduces to *-s* in black dialect. Her response to the teacher was "My mommy told me never to say that word."

Grammatical Interference. The grammatical rules of black dialect do not generally create utterances whose overall meaning would be misunderstood by the teacher. There will be some features, however, which are likely to escape her. I quote again from Stewart: A student says, "He ain't like that," which the teacher understands to mean, "He isn't like that," whereas the child meant, "He didn't like that" (1967). There is also the likelihood that the teacher will miss the *durative aspect* when it is intended by the speaker in the expression "He be working," which the teacher would most likely interpret (sometimes correctly) as "He'll be working," but which can mean, at other times, "He is generally or habitually working," as in the expression "You can't see him this afternoon; he be working."

More important, the teacher may interpret failure to conjugate verbs like *come* and *say* to the preterit in "He come yesterday," as a failure to perceive past time, whereas, according to Ralph Fasold, *come* and *say* in Black English fall into the same class of verbs as *hit* and *put* in standard dialect, i.e., they are perceived within the context of the utterance as present or past but not marked for past tense. For other possible interference in this area the teacher is urged to read Ralph Fasold's and Walt Wolfram's most recent summary of what has been written to date about the grammar of black dialect (1970).

Vocabulary Interference. Besides the use of black idiom, which the teacher would not be likely to know and have to learn, there are occurrences of other kinds of vocabulary interference, much as would occur among all students. The following is an example as reported to me:

Teacher: I know you didn't mean that.
Student: I am not mean!

One important consideration here having to do with vocabulary is the assumption often held by the teacher that the number of conventional vocabulary items (those which appear on tests) that the black child knows approximates his total lexical inventory. This assumption might be more true of the middle-class white child. The black child, however, knows a significantly large other vocabulary, which the teacher is likely to regard as slang, for which the child receives no credit on tests, yet which should be taken into account in evaluating his total verbal resources. Others have argued that since this other vocabulary is not used in books the child is expected to read, this knowledge need not be considered. However, a curriculum that was more responsive to the culture of the child, as one operating out of a pluralistic perspective would be, would find some way of incorporating more of what the child knows.

For example, the black child knows *cut out* means *to leave,* in addition to the meaning known to the white middle-class child, and *behind* means *as a result of* in the expression "So I figured it all happened behind them women, because I heard one of they say that he won't mess with nobody else wife no more" (Conot, 1967, p. 335), and so on. If the *total* lexical bank of black and white children were compared instead of just *conventional* lexical items, black children would appear better by comparison than they presently do.

Intonation Interference. This is an extremely small category. I have only one example. Present distinctive black use of *really* is said with falling intonation and is used to affirm what has just been said. It is equivalent to *yes* or *I agree.* Whites frequently hear this *really* and assume it is the one that they have with question-asking intonation, which is an affirmation of doubt and a request for confirmation. In inter-ethnic contexts in which a black person says, "Really," with falling intonation, whites respond with, "Oh yes! I've found that . . . ."

The Demand for Relevance: A Black English Curriculum

The demand for relevance is often a request by the student of the teacher to demonstrate that what she is teaching is functional within the student's present or expectant life experience. The curriculum of the school is, consciously or subconsciously, continually being put to this "relevance" test by the student body. Their academic interest depends on how successfully the school curriculum satisfies this criterion for them.

Often what the teacher does is based upon what she sees as relevant (functional) for future use but which, for the moment, is far beyond what the student expects to realize for himself. The language arts curriculum that I am advocating here strives to reconcile these opposing views by offering content that is not only immediately functional within the student's present life experience but also preparatory toward developing skills that are necessary for future use.

For example, developing elaborated style in the native dialect would have the effect of creating a use of language that has the same functional capacity as standard dialect, yet would not tamper with the student's identification with and self-realization through his native dialect. By developing elaborated style through expressive forms and within contexts that are culturally functional and prestigious, one takes advantage of the motivation that has already been built into the informal (cultural) learning experience.

Also, by concentrating on performance rather than on system, the teacher not only bypasses the cultural conflict inherent in getting a child to switch to standard but accomplishes what would have to be done in any event within whatever system the child uses, namely, developing performance versatility.

In effect, it leaves the decision to switch to standard dialect in the hands of those who would wish to perform in it but will have already equipped the student with performance capability in standard, since such ability between nonstandard and standard will have been equalized under the program espoused here. Also, once performance capability is equalized between two dialects (as with two languages), switching (translation) is facilitated, since intereference between modes (styles) will have been generally resolved, leaving only the necessity of establishing equivalences within respective systems.

In other respects I have considered implications of cultural data in general terms that should be considered guidelines for those who wish to extend the matter further. I have not drawn up specific lesson plans that the teacher could take and use tomorrow. I would hope, however that inner-city teachers and writers of curriculum could use the information herein to rethink and revise their methods and objectives. To begin with, I would urge those teachers whose first interest has always been the student to use their imagination, creativity, and ingenuity, to utilize the cultural data herein and make the classroom the relevant and exciting place of learning it can be. I would hope that this article might also ease the conscience of those caught in the dilemma of whom they are to serve, the dominant culture or the child, and place a supportive hand on the shoulder of the teacher who considers foremost what is best for the student even if she has to defy her principal to do it and throw out her present lesson plan guide as immaterial and prejudicial.

Finally, I would hope that some of the points made here with respect to cultural distinctiveness would serve to promote cross-cultural respect and consideration and replace cross-cultural antagonism. For that to happen, teachers and administrators involved in teaching culturally different children need to extricate themselves from their aesthetically narrow Anglo ethnocentric "bag." So, in fact, does all of middle-class America. Perhaps they will eventually have their own aesthetic transformed to the extent that they, too, will be able to remark appreciatively, as did a Mexican graduate student of mine, listening to a lecture on Afro-American folk music *performed* by an African colleague: "Isn't it great to be so free and uninhibited?"

Bibliography

Abrahams, Roger D. "The Changing Concept of the Negro Hero." *The Golden Log* 31 (1962a): 125 ff.

———. "Playing the Dozens." *Journal of American Folklore* 75 (1962): 209–220.

———. *Deep Down in the Jungle.* Hatboro, Pa.: Folklore Associates, 1964.

———. "Public Drama and Common Values in Two Caribbean Islands." *Trans-action* 5 (July-August 1968): 62 ff.

Animal Tales Told in the Gullah Dialect. Told by Albert H. Stoddard. Vol. I (L 44). Washington, D.C.: Archive of Folk Song of the Library of Congress, 1949.

Bailey, Beryl Loftman. "Toward a New Perspective in Negro English Dialectology." *American Speech* 40 (1965): 171–177.

Baratz, Joan C. "Linguistic and Cultural Factors in Teaching Reading to Ghetto Children." *Elementary English* 46 (1969a): 199–203.

———. "Teaching Reading in an Urban Negro School System." In Joan C. Baratz and Roger W. Shuy (eds.), *Teaching Black Children to Read.* Washington, D.C.: Center for Applied Linguistics, 1969b.

Baratz, Joan C.; and Baratz, Steven. "Early Childhood Intervention: The Social Science Base of Institutional Racism." Paper presented at the Society for Research in Child Development, Santa Monica, California, March 1969a.

————. "Negro Ghetto Children and Urban Education: A Cultural Solution." *Social Education* 33 (April 1969b): 401–405.

Bereiter, Carl; and Engelmann, Siegfried. *Teaching Disadvantaged Children in the Preschool.* Englewood Cliffs, N.J.: Prentice-Hall, 1966.

Bernstein, Basil. "Aspects of Language and Learning in the Genesis of the Social Process." In Dell Hymes (ed.), *Language in Culture and Society.* New York: Harper & Row, 1964a.

————. "Elaborated and Restricted Codes: Their Social Origins and Some Consequences." *American Anthropologist* 66 (December, 1964b): 6.

————. "A Social-Linguistic Approach to Socialisation: With Some Reference to Educability." In J. J. Gumperz and D. Hymes (eds.), *Directions in Sociolinguistics.* New York: Holt, Rinehart and Winston, 1970.

Board of Education, City of Chicago. "Psycholinguistics Oral Language Program: A Bi-dialectal Approach." Experimental Edition, Part 1 (1968).

Capell, A. *Studies in Sociolinguistics.* The Hague: Mouton and Co., 1966.

Cadzen, Courtney. "Subcultural Differences in Child Language: An Interdisciplinary Review." *Merrill Palmer Quarterly* 12, No. 3 (1966): 185–219.

Cohn, Werner. "On the Language of Lower-Class Children." In Staten W. Webster (ed.), *The Disadvantaged Learner: Knowing, Understanding, Educating.* San Francisco: Chandler Publishing Company, 1966.

Conot, Robert. *Rivers of Blood, Years of Darkness.* New York: Bantam, 1967.

Cooke, Benjamin C. "An Initial Classification of Non-Verbal Communication Among Afro-Americans." In Thomas Kochman (ed.), *Rappin' and Stylin' Out: Communication in Urban Black America.* Champaign-Urbana: University of Illinois Press, forthcoming.

Deutsch, Martin; Katz, Irwin; and Jensen, Arthur R. (eds.). *Social Class, Race, and Psychological Development.* New York: Holt, Rinehart and Winston, 1968

Deutscher, Irwin. "Notes on Language and Human Conduct: Some

Problems of Comparability in Cross-Cultural and Interpersonal Contexts." Syracuse University, March 1, 1967. Mimeographed.

Dillard, J. L. "Negro Children's Dialect in the Inner City." *The Florida FL Reporter* 5 (1967): 7–10.

————. "Non-Standard Negro Dialects—Convergence or Divergence?" *The Florida FL Reporter* 6, No. 2 (1968), 9–12.

Dollard, John. "The Dozens: The Dialect of Insult." *American Image,* 1 (1939): 3–24.

El Grito, vol. 2. Berkeley, Calif.: Quinto Sol Publications, 1968.

Erickson, Frederick David. "Discussion Behavior in the Black Ghetto and in White Suburbia: A Comparison of Language Style and Inquiry Style." Doctoral dissertation, Northwestern University, 1969a.

————. "'F' Get You, Honky!: A New Look at Black Dialect and the School." *Elementary English* 46 (April 1969b): 495–499, 517.

Fanon, Frantz. Chapter 1, "The Negro and Language." In *Black Skin, White Masks.* New York: Grove Press, 1967.

Fasold, Ralph W. "Orthography in Reading Materials for Speakers of Black English." In Joan C. Baratz and Roger W. Shuy (eds.), *Teaching Black Children To Read.* Washington, D.C.: Center for Applied Linguistics, 1969a.

————. "Tense and the Form *Be* in Black English." *Language* 45 (1969b): 763–776.

Fasold, Ralph W.; and Wolfram, Walt. "Some Linquistic Features of Negro dialects." In Ralph W. Fasold and Roger W. Shuy (eds.), *Teaching Standard English in the Inner City.* Washington, D.C.: Center for Applied Linguistics, 1970.

Feigenbaum, Irwin. "Using Foreign Language Methodology to Teach Standard English: Evaluation and Adaptation." *Florida FL Reporter,* 7 (1969).

————. "The Use of Non-standard English in Teaching Standard: Contrast and Compassion." In Ralph W. Fasold and Roger W. Shuy (eds.), *Teaching Standard English in the Inner City.* Washington, D.C.: Center for Applied Linguistics, 1970.

Ferguson, Charles A. "Diglossia." In Dell Hymes (ed.), *Language in Culture and Society.* New York: Harper & Row, 1964.

Fishman, Joshua. "Review of Hertzler 1965." *Language* 43 (1967): 586–604.

Gold, Robert S. *A Jazz Lexicon.* New York: Alfred A. Knopf, 1964.

Gumperz, John J.; and Hymes, Dell (eds.). "The Ethnography of Communication." *American Anthropologist* 66, No. 6 (special publication, 1964).

Haraty, Peter. "The Separatist's Fig Tree." *Liberator* (August 1969).

Hertzler, Joyce O. *A Sociology of Language.* New York: Random House, 1965.

Holt, Grace S. "The Ethno-Linguistic-Oral Language Approach." *Inner City Issues* (June 1969).

Horton, John. "Time and Cool People." *Trans-action* 4 (April 1967): 5–12.

Hymes, Dell H. "The Ethnography of Speaking." In Joshua Fishman (ed.), *Readings in the Sociology of Language.* The Hague: Mouton and Co., 1968.

Iceberg Slim. *Pimp: The Story of My Life.* Los Angeles: Holloway House, 1967.

Jensen, Arthur. "Social Class and Verbal Learning." In Deutsch, Martin; Katz, Irwin; and Jensen, Arthur R. (eds.), *Social Class, Race, and Psychological Development.* New York: Holt, Rinehart and Winston, 1968.

John, Vera. "The Intellectual Development of Slum Children: Some Preliminary Findings." *American Journal of Ortho-psychiatry* 33 (1963): 813–822.

Johnson, Kenneth R. "The Language of Black Children: Instructional Implications." In Robert T. Green (ed.), *Racial Crisis in American Education.* Chicago: Follett, 1969.

———. "Pedagogical Problems of Using Second Language Techniques for Teaching Standard English to Speakers of Nonstandard Negro Dialect." Linguistic-Cultural Differences and American Education. *The Florida FL Reporter* 7 (Spring/Summer 1969).

Joos, Martin. *The Five Clocks.* New York: Harcourt, Brace and World, Harbinger Books, 1967.

Kenyon, John S. "Cultural Levels and Functional Varieties of English." *College English* 10 (October 1948): 31–36.

King, Woodie, Jr. "The Game." *Liberator* 5 (1965): 20–25.

Kochman, Thomas. "The Kinetic Element in Black Idiom." In Thomas Kochman (ed.), *Rappin' and Stylin' Out: Communication in Ur-*

ban Black America. Champaign-Urbana: University of Illinois Press, forthcoming.

———. " 'Rapping' in the Black Ghetto." *Trans-action* 6 (February 1969a): 26–34.

———. "Social Factors in the Consideration of Teaching Standard English." *The Florida FL Reporter* 7 (1969b).

———. "Toward an Ethnography of Black American Speech Behavior." In Norm Whitten and John Szwed (eds.), *Afro-American Anthropology.* New York: The Free Press, 1970.

Labov, William. *The Social Stratification of English in New York City.* Washington, D.C.: Center for Applied Linguistics, 1966.

———. "Some Sources of Reading Problems for Negro Speakers of Nonstandard English." In A. Frazier (ed.), *New Directions in Elementary English.* Champaign, Ill.: National Council of Teachers of English, 1967. Reprinted with additions and corrections by the author in Joan C. Baratz and Roger W. Shuy (eds.), *Teaching Black Children To Read.* Washington, D.C.: Center for Applied Linguistics, 1969a.

———. "Rules for Ritual Insult." In Thomas Kochman (ed.), *Rappin' and Stylin' Out: Communication in Urban Black America.* Champaign-Urbana: University of Illinois Press, forthcoming.

———. The Logic of Non-Standard English." In James E. Alatis (ed.), *Linguistics and the Teaching of Standard English.* Monograph Series on Languages and Linquistics, No. 22. Washington, D.C.: Georgetown University Press, 1969.

Labov, William; and Cohen, Paul. "Some Suggestions for Teaching Standard English to Speakers of Non-standard Urban Dialects." In *Oral Language for Speakers of Non-standard English.* English Language Arts Curriculum Revision Project, Grades 5-12 (Strand Four, Developing Oral-Aural Skills). New York: Board of Education of the City of New York, Bureau of Curriculum Research, 1967.

Labov, William; Cohen, Paul; and Robbins, Clarence. *A Preliminary Study of the Structure of English Used by Negro and Puerto Rican Speakers in New York City.* Final report, Cooperative Research Project No. 3091. Washington, D.C.: Office of Education, 1965.

Labov, William; Cohen, Paul; Robbins, Clarence; and Lewis, John. *A Study of the Non-Standard English of Negro and Puerto Rican*

Speakers in New York City. Final report, Cooperative Research Project No. 3288, vols. I and II. Washington, D.C.: Office of Education, 1968.

Legum, Stanley E.; Williams, Clyde E., and Lee, Maureen T. *Social Dialects and Their Implications for Beginning Reading Instruction*. Inglewood, Calif.: Southwest Regional Laboratory for Educational Research and Development, 1969.

Liebow, Elliot. *Tally's Corner* Boston: Little, Brown, 1966.

Lin, San-su C. "Pattern Practice in a Freshman English Program." In Roger W. Shuy (ed.), *Social Dialects and Language Learning*, Champaign, Ill.: National Council of Teachers of English, 1965a.

————. *Pattern Practice in the Teaching of Standard English to Students With a Non-Standard Dialect*. New York: Teachers College Press, 1965b.

Loban, Walter D. *The Language of Elementary School Children*. Champaign, Ill.: National Council of Teachers of English, 1963.

————. *Problems in Oral English*. Champaign, Ill.: National Council of Teachers of English, 1966.

Loflin, Marvin D. "A Teaching Problem in Non-Standard Negro English." *English Journal* 56 (1967), 1312–1314.

Maryland, James. "Signifying at the Outpost." Term paper for the course entitled "Idiom of the Negro Ghettos," Center for Inner City Studies, Northeastern Illinois State College. 1967.

McCormick, Mack. "The Dirty Dozens: The Unexpurgated Folksongs of Men." Arhoolie Records.

McDavid, Raven I., Jr. *American Social Dialects*. Champaign, Ill.: National Council of Teachers of English, 1965.

————. "Social Dialects: Cause or Symptom of Social Maladjustment?" In Roger W. Shuy (ed.), *Social Dialects and Language Learning*. Champaign, Ill.: National Council of Teachers of English, 1965.

————. "Dialect Differences and Social Differences in an Urban Society." In William Bright (ed.), *Sociolinguistics*. The Hague: Mouton and Co., 1966.

————. "System and Variety in American English." In Alexander Frazier (ed.), *New Directions in Elementary English*. Champaign, Ill.: National Council of Teachers of English, 1967a.

————. "A Checklist of Significant Features for Discriminating Social

Dialects." In Eldonna L. Evertts (ed.), *Dimensions of Dialect.* Champaign, Ill.: National Council of Teachers of English, 1967b.

McDavid, Raven I., Jr.; and Austin, William M. (eds.). *Communication Barriers to the Culturally Deprived.* Cooperative Research Project No. 2107. Washington, D.C.: Office of Education, 1966.

McDavid, Raven I., Jr.; and McDavid, Virginia. "The Relationship of the Speech of American Negroes to the Speech of Whites." *American Speech* 26 (1951):2–17.

Miller, Warren, *The Cool World.* Boston; Little Brown, 1959.

"Minority Groups in America." Fybate Lecture Notes, *Sociology* 110 (October 1968).

Mouckley, Florence. "The Old Accent Changeth." *The Christian Science Monitor,* February 1, 1969.

Newman, Stanley M. "The Gouster: A Functional Analysis of a Ghetto Role." Northeastern Illinois State College, 1967. Mimeographed.

Nygren, Carolyn. "Basil Bernstein and Black English." Master's thesis, Center for Inner City Studies, Northeastern Illinois State College, 1969.

Pederson, Lee A. "Non-standard Negro Speech in Chicago." In William A. Stewart, (ed.), *Nonstandard Speech and the Teaching of English.* Washington, D.C.: Center for Applied Linguistics, 1964.

————. "Some Structural Differences in the Speech of Chicago Negroes." In Roger W. Shuy (ed.), *Social Dialects and Language Learning.* Champaign, Ill.: National Council of Teachers of English, 1965.

Poussaint, Alvin F. "A Negro Psychiatrist Explains the Negro Psyche." *The New York Times,* August 20, 1967.

Powell, Annette. "The Dynamics of a Black Audience." Term paper for the course "Idiom of the Afro-American Community," Center for Inner City Studies, Northeastern Illinois State College, 1969.

Rapsodi in Black: A Message in Soul Dances from 1953–1968. "Culture of Poverty" class project, Center for Inner City Studies, Northeastern Illinois State College, 1968.

Romeo, A. "The Language of Gangs." New York: Mobilization for Youth, n.d.

Rona, José Pedro. "The Social and Cultural Status of Gaurani in Paraguay." In William Bright (ed.), *Sociolinguistics.* The Hague: Moulton and Co., 1966.

Schatzman, Leonard; and Strauss, Anselm. "Social Class and Modes of Communication." *American Journal of Sociology* 60 (1955): 329–338. Reprinted in A. G. Smith (ed.), *Communication and Culture*. New York: Holt, Rinehart and Winston, 1966.

Stevens, Shane. *Go Down Dead*. New York, William Morrow and Co., 1967.

Stewart, William A. "Nonstandard Speech Patterns." *Baltimore Bulletin of Education* 43 (1956): 52–65.

————. "Urban Negro Speech: Sociolinguistic Factors Affecting English Teaching." In Roger W. Shuy (ed.), *Social Dialects and Language Learning*. Champaign, Ill.: National Council of Teachers of English, 1965.

————. "Sociolinguistic Factors in the History of American Negro Dialects." *The Florida FL Reporter* 5 (1967): 11, 22, 24, 26.

————. "Continuity and Change in American Negro Dialects." *The Florida FL Reporter* 6 (1968): 3–4, 14–16, 18.

————. "On the Use of Negro Dialect in the Teaching of Reading." In Joan C. Baratz and Roger W. Shuy (eds.), *Teaching Black Children to Read*. Washington, D.C.: Center for Applied Linguistics, 1969.

Stewart, William A. (ed.). *Non-Standard Speech and the Teaching of English*. Washington, D.C.: Center for Applied Linguistics, 1964.

Strauss, A.; and Schatzman, L. "Cross-class Interviewing: An Analysis of Interaction and Communicative Styles." *Human Organization* 14 (1955): 28–31.

Thomas, Piri. *Down These Mean Streets*. New York: Alfred A. Knopf, 1967.

Turner, Lorenzo D. *Africanisms in the Gullah Dialect*. Chicago: University of Chicago Press, 1949.

Williamson, Henry. *Hustler* (R. Lincoln Keiser, ed.). New York: Doubleday, 1965.

Zintz, Miles V. *Education Across Cultures*. Des Moines, Iowa: Wm. C. Brown Co., 1963.

PART III

Varieties of
Communicative Strategies

PART III

Varieties of
Communicative Strategies

First-Grade Classrooms

Implications of Teacher Strategies for Language and Cognition: Observations in First-Grade Classrooms

Elliot G. Mishler

Harvard Medical School and Massachusetts Mental Health Center

Introduction

In this paper, in presenting some verbal exchanges between teachers and pupils in several first-grade classrooms, we will attempt to show how different cognitive strategies as well as different values and norms are carried in the language used, primarily in the structure of teachers' statements and in the types of interchange developed between them and the children.

The problem defined for study and our approach to it draw directly upon current views in sociolinguistics and ethnomethodology about the functions of language (see particularly Hymes, 1966; Garfinkel, 1967; and Garfinkel and Sacks, 1967). A central theme

This report is based on materials collected as part of a larger project, "Social Context Effects on Language and Communication." The cooperation of the principals and first-grade teachers of the several schools included in the study is gratefully acknowledged; they were open and receptive to our request to observe and record classes, and I regret that in order to maintain confidentiality they cannot be acknowledged by name. All classrooms reported on in this paper were observed by myself and Lea Baider; the analyses and interpretations presented have benefited from discussions with her. Critical comments on an earier draft of this paper by Courtney Cazden and Nancy E. Waxler proved helpful in its revision.

in this work is an emphasis on studying language in its social context. These theorists have cautioned against accepting idealized accounts of language use as descriptions of actual communication and have suggested that we must find ways to understand, in a general and theoretical sense, the social functions of particular forms of language used in specific contexts. If we take these proposals seriously, then we need to learn how to describe, analyze, and theorize about what is actually said, by whom and to whom, when and where.

The classroom has not suffered from lack of attention; there is a large body of research on relationships between the behavior of pupils and teachers in the classroom and various educational and psychological criteria. However, for purposes of sociolinguistic study, reports of this work are of limited usefulness. The difficulty may be stated briefly—the language used, that is, what teachers and students actually say to each other, is almost never reported and is therefore not available for examination, reanalysis, and possible reformulation. Typically in these studies, speech is processed at the time of observation by systems of behavior-rating categories. On the whole, the structure of teacher-student speech has not been taken seriously; work has been oriented toward abstract dimensions that are viewed as useful for characterizing different types of social relationships in the classroom, for example, as dominative or integrative, or to index whether the emotional climate in the classroom is warm or hostile, or to permit classifying teaching styles as student- or teacher-centered. (For reviews of this work, see Medley and Mitzel, 1963; and Withall and Lewis, 1963.) One result of this methodological emphasis on rating scales and category systems is that little in the way of speech protocol material may be drawn upon for sociolinguistic hypotheses and generalizations.

Verbatim accounts are an initial and minimal requirement for developing appropriate analytic categories for the study of language functions. This paper focuses on the analysis of several excerpts of teacher-pupil exchanges in first-grade classrooms. These were transcribed from stereo tape recordings made during routine class instruction, and the transcriptions are as verbatim as possible. We shall try to show that there are ways of analyzing such material that, on the one hand, preserve the particular features of interactive speech and, at the same time, are relevant to general theoretical concerns with relationships among language, cognition, and socialization.

More specifically, we shall argue that specific cognitive strategies and social values are manifest in how a teacher talks to and responds to pupils. As a first step, we will examine several components of cognitive strategies: how attention is focused, the structure of alternatives presented, and the procedures for information search and evaluation. In the related but broader area of social values and norms, we shall look at the emphasis given to language itself, the role of authority, and the type of connection made between individual and group experience.

Our aim is to explore the range and variety of strategies and norms that may be found in classroom talk. We will approach the problem by contrasting the speech of different first-grade teachers with each other, with the intent of extracting a number of differentiating features in the language used and of showing how these features reflect both different constructions of reality and different ways of learning about it.

Cognitive Strategies

As a primary socializing institution, the school has the task of instructing children about the content of their culture. A wide range of information is transmitted from what things are called and how they are socially classified and organized, through basic adaptive and instrumental skills, to social values and codes of conduct. Despite the enormous literature on learning, it would not be an unfair generalization to assert that how children actually learn what they do learn in school remains very much a mystery.

We begin with the well-documented observation that there are different ways to learn, that is, that there are different approaches to gathering information, forming concepts, and solving problems. Further, these appear to be systematic individual preferences in these modes of cognizing and learning. For example, Bruner, Goodnow, and Austin (1956) describe alternative selection strategies, that is, "regularities in decision-making" that are used in the search for and attainment of correct concepts in categorization problems. Variations in how individuals orient toward their environments to gain relevant information have been classified as differences in cognitive control principles and cognitive styles (Gardner, Jackson, and Messick, 1960). As a last example, Cohen (1969) has reported social-class differences in conceptual styles, defined as "rule sets for the selection and organization of sense data."

Given the central task of the school and the evidence on variations in how individuals learn, we thought it would be of interest to look at different cognitive strategies used by teachers. We use the term "strategy" to refer to the principles implicit in an individual's approach to the world with the aim of learning about it. Neither rationality nor consciousness is implied, any more than when we speak of grammatical rules. Rather, we are concerned with discovering rules that underlie and guide ways in which information is sought, concepts attained, and problems solved. In their totality, these rules compose an organized approach to "what" is learned and "how" it is learned.

We shall be trying to find these rules in the language used by teachers in the classroom when they are engaged in "teaching" something. There are a number of components to a strategy. We have selected three for examination: how attention is focused, the search and evaluation procedures used, and the structure of alternatives presented.

Focusing of Attention

The following excerpts from teacher-pupil exchanges in two different classrooms provide useful points of contrast and comparison in how teachers orient themselves and the pupils to a topic for discussion.[1] Both sets of exchanges are taken from the initial phase of episodes in which the teachers are leading discussions.

1a. The teacher has just finished reading a story to the whole class about a detective, Big Max, who had been hired by a king to find a lost elephant.

---

[1] These excerpts were not selected as typical of or representative of particular teachers observed, but rather were chosen as instances that contrasted in various ways with each other. They are being used as illustrations, or exemplars, of different cognitive strategies and are not intended as grounds for evaluating the quality or effectiveness of different teachers.

TEACHER: Big Max (*pause*) used some words that go with detectives. Can you think of any? Right over here, someone.

(*Several children speak at once; unclear responses*)

T: What does a detective have to look for when he's on his way to solving a case? Bill.

CHILD: A clue.

T: A clue. Can you think of any clues that Big Max found in this story, Eric?

C: Hmm. (*pause*) Tears.

T: And who do those tears belong to?

CLASS: Crocodile.

2a. The children have finished cleaning up after a free period of play, games, and art. The teacher has assembled them around her.

TEACHER: Can I see everybody over here? We're going to be seeing a very unusual movie this morning.

CHILD: What's it about?

T: I don't think I'm going to tell you, Stephen. I'm going to let you wait and find out.

CLASS (*chorus of complaints from several children*): Aw!

T: It's done with colors.

CLASS (*several children calling out; unclear*): Colors . . .

T: I don't think it's a story.

Although our concern in this paper is primarily with the description and analysis of different strategies and not with their evaluation, our intuitive sense that the first exchange is "better" than the second provides a useful point of departure. The first episode appears to be more directed and focused than the second. Our central problem here, as elsewhere in our analysis, is to specify particular features of the language used as indicators of different cognitive strategies.

In the first excerpt, *1a,* the teacher works directly out of and with explicit reference to a shared collective experience. Her first statement provides continuity between the story they have just heard and what they are now to do together. This transition is displayed by variations in tense in the sentences that compose her first statement: "Big Max used . . ." and "Can you think . . . ?" Further, she focuses their attention on one figure in the story and on one aspect of his behavior, namely, his use of special words.

There are several implications for language-learning in this teacher's way of providing a transition between past and present and in how she focuses the attention of the class on certain specific features of their experience. First, she underscores the importance of language. The use of different verb forms, which we have already observed, is one device that serves this purpose. In addition, she is pointing out that there are special words that "go with" particular occupations and, by implication, with particular settings and persons. Words, therefore, can carry a great deal of information about the world. Finally, in this classroom at least, the children are being told that it is important to pay attention to particular words, since they may later be held accountable for having heard and understood them as the teacher is now holding them accountable by asking them for words that Big Max actually used.

At the same time she has selected a specific feature of the situation for their attention, this teacher generalizes the issues involved and moves the discussion from a concrete to a more abstract level. The shift from the particular concrete instance to the more general abstract class of events is accomplished by her use of the plural noun "detectives" in her first sentence and her use in her next statement of the indefinite article, "What does *a* detective . . . on his way to solving *a* case?" When there is a correct response, "A clue," to the general question, she confirms its correctness by repeating it and then requests specification with references to concrete instances in the story.

Thus, in a brief interchange consisting of a series of eight statements by the teacher and pupils, we find that this teacher provides a highly specific way of cognizing the world. Briefly, it is a world where there is continuity through time and ways in which past and present may be connected, where words help to differentiate aspects of the world and of experience, and where there are different, though related, levels of abstraction and generalization. In a sense it is a complex yet ordered world; it is organized, and language is one of the basic principles of its organization.

What sort of a world is contained in the second excerpt, *2a?* Attention is directed to a future event about which only the teacher appears to have knowledge: "We're going to be seeing a very unusual movie this morning." The teacher's first statement is controlling and motivational as well as informative; she directs the children to assemble and then stimulates their interest by the adjectival phrase, "very unusual." No specific reason is given as to why they are to gather together, and no specific information about the movie is provided beyond its "unusual" character. In addition, the statement serves implicitly to direct attention to the teacher rather than to the event itself—she seems to "know" why they are being brought together and what will happen.

The first statement by a child is a question. The teacher's opening remark has "worked" motivationally in that the children are oriented toward the future event. The teacher's response to this question is of special interest because it not only does not provide new information but essentially denies the legitimacy of the question. This serves not only to deepen the mystery about why they have been brought together and what will happen, but introduces a teasing and provocative quality to the interchange. The teacher seems to be proposing a game in which they will have to try to find out what she knows, with the proviso that in the end she may not tell them. In this way, she reinforces the focusing of attention on her rather than on the event itself.

The children's collective complaint, "Aw," is ritualistic in quality. It is as if they "know" this game and understand that the way to get information from the teacher and determine what she wants of them is to express their feelings rather than to ask a question. They are demonstrating both that they are "properly" motivated and that they know the rules of this game.

The teacher's response to their complaint, "It's done with colors," is interesting in several respects. First, it contains no detailed information about what the movie is about, so the actual content of the future experience remains vague. In some contexts "colors" would be an informative datum about an object or event, but for a movie to be "done" with colors could mean almost anything. Second, the observers learned that the teacher had not seen the movie prior to this discussion; her response reflects knowledge only of its title, *Orange and Blue*. In actuality she could not answer the question of what it is about, but despite this she does not qualify

her response with "From its title, I think /or/ I would guess . . .";
her response is a flat assertion implying real knowledge. A qualification would put her in the same situation as the children, but the unqualified statement reinforces the knowledge and status differential between her and the children.

Finally, although she qualifies the last response in this excerpt with "I don't think," specific information is still not provided. The statement that the movie is not a "story" is of limited value because it neither clearly reduces the range of possible alternatives nor indicates types of possible answers among which one might search for the correct one.

In the world constructed by this teacher, the salient dimension is the relationship between herself and the children, and this relationship is organized hierarchically. The world of objects is vague and undifferentiated, and the children will be able to learn about it not by a directed search or inquiry but by behaving in an acceptable way to the teacher. There is no substantive or logical continuity between what one child says and what another says, and the connections between responses are mediated by the teacher.

A third classroom provides some additional points of contrast and comparison on how attention is focused.

3a. A parochial school classroom after morning pledge, prayer, and song. Each child has a brochure with pictures and text.

TEACHER: Let's look at the cover. What do we see on the cover of this magazine? David, what do we see on the cover of this magazine?
CHILD: A church.
T: A church. Does it look like our church?
C: No, it doesn't.
T: Why doesn't it?
C: Mmm. The. The people are the church.
T: All right, James.
C: It's a small church.
T: It's a small church. All right. Where did the church come from? Have you any idea where the church came from, Glen?
C: God.
T: Yes, it did come from God. Can you think of anywhere else?
C: Jew.
T: Lisa?

C: Jew.

T: From where, Lisa?

C: Jew.

T: Can you tell me that in a sentence?

C: The church came from Jews.

T: All right. It came from a long, long time ago, didn't it? The Christ Church was started by Jesus. Remember from that story I told you of the day that Jesus had breakfast with his Apostles and he made Peter the (...) of the church. It was a small, baby church and it has grown throughout the years. Is the church a building? Think of what your church looks like. We all have different churches. Other people go to X church. Can you tell us what X church looks like, David?

In contrast to the first teacher's emphasis on the immediate past and the second's on the future, this teacher focuses the class's attention on a concrete and visible present. Her first questions request descriptive replies, yet at the same time are relatively open-ended and global: "What do we see ..." and "Does it look like ... ?"

One early response, "The people are the church," seems off the mark and is ignored. However, after a correct descriptive answer, that is, "It's a small church," the teacher then follows up on the second and more abstract meaning of the word "church." Although she uses the term both in its concrete and abstract meanings throughout this exchange she does not make the difference explicit; rather, the meaning intended is implicit in the form of the question asked. Thus, "What do we see ..." and "... tell us what X church looks like" can only refer to it as a concrete building, but "Where did the church come from?" and "It was a small, baby church and it has grown throughout the years" refer to the church as an abstraction. Whereas the teacher in *1a* shifted back and forth between levels of abstraction by making explicit use of the relationship between a general term, "detectives," and its particular instance, "Big Max," this teacher shifts levels implicitly by using the ambiguity inherent in one word. There is no underlying semantic relationship between "church" as it refers to particular types of buildings and "church" as an abstraction referring to the people who share a body of doctrine. In order to keep the reference clear, she varies the frame of the statement within which the word is used. One implication is that the children must attend to her full statement in order to know "what" she is talking about.

In the last statement in the excerpt, a more elaborated and detailed comment than any offered by the other teachers, we find this teacher presenting a framework of interpretation. There is a "story," part of a more general set of stories, within which they can "fit" the picture they are looking at and the discussion they are having. The continuity and coherence being provided differ from that in the first classroom in that here they involve linking the present topic to a general scheme of interpretation about the world. It is not so much that the discussion of the church is an instance of a general concept as that it is another element to be joined to others that together compose the overall system; the discussion takes its significance and relevance from its connection to this larger framework.

Information Search and Evaluation

In the previous section we examined different foci of attention as they are manifested in how teachers talk about a topic and respond to their pupils' statements. We turn now to the ways in which these teachers structure the process of searching for and evaluating information.

The first excerpt, *1a,* continues as follows (*1b*):

TEACHER: And who do those tears belong to?
CLASS: Crocodile.
T: When they talk about crocodile tears, (*pause*) what could that mean?
CHILD: Fooling tears.
T: Fooling tears.
C: (*Unclear*)
T: I wonder (*pause*) if you think this would be true, (*pause*) boys and girls. If Mark or Eric or Genia or Jim or any of you ever have crocodile tears?
C: No. Yes.
T: Raise your hand and tell me if you think so. David.
C: When you're faking.
T: When you're faking. What do you mean by that?
C: Well, I'll tell you. When you're faking it means that you're not really sorry [. . . and] you're not really [. . . doing] that thing that you wanted to do and then to get the thing that you wanted.
T: Can you think of a child who might fake in other things?

In the ordered and complex world as a point of reference and attention that she has constructed with the pupils, this teacher now sets in motion a divergent cognitive process. (The term is borrowed from Guilford [1967], who uses it to refer to the elaboration of instances that fit a particular class or category, in contrast to a convergent process that involves searching for the one correct answer.) "What could that mean?" and "What do you mean by that?" are open-ended questions that encourage the children to generate their own individual responses and that contain the implicit recognition that there are various and alternative responses that may be equally appropriate and correct. Further, continuity is maintained through the sequence, so that as the network of meanings is elaborated it includes the contributions of the several children who have spoken.

She continues the previously observed pattern of switching back and forth across different levels of abstraction. Here, she shifts from the story's crocodile with tears to the abstract metaphor used by "they," that is, by people in general. It would appear that the use of "they" as a general term of reference and the transformation of "crocodile" into an adjective are both critical to this effective transition from a concrete to an abstract level of discourse. They mark the shift in ways that seem, from their responses, to be clear and recognizable to the children.

A second shift in levels of discourse is the move from this particular feature of the story to personal experience. This is accomplished not by referring to the actual event in the story, i.e., a crocodile with tears, but by the use of the metaphor as a mediating concept. Thus, both the events in the story and their experiences are linked together indirectly by their separate connections with an abstract term. As before, the shift is marked explicitly, here by using the names of particular children in the classroom.

This teacher's emphasis on the cognitive elements in the task is also worth noting. A rough index is given by her use of the words "think" and "mean"; in her ten statements across both excerpts, the first is used in five and the second in two of them. We will return to other features of this exchange after examining a continuation of the discussion in the second of our classrooms (2b).

TEACHER: I don't think it's a story.
    (*Several children speak at the same time; unclear*)

T: Excuse me, I can't hear Beth. I can't hear Beth.
           (*Unclear general noise*)
T: John.
CHILD: Is it a fable?
T: No.
C: Is it Batman?
T: Does anyone have any questions to ask?
           (*Unclear general noise*)
T: Beth had a question to ask.
C: Is it a movie about how we hear?
T: About how we hear? No, it's not about how we hear.
           (*Unclear general noise*)
C: Is it a cartoon?
T: No, it's not a cartoon, Rodney. What else could it be?
           (*Unclear general noise*)
T: I think you like [. . .], don't you, Jerry?
           (*Unclear general noise*)
C: Will you tell us what it is?
T: I can't tell you anything because no one's ready.
           (*Unclear general noise*)
C: It's Mickey Mouse.
T: I think maybe the group doesn't get to see it.
        (*General complaining sounds; noise subsides*)
C: Stuart knows what it is.
T: Excuse me?
C: Stuart knows.
T: No. He doesn't know what it is.

There are several other guesses—horses, Abraham Lincoln, animals, rattlesnakes, cooking, and *Chitty Chitty Bang Bang*—all responded to in much the same way as before. The teacher terminates the discussion by stating, "When I see people controlled, the lights will go on and we'll be able to go in." And her last series of statements, as the class lines up to go to another room for the movies, compose the following sequence: "Let me see who's ready. Peter, you're ready. When you're ready. Who's ready to go next door? Nobody in here seems to be ready yet."

This teacher has generated a sequence of random guesses—story, fable, Batman, how we hear, cartoon, Mickey Mouse, horses, Abraham Lincoln, animals, rattlesnakes, cooking, *Chitty Chitty Bang Bang*. There is no connection among the answers, information does not accumulate, the sequence in which the answers are produced has no significance, and the children have no basis for knowing whether they are closer to the correct answer at the end than at the beginning of the episode. The children have introduced content in an ad hoc way, either from other experience about what movies are about, that is, Batman and cartoons, or from the immediate environment; for example, the "how we hear" refers to a diagram of the ear on the wall behind the teacher. The process also seems to obscure certain logical relationships that might be helpful to an effective search procedure; for example, being told that the movie is not in the general class of cartoons does not eliminate a question about whether it is a specific cartoon, Mickey Mouse.

In contrast to the teacher in the previous excerpt, *1b,* this teacher is engaged in a convergent process in which there is one correct answer. However, since she provides no positive information that would help to limit the number of alternatives, each guess seems to be independent of what has gone before, that is, there is no history to the discussion. Or, to be more exact, whereas the cognitive work appears to have a random and disjointed quality, the relationship to the teacher is more developmental. For example, the children's understanding of the rule of this game, namely, that they must behave properly in order to learn, gains in clarity, as is indicated by the change from the initial question, "What's it about?", to "Will you tell us what it is?" near the end of the episode. Thus, they recognize their dependence on her and on her approval of their behavior.

The process is not only convergent, it also has the form of an interrogation, in which the children are required to direct questions to the teacher. This differs from both of the other classrooms that have been discussed, where the question-answer pattern was based on the teacher as questioner. When a teacher asks questions, it is possible for children to follow each other in the sequence of discussion and even to interact together. However, such patterns are precluded when the children must question the teacher, who has all the required information, since there is no meaningful basis on which one child's response can be related to another's unless it is first mediated by the teacher.

The exchange at the end of the excerpt is of particular interest, since the teacher, rather than responding to substance, again denies the legitimacy of a child's report both directly and then indirectly by refusing to explore the claim; "No. He doesn't know what it is" effectively aborts any discussion of Stuart's possible knowledge. Further, since Stuart has violated one of the implicit rules by whispering to a classmate, the teacher's response serves notice on everyone that such violators will not have a legitimate claim on her attention or on the attention of the group.

Of the sixteen statements by the teacher over the period covered by the two excerpts (2a and 2b), seven of them may be classified as "administrative," a classification that includes directives, efforts at control, and calling on students without further content in the statement. Of the nine that are more "substantive," six refer to the object under discussion—namely, the movie—as "it," a pronoun without explicit content and gifted with ambiguity. In contrast, among the teacher's ten statements in the discussion of Big Max (1a and 1b) there is only one that is solely administrative, and none of them uses "it" as a term of reference. The contrast between the divergent and convergent approaches represented by these two teachers is also marked by the differences between them in their use of the word "think" and its equivalents. We have already noted the frequent use of this cognitive term by the first teacher; it is important to note that it is used usually in the frame of a question directed to the children, that is, "What do you think . . . ?" The word is used by the second teacher in only three of her sixteen statements, and in each instance it is with reference to herself, that is, "I think . . . ."

The classroom is a socializing context where children are expected to learn about "something" and at the same time to learn certain rules of proper and appropriate behavior. Our classrooms do not differ in this respect, for both types of learning go on simultaneously. However, there are differences in how these two functions are related to each other—for example, which of them is given primacy. For the first teacher, rules for "how" to behave are subordinated to the exploration of content; when several children talk at once, for example, she says, "Raise your hand and tell me if you think so." For the second teacher, stress is placed on the control of behavior, and the discussion of the film is used primarily as a medium for learning general rules, with only peripheral interest in the actual content itself.

The following excerpt comes from the third classroom (*3b*); it is from a later point in the continuing discussion about the church and its meaning.

TEACHER: We've talked about what our churches look like. Do you think that a building, the outside, really makes up the church? Do you think the building is what we call the church?
CHILD: No.
T: What is really the church? Jesus?
C: God's house.
T: Yes, it is God's house. I wonder what really makes up the church. Joseph.
C: The Mass.
T: Mmm. That's not what I am thinking of. Who goes to Mass? Joseph.
C: The people.
T: The people. What do we call the people who go to church? We have a name for them. Margaret.
C: Catholics.
T: There is another name for them.
C: Christians.
T: Theresa.
C: (*Unclear*)
T: No, dear. John.
C: God's family.
T: God's family. All right, so God's family really makes up the church. That's what the church is, is God's family. It doesn't make any difference what church you go to, it's God's family that really makes up the church. The people are family related with Jesus.
   Who can read that question on the board under this first page?

   The process here is a convergent one, as was that in the second classroom, but it differs from the latter in several critical respects. First, the teacher both asks the questions and evaluates the answers. Most importantly, her successive questions take previous answers into account. Thus, when her question about what "really makes up the church" does not produce the correct answer, she reformulates her question in such a way—"Who goes to Mass?"— as to take the wrong answer into account and at the same time to orient the children in the right direction. The full process includes immediate corrective feedback so that errors are not permitted to hang in the air, successive reformulations of the question so as to narrow down the range of possible alternatives, and explicit confirmation of the correct answer when it is expressed.

As in the earlier part of this discussion, continuity is maintained through the teacher's use of a larger, general framework of ideas and accounts to make sense of the discussion. The level of her activity is much higher than that of either of the other two teachers we have been describing. One crude measure is the number of lines of typescript per statement for each teacher. The first teacher (Big Max) generates fifteen lines of typescript from ten statements for a mean of 1.5; only one of her statements has three or more lines. The second teacher (movie) has eighteen lines for sixteen statements for a mean of 1.1 with no statements as long as three lines. Our third teacher provides forty lines for nineteen statements for a mean of 2.1; four of her statements have three or more lines. Thus, although the process at one level is convergent, it differs from the movie discussion in that the answer the children are being asked to find changes over the course of the discussion, as the teacher actively reformulates her questions and relates answers to a larger framework of meanings.

The Structure of Alternatives

In discussing how a teacher focuses children's attention on a problem and how she guides their search for answers, we have already referred to sets of alternative possible answers that seem to be implicit in the discussion. Differences among the teachers merit separate, though brief, comment, particularly since these three components of cognitive strategies have some degree of relative autonomy from each other; that is, a specific way of defining an alternative set does not constrain the way of searching for and evaluating evidence.

By the structure of alternatives, we mean the number and types of alternative answers to a question and their relationship to each other. From the typescripts examined, one may distinguish graphically among the three teachers in the following way: the first implies a set of alternatives organized as a "tree" with earlier answers branching into later possibilities; the second offers an array of points scattered about a topological "region"; and the third provides a "matrix" within which the answer is to be found.

In the tree, one answer leads to another—from the crocodile with tears, to fooling tears, to crocodile tears, to "when you're faking." In this teacher's divergent style, each new question depends upon the previous answer and the branching process does not appear to have a predetermined end. Hypothetically, of course, it would be possible to begin with a tree that had a predetermined set of points and a "correct path" through them to the final answer. It is for this reason that we view the structure of alternatives as relatively autonomous from the attention-focusing and search procedures used.

The region of possibilities offered by the second teacher is unstructured. The points within it are not connected with each other, nor divided into clusters. All that one knows is that the correct answer is to be found "somewhere" within it. Neither later questions nor later answers in the sequence depend upon what has gone before. Rather, the question remains the same throughout: "Can you guess what the movie is about?" If the correct answer were finally found, this would serve only to divide the region into two parts: one containing the one correct point, with all the wrong answers in the other part.

Finally, for the third teacher, there appears to be a fixed set of alternative answers, among which is the correct one. Although the dimensions of the matrix and the number of alternatives are unclear, the process involves narrowing down to one answer and excluding others along the way. In this respect, it is more organized than the region of points, and the term *matrix* seems applicable. It is not the case that one answer leads to a related question and new alternatives, as in the tree, but that errors are corrected in such a way as to direct the search, as in the sequence: "I wonder what really makes up the church?" "The Mass." "That's not what I am thinking of. Who goes to Mass?"

We have been using the notions of tree, region, and matrix in a metaphoric sense, as an aid to visualizing certain aspects of cognitive processes in the classroom, but it is evident that such descriptions could be given a more formal definition. It is also clear that the three classrooms observed do not represent a full range of types of alternative sets. For example, the problem might be that of classifying or categorizing objects according to a principle: "Which of the following words are verbs and which are nouns?" Or, in a more open-ended fashion, "Which of the following animals go together?" Another type of problem might use continuous variables, such as height and weight, as coordinates, the task being that of identifying an object representing a pair of measures.

The aim of these remarks on different structures of alternatives has been to point to an important feature of teachers' cognitive strategies that is somewhat more hidden from view than how they focus attention or guide the search for answers. Nonetheless, this aspect of their approach is of equal importance if we are interested in understanding how children learn "how to learn" about their environments.

Social Values and Norms

Although it is somewhat artificial to separate cognitive strategies from social values and norms, since the former represent one type of instance of the latter, distinctions can usefully be made between specific problem-solving operations that are features of special contexts like classrooms and more general social standards and rules that may be found in various contexts. We have selected three "topics" to examine: the orientation to language itself, modes of authority and control, and relations between the individual and the group.

Orientation to Language

We might begin by asking whether the teachers vary in how seriously they view language. We have already observed that the first teacher selected the actual words used in the Big Max story as a focus of attention. In her question about words that "go with" detectives, she is orienting the children to more than the dictionary meaning of words. She is pointing out that words may have a special social reference, that is, that they are associated with certain types of persons and certain types of situations. Further, she is underlining the fact that the social meaning, in contrast to the narrow semantic meaning, is actually used in order to "tell" something about the world; thus, the author of the story used special words to confirm that it was a story about a special type of person, namely, a detective. In this way, she is showing how language is a resource to differentiate and articulate the world. And, of course, this rests on the assumption that it is a differentiated world.

The awareness of language as a resource is extended further by this first teacher through her introduction of the metaphor *crocodile tears*. In showing that words may have several different types of meaning—literal, social, and metaphorical—she is sensitizing children to both the complexity and the utility of language.

The third teacher in her question about the meaning of the "church" also displays a serious interest in the words that she and the children are using in the discussion. However, here the emphasis seems to be placed on the singular meaning of certain special words, a meaning that they have because of their use in a specific story. The words are labels for events, but although words function in this way because of social consensus and although the connection between a particular word and its referent is an arbitrary convention, this teacher conveys the sense that words and objects are connected integrally. In part, this occurs because she does not explore the ambiguity and range of meaning of different words; for example, we have noted that she does not deal explicitly with the two different referents for *church,* although her questions require at one time the use of one meaning and at another time, its alternate meaning. Nor does she ask the children what they mean by or understand of the words they use. Further, she implies that there is a universally recognized meaning to words and that she is simply helping them to learn them. This is evident in her frequent use of the adverbial modifier *really* in such statements as "What is really the church?" and "I wonder what really makes up the church." Her confirmation of the right answer is assertive and decisive—". . . All right, so God's family really makes up the church. That's what the church is, is God's family. . . ."

There is little evidence in the discussion about the movie of a concern with language as a resource. The convergent guessing process tends to generate simple questions from the children, with single words rather than phrases or clauses in either the predicate or object positions. The syntax of the teacher's statements is also simple in structure. She uses no relative pronouns or conjunctions, and there is only one complex sentence in her sixteen statements: "I can't tell you anything because no one's ready."

In the discussion about the church, the questions and statement of the teacher are somewhat more complex structurally; although many of her sentences are simple in form, there are more dependent clauses and the associated use of relative pronouns—*when, what, who, that*. However, the convergent process, with the teacher asking the questions, tends to generate responses from the children that are equivalent in the simplicity of their structure to those found in the second classroom.

The first teacher's statements are the most complex of the three. She not only uses relative pronouns, but the conjunction *and* and the conditional *if*. When we recall that in the excerpts presented above the first teacher's contributions cover fewer total lines of type-script than either of the other two, then the relative degree of complexity in her language becomes even more striking. The children's responses remain relatively simple in structure, although there is one statement at the end of *1b* that is elaborate and complex. It is worth noting, however, that in a later discussion on this same morning that was more open-ended and focused on the general problem, as the teacher phrased it, of "Why do people blame things on each other?", these children responded at length and with complexity. One indicator of this increase in complexity in this later discussion is that 20 percent of the statements made by children were two or more lines of typescript, and 15 percent were three or more lines.

This "blame" discussion provides good examples of the level of complexity and abstractness that may be reached by first-grade children. Excerpts are included here (*1c*) and we shall return to some features of this discussion in the following sections.

The class has just returned from an art room. The teacher has assembled them around her and sits in the circle with them. There is a song. The teacher then begins what she had scheduled and announced earlier as a "discussion." The full discussion, from which this is excerpted, runs about thirty minutes.

TEACHER: Boys and girls, (*pause*) as you know, (*pause*) yesterday we had a little problem between two boys. And, I thought we might talk about it a bit today, because all of us have this problem at some time or another. It might make things better. Yesterday two boys had a quarrel, and they finally had to start with their fists to try to solve it. And when it was all over with they were blaming each other for things. It was very hard to tell unless a person had seen it start who really was to blame. I was wondering if we could talk about the idea, why do people (*pause*) blame things (*pause*) on each other. Why do they blame things on each other? Why does one boy try to blame the other boy for an accident that happened? (*Name of child.*)

CHILD: They don't want to get into trouble.

T: They don't want to get into trouble . . .

C: . . . and they blame the other person for it.

T: That's one reason, I'm sure. Dana.

C: . . . a person like if a person knows that, uh, and he blames the other person . . . like if I blame it on someone that he did it, when I really did it.

T: Why would you do that?

C: Well, I didn't want to get in trouble.

T: All right, that would be something like Angela's idea. That you don't want to get in trouble because of what happens. Right. What kind of troubles do you think could happen? What kind of trouble do you stay away from by blaming Seth? What might happen to you, do you think? . . .

* * *

T: It might be much better. But why do you think, what kinds of trouble do you try to stay out of? Do you think something would be done to you because of what happened?

C: I think like a punishment. . . .

* * *

T: Like a punishment. Well, what kind of punishment might be done to you? . . . what kind of punishment don't you like? . . .

* * *

C: Go to bed.

T: To be sent to bed early, you mean. Is that punishment for you? . . .

* * *

T: Can you think of ways then we wouldn't have to take out that punishment? All right. Can you think of other reasons why people might try to blame someone else? Why Kris might try to blame her brother. Can you think — or people in this room. Lisa. . . .

* * *

T: Can you think of any other reasons why you might blame somebody for something you really did? Peter.

C: Well, somebody starts fighting with me . . . and the other person started it, and then another time the other person started it, and the person who started the last time didn't get hurt, and the next time the other one gets hurt.

T: Can you tell us in one sentence now, why?

C: (*interrupting*) . . . getting hurt.

T: Oh, because one time you might have gotten hurt, another time he might have hurt you.

C: No, somebody starts a fight and the person that started didn't get hurt then the person who didn't get hurt and the one who did and the next time starts a fight.

T: So, suppose Peter and Seth were doing something together, playing together, and then Seth started a fight with you and after it was all over Peter was hurt, and Seth who started it didn't get hurt. So, you'd try to blame him for starting the trouble.

C: No, and I start the fight and Seth gets hurt . . . a way of getting back.

T: Oh, I see, so you get your revenge for next time by starting a fight and pretending it was Seth that started the second fight and it really wasn't but it was your way of getting back.

C: Yes.

T: Right, so a way of getting back at people is one reason, cause you're afraid what punishment you might get. All right, can you think of any other reasons why people might blame their friends for something that they did to themselves? Susan. . . .

* * *

T: Anyone have any other ideas about blaming, putting the blame on someone else? David.

C: Well, sometimes people blame each other because they want to know what's happening to . . . they want to know what's going to happen to them, so they blame the other person and when the other person gets hurt then they know that they might get the same punishment, the same kind so then they won't fight. . .

T: I see. Is that what . . . your daddy's home now and David and his brother are having a fight. If David really started the fight, but he blames his brother, so his brother will get punished, and then David will find out what kind of a punishment his father will give his brother so the next time David will be expecting what kind of punishment he'll get himself.

CLASS: Yeah. . . .

* * *

T: Right. Now we were thinking about, we've worked in these make-believe things . . . we're talking about real things now, like people like ourselves, about things that we might do. Is there any time that you ever tried to let someone, that you didn't get the blame for something that you did? Can you think why you did that? You don't know why.

C: . . . when Debby hurts my feelings and I went back home.

T: What do you mean by Debby doing something to hurt your feelings? What would that mean? *(Children's voices)* How could your feelings get hurt?

C: If she said a bad thing to me. . . .

* * *

T: That would be another reason why you might try to blame another person, cause they hurt you not with their fists but with the words, or the way they use their words. Right? Debby. . . .

* * *

T: Getting back to the idea of who's blaming other people sometimes. Can you think of any reason why you might want to blame someone else for something? . . .

* * *

C: . . . Erik started the fight with me . . . and he blamed that I started the fight and he would get in trouble but I wouldn't . . . and the next time. Like Peter said.

T: Something like Peter said. You'd get even with him the next time it happened. Even if he wasn't the one who started . . . get him in trouble. Get even. . . .

* * *

T: So far, before I forget anybody's response, Susan. We've said that sometimes we blame people for something that we did, because we're afraid of what punishment we'll get, sometimes we do it to get even with them when they've done something nasty to us. What is another reason? Jim. . . .

* * *

T: Why do you suppose that Eric did that? Maybe it would be a good idea to ask Eric. Maybe he could straighten it out for us. You mentioned that yesterday. Something between you and David. He heard you tried to blame David. Could you tell us how you felt yesterday? Why you were trying to blame David? What was happening? . . . You don't remember.

C: He always says that.

(Children's voices)

T: . . . is it hard to know, Eric, why you try to blame someone?

C: Well, I was very sad.

T: Why were you sad?

C: I don't know.

T: You mean you were sad about what was happening because David was fighting or were you sad before that?

C: I was sad before that.

T: . . . and was it this sadness that made you forget and try to blame someone else?

C: I was sad . . . .

T: I know you were very sad when you first came. And it was this sadness that made you forget about taking the blame yourself . . . and so you tried to blame someone else for it because you were so upset and sad about what happened. . . . That happens a lot of times. I know I've gotten very mad at times and got so upset or angry. . . . I could see that you might be so mad about that you could forget you were the one who started it. Do you think it is easy sometimes when a fight starts that when it is all over, you forget which one started it? . . .

* * *

T: Do you think this is a good question, do you think it is always just one person who starts, or can it ever be that both of you had a little bit to do with starting it?

C: Yeah, it could be. Umm . . . . And then—umm—and then I blamed him I thought that he started it first and that's not true, and then we had another fight and then she started to . . . and then we both got punished then because we both blamed each other. . . .

* * *

T: Well, I think my question was, do you think sometimes, do you think that it's always one person's fault or possibly sometimes it starts and you both have a little bit to do with starting it, both are a little wrong, do those things ever happen when both of you were doing a little . . . to start the fight. . . .

* * *

T: All right. We're still thinking about that idea of how can you tell whose fault it is when something happens. . . .

* * *

T: All right, we did say something about whether using your brain would be a much better way to stop a fight than your fists. Do you think, boys and girls, that in a classroom when we're talking about getting people into trouble and punishing and things like that and who is to blame, is it an easy or a hard thing to figure out who is to blame for something when you haven't seen it while it was happening? Mark, what do you think?

(Silence)

T: Is it easy or hard to figure out who's to blame for something when you haven't seen it?

C: It is hard.

T: Very hard. Right, then sometimes we blame other people, like right now, lots of people are trying to blame Eric for something, or some people are trying to blame David for something, someday it might be that they're trying to blame Peter for something or Janis or Jean, and if we haven't seen the whole thing, do you think we are in a very good spot to tell who . . .

C: No. . . .

* * *

T: Then from all the things that we've said, maybe, . . . in here, . . . Eric, do you think it would be a good idea for us then when things happen in the classroom, Eric, we try not to blame that person, especially if we haven't seen the whole thing happen, that's very hard, isn't it? All right, I think that inside a person's heart they know themselves which one is to blame, and sometimes it may be two people to blame. But we'll have to let that party settle it themselves instead of us trying to say who caused it when we didn't see it. Okay? Pamela.

Role of Authority

In all classrooms, the power of the teacher to organize and direct activities, to impose sanctions and distribute rewards, is clear to her and to the children. On this dimension, as on the others we have been examining, the several episodes reveal different ways in which teachers exercise their authority. One important limitation to our data for exploring these differences should be pointed out— namely, that the classes were observed during the spring. Some of the ways of imposing discipline and of defining particular forms of power relationships between teacher and child, which may have been explicit at the beginning of the school year, have already become implicit. That is, certain modes of sanctioning and responding may be so routine and automatic as to be difficult to detect in the verbal interchanges. A systematic study of authority relationships would require the observation of classes over a period of time to determine how particular patterns developed and were established. This late in the year, one might expect to find differences on this dimension when the teacher's authority has to be reaffirmed or reinstituted, that is, when there is a disruption in or breakdown of the established rules or when a new situation arises that requires a reformulation or new application of the rules. We shall focus on instances that seem to be of this type.

In general, the first teacher functions as a "task leader." First, she sets up the problem for the group. In the Big Max discussion, for example, she directs their attention to "some words that go with detectives," and asks if they "can think of any"; in the discussion of "blaming" she provides background information and then specifies what they are to talk about: "I was wondering if we could talk about the idea, why do people blame things on each other." There is some tentativeness to her phrasing, as in the use of the conditional verb "can" and the "I was wondering" clause, and this suggests that her initial statement of the problem is negotiable. After introducing the problem, she actively guides and directs the discussion by recognizing and calling on children by name and by restating and summarizing what has been said, for example, "All right, that would be something like Angela's idea"; and "So far, before I forget anybody's response . . . ." Finally, she terminates the discussion with a statement of what they have arrived at: "Then from all the things that we've said . . . we'll have to let that party settle it themselves instead of us trying to say who caused it when we didn't see it. Okay? . . ."

The extent to which the class as a group is asked to share responsibility for developing and confirming norms for behavior is a distinction among different modes of authority relations. The first teacher makes a number of explicit attempts to share her authority. Her frequent use of the plural pronoun "we" is one way in which she indicates that they are engaged in a common task of trying to arrive at an acceptable rule for situations where individuals "blame things on each other." Another, similar device is question frames that invite children to introduce their own reasons and experiences as legitimate grounds for a common norm, such as "Do you think . . .," "Why do you think . . .," "Why do you suppose . . ." Finally, in her terminating statement that formulates the rule for behavior, she makes it clear that it is not only a decision they have arrived at together but that it is now to apply to all of them, including herself.

The behavior of the second teacher contrasts in a number of ways with that of the first teacher. With respect to the source of norms, she tends to state a rule using her position as the teacher as the grounds for its authority. For example, initiating a new class activity at a later point during the same morning, she states: "Listen carefully. Several of the boys in the Green Dot group started to build something with LEGOs. They asked if they could leave it up, and no one else work on it today. And tomorrow, they'll share it with you. You may use other things in the room. I don't want to see anyone inside that or near it."

Whereas the first teacher is a task-oriented leader, the second is more coercive and directive, focusing on the control of behavior rather than on the accomplishment of a task. We have already noted the latter's relatively high proportion of administrative and control statements. It appears that authority is "external" and sanctions for misbehavior must still be made explicitly and frequently. We are not suggesting that this teacher is "more" of an authority than either of the other two, or that in reality she controls more resources and rewards, but rather that she relies more on direct sanctions in order to control behavior. Each of the other teachers structures the tasks in such a way as to hold the attention of the children, and as a consequence to control their behavior. Thus, the directed questioning that they engage in may also be looked at as an alternative way of exercising control.

Two other qualities of the second teacher's mode of exercising authority are worth noting. First, the process is one of control by threat, that is, that they will be deprived of a reward unless they behave: "I can't tell you anything because no one's ready." "I think maybe the group doesn't get to see it." "When I see people controlled, the lights will go on and we'll be able to go on." Second, the threats are directed against the group rather than particular individuals. It is of some interest that whereas responsibility in the cognitive area is placed on individual pupils—that is, each child is expected to try individually for the correct answer—the sanction for the control of behavior is directed at the group, which therefore is held responsible for the proper behavior of its individual members.

In response to a typical classroom problem, namely, two or more children talking at once, the first two teachers differ in ways that again reflect differences in how control is exercised. The first says, "Raise your hand and tell me if you think so." The second, "Excuse me, I can't hear Beth. I can't hear Beth." The first has recourse to a general and abstract rule, and at the same time asks them to engage in a specific positive act. The second keeps the focus

on herself and her requirements, implying that they are interfering
with her needs, and is nonspecific and vague about what they should
do; they are being asked to "do" nothing.

A mixed picture emerges from the "church" discussion, in that
the third teacher is both directive and task-centered. She controls
the discussion firmly, and all the children's comments are directed
to her in response to her specific questions. During the full morning
of observation, there were few instances in which she used an explicit sanction to control behavior. There was no apparent need for
her to do so, since the norms—to be quiet unless called upon, not to
talk to neighbors—were apparently well internalized and violations
were rare. Longitudinal observations would have been particularly
useful in this classroom for understanding the nature of the authority relationship and its development.

The Individual and the Group

A critical feature of the classroom as an educational and socializing context, and a feature that contrasts markedly with the
family setting, is that it involves a group of children of the same age
who experience the process together; even when a child works alone
or is responded to individually, this still takes place within and with
reference to the group. We shall examine differences among our
three teachers in whether and how they elicit and use individual experiences as material to be shared with the group and the degree to
which they explicitly focus on the class as a group.

In the excerpts presented earlier, both the first and third
teachers invite the children to share their own personal experiences
with the group. The first, for example, asks "If Mark or Eric or
Genia or Jim or any of you ever have crocodile tears?" and "Is there
any time . . . that you didn't get the blame for something that you
did? Can you think of why you did that?" and the other asks "Can
you tell us what X church looks like, David?" The first teacher is
asking for a report of feelings and ideas, the third teacher is asking
for information. The second classroom contrasts with both of these.
For example, in one interchange not included in the excerpts, one
child states that her mother had told her what the movie was about
and then makes a vague statement about this. The teacher's response is: "Well, that's good. Now we're getting warm." She does

not, however, invite the child to elaborate or clarify the statement. Here, as in her other response to Stuart's claim to know, she tends to close off the possibility of further report and limits what the child might bring into the situation from outside the classroom.

In the "blaming" discussion, the first teacher is continually asking *why*. She is asking the children to share their interpretations and understandings of the world, particularly their attributions of motives, that is, their explanations of behavior. In the church discussion, the analogous question is *what*. The emphasis is on the description of the world, particularly its physical characteristics or the proper labels for people and events. Her typical questions are: "What do we see on the cover of this magazine?" and "Does it look like our church?" and "What do we call the people who go to church?" This contrasts with the first teacher's "Why would you do that?" and "What would that mean? . . . How could your feelings get hurt?"

The first teacher focuses on and actively elicits interpretive reports of personal experience. For example, at one point when the discussion has become somewhat general, she says: "Right. Now we were thinking about, we've worked in these make-believe things . . . We're talking about real things now, like people like ourselves, about things that we might do. Is there any time that you ever tried to let someone, that you didn't get the blame for something that you did? Can you think why you did that?" At another point, as she brings the discussion back to the concrete incident with which she began, she turns directly to one of the boys involved: "Why do you suppose Eric did that? Maybe it would be a good idea to ask Eric. Maybe he could straighten it out for us. You mentioned that yesterday. Something between you and David. He heard you tried to blame David. Could you tell us how you felt yesterday? Why were you trying to blame David? What was happening? . . ."

Note also this teacher's use of the first person plural pronoun "we" in such a way that she identifies herself with the class: ". . . as you know, yesterday we had a little problem between two boys. And, I thought we might talk about it a bit today, because all of us have this problem at some time or other"; and its reiteration in her later statement in the discussion: "We've said that sometimes we blame people for something that we did, because we're afraid of what punishment we'll get, sometimes we do it to get even with them when they've done something nasty to us. . . ." It might seem that the use of "we" could serve as an index of a teacher's way of referring to the class as a group with a clear affirmation of her own membership in it. However, the meaning of "we" varies with different contexts. For example, it is used in a more ambiguous way by the third teacher in her discussion of the "church." When she says, "What do we see on the cover of this magazine?" she is clearly referring to herself and the class. On the other hand, when she says, "Who do we call the people who go to church? We have a name for them . . .", "we" appears to have a more general collective referent, that is, to all people like themselves. Here, as in the way in which she focuses attention and orients to language, this teacher is linking what happens in the classroom to a larger world of meanings. We pointed earlier to the second teacher's focus on the class as a group when it was a matter of applying sanctions for behavior. This teacher uses "we" only in repeating a child's guess as a collective term of reference, and in other ways consistently separates herself from the group. For example:

CHILD: Is it a movie about how we hear?
TEACHER: About how we hear? No, it's not about how we hear.

In summary, the first teacher places herself within the group, and membership in this group is specific and distinctive. The second teacher treats the class as a group of which she is not a part; she is the separate teacher-authority. The third teacher locates both herself and the class in a larger group that exists outside the confines of the classroom.

Discussion

This paper has been divergent in style. We have tried to show that the language used by teachers in classrooms can be analyzed in ways that yield information about important aspects of the educational-socialization process. We have focused on certain implicit rules for learning, that is, cognitive strategies, and on norms and values with regard to the use of language, the role of authority, and the relations of an individual to a group. We began with stated reservations about the value of idealized linguistic descriptions and of summary indexes or ratings of verbal behavior that did not take seriously the actual particulars of the language used. In directing attention to what teachers say and how they say it, our work is consistent with the general program of sociolinguistics, and in particular with Hymes' (1966) emphasis on the study of language use within specified contexts as the key to understanding social relationships and the social functions of communication.

To a large extent we have been concerned with discovering rules of appropriate or acceptable usage, as Hymes distinguishes these within rules of competence. It is clear, even from the limited materials presented in this paper, that we must go beyond the vague idea that the school represents only one type of context or that the teacher-pupil relationship is a particular and singular type of social relationship. Each of the three teachers observed behaved "appropriately" for her role; yet, we have been able to show that they behaved very differently from each other. Most importantly, the differences can be found easily in their respective styles of speech. Hymes argues that we must investigate what is linguistically possible, feasible, and appropriate. From our observations we must recognize that many variants are appropriate, even in well-defined and restricted contexts, and add another level of analysis that might be called preferential.

In examining these speech samples, we have been relatively eclectic in the types of linguistic units used in drawing inferences. Some of the differences between teachers are at the level of words, for example, in whether words in a particular grammatical category are used, such as first person plural pronouns; other differences are syntactic, as in variations in the use of dependent clauses; still others include the interchange between speakers, as in question-answer sequences. At this stage of knowledge and research, we believe it would be an error to restrict inquiries to one or another of these levels. We know very little about the communicative functions of variations within each of these levels; we know even less about relationships across levels. For sentences and smaller linguistic units, systems of classification are available that may be used to code and analyze these units of speech. Much work remains to be done with the larger units—interchanges, tri-acts, arguments, discourse—to develop classification systems that are of equal power and utility.

Finally, it is worth repeating a point made earlier, namely, that verbatim protocols like those provided in this paper are only the first step. For those concerned with the process of education, a question of critical interest is whether variations in the verbal behavior of teachers make any difference to the learning and cognitive development of children. This requires more systematic study, in both field and laboratory settings, of the ways in which children with different verbal and cognitive skills respond to different instructional styles.

Bibliography

Bruner, Jerome S.; Goodnow, Jacqueline J.; and Austin, George A. *A Study of Thinking.* New York: Wiley, 1956.

Cohen, Rosalie A. "Conceptual styles, culture conflict, and nonverbal tests of intelligence." *American Anthropologist* 71: 5 (October 1969), 828–856.

Gardner, Riley W.; Jackson, Douglas N.; and Messick, Samuel J. "Personality Organization in Cognitive Controls and Intellectual Abilities." *Psychological Issues,* Vol. 2, No. 4, Monograph 8. New York: International Universities Press, 1960.

Garfinkel, Harold. *Studies in Ethnomethodology.* Englewood Cliffs, N.J.: Prentice-Hall, 1967.

Garfinkel, Harold; and Sacks, Harvey. "On setting in conversation." Paper presented to Annual Meeting of the American Sociological Association, August 31, 1967. Mimeographed.

Guilford, J. P. *The Nature of Human Intelligence.* New York: McGraw-Hill, 1967.

Hymes, Dell. "On communicative competence." Paper presented to Yeshiva University Conference on Language Development Among Disadvantaged Children, 1966. Mimeographed (rev.).

Medley, Donald M.; and Mitzel, Harold E. "Measuring classroom behavior by systematic observation." In N. L. Gage (ed), *Handbook of Research on Teaching.* Chicago: Rand McNally, 1963.

Withall, John; and Lewis, W. W. "Social interaction in the classroom." In N. L. Gage (ed.), *Handbook of Research on Teaching.* Chicago: Rand McNally, 1963.

The Meaning of Questions and Narratives to Hawaiian Children

Stephen T. Boggs
University of Hawaii

Aina Pumehana is a modern community located within commuting distance of Honolulu. As a Hawaiian Homestead community, a sizeable part of its population can trace ancestry to the original inhabitants of the islands, since it is necessary to establish 50 percent Hawaiian ancestry in order to lease a lot on the Homestead. The people of Aina Pumehana consider themselves to be Hawaiian in the overwhelming majority of instances, the younger as well as the older. The community has the reputation of being a country place. It lacks agricultural employment, however, and is bordered on one side by modern, inexpensive tract houses.

In the latter houses live military families, a few professionals

The present study was stimulated by the work of William Labov in Harlem (see Labov, et. al., 1968). Valuable guidance was also obtained from Slobin (1967). I am indebted to Ann Peters for calling my attention to several important unpublished papers and to Courtney Cazden for allowing me to read a preliminary draft of her paper, "Children's Questions: Their Forms, Functions and Roles in Education" (1970). Her advice contributed materially to the present paper.

The study has been conducted with financial assistance from the University Research Council and the Head Start Evaluation and Research Center, both of the University of Hawaii.

The research reported herein was performed pursuant to a contract (No. OEO 4121) with the Office of Economic Opportunity, Executive Office of the President, Washington, D.C. 20506. The opinions expressed herein are those of the author and should not be construed as representing the opinions or policy of any agency of the United States Government.

I am indebted to the Social Science Research Institute, University of Hawaii, for typing services.

and operators of businesses, and workers in local industries, in retail businesses, and on military installations. Aina Pumehana is in fact a suburb in the state's largest metropolitan area. The people of Aina Pumehana are employed in Honolulu and other parts of the area, but not in as many occupations as their immediate neighbors. Half of the employed men in Aina Pumehana are in semiskilled occupations. They are heavy equipment operators, truck drivers, policemen, and firemen. One-fourth are in such skilled occupations as pipe fitting, cable splicing, carpentry, or foreman work. Fewer than 5 percent are in any kind of white-collar occupation, and none is a proprietor, executive, or professional. The remaining 19 percent, mostly younger men, are in unskilled jobs (see Boggs and Gallimore, 1968).

The educational level of the men is rather high: 65 percent of the men under thirty years of age have finished high school, and the number appears to be increasing (Boggs and Gallimore, 1968, table 2). Despite its popular image, it is not a poverty community. It lacks the high rates of unemployment, low average wages, and fatherless families typical of poverty communities. Family income averaged $600 per month in 1967, in part because wives and other family members typically work (Boggs and Gallimore, 1968). Since housing costs are so minimal, this income is available for other expenditures.

Families are large. Households with children average 4 children and 2.46 adults each. Women over forty-five years of age have had, on the average 6.17 children.[1] Children are welcomed. Many parents are eager to adopt children in addition to their own (Howard, 1968).

Given these facts one might expect the children of this community to do rather well in school, compared with those from poverty communities on the United States mainland. Some do, but the great majority perform well below national norms in school. Nearly 100 percent of the students in the first three grades, for example, scored below the fifteenth percentile on reading tests in 1966. Approximately 70 percent of the tenth grade in that year scored below the twenty-fifth percentile on standardized achievement tests, and a

[1] Data obtaned from the Hawaiian Community Research Project files, courtesy of the Bernice P. Bishop Museum.

large proportion of the fourteen-year-olds read at about the second-grade level of competence (Gallimore, MacDonald, and Boggs, 1968).[2] Such an astonishing outcome is difficult to explain. Although prejudice with its self-fulfilling prophecy of poor performance cannot be ruled out in this case, teachers are inclined to insist that Hawaiian children are no different from any other, and can be taught in the same way, thus justifying the view that they are not different.

The primary assumption of the present study was that poor performance in school was a result of the lack of fit between attitudes and behavior patterns of the children and those required by the school. Behavior patterns required by the school might be lacking in the children, or the school might interfere with attitudes and behavior patterns of the children and fail to take advantage of them. The attitudes and behavior patterns that have the most important effect upon the children we have found to be those involved in communication. This is more than a matter of language. Although the children's speech has often been suspected as a cause of poor performance in school, our observations lead us to suggest that other aspects of communication may be more important for Hawaiian children. The form of exchange between child and adult and the conditions in which it occurs will affect not only what is said, but how involved the child will become. His competence in producing forms of speech is just one factor.

The present study explores these aspects of communication, their consequences, and their possible causes. For example, recitations in observed classes were puzzling, and often frustrating to the teachers. When the teacher asked a question at least a dozen hands would usually shoot up and then, before anyone could be recognized and reply, several would blurt out the answer. When an individual did have the floor he sometimes spoke confidently and sometimes shyly, but did not volunteer any information not called for. Often a child would gain recognition and then have nothing to say. Reports to the teacher on the behavior of other children meanwhile would interrupt any other communication. We have attempted to write generalizations that will make sense out of these observations and

[2] Information on the reading scores was obtained from the Language Arts Project in the Aina Pumehana Elementary School. This project was funded by PL 89-10.

simultaneously relate them to other behavior observed, such as the children's strong preference for interacting with one another, rather than with adults.

Most of the data were obtained by means of participant observation in one first-grade classroom of the elementary and intermediate school in Aina Pumehana, which is attended almost exclusively by students of the Homestead and nearby area.[3] Only one of the approximately thirty students in this class was a Caucasian; four were Samoan, and the rest Hawaiian. The teacher was a Caucasian, recently arrived from the West Coast. Some data were obtained in a second first-grade class, of whom three students were Caucasian and twenty-four Hawaiian. Both classes comprised average children, not selected in any way. The former is referred to hereafter as Class One, the latter as Class Two.

Class One was visited by the author at approximately biweekly intervals from September 1966 until February 1968, that is, into the second grade. Each visit lasted the whole day. Through interaction in the classroom and on the playground the observer was able to develop several roles. He was (1) a kind of adult friend; (2) a teaching assistant, when left in charge of the class alone or with the regular teaching assistant, a mother from the community; and (3) a teacher, when conducting certain assignments on behalf of the teacher. The latter were Reading Readiness exercises, which were tape-recorded by the teacher. Since the children had played the tape recorder for these assignments before the observer appeared, they were accustomed to it. When offered an opportunity to record their voices and hear themselves played back, they were both interested and frightened, at times. Such opportunities were offered throughout the day, and during the first year all of the children conversed with the observer on tape. Most of them also recorded their performance in the assignments referred to, as well. However, only fourteen of the children in Class One have been included in the present analysis, because some said too little in their conversa-

[3] I am very much indebted to Mr. Kazuo Ikeda, principal of the school, for permission to conduct the study; and to Mr. Walter Tanaka, vice-principal, Miss Carolyn Loper and Mrs. Roberta Tokumaru, directors of the Language Arts Project at the school, for their assistance in making arrangements with the teachers. For the teachers, who tolerated the observers' presence so graciously, I feel great admiration and an unbounded gratitude.

tions and others lacked recordings of their performance in the assignments.

Three kinds of data from this class are reported: observations, recorded conversations with the observer, and performance in Reading Readiness assignments. Communication patterns are analyzed according to circumstance: children interacting with the teacher, the observer, and one another. Comparison of communication patterns in these different circumstances depends almost entirely upon observations, since the techniques used did not allow recording of speech among children or between them and the teacher, although a few verbatim communications in these circumstances were recorded in the observations.

The report begins with a comparison of the children's responses to questions, volunteering of information, and questions asked in the various circumstances referred to. A detailed consideration of the differences in the productivity of responses to questions and volunteered narratives in the recorded conversations with the observer follows. Since competence in formulating questions is one of the possible causes of these differences, evidence pertaining to competence is presented and its relationship to the productivity of answers to questions is discussed. Further details of the procedures used by the investigator are presented, along with the relevant findings. A test given in Class Two, for example, apparently stimulated the children to ask a number of questions, and these provide some of the evidence of the children's competence in producing question forms. In the final section some implications of these findings for the teacher are set forth. Here the effects of preferred patterns of communication upon the child's performance in the classroom, including performance on Reading Readiness exercises, are presented and discussed.

Circumstances Affecting Communication Patterns

By comparing the circumstances in which children answered questions or failed to answer them, volunteered information, or asked questions, one can make some inferences about the meaning questions and narratives may have for them. One circumstance that made a significant difference in answers to questions was whether the child was answering a question directed to him or not. When called upon to answer a question in class, a child was likely to answer minimally, if he answered at all. When the question was addressed to another child or to the whole group, however, children who volunteered were more voluble.

One example of the latter circumstance occurred when the teacher wrote the answer to a question she was going to ask on the board and covered it up, telling the children before she did so to hide their eyes. Of course they did not do so, as she anticipated; and as soon as she asked the question, calling for what they were not supposed to know, many blurted it out. The strength of this impulse was unmistakable. They also answered frequently when she addressed questions to the group, as in the following discussion:

At the end of the count of ten when the whole class is supposed to be sitting on the floor, D——— is not there. Instead he goes out the door of the class. One of the children calls the teacher's attention to this and she says, "D——— is being stubborn." She then engages the class in a conversation about being stubborn, asking them if they know what it means to be stubborn. Someone suggests that it means to be sad. Someone else says it means bad. The teacher says that you are stubborn if someone asks you to to do something and you say *(demonstrating)*, "No, I won't do it!" At this point one of the children says, "Yes. They ask you and you no like."

They also tended to answer questions addressed to another child, as discussed below. But when called upon themselves, answers were often not forthcoming, and were never voluble. Thus it sometimes happened that a child would wave his hand in response to a question asked before the class, blurt out an answer, and then not deliver the answer he had just uttered when called upon.

Another circumstance that typically led to a refusal to answer a question was when an adult was checking up on a child's work, or supervising in some manner. In the following episodes, that was not the observer's intent, but the child appears to have so interpreted it:

I came up to O———, who was sitting and daydreaming, asking him what he was supposed to do. He smiled but did not begin work. N——— did not answer at all when I asked her what she was supposed to be doing. She went on coloring.
When I was checking the work, I asked T——— what he was doing and

he said coyly, "What you want to know for?" He did not show me what he was doing.

Thus, attempts to initiate conversation by asking about a child's activities or work were frequently unsuccessful, although the same children would be quite voluble when approached differently.

Questions were likewise not answered in circumstances in which the adult was frustrating the child. For example:

A boy and a girl asked me to help them with an assignment: to draw a line from one numeral to the next larger one, thus outlining a figure. When they asked me where to draw next, I asked each to count. They did well at this at first, but then started to balk at counting. As it continued they would not answer, saying that they did not know what followed two, and even one.

One common feature of a failure to answer a question may be the child's perception of being put on the spot—i.e., threatened with negative consequences. In the last episode, for instance, the likelihood of failure is increased both by the adult's refusal to provide the information sought and by his questions.

The circumstances that encourage children to volunteer information to an adult are mostly the opposite of those in which questions are not answered. These circumstances have one thing in common: cues that the adult is receptive. One has already been noted: the teacher's invitation to the group to discuss. In such a circumstance she did not scold or ridicule, but even performed herself on occasion. Some individuals who rarely talked at any time would then volunteer remarks. Moreover, the children would wait, not speaking until called upon—in sharp contrast to their behavior when answering questions directed to other children or to the group. Whether intended or not, their behavior in the latter circumstance had the effect of preventing individual recitations. Since the teacher scolded them for such behavior, it seemed to the observer to have the characteristics of a struggle with the teacher for control of the class. Needless to say, the children usually won. When invited to narrate, however, they were willing to await their turn, as if they were acting in accordance with a convention.

Cues that the adult was receptive also encouraged communication in dyadic interaction. Such cues often went unnoticed by the observer, as in the following episodes:

At naptime the teaching assistant came into the room. She said as soon as she entered the door, "There's too much noise in here. Quiet down." The observer had been saying nothing and continued in the same way. M—— put his mat on the floor nearby and said to the observer, "Are you going to stay over here?" or words to that effect. K—— was already lying in front of the observer. He asked, "What's my name?" Then M——, while lying down, told the observer where he lived and called attention to his paper, which was up on the board.

Twice in a few minutes, N—— fell off her chair at her desk, which she had been kicking. She was ashamed of herself and looked at the observer shyly. The teacher was trying to conduct a lesson before the whole class. N—— leaned over to tell the observer that she used to live on Maui. He then smiled at her and she repeated this information, adding that she used to live on the Mainland also.

In these cases, and many others recorded in the field notes, the observer was apparently seen by the child as overlooking some immediately preceding misbehavior: the noise in the first episode and the falls interrupting the teacher in the second. Because he was not aware of this import, the observer was surprised on these occasions by the sudden approaches of the children, and the volubility of their volunteered information.

More obvious cues of the adult's receptivity occurred in other cases: consoling another child or holding a child in his lap. When these things happened, the child being held, and one or more looking on, would volunteer news and remarks and would open conversations. The tape recorder also came to symbolize the observer's receptivity. When it was set up children would come over to report news and ask to record. When in use, bystanders would often walk up, grab the microphone, and speak.

Finally, children were eager to volunteer information they thought the adult wanted to hear, under any circumstances. They reported that they had done what they were supposed to do, or that another child had not. In all of these cases the children spoke when they assumed that the adult would be receptive to the communication: either generally or to a specific piece of information. With the exception of asking questions themselves, the field notes reveal no instances that contradict this generalization.

The difference between the circumstances that elicit answers to questions and volunteered information and those that do not provides a context for the finding, reported in detail below, that questions were less productive than other kinds of remarks in the recorded conversations with the observer. These conversations had characteristics that would tend to inhibit answers to questions and to promote volunteered information. By conversing and showing interest, the observer was indicating his receptivity, but his questions were also directed to an individual. It is my hypothesis that it is basically unpleasant for a Hawaiian child to have a question directed to him by an adult, even if it is an attempt at friendly conversation.

If this interpretation is correct, then it might follow that attempts at conversation made up entirely of questions should fail to produce much response at all. Inadvertently, such an experiment was conducted during the second year, when the observer was better known, and should have been more approachable. During this time the focus of interest was in discovering the nature of the categories the children used in their thinking. For two months the observer attempted to elicit by repeated questions the items that contrasted with one another in a particular set. He therefore asked many questions and made few comments. Such questions produced sparse answers, even on popular subjects such as food, animals, and people. Rarely did children volunteer narratives during this time. In approximately three hours of recorded speech only six narratives comparable in length to those of the first year were recorded. The attempt to elicit information in this way was then abandoned. Thereafter the observer restricted his role to talking with individuals on their request, expressing interest by comments, and occasionally asking questions, as in the first year. During this three months, five hours of speech were recorded, virtually all of it narrative in nature, and these narratives were much more voluble than those of the first year. It is hard to escape the conclusion that individually directed questions inhibit response in the child addressed, whereas expressions of receptivity by the adult encourage response.

Conversations with the observer differed in several respects from communication among the children themselves, as one would expect. Questions among children are more likely to be answered, and children are more likely to ask one another questions. Answers to questions are more voluble, since they usually involve an argument, and other kinds of remarks are filled with more information than when conversing with an adult, except under the best of circumstances. Unfortunately, these points cannot be documented in quantitative terms, since recordings were not obtained of speech between children, except incidentally.

These aspects of communication among children reflect an almost continual orientation to one another, rather than toward adults. They were frequently observed to help, amuse, copy work from, and compete, argue, and fight with one another. In many instances they appeared to be striving to avoid being outdone in an activity they valued, and to be sensitive to any slight. The following is an argument, recorded while the observer was attempting to converse with a single child:

C——: We got our [Christmas] tree, way, way . . . ova der on Kauai.
T——: Where is Kauai, which place is Kauai?
C——: Down der!
T——: Where? Ova der? Not ova der! 'As one islan, one differ[?] islan stay ova der. . . .

This also illustrates the aggressive use of questions by children. The girl, C——, did not respond as volubly as usual on this occasion because the observer intruded and agreed with T—— before she could do so. A more typical response is the following, in which other children, anxious not to be outdone, rush to answer a question directed by the observer to one of them:

Obs: How do you fix a nini [nursing] bottle, D——?
C——: I fix a . . .
D—— (interrupting): I put the milk first and then I put the wata.
C——: Like me, I put the milk firs, then I put the hot wata an then I (put some on arm—gesturing) to see if hot (speaking rapidly, but interrupted twice before she can complete this much). . .
D——: Ya [yeah].
M—— (speaking rapidly): Na! You make em drip on top your arm and say, "Feel the thing hot?" Then you give the bebe . . .
C——: (interrupting, likewise speaking rapidly): Then you give the bebe (mimicking sardonically).

This pattern is similar to that observed when the teacher addressed a question to another child, or to the class, and a number of children rushed to answer. In both cases answers tended to be voluble, as long as the speaker was not the one called upon. In the episode below, C—— had been asked the same question cited above a few moments earlier:

OBS. *(to M——)*: Have you made nini bottles for baby?
M——: Plenny time, you can make um.
C——: And make um hot.
OBS. *(to C——)*: You know how to do it?
C——: I do' know how.
OBS.: You don't know how? You never did?
(Other children answer.)

Instances such as this tended to increase the volubility of responses during the recorded conversations with the observer, whether the children were answering questions or not.

Finally, children were observed to ask questions in a variety of circumstances, including some in which they would not answer questions, or would not volunteer information—when being supervised and when it interrupted the adult, for example. One can understand this by assuming that it is a natural trait for children to ask questions when they need information or assistance. This is no doubt true. But it will not explain a few circumstances in which they do not ask questions, or do so rarely: (1) when conversing individually with the observer and (2) when called upon in front of the class. Over a twelve-month period approximately twenty children produced about thirty-four questions in their recorded conversations with the observer, except for one exchange to be mentioned. The notes record no instances in which children called upon to recite asked a question, although they would, of course, ask questions if someone else were called upon. It was also puzzling that children would address questions to the observer individually or severally when attempting to initiate a conversation with him, but not when he was attempting to converse with them individually. In the latter case, and when called upon in front of the class, children appear to have assumed that it was the adult's prerogative to ask the questions, not theirs. This became an issue one day when the observer invited a girl to talk and she replied:

E——: What talk about?
OBS.: Well, what would you like to talk about?
E——: You! firs.

And she then proceeded to interview the observer before he realized what was happening, asking some twenty-five questions. Her behavior may have been idiosyncratic, since no other child behaved this way.

It is interesting to compare the circumstances just discussed with supervision, i.e., when the adult asks a child about schoolwork under way. In those circumstances the child is being put on the spot, and tends to answer minimally, if at all. But when supervised he appears to assume that it is as much his right to ask questions as the adult's. Such an assumption is consistent with the children's school experience, which also leads them frequently to request assistance and to persist in their attempts to get it, even though they approach the adult hesitantly at first.

Most of the findings in this section can be summarized in the following table. Comparison of 1, 2, and 3 in table 1 indicates that the likelihood of some response to a question increases as the threat of being put on the spot by an adult decreases. Similarly, information and narratives are more likely to be volunteered. But responses to questions are minimally productive whenever an adult is addressing a question to an individual child, regardless of the more specific circumstances. Minimal productivity, then, indicates defensiveness with adults. From these findings one might infer a rule such as:

TABLE 1
Summary of Findings

Relationship and Circumstances	Response to Questions		Volunteered Information and Narratives	Questions Asked
	Per cent response	Productivity		
1. Author to individual: Supervision	0	Minimal	Low	Frequent
2. Teacher to individual: Recitation	50	Minimal	Low	Rare
3. Author to individual: Conversation	90	Minimal	High	Rare
4. Teacher to children collectively	50	Voluble	Moderate	Frequent
5. Child to child	100	Voluble	High	Frequent

when queried individually by an adult it is safer to answer minimally, if at all.

The fact that answers to adult's questions are minimal even when the child is attempting to reply may signify, moreover, that there is something involuntary about the defensiveness that is hypothesized.

Children appear to be reacting to two dimensions, judging from these findings: (1) authority, as in the child-adult relationship compared with the relationship among children; and (2) dyadic relationships compared with collective ones, relationships among children often being collective. A collective relationship with an adult seems to be equivalent to relationships among children, so far as patterns of communication are concerned. It has been suggested that the response of children when questioned in class had the effect of shifting dyadic relations to collective ones. The reason may be that the child finds protection in collective relationships with adults. These findings might be summarized in the following rule: Other children can be queried, answered, and talked to at any time, and so can adults when relating to a group of children.

Other findings, not summarized in table 1, suggest the following additional rule: When an adult is receptive one can volunteer information individually, or initiate a conversation. A conversation consists of an ordered exchange of narratives. In fact, such conversations tend to become collective, rather than dyadic, since the children appear to assume that an adult who is receptive to one will be receptive to all. Even though children strive to outdo one another, they never appear to claim an exclusive right to the attention of the adult. Thus, their whole system of relating to adults collectively appears to be self-consistent.

The Length of Responses to Questions in Conversation

As already noted, questions tended to produce briefer responses in recorded conversations with the observer than did other kinds of verbalizations. In this section this finding will be described in detail, some alternative explanations of it mentioned, and one of them examined.

The children's responses in conversation generally tended to be narratives, and narratives, of course, tend to be longer than answers to questions. Operationally, however, it is not easy to distinguish between the two. Attempted narratives were often brief. Since there was also a possibility that questions could elicit narratives, especially the kinds of questions illustrated below, the analysis attempted to assess simply the length of responses to questions and to other kinds of verbalizations by the observer, rather than to classify each response as an answer to a question or a narrative. The finding described here, in other words, can be interpreted as indicating that questions are less likely to elicit narratives than are other verbalizations.

But such an interpretation still requires explanation. The explanation already offered is that children are inhibited by questions directed at them individually by adults. There are two other plausible explanations: (1) that the shorter length of answers to questions might be an artifact of the analysis; (2) that children had difficulty in responding to questions because of differences in the form of questions in their style of speech, as compared with the standard English spoken by the observer. The latter explanation will be considered in the following section. The former will be examined in the following paragraphs.

The speech analyzed came entirely from the conversations with individual children that were tape-recorded during the first year. As mentioned earlier, invitations to talk were offered by the observer in the course of a variety of activities in the classroom. After a while children would come over and volunteer to record. Conversations might begin with a child saying, "I want to talk," or they might begin with an affirmative answer to the question, "Do you want to talk for me?" When the machine was switched on, the child usually began to speak in response to a comment like, "Okay, go ahead," or a question like, "What do you want to tell me?" Once started, the observer's only purpose was to prolong the conversation in order to obtain as much speech as possible. In order to do this he asked questions intended to pursue topics mentioned by the child, expressed interest by brief comments, and occasionally suggested topics by means of questions or expressed surprise, disagreement, or a challenge. He allowed time for response and in general avoided speaking when the child seemed likely to continue. While efforts were made to restrict the conversations to an individual child by using the concept of turns, and by discouraging interference by other children, other children did interfere on occasion. This is another example of the children's tendency to shift dyadic interaction into collective form. It has not been possible to detect this influence on the tapes in every case.

All of the tapes were reviewed, and each conversation that appeared to be long enough to analyze according to the following criteria was transcribed approximately, without attempting phonemic accuracy. Thirty-seven conversations obtained with fourteen children were included in the analysis. The only conversations excluded were those that were too brief, and several from children who had recorded frequently. In the latter cases, the conversations selected were those that varied most in length of responses and time of recording—early in the year, late, and intermediate. The number analyzed from each child is indicated in table 2.

Each conversation was analyzed in the following manner by a research assistant, who prepared a transcript of the tapes.[4] First, every continuous verbalization by the observer was noted and classified as either a question or a comment. Any verbalization the assistant did not recognize as a question in standard English was classified as a comment. This was accurate, since the observer used only standard English. A verbalization was treated as a single question, no matter how many separate questions it contained. When a verbalization contained both a comment and a question, it was treated as a question in the analysis. Examples of comments and questions are provided in the protocol on pages 314-315. The comments illustrated there are typical. In a few cases they consisted of a repetition of the child's phrase, followed by "yeah."

The question or comment was regarded as the start of a unit and the child's response to it as the end of that unit. A response was considered to be any verbalization by the child that followed a given question or comment and continued until the observer spoke again, unless the observer's speech coincided with that of the child and did not cause him to pause. On the few occasions on which this occurred, the observer's interruption was ignored in the analysis that

---

[4] This analysis was carried out by Ann Berens, who contributed as well to the development of other codes not included in the present report.

Protocol

Line	Length	Interrupts child's response
16 Q YEAH, AND THAT'S WHEN YOU SEE IT, SEE YOUR HOUSE, HUH?		No
Yeah, an the dog no bite me.	1	
17 Q IT'S RIGHT NEXT TO J——?		Yes
Next by J—— granma.	1	
18 Q NEXT BY J——'S GRANMA?		Yes
Next by J—— papa.	1	
19 C YEAH, YEAH, THAT'S RIGHT.		No
Any everytime I touch the dog nose the dog no bite / an my mother come up / an my mother pick up flower for the graveyard, / an my mother said the, uh,	1	
dog go away / an the dog no go away.	4	
20 C UM-HUH.		Yes
Say, the dog just stand there by that, um, fence.	1	
21 Q WHEN DID SHE PICK THE FLOWERS? JUST TODAY, OR YESTERDAY? HMM?		No
I don't know.	1	
22 (Omitted because of blank space on tape)		
23 Q YEAH, TO THE GRAVEYARD, HMM?		(Omit)
Yeah, I got my sister, my aunty an only two dead, / an my other sister.	2	
24 Q ARE THEY DEAD?		No
Yep.	0	
25 Q DID YOU GO TO THE GRAVEYARD, TOO?		No
Huh?	(Omit)	
26 Q DID YOU GO TO THE GRAVEYARD, TOO?		(Omit)
Only my mother wen.	1	

Protocol (Continued)

Line		Length	Interrupts child's response
27 C	OH.		No
	Us, cause us was, uh, home an, an pau graveyard, uh, my N——, my sister N—— go buy one cake, / an us had cake. / First us go eat, / us n'eat / an us go bath, / an us cn eat cake an ice cream.	6	
28 C	YEAH.		No
	An I got one half-dollar.	1	
29 Q	YOU DO?		Yes
	I can tell my mother I like my dollar for buy something.	1	
30 Q	THAT FEELS GOOD, DOESN'T IT, WHEN YOU HAVE A HALF-DOL-LAR?		No

Key
Q = Question
C = Comment
OBSERVER'S REMARKS IN CAPITAL LETTERS
Child's remarks in small letters

followed. A response was considered to be a response to a question if it followed a question, unless it ignored the question completely, in which case it was grouped with responses to comments. This was done in order to refer to responses to questions as *answers* and also because such responses gave no evidence that the question had been processed by the child. All of the responses to questions illustrated in the protocol were considered to be answers.

The next step was to assign a score to the length of each response. A score of 1 was assigned to each part of a response that could be interpreted by ignoring conjunctions as an independent declarative statement in standard English without referring to a preceding question. Parts with compound subject or object and a dependent clause were scored 1. A score of 1 was given to a single phrase or even a single word, if it were an adequate answer to a question, except for affirmatives and negatives. The latter were scored 0, as were exact repetitions of a child's own preceding utterance of two or more words and any other utterances not meeting these criteria. All scores for a single response were totaled. Examples are provided in the protocol. The first part of the response to line 27 was scored 1 rather than 2 because the phrase "cause us was home, an pau graveyard" is not an understandable declarative statement independent of any question preceding it. "My sister go buy one cake" is such a statement. The child may have meant, "when we were finished at the graveyard, my sister . . .," but the scoring is the same, whether this assumption is made or not. The response to line 19 should have a total score of 5, but because we were interested in the length of responses when a new topic was introduced, the parts related to this new topic were counted separately. In this response the child shifts from talking about the dog biting him to talking about the visit to the graveyard. It would be preferable to score length on the basis of rules for this dialect, but such rules were not known.

The analysis described so far is sufficient to provide the data that appear in table 2, comparing the average length of responses to questions and to other verbalizations. Consideration of the data in the protocol leads, however, to the thought that some of the child's intended responses may have been cut off by the observer's comments or questions, and if responses to questions were cut off more often than other responses were, this alone could explain the results in table 2.

To check this possibility a further analysis was carried out, which was intended to estimate whether any response may have been interrupted by the observer. This estimate was based solely upon content. No attempt was made to estimate interruptions on the basis of oral criteria, except in the case of simultaneous speech, mentioned above. Each response was compared with all following responses to determine whether any of the latter could be construed as continuing an idea contained in the former. Thus, the idea mentioned in the response to line 28 is expanded in the response that follows line 29; the last idea expressed in the response to line 19 is continued in the response to line 20; and so on. Whenever this occurred, the comment or question that followed the response being compared was considered potentially, at least, to have interrupted that response. This judgment was not made, however, if the association occurred in a subsequent response that the rater judged would not have occurred in the absence of a question by the observer. For example, the child's correction of his response to line 17, which is given in line 18, would have been judged as having been caused by the question in line 18 were it not for the fact that the child had similarly corrected himself in the response that preceded line 16, which reads in part, "if you see J—— granma, no, no, J—— granma, papa stay, you go over there. . . ." This method of analyzing possible interruptions does not include the possibility that a child might never have mentioned an idea again because of one question or a series of questions. But there is no way of knowing when this happened.

In ten conversations from eight children there were sufficient data to compare the length of answers and other responses when they were interrupted and when they were not. In seven of these conversations answers are shorter than other responses when both are not interrupted, removing interruption as a factor accounting for the shorter length of answers, to the degree that interruptions have been validly assessed. In one of the remaining conversations, interrupted answers are not shorter than those that were not interrupted, again indicating that some other factor may be involved. In only two of ten conversations are the facts in accord with the hypothesis: i.e., answers are shorter than other responses only when interrupted, and interrupted answers are shorter than those that are not interrupted. Moreover, in nine of the ten cases answers are no more likely to be interrupted than other responses. There is no positive evidence, therefore, that interruptions by the observer will account for the shorter length of answers, compared with other responses.

Table 2 reports the average length of each child's answers to questions and other responses. Separate conversations for each child have been averaged, and the number of responses on which each average is based is given in parentheses. As the analysis of variance shows, the greater length of other responses is statistically reliable.

TABLE 2
Mean Length of Responses

No. of Conversations with each child	Answers		Other Responses	
4	0.85	(58)	1.75	(30)
4	1.62	(16)	4.70	(20)
2	0.35	(14)	1.40	(14)
4	1.63	(44)	2.53	(48)
3	1.00	(10)	2.30	(13)
2	0.60	(21)	1.50	(16)
3	1.53	(56)	2.07	(38)
1	0.50	(4)	4.00	(2)
4	0.83	(61)	1.23	(39)
3	1.27	(46)	2.43	(27)
2	1.15	(18)	3.90	(17)
1	1.25	(4)	2.11	(9)
1	1.50	(4)	6.00	(1)
3	0.77	(15)	2.10	(21)
Mean	1.06		2.72	
Standard deviation	0.43		1.40	

Summary of Analysis of Variance

Source of Variance	Sum of Squares	Degrees of Freedom	Mean Square	F Value	Probability
Total	47.11	27			
Subjects	17.57	13			
A vs. O	19.17	1	19.17	24.02	<.001
Error	10.37	13	.798		

Key
A = Answers
O = Other responses
Note: Numbers in parentheses are the number of responses on which the mean is based.

More detailed comparisons, not shown in the table, were carried out. Thus, one kind of response included in the other response category was the one that began the recording. These were called *initial responses*. They were analyzed separately because they were different from other responses in at least two respects: (1) the child had a longer time to prepare them than in the other cases, and (2) they were basically responses to an invitation to speak. Also, questions were classified as yes/no or wh– questions. The former are all of those that could be answered by a yes or no. The latter begin with a word like *what, where,* or *how,* and cannot be answered with a yes or no. The length of answers to each type of question can be compared with the length of initial responses and/or the residual category (responses to comments and responses that ignored questions) in seventy-four instances. In fifty-eight of these seventy-four comparisons answers to each type of question were shorter than each of the other types of response. Thus one can conclude generally that answers to questions are briefer than other responses.

Competence in Production of Question Forms

Another reason for the minimal length of answers to questions asked by adults in this study might be a difficulty in comprehending question forms in standard English, which was spoken by the teacher and the observer. Evidence presented here indicates that the most common structure of questions in the children's speech is different from that common in Standard English. The evidence summarized in table 1 is consistent with such a hypothesis: children respond volubly to one another's questions because they are familiar with the forms, while those volunteering answers when not called upon in class may be the ones who are more competent in handling the form of questions in standard English.

Evidence of comprehension is provided when a child produces a given question form. If a child is capable of producing a question with a certain form, the rules of language are such that he is capable of interpreting questions of that form syntactically, although it does not follow that he lacks such an ability if he fails to produce the form himself. Briefly, the evidence presented here indicates that the children of two classes rarely produced questions that inverted subject and verb. But a few did so occasionally, and these children do not appear to have produced longer answers to questions than some who did not give evidence of such competence. Thus, the brevity of answers to questions does not appear to be a consequence of failure to comprehend standard English questions.

All of the recorded conversations with the observer in Class One during both years, already described, were searched for questions produced by the children, and a few were added from verbatim notes of observations. As already noted, these children produced about fifty-nine questions during this time, not counting "Huh?" and "What?" The children in Class Two produced forty-four questions in one circumstance. This was during the administration of the Oral Production Test II, developed by the Dade County Board of Education in connection with the Miami Linguistic Readers. The observer, who in this class had participated at frequent intervals in classroom and playground activities, administered the test during the last month of school.[5]

The test consists of a series of six cartoon pictures depicting a boy and his father going fishing and the family meal that follows. The situations depicted were understandable on the whole, and aroused interest, as evidenced by the requests to take the book home and the number of narratives that were volunteered. Each child looked at the pictures and talked about them with the observer first. After talking about the pictures the children were asked a series of standardized questions. Their answers, together with everything they said in the situation, were recorded. These recordings were likewise searched for questions they asked.

The questions asked by the children of both classes are summarized in table 3 according to their form. More complex questions in standard English involve an ordering of subject and verb inverse to that of declarative sentences, plus such additional words as auxiliary verbs and/or wh– words (see Bellugi, 1965; Klima and Bellugi, 1966). Forms 1 and 2 in table 3 are not of this type, although some of them, such as "You mean this hand?," are forms used in standard English. The point is that forms 1 and 2 provide no evi-

---

[5] I am indebted to Stoughton K. White for collecting these data. Vi Mays transcribed the children's questions and contributed other analyses of these data.

TABLE 3
Frequency of Question Forms Produced by Children

Form	Type of Question		
	Yes/No		Wh–
1. S or V lacking	get swings (14/44)		
	(9/59)		
2. a. S + V + (O)	(16/44)		(5/44)
	(31/59)		(4/59)
	I not going hear		how come they no put the house in
	at's bird, fish, yeah		what you talking
	you mean this hand		about
b. (O) + S + V			what question he is asking
			(1/44)
3. Aux + S + V + 0	can I take off (8/44)		
	your eyeglass (6/59)		
4. Wh– + aux + S			what's she doing (0/44)
+ V + O			(3/59)
5. Wh– + O + V + S			what kind is this (0/44)
			(2/59)
6. Wh– + V + NP			what's your mail- (0/44)
			box number (4/59)

Key
(—/44) = Number produced in oral test situation, Class Two
(—/59) = Number produced in recorded conversations, Class One
S   = Subject
V   = Main verb
O   = Object
Aux   = Auxiliary verb
NP   = Noun phrase

dence that the child can produce more complex forms of questions; in fact, the large majority of questions asked by children in both groups were of this form. More complex forms (3–6 in the table) were produced, however, nor was this a result of hearing such questions in the oral test situation. Indeed, more of the complex question forms, particularly of the wh– type, were produced in conversations than in the oral test situation.

These findings are generally similar to those reported by Bellugi, *et al.* (see Cazden, 1970), except that auxiliary verb and subject are not always inverted in yes/no questions by these children. For example:

I can go fishing with you, okay?
Dey guys can play?
They don't kick?

This is a stage characteristic of younger children, according to Klima and Bellugi (1966). This finding, like the inversion of auxiliary verb and subject by some children, may reflect individual differences in rate of development.

Children who produced the more complex forms of standard English questions were no more productive in their answers to questions, however, than those who did not produce such questions. Questions of forms 3–6 were produced by six children during the twelve months of recorded conversations. Data on the length of answers to questions are available for four of the six. As table 4 shows, these four were no more likely than the other children to attempt to answer questions, or to produce longer answers. It may be that the children who did not produce the more complex question forms were as competent in comprehending them. In any case, the evidence does not support the hypothesis that the children failed to answer productively because they did not comprehend the standard English forms of questions addressed to them.

TABLE 4

Use of More Complex Question Forms and Productivity of Answers

Type of Question Used by Child	Average Length of Answers				Percent of Questions Eliciting an Answer		
	< 1.0	1.0–1.4	1.5+	(Total)	< 90	90–100	(Total)
Number of children using more complex questions	2	0	2	(4)	1	3	(4)
Number of children not using more complex questions	4	4	2	(10)	5	5	(10)

Implications for Teaching Hawaiian Children

Since the study was undertaken originally in an attempt to analyze problems in learning to read, data were systematically collected on the children's performance in regularly assigned tasks that were supposed to prepare them to learn to read. Science Research Associates, Inc., had published at the time three booklets of Reading Readiness exercises that were used by the teacher as a basis for tape-recorded lessons. In these lessons the teacher gave the instructions contained on a page of one of the booklets: for example, to mark the picture corresponding to a word spoken, the first of two events in a presumed sequence, the larger of two items, the one with wheels, etc. The children had individual copies of the page in front of them. After playing these tapes, or occasionally instead of playing them, the observer would review the task with a group of four to ten children, ask questions intended to elicit information about the items pictured, answer requests for information, and repeat the correct answers several times.

This ideal description should all be qualified by the phrase "if possible." The lessons were not very successful, especially with the less able children, and became less so as the year progressed. There were many reasons for this, including cultural unfamiliarity with many of the items (e.g., medieval castles, creamers, igloos), phonological interference (e.g., *towel* vs. *tower, glass* vs. *glasses*), and certain motivational factors, such as the children's preference for initiating and completing tasks on their own and their dislike of paying attention as a group to an adult giving instructions.

In view of the many potent sources of problems in this task, it is interesting to note that the children's individual performances correlated to a marked degree with the volubility of the narratives they recorded during the conversations analyzed earlier, but their volubility in answering questions in conversations did not. Performances on the Reading Readiness tasks were recorded immediately following the instruction described above, in response to invitations and urgings by the observer. Each answer was elicited with a question. If a child answered incorrectly, the observer repeated the question until the child answered correctly, or failed to answer. Each child's score for the test was the number of correct answers as a percent of the number of questions asked.[6] From two to five tests were recorded for each of thirteen children who also recorded in conversations. The percent of correct answers on each test were averaged. One measure was limited to those tests in which the child was in the first half of the children recording their answers. A second measure included all of his tests.

The correlation between the length of narratives and the first of the two measures is .50, while that between the length of responses to questions and the same measure is .10. With thirteen cases a correlation of .55 is significant at the .05 probability level.[7] We can conclude that, when agreeing to record during the first half of a testing session, the children who tell longer narratives tend to be the ones who give more correct identifications to the pictures. This might be interpreted as due to a greater willingness to talk with the adult, or to greater vocabulary. In either case the child's ability seems to manifest itself in narrative, rather than in response to individually directed questions from adults.

Observations in several classrooms comprising Hawaiian and part Hawaiian teen-agers in other parts of the state suggest that the success of teaching techniques is related to whether or not they take advantage of the behavior patterns that have been described. One observer writes as follows of a teacher, herself part Hawaiian, who succeeds in eliciting extensive communication from a class of such students:

There was no direct questioning of individual students and most questions were asked of the entire group. All responses were absolutely voluntary; no one was forced to say anything. Voluntary responses were very good, and often students would blurt out an experience or an answer without being recognized by the teacher. There were instances when students talked continuously without anyone being recognized (Chong, 1969).

This teacher is obviously taking advantage of the children's preference for relating to adults as a group, and using it creatively.

---

[6] Robert P. Edmondson very kindly volunteered to score these data.

[7] This measure was chosen in order to control the effects of practice resulting from observations of others' answers. Overall scores did not correlate as highly, perhaps because of such an effect. Placement in reading groups correlated in the same way, but not to a significant degree.

Compare the following teacher in a rural school, who knows her part Hawaiian pupils equally well, and makes use of their fear of individual recitations and supervision to keep them under control:

The teacher directs the class to the blackboards. L. was the first at the board as if their mental powers were working. However, they were them if they were in trouble. T. and M. began scribbling numbers on the board as if their mental powers were working. However, they were actually faking around, completely lost, not knowing what to do. Occasionally, both boys would take a glance at L. to see if he completed his problem. But L. was also lost. M. was really worried, now that L. couldn't help him. He turned to me and signalled. But before I could assist him, the teacher was on him. Now he was really lost, quite frightened, mumbling numbers to himself (Riola, 1969).

This technique not only fails to promote learning, it may also fail as a means of maintaining control if students respond collectively, especially if the teacher does not understand the functions and purpose of the students' behavior. Thus, a "special class" comprising part Hawaiian children, who were selected because of discipline problems, uses its collective strength in the following manner, according to Louise Bernstein:

When the group as a whole is relating to a teacher in the class context, the humor relationship is that of ridiculer (class) to ridiculed (teacher). The children enjoy making the teacher the brunt of their jokes, confusing her and pushing her to the breaking point. The teacher is definitely shown that she is not part of the in-group. . . . Joking behavior is also used to show the authority and each other that they (the children) are not "selling out" (Bernstein, 1969, pp. 26–27).

. . . the class bears the stigma of the word "special." . . . Most of the students in the special class feel that they really are "dumb-dumbs." So, to make up for this, they take pride in their physical strength. . . . The visible signs of their stigma (such as clothing and language differences) which set the Hawaiians apart from the other students, are often used as symbols of defiance (Bernstein, pp. 28–29).

Obviously, preferred patterns of communication are not the only cause of the adaptation described in these last paragraphs. But if the hypothesis advanced here is correct, then it is a reasonable inference that failure to make proper use of them has played some part in producing the sense of irrelevance that grows in all too many Hawaiians as they go through the grades. When they choose to defend themselves from this world in which they constantly fail, they rely upon means familiar to them from childhood—they force the adult to relate to them as a group. It is in this context that one can understand the frequent complaints of Hawaiian children that teachers "pick on me" and "just scold us." The former means simply that individuals are involuntarily selected for specific attention. The latter is a reflection of the struggle for control that goes on between the teacher and the group.

Bibliography

Bellugi, Ursula. "The Development of Interrogative Structures in Children's Speech." In Klaus F. Riegel (ed.), *The Development of Language Functions.* Report No. 8. Ann Arbor: Center for Human Growth and Development, University of Michigan, 1965.

Bernstein, Louise. "Humor as an Indicator of Social Relationships Among Twenty Hawaiian Children." Senior honors thesis presented to the Department of Anthropology, University of Hawaii, 1969.

Boggs, Stephen; and Gallimore, Ronald. "Employment." In Ronald Gallimore and Alan Howard (eds.), *Studies in a Hawaiian Community.* Pacific Anthropological Records No. 1. Honolulu: Bernice P. Bishop Museum, 1968.

Cazden, Courtney. "Children's Questions: Their Forms, Functions and Roles in Education." *Young Children* 25 (1970):202–220.

Chong, Edison M. C. Term paper for Anthropology 480(3), University of Hawaii, December 1969.

Gallimore, Ronald; MacDonald, W. Scott; and Boggs, Stephen. "Education." In Ronald Gallimore and Alan Howard (eds.), *Studies in a Hawaiian Community.* Pacific Anthropological Records No. 1. Honolulu: Bernice P. Bishop Museum, 1968.

Howard, Alan. "Adoption and the Significance of Children to Hawaiian Families." In Ronald Gallimore and Alan Howard (eds.), *Studies in a Hawaiian Community.* Pacific Anthropological Records No. 1. Honolulu: Bernice P. Bishop Museum, 1968.

Klima, E. S.; and Bellugi, Ursula. "Syntactic Regularities in the Speech of Children." In J. Lyons and R. J. Wales (eds.), *Psycholinguistic Papers: The Proceedings of the 1966 Edinburgh Conference.* Edinburgh: Edinburgh University Press, 1966.

Labov, William; Cohen, Paul; Robbins, Clarence; and Lewis, John. *A Study of the Non-Standard English of Negro and Puerto Rican Speakers in New York City.* Final report, Cooperative Research Project No. 3288. Washington, D.C.: Office of Education, 1968.

Riola, Bernard C. Term paper for Anthropology 480(3), University of Hawaii, January 1969.

Slobin, Dan I. (ed.). *A Field Manual for the Cross-Cultural Study of the Acquisition of Communicative Competence.* Berkeley: Department of Psychology, University of California, 1967.

The 'Silent' Indian Child

Styles of Learning— Styles of Teaching: Reflections on the Education of Navajo Children

Vera P. John
Yeshiva University

The poor receive in an exaggerated form the worst a society has to offer. The quality and prices of meat are abominable in ghetto areas; mail-ordered clothes disintegrate when washed in hard water by the rural poor. In the Southwest, the noisiest and least shady parts of town are where the Chicanos have to live. The education of Indian children reveals the worst distortions of the educational fads that plague our public school system.

The fact that Indian life is so alien to the Anglo teachers intensifies their efforts to remodel children. They attempt to shape the children's attitudes, skills, and classroom behaviors into familiar patterns. These efforts, whether carried out by gentle coaxing, programmed reinforcement, or harsh and punitive methods, result in a lack of participation on the part of Indian children in their own education and in a high drop-out rate. It is not my intention to detail, once more, the facts of Indian miseducation, ably summarized in Senator Kennedy's report of Congressional hearings on this topic (1969). Instead, I would like to raise specific questions concerning the use of language in Indian classrooms—questions relevant to both form and function in communication.

The major goal of education for Indian children, according to most of their teachers, is to instruct them in the English language.

Whether they are speakers of a tribal tongue, or speakers of "Indian style" English, the objectives are usually described as developing in these children speech that is both unaccented and characterized by standard grammer. It is in pursuing this goal of fluency in English that the analogy described above, concerning life in poor communities, is most applicable.

The boarding school child is confronted with a chain of language-oriented experiences. Frequently, his meals are served on the condition that he asks for the right dishes in the right way. Choral speaking, pressures for oral performance at school celebrations, all add up to an inexorable demand: he is expected to become a fluent speaker of the national language and thus, it is believed, a well-adjusted member of mainstream society.

Styles of teaching are, in part, an expression of the goals of education. When working with Indian children, educators choose methods of instruction that zero in on what they wish to accomplish instead of methods that reflect the developmental stages of children or respond to the specific features of tribal life. Thus, exercises in language become the ever-present reality in reservation schools.

In this paper, my particular interest is to explore the way Navajo children learn, and how they are taught. The clash of cultures is most obvious, to me at least, in the schools of the vast Navajo reservation. The more subtle conflicts in instruction and communication that occur in other tribal settings are described by Robert Dumont for Plains Indians ("Learning English and How to Be Silent: Studies in Sioux and Cherokee Classrooms," page 344), and Susan U. Philips for the Indians of the Northwest ("Participant Structures and Communicative Competance: Warm Springs Children in Community and Classroom," page 370).

Children on Navajoland

Carol Bitsui evokes a traditional Navajo childhood in an oft-quoted poem:

I was raised on the reservation in a hogan with neither running water, nor a button to press for warm heat. My bed was cradleboard, a sheepskin and the earth. My food was my mother's breast, goat's milk, berries, mutton, and corn meal. My play partners were puppies, the lamb and lizards (Steiner, 1968, p. 29).

The varied life of the young Navajo child is finding its way into stories and tales. In *The Black Mountain Boy* (1969) a six-year-old boy's responsibilities for his family's sheep are described in amusing detail. Though by urban standards life is poor on the reservation, many children raised in that vast area of desert and mountains develop slim and strong bodies, and they learn to care for animals at an early age. Through these efforts they develop a keen and observant eye for motion, forms, and shades. The Navajo educator, Herb Blatchford, described to me how the children of his tribe learn by looking. They scrutinize the face of adults; they recognize at great distances their family's livestock. They are alert to danger signs of changing weather or the approach of predatory animals.

Impressions formed by these careful observations are lasting. Art instructors working with young children or young adults laughingly complain that once you give a Navajo something to draw on he will inevitably sketch a horse. Any visitor to the reservation will concur; these gradeful and ever-present animals leave one with a dramatic memory.

There is considerable agreement, then, on the part of social scientists, educators, and others that the Indian children of the Southwest are visual in their approaches to their world. Mrs. Anita Pfeiffer, principal of the Rough Rock Demonstration School, found her pupils precocious in their prereading skills. They display above-average visual discrimination and fine motor coordination. Though research is limited relevant to this observation, experienced early childhood teachers seem to concur with Mrs. Pfeiffer.

Teachers have sometimes noticed that 5-year old (Indian) children use scissors as well as 3rd graders, that their preschool children understand how to use modeling materials, and show other evidence of fine motor coordination (Feldman and Dittman, 1970).

And in a study done in the thirties, Wayne Dennis (1940) found above-average performance on the part of Hopi children on the Draw-A-Man test (see Cazden and John, 1971).

In my own wanderings on and around the reservation, I am

always struck by how freely Navajo children play. Whether they are in front of their hogans or eating in a restaurant in an off-reservation town, the children move around and touch things, enjoying their explorations. Their parents allow them this freedom, even in unfamiliar settings, where they themselves are not necessarily at ease. Older children assume responsibility for younger children, without bossiness, the young Indians use gestures and touch, seldom words.

Navajo children who have not experienced severe environmental stresses (malnutrition and frequent illnesses) avidly absorb the world by sight and touch. Their elders give them considerable leeway in exploring the mountains and mesas; Navajos, young and old, walk and ride great distances. In kindergarten classrooms that are tailored to their developmental needs, reservation children enjoy all the materials (blocks, trucks, etc.) that invite active manipulation. Though attentive to the teacher's voice, these children tend to watch her actions.

Our knowledge about the functions of language in the Navajo home are limited. In some of the traditional communities, during long, cold nights young children hear their grandfathers tell the winter tales. But many other children, living in more modern, often BIA communities, are not exposed to the rich lore of their forefathers, and older children are usually in boarding school during the winter when the tales are told. While listening to each other's words with respect and patience is a crucial part of Indian cultures (witness the seven-hour board meetings at the Navajo-controlled school of Rough Rock), in the life of children it is actions that tend to bring special rewards and attention. In contrast with urban middle-class children, whose realm of effective operations upon their environment is limited, and who are expected to display their growing skills through language, the Navajo child is a doer.

Schooling on the Navajo Reservation

The tall water tower of the Bureau of Indian Affairs school dominates the landscape in many sparsely populated areas of the reservation, and around the school cluster the small, neat, identically built houses of the teachers. A fence frequently surrounds the "compound" to protect the grass and the buildings from livestock. Some parents and their young children approach these alien buildings with trepidation and fear.

Indeed, the physical appearance of the school has such a striking impact on the pupils that it plays a significant part in the socialization process they undergo. It assails as well the outsider who comes to work in the "compound." In the bilingual and bicultural kindergarten program, initiated a couple of years ago by the BIA and the National Association of Education for Young children, some steps were taken to minimize the awesome effects of the school. Members of the Dilcon community built a brush shelter and a hogan in the barren play yard of the compound. Seated on sheepskins in the brush shelter, parents and their children first met the staff and shared some food.

My own introduction to the education of Navajo children was in a somewhat different setting. As a consultant to a summer institute held in Gallup, I joined with others in observing a demonstration class in English for children in the early grades. The room was carefully structured to ensure the children's maximum participation in verbal activities. The lesson being taught consisted of phrases, valiantly varied by a gifted teacher, such as: "Mrs. X teach*es* every day," in contrast with "Mrs. X is teach*ing* right now." The program was aimed at teaching patterns of English that are particularly difficult for native speakers of Navajo.

Language lessons are introduced as the most valued aspect of education, but they are presented in ways that contradict aspects of Navajo children's preschool life. The shape and cold feel of the buildings in which they live and are taught deprive them of sensory impressions they are used to: the look of the sky, the feel of the wind, the smell of smoke. I was struck, watching children during my first summer out West, how often the little ones clustered around each other, touching their buddies' hair and arms or holding hands even during lessons. This is one of the ways in which they keep literally in touch with the familiar.

In class, the words frequently seem empty of meaningful content; in order to strengthen the connection between the words and motion, children are asked to accompany "their phrase" with a "favorite" activity.

In contrast with the pressures of this approach, aimed at changing the Navajo child into a potentially urban citizen, are the approaches of the Rough Rock Demonstration School. Their goal is to respond to the educational needs of the surrounding Navajo communities. In the process of attempting to fulfill these needs, the school has developed some important innovations in Indian education.

Though Teaching English as a Second Language (TESL) was part of the early program of the Navajo-controlled school, it has given way, more and more, to bilingual instruction. At present, the development of the native tongue is the educational foundation of the school. The Navajo teachers on the staff are developing their own curriculum materials; the aides are acquiring literacy skills in their native tongue at the Navajo Community College. Though the school is housed in typical BIA buildings, changes have been brought to the physical plant as well. A large corral for horses and cows borders the western end of the "compound"; hogans built for community programs furnish a welcome relief from the monotonous rows of neat little houses. A specially designed science building, whose modern architecture has been combined with native plants and materials, is the pride of the campus.

But schooling is not limited to the main campus of the Rough Rock Demonstration School. A summer school for children who live on top of a hard-access mesa was initiated a couple of years ago. In the midst of a traditional Navajo community with no electricity or running water, teachers live in tents surrounding the school, which is held in brush shelters. A bus driver of exceptional skill makes daily trips with food, water, movies, and other essentials. Often, a strong wind blows through the brush-shelter classrooms. The children cluster around their teachers, who have learned to develop more direct ways of teaching in this environment than they were taught in their training institutions.

The intimacy of the brush shelters contrasts with the many classrooms I have seen on the reservation. Instead of the physical and emotional separation heightened by the distance between rows of pupils' desks and the teacher's desk, everybody in these summer shelters works around the same table. A single blackboard is used by teachers and students alike. The Navajo children, who have been described as shy, are alert and vocal in this familiar environment.

Throughout the day, sheep and horses wander from pasture to water trough in front of the "classroom." At lunchtime, some parents join their children. They ask questions about their children's work and are answered by the teachers, who speak Navajo. They pick up books, are offered translations; in this environment, the attempt to bring school and home together is no longer a slogan.

Another program, which reflects strong parental participation, is the home-study week. This approach is of particular interest in our discussion of styles of learning. Children return to their homes (whether they live on campus or commute) during a period when home chores are light and the parents have time to teach. Each child is accompanied by a staff member, who works out with the parent the specifics of the program during the home-study week. During this week children explore with their parents, learning about medicinal plants, observing carefully the shape and color of many things they have never paid attention to before. They learn to recognize such plants as *Ch'il dilvesii,* or bottlebrush, the root of which is boiled in water and used in the cure of colds, fevers, and sugar diabetes. Learning by careful observation is a dominant mode of adjustment for the many people who live close to nature, and the child who returns to Rough Rock after his home-study brings back with him a freshness and curiosity that often gets blunted in the best of schools where classroom teaching is the order of the day.

Words and Thoughts and the Education of Navajo Children

In contrasting different approaches to teaching Navajo children, we become aware of some new questions concerning the role of language in instruction and the role of language in the individual cognitive development of the reservation child.

Children whose language is dramatically different from that of their teachers are believed to suffer from deficits of thought as well as communication. The best-known expression of this notion is found in the writings of Bereiter (1966), whose concern is with low-income Negro children, but a similar set of convictions characterizes many teachers of Navajo children, whose zeal in English instruction resembles that of the missionary bringing the true God to the heathens. The magnitude of resources devoted to the study of the national language (in money and school time) further illustrates the central role of this endeavor in schools for the Navajo.

Beside the political considerations of teaching English to Indians (some of the treaties have included such instruction in their provisions), there are other reasons for its central position in education. The production of language is an overt process, and its acquisition, therefore, is usually thought of in terms of overt practice. The teacher, an undisputed authority in his knowledge of the language, monitors the student's progress by watching for improvements in his syntax and pronunciation. Imitation and repetition, as exemplified by the pattern drills aimed at the accurate reproduction of word endings described above, are considered key factors in the acquisition of English. These methods of teaching also facilitate classroom organization: the children perform together, often in unison.

But is this style of teaching truly beneficial to the Navajo pupil? Contemporary linguists minimize the importance of overt processes of learning in language acquisition. Cognitive principles of hypothesis formation and testing, and the development of receptive competence, are emphasized in the writings of Troike (1970) and Ervin-Tripp (1970). But over and above questions raised by linguists regarding effective ways of teaching a second language to children, I am greatly concerned about the clash of learning and teaching styles brought about by TESL approaches.

If the description of the ways in which young Navajo children learn is correct, that is, that they tend to aproach their world visually and by quiet, persistent exploration, then a style of teaching stressing overt verbal performance is alien to such a child. In contrast, teaching approaches that capitalize upon his own styles of learning might be very effective. A study with Sioux Indian children is of interest in this respect. The Swiss psychologist Gilbert Voyat (1970) worked with six- and seven-year-olds from the Pine Ridge Reservation. His subjects showed the same level of development on Piagetian tasks of cognition (such as seriation, number, and conservation problems) as their European and American peers. As yet, such findings do not seem to affect teachers of Indian children. Most of them appear convinced that their students suffer from severe intellectual deficits; they have arrived at these conclusions through their assessment of the children's verbal performance. The development of educational approaches based upon cognitive competencies specified by Voyat is an alternative well worth exploration.

Though no comparable evidence exists about Navajo children, it is likely that they too will show a high level of performance on Piagetian tasks. In addition to the descriptive evidence presented above, the success of curriculum approaches based on nonverbal approaches (for instance, the ESI pre-science curriculum was found to be effective with first-graders) points to such an inference.

But teachers trained in the TESL tradition are greatly limited in their approach to the development of language and cognition in Indian children, and for that reason this paper will propose some alternatives. In exploring such alternatives it is useful to recognize that the learning of language and the development of cognition have certain intellectual processes in common. The search for commonalities in sorting out the multitude of sense impressions that impinge upon children is one such shared feature of language and cognition. In conservation tasks children learn to ignore irrelevant variables (i.e., the shape of the beakers) when examining the amount of liquid transferred from one container to the other. Similarly, they learn to ignore variations in pronunciation in their attempts to unravel the meaning of words.

The crucial discovery of using language to deepen and express thoughts is much hampered when students are pressured to acquire a second language, and unfortunately the onset of these educational pressures does coincide with a stage of development in which young children learn to use language as a conceptual tool. The seventy percent of Navajo children who lack sufficient command of the English language to handle first-grade work (Spolsky, 1970) are currently being exposed to a TESL approach in learning the national language.

In contrast to the TESL approach, one of the arguments in favor of bilingual education is that it offers an opportunity for non-English-speaking children to develop their native language for the purposes of learning, memory, and thought. Using this method of teaching, the children are not expected to acquire all their subjects in their weak language. Once the native language has become the medium of instruction, English is introduced as a second language.

If such a step is adopted throughout the Navajo reservation, genuine progress could result. However, instruction in the native language by itself does not meet the need of closely meshing styles of learning with styles of teaching. A serious effort is needed to develop generalized knowledge concerning thought and language and to test such notions in work with Navajo children. Stereotyped approaches to thought are not limited to educators of Indian children. Indeed, most psychologists either avoid this area or are wedded to rather simple theories. Most educators and learning theorists assert that the use of language in thought is the only way man develops abstraction. On the other hand, an important approach to cognition, that of the Gestalt theorists, emphasizes perceptual processes. To them, problem solving is a rearrangement of relationships, and the term "I see!" is just one example of the visual nature of cognition. The term "insight" is a further example of such an orientation.

The paucity of tradition that characterizes the study of thought by psychologists (often relegating this topic to philosophers) may account for the limitations of extant approaches. In addition, behavioral scientists tend to choose their own cognitive processes, though unconsciously, as the basis of their theory building. The verbally brilliant Jerome Bruner has developed a model of cognitive growth that culminates in a symbolic-verbal stage. In my own work I have been partial to theories of thought that emphasize the preeminent role of language. But during the last couple of years, I have come to recognize the limitations of such approaches. Many factors, including my learning and teaching experiences on the Navajo reservation, have contributed to an interest in exploring the visual abstract as well as verbal processes of thought.

In an impressive series of experiments, William Rohwer (1969) has shown that verbal and visual processes were equally effective in children's elaborations of paired associate stimuli. If the process is an active, imaginative one, the child remembers what he has to learn many times better than when asked simply to link two words.

The long-standing emphasis upon language, as a dynamic inner process, rings introspectively true to many thinkers. However, some individuals rely on a visual flow of abstract imagery when hard at work on a new idea. Einstein described his own approach as follows:

What, precisely, is "thinking"? When at the reception of sense impressions, memory-pictures emerge, this is not yet "thinking." And when such pictures form series, each member of which calls for another, this too is not yet "thinking." When, however, a certain picture turns up in many such series, then—precisely through such return—it becomes an ordering element for such series, in that it connects series which in themselves are unconnected. Such an element becomes an instrument, a concept. I think that the transition from free association or "dreaming" to thinking is characterized by the more or less dominating role which the "concept" plays in it. It is by no means necessary that a concept must be connected with a sensorily cognizable and reproducible sign (word); but when this is the case thinking becomes by means of that fact communicable (Schillps, 1959, p. 9).

It is difficult to assess how a growing child conceptualizes his world, but it is likely that in every classroom there are some children to whom visual imagery is a powerful tool of fantasy and thought, while other children in the same room may be primarily verbal in their ways of imagining and discovery. Cultural conditions may affect the distribution of the number of children for whom inner vision or inner speech is of primary importance, but too little is known at present to argue definitively for such a relationship.

It is crucial, however, to allow for the development of varied ways of thought in school. Nowhere is this injunction of greater importance than in the classrooms of Indian children, who bring with them a rich oral and visual tradition, an asset seldom understood or developed in their school years.

The ideas that form this paper have been developed over summers working in Dilcon, Greasewood, Gallup, and Rough Rock. And though I firmly believe that there is a need for alternative approaches to the education of Navajo children, some of which are being enthusiastically developed at the Rough Rock Demonstration School, I fought with myself throughout the writing of this paper, questioning my ability as an outsider to observe accurately the flow of life in a culture distinct from my own.

In the near future Indian scholars will have reached a sufficient number so that it will be unnecessary to rely upon the participation of such enchanted strangers to the Navajo reservation as my-self. In the meantime, it is my hope that these observations aimed at contrasting the teaching style of predominantly white teachers and the learning style of Navajo children will receive criticism and correction from my Navajo colleagues.

Bibliography

Bereiter, Carl; Engelman, S.; Osborn, J.; and Reidford, P. A. "An Academically Oriented Pre-School for Culturally Deprived Children." In Fred M. Hechinger (ed.), *Pre-School Education Today*. Garden City, N.Y.: Doubleday, 1966. Pp. 105-137.

The Black Mountain Boy. Rough Rock, Arizona: Rough Rock Demonstration School Curriculum, 1969.

Cazden, Courtney B.; and John, Vera P. "Learning in American Indian Children." In M. Wax, S. Diamond, and F. Goering (eds.), *Anthropological Perspectives on Education*. New York: Basic Books, 1971.

Dennis, Wayne. "The Performance of Hopi Children on the Goodenough Draw-A-Man Test." *Journal of Comparative Psychology* 34, No. 3 (December 1942).

Ervin-Tripp, S. "Structure and Process in Language Acquisition." In James E. Alatis (ed.), *Bilingualism and Language Contract: Anthropological, Linguistic, Psychological, and Sociological Aspects*. Monograph Series on Languages and Linguistics, No. 23. Washington, D.C.: Georgetown University Press, 1970.

Feldman, M.; and Dittman, L. *Curriculum for Indian Children*. Washington, D.C.: National Association for the Education of Young Children, 1970.

Kennedy, Edward. *Indian Education: A National Tragedy—A National Challenge*. Report of the Special Subcommittee on Indian Education of the Committee of Labor and Public Welfare, U.S. Senate. Washington, D.C.: U.S. Government Printing Office, 1969.

Rowher, W. D., Jr. *Language, Race, and School Success*. Unpublished manuscript. Berkeley: University of California, 1969.

Schillps, P. A. *Albert Einstein: Philosopher, Scientist*. Vol. I. New York: Harper Torchbooks, 1959.

Spolsky, B. "Navajo Language Maintenance: Six-Year-Olds in 1969." *Language Sciences*, No. 13 (December 1970): 19-24.

Steiner, Stanley. *The New Indians.* New York: Harper and Row, 1967.

Troike, R. "Productive Competence and Performance." In James E. Alatis (ed.), *Linguistics and the Teaching of Standard English.* Monograph Series on Languages and Linquistics, No. 22. Washington, D.C.: Georgetown University Press, 1969.

Voyat, Gilbert; and Silk, Stephen. "Cross-Cultural Study of Cognitive Development on the Pine Ridge Reservation." *Pine Ridge Research Bulletin,* No. 11 (1970): 50-74.

Learning English and How to be Silent: Studies in Sioux and Cherokee Classrooms

Robert V. Dumont, Jr.

Discussions, questions and answers, dialogues, or informal conversations form such a natural and fundamental part of education that we do not usually think of students deliberately choosing not to talk. When they do, we have few resources to find out what the silence means. Education as we know it stops, and in its place there is something foreign and incomprehensible, taking place almost entirely at the will and discretion of the students.

Over the years, beginning with our first study in Sioux classrooms in South Dakota to our most recent work in Cherokee classrooms in eastern Oklahoma, we have found that student silence characterizes much of what goes on in the formal schooling of American Indian children. It is noticeably present as early as the third grade and is fully and systematically put to use by the seventh and eighth grades. In our first attempts to understand what was taking place, we saw the silence simply as a response to what was not known or understood, a result of language difference, a symptom of fear or shyness, or a trait peculiar to certain cultural groups. As we were to find out later, these were but the most observable and easily understood forms of silence.

344

The Sioux and the Schools

From the first days in the Oglala Sioux classrooms (Wax, Wax, and Dumont, 1964), it was pointed out by many educators that silence was a nerve center of the classroom through which teaching and learning did or did not take place. Education and learning were equated to talking while silence was equated to the absence of learning. At the teacher orientation before school started we were informed about the shyness, fear, indifference, stoicism, unwillingness to compete, and withdrawal of the Sioux students. One factor central to many of the problems was language, their inability to speak and understand English very well, which was attributed to parental indifference to education, and the continued use of the native language in the home. Considerable emphasis was placed on getting students to talk, and if they did, it was necessary to get them to "talk up."[1]

When classes began we did not expect the intensity of the constrained and cautious behavior of the students nor the long and sometimes embarrassing periods of silence. Teachers requested, pleaded with, shouted at, commanded, badgered, and cajoled students to talk. When they did their replies could barely be heard or else the word was mouthed. Most often their answers were little more than "Yes," "No," or "I don't know." Inevitably, the days were long periods of desk work, teacher monologues, or lectures and rhetorical questions. Remarkably, we rarely met a teacher who had given up, who did not try to get her students to talk, to ask questions, or to take an open interest in classwork, but whatever was tried seemed to be of little use.

Our residence in the Indian community allowed us to see that these same children were amazingly different outside the classroom: they were noisy, bold, daring, and insatiably curious. Talking and language were hardly problems once they decided to find out something. If they did not know the right words, they found someone within their ranks who would act as an interpreter; at times, many

---

[1] "Talk up" is the same as "speak loudly." Teachers felt that if they could get their students to talk or read loudly they would learn more. A very similar phenomenon was present with the Cherokees and their teachers.

had to be used in one conversation. Even the very young would engage the non-Sioux speaker in language lessons they kept going with considerable laughter and teasing. Occasionally they would even let it be known that they were closely attuned to what went on in school.

As the observations continued we began to see that the Sioux children had developed an amazingly complex system of communication and control within the classroom. One part of it was nonverbal—a mouthed word, a shift in the body, a gesture, or a glance. The other part was verbal, in both English and Sioux, deftly used so that either noise levels were kept just before the point at which they would warrant punishment or else they were of such a nature that any one person could not be singled out. When they did what the teacher asked they showed neither interest nor excitement. Many times there was no response. When singled out to read or answer questions they could not avoid they did so with hesitancy, constraint, and sometimes fear. Nonetheless, silence governed teaching and learning, representing a student-developed and -controlled tactic that excluded the teacher from almost all student activities and that made school a rather pleasant experience. However, in the absence of adult supervision—by either the teacher or the Sioux parents— they could, at times, be brutal to the weak and those who deviated from the norms of what we could only call the Sioux school society. (This notion is discussed in Dumont and Wax, 1970.)

Quite rightly, language was a major and overwhelming problem, but it was neither Sioux or English but the absence of either. It was quite evident that the children had knowingly decided not to talk. Seeing the difference between the children in school and at home, we came to call their classroom behavior a "mask of silence."

Although there were isolated instances, sometimes lasting no more than a few minutes and never more than half a day, in which students talked with the teacher openly and naturally, we did not find a classroom where student speech was the tenor of student activities. From these isolated instances, we did get some idea of what to expect if they chose to talk, but we had no knowledge of how this came about, how it was sustained, how it affected teaching and learning, or how it was related to silence.

At the end of the Sioux study it was all too easy for us to conclude that the educational system was a near total failure. Like the educators who equated learning to how much students did or did not talk, so, too, did we as social scientists evaluate the quality of education by the degree to which teachers did or did not get their students to talk. It is a common error—perhaps one that comes about because of the complex nature of and the difficulty in dealing with cultural differences when they take place in the classroom. Consequently, because we did not know how to ask the right kind of questions, our understanding and interpretation of silence as a student response or as directly related to their being Sioux kept us from finding out why they used silence and what they used it for.

Disturbed by the absence of alternatives in the classrooms and compelled by the vitality of the Sioux children, we returned the following summer with an experimental community-based educational program to see if the silence of the classrooom could be broken (Dumont, 1964). We lived and taught in the community —everyone talked. But there were times when there was silence as tortuous and incomprehensible as it was in the schools; the normal course of activities, however, was talking and not silence.

From the summer's experience we learned that the more teaching and learning was moved into the cultural complex of the Sioux community, the more students talked, and as it moved within the cultural complex of the school, the more silent they became. This understanding of how the intercultural classroom worked, as general and basic as it was, forced us to see that silence was a result of the teacher-student learning exchange. Conventional ways of exercising authority and other methods of teaching and school definitions of learning once enforced had the potential of exploding a classroom, whether it was in the community or school, into sustained, student-controlled silence.

In order to learn this, we had placed the odds in our favor: residence in community homes, classrooms located in community buildings, community people making up part of the staff, and a constant involvement in community affairs. The possibility for anyone from the school to involve themselves in the day-to-day world of the Indian community was there, but they were bound to the tradition and rules of the school, which remained isolated and apart from the Indian community. We condemned the school for its cultural superiority maintained at the expense of the children; we could run programs such as we did, but we quickly learned they were of little value when they had no effect upon the school. The crucial and overriding question was whether or not the conditions within the school could be changed to the degree necessary to get students to talk. Talking, a continued dialogue between teachers and students, is an intercultural classroom at its best, while silence is indicative of the most dysfunctional form, which excludes cultural differences.

Two Cherokee Classrooms

Three years later, in a study of Cherokee education in eastern Oklahoma, we found many of the same conditions of silence.[2] In one school we came upon a fifth- and sixth-grade classroom where students talked with the teacher. By any standards it was an extraordinary classroom. In comparing this room to the more conventional ones, we began to understand something about the dynamics of silence and how it functioned as a medium of communication to both promote and defeat courses of instruction. Not only was there a "language of silence," but in classrooms where students talked we found that neither Cherokee nor English was the medium of communication, but a language employing conceptual forms from both was used and further developed each class day by teacher and students.

The classroom where students talked was more important to us, but in order to understand what was taking place we had to return constantly to the silent rooms, because it was silence, from any point of view, that dictated the course of education. In the course of our work we found that, in addition to what we already knew about silence, it was also a retreat from the word, intended

[2] This section of the study is a product of the Indian Education Research Project sponsored by the University of Kansas under contract with the U.S. Office of Education according to the provisions of the Cooperative Research Act. The principal investigator was Murray L. Wax, and the field research on rural schools was conducted by Robert V. Dumont, Jr., and Mildred Dickeman, with the assistance of Lucille Proctor, Elsie Willingham, Kathryn Red Corn, and Clyde and Della Warrior. Sole responsibility for this text rests with the author.

to sever communication and to serve as a strategy in a network of student defense needed to deal with the conflict resulting from cultural differences. Employed in this manner the teacher has little control over what students learn and, especially, over how they structure the experience of school. Also, it is not merely a retreat from the word but serves to characterize that reality for which there are no words. Cultural differences are the unknown, the foreign, and the strange; and if there are no words for this in either the students' or teacher's vocabulary there hardly can be any in the language they share. If the teacher is sensitive to this, compromises, and alters the style and methods of teaching, silence can be dispelled. Even then it recurs, but in this case it is functional, serving as a check and balance and a signal within the teaching-learning exchange indicating that there is a momentary difficulty that has to be corrected. In this case, both teacher and students know what it means. Lastly, silence can be the final resolution to the cultural differences. As such, it is as total a breakdown of education as can take place without the school's closing.

Cherokee children take school seriously, much more so than any other children that I have met. To be competent with and have a good mastery of academic skills is vastly important to them. After school older brothers and sisters teach the younger children English or arithmetic. In class they are attentive and remarkedly well disciplined. Second-graders sit for periods of over an hour with near-perfect posture, engrossed in reading or other activities and rarely moving or talking to their neighbors. The restraint and caution learned at home as the proper way of dealing with others governs their behavior, making discipline an almost unnecessary task. Ironically, few teachers understand the cultural implication in this behavior for the classroom, and many explain away the difference in the most simple of terms, in much the same way as one teacher who said about the Cherokee children, "They like to play school."

This teacher, like many of the others in the small, rural, independent schools that serve the Cherokee, is of Cherokee descent but she is not a Cherokee. This is the first thing you are told after being introduced to her and the others like her. The distinction is important, for if one is descended from them one does not have to acknowledge the present-day Cherokee but only what took place in the past—the schools, academies, and other highly developed institutions, the written language, and the literature, which were developed in the East prior to Cherokee removal by President Jackson and rebuilt again in Oklahoma, only to be destroyed again and never rebuilt. It is an admirable past which stops at the Oklahoma destruction for the remaining Southern aristocrats of this area and many of the new middle class, who, if they can, claim it by descent or as a matter of heritage and take excessive pride in that fact. However, they make it quite clear that they are not Cherokee and that they are not related to those people living in the hills. They prefer to call them "Indians," denoting the lower class and the socially unacceptable.

The tree-covered hills protect, forming a cover and camouflage and hiding the Cherokee and the poor whites as well as allowing them to hide. In the towns one does not see Cherokee faces unless one looks closely, but in the hills, away from the main roads and the center of white population, some 10,000 traditional Cherokee live. It is one of the more economically impoverished areas in the country, and the Cherokee find the means to provide for their families only with the greatest difficulty.

Like many poor people they believe that an education will provide economic stability, but very few have either finished school or can find other than low-paying transient or seasonal labor. Many of the rural schools and teachers as well exist on a level close to basic subsistence. In some of these schools closer to the larger towns, a long-practiced system of reverse busing continues as a necessary part of the local economy. The one or two teachers, who have been there most of their teaching careers, drive into the towns, pick up the Cherokee children (competing for them in some cases), and take them to "their" schools. Related to this is the accepted fact that the majority of the students do not go beyond the eighth grade (which is as far as the rural schools go), which very conveniently keeps the majority out of the white town schools.

In addition, consolidation had started during our residence. The teacher who understands no more about her students than that they liked to play school had been the only teacher at a remote school for some time. In the consolidation she had to be rehired, which her new principal did not like, because she had gained a notorious reputation for doing little more than putting in time and drawing salary. Such conditions were more widespread than many realized. We talked with a local college professor (of Cherokee descent), who emphatically stated his concern for the fate of Cherokee students when they would have to go to the consolidated schools. Would it not be better in the present system to get them through the eighth grade and then have them quit, instead of having them drop out earlier?

The rural schools as they now exist are destructive to the children, but in many ways they offer the potential basis for an excellent education. They are small and personal, and usually the teacher is resident in the community. There is time for everyone to become acquainted and to move through the early school years with the same people, which more closely meets the needs of the Cherokee than any consolidated school ever could. But it does not work this way. In the Harris School, which is the subject of the following classroom discussions, Mr. Howard's class is what an intercultural community school could be, while Mr. Miller's is all that should not be done and that which makes these schools and their surrounding communities like small feudal systems. Mr. Miller stated after being ruthlessly used (and allowing himself to be) in a power play in regional politics, "Outside I have no control, but here (community and school) I am the boss."

The Harris School, built in the public works era, has four classrooms from kindergarten through the eighth grades. Later construction was stopped halfway on what was to be a gymnasium and is now the cafeteria as well as doubling for special classes and an auditorium. Like the rest of the school, it shows the wear from too many years of service and not enough funds or concern to make but minor repairs. The school is more than just run down, for everywhere one turns there are marks of indifference. Dust and winter soot coat the walls, and the blackboards should have been discarded years ago. In one room above the board there is a long piece of cardboard sprayed gold for a backdrop to the alphabet, but it reaches only halfway across and the letters spill haphazardly onto the wall. On the closet doors there are curtains of flimsy material reaching halfway to the floor, more cheap pretense than functional. There is not enough space, and Mr. Miller's ten seventh- and eighth-graders meet in the short, wide hallway that connects the old building with the newer cafeteria addition. Children from other classes continually pass through on their way to the rest rooms or to lunch or to special classes, cutting through the narrow aisle separating the desks, but no one seems to mind.

Mr. Miller

At our first meeting, Mr. Miller, who is also the principal, was very much the young executive, firm and authoritative, directing and leading the conversation, and very expertly creating that southern mood of friendliness and distance. He is much like the politicians one hears at the outdoor courthouse rallies, using words in much the same way so that they convey a variety of tones and moods within a few sentences, underscoring, emphasizing, implying, and thereby saying what the words cannot. In the classroom all the words and much of the tone are there, but the vitality and assuredness of unerring right (the mark of a good politician) are missing. He talks too quickly and uses too many different ways of talking, trying to find some way to make the students respond without having to resort constantly to endless questions.

"Well, Townsend won. It was the upset of the year . . . from all the indications it looked like Glasgow would take off with the game but at the half Townsend took off. . . . It was an example of good physical shape. Townsend is smaller and younger. I only wish Bill was here today; this might dawn on him. Townsend's team is juniors and sophomores. This just proves that size makes no difference. It is just the will to win. They had the desire . . . . "

He preaches. It is as if he has come to the conclusion that if they choose not to talk with him they, nonetheless, must listen; the only suitable alternative is to instill a set of rules and guidelines that will give them the fundamentals for a good and moral character. Whether he intends this or not, it comes to mean such, for the many rules and guidelines are not for expediency in learning academic materials but are directed at the person and his performance. How well the student does or does not abide by them is a reflection upon his character.

They have just finished their spelling. Sue: "Is it a miss if you got a capital where it's suppose to be a small letter?"

Mr. Miller: "Is it Alice's?"

"Yes."

"She'll probably get enough wrong anyway." Turning to Alice: "Now, we'll just have to correct that. You're old enough ... You've been making capital letters lately, Alice, and you're old enough to know not to do that." He becomes more stern, "Now, I'll give you a week to correct that. I want you to correct that by next week."

Although he tries to be friendly and easygoing, he suddenly erupts in undue sternness or he pressures a student with an intensity and persistence not warranted. Students become tense, even more quiet, and at times there is something that looks like fear, but they are much too guarded to let it show for long. As much as students are afraid of what they cannot understand, control, or order, so, too, is the teacher. While they protect themselves by their silence, the teacher talks, trying to find through words that reality with which he is familiar and which he can control.

"How many twelfths are there in a whole?"

Debra has been at the board for some time and is unable to do the problem.

Mr. Miller: "How many thirds in a whole?"

Silence.

"How many halves in a whole?" Since he is getting no response from the rapid-fire questions, he changes tactics. "Did she miss it?"

Bob, who is correcting her papers, murmers, "Ya."

"Debra, now, how many halves are there in a whole?" She looks toward the board. "It isn't on the board—just imagine. If you divide something twelve equal times, how many parts are you going to have?"

"Twelve." It is weak and can barely be heard. She now works the problem with Mr. Miller's help. All he was trying to get her to do initially was to take one away from eight.

Mr. Miller: "Let's try another one. Let's write those numbers large. That helps." She starts the problem and he continues, with each statement more intense and pressuring than the one before. "You have borrowed one whole number. The object is to get this numerator large enough to subtract. You are going to have to change this number ... you've got to learn to borrow."

He gives her another problem. "Forget about those whole

numbers, except you have to borrow from them. Then you will have it licked . . . you may add on this side if you want."

Debra has her hand poised at the board. She is figuring in her head, and her hand makes quick, intense gestures. Mr. Miller stares at her intently. You can feel the tension.

Mr. Miller, irritated: "Wait a minute. Wait a minute." His voice softens, as if he has caught his irritation. "That's okay, Debra." He adds brusquely, "Sit down." He erases everything at the board and rewrites the same problem. "We must find the common denominator. What is it, Debra?"

"Twelve" explodes as a conclusion to the intense fear and constraint. It is a tone and a loudness I had not heard before in the room.

He requires Debra to go beyond the limits of Cherokee propriety, to forget the rest of the people in the room. To disassociate one's self from those present without cause is unthinkable and unpardonable, but it is what the teacher requires and he does it with ease. He imposes and intrudes, denying her any respect. The Cherokee value individual autonomy to such a degree that even to stare is considered rude. At the same time, they are trained to the subtlety and nuance of words and tones and moods; for them words and the way they are said convey action—words spoken are acts completed, affecting those with whom one speaks. Mr. Miller's multitude of words, tones, and moods represents not only conflicting emotions and attitudes but also carelessness and incompetency. It is even more perplexing and incomprehensible because of his anger, which appears to have no well-defined cause.

The key to much of what has gone wrong is in his sometimes off-hand but very pointed remarks, which when added up can be called "classroom morality," and in the outbursts of anger when students do not perform according to accepted standards. They are representative of the value he places on education; it is an unquestionable form of socialization that is as much to convey fundamentals for academic proficiency as it is to mold the character. For the Cherokee this is not so; they do not accept the value and norms inherent in character development, and for them school is a place to learn English and a means by which one can gain economic stability. They do not see that the school can make the "good person," and it could only do so if Cherokee norms of the "good person" shaped the form and structure of the educational process.

Nonetheless, academic ability and skill are important to both teacher and students, but the ways in which they are defined and attained by either are disparate enough so that without choice, compromise, and adaptation the behavior of either one becomes an anathema to the other. Each persists, at times ruthlessly, in structuring the classroom so that it is wholly within his own cultural world. Both sides have a somewhat equal power with an equal number of controls at their command so that neither achieves what he wants.

Mr. Miller's classroom is one of the most diffiicult to be in, for even if it is quiet—at times a long breath has a piercing quality—that silence tells more than any number of words can. It is threatening, frustrating, condemning, rage-filled, and it expresses understanding, compliance, acquiescence, and defeat. The slightest motions, a change in posture or a facial expression, are cause for immediate attention, for they mean a shift in the meaning of silence. Every different form that it takes is also a different kind of tension, which is never absent but only varies in intensity depending upon what Mr. Miller does.

The conflict is not open and rarely, if ever, is it brought to a verbal level—the following incident is the closest that it ever came. However, it is only the emotion that is displayed; the cause of that anger remains unknown to Mr. Miller, because it is only conveyed by actions, not words. At first glance it might appear to be game playing, but it is psychologically brutal. Mr. Miller is an expert, but so, too, are the students.

Mr. Miller: "All right, Sandra, I assigned you page thirty in the eighth-grade book. Bring your paper to me and come up to the board."

Sandra, a seventh-grader and considered to be one of the brightest students in school, has been advanced to the eighth-grade math, but since she is behind the regular eighth grade she works alone. At the board she starts a problem, using a multiplication sign instead of the division sign.

"Are you sure that is what you want?"

Sandra erases and writes it again.

"No."

She erases and writes the same sign over, making the chalk click in her quick, brusque manner.

"No, you want this." He writes just as emphatically.

She writes the problem again and leaves a blank between the two numbers. She makes it very clear that she knows what to do and how to do it, and Mr. Miller is keeping her from working. On the next problem she favors the right side of the board, keeping as far away from Mr. Miller as possible, although the board is only about six feet wide.

"Get over here where you have enough room. Don't work in corners. You crowd yourself." She moves over one step but writes the problem in the same place. "Goodness, Sandra, scoot over here." She shifts around but does not really move. Most of the other students are watching now; some talk to each other and others smile.

"Sandra, I'm surprised you are so slow. I should put you back in the seventh grade. Your numbers are so small."

She slams the chalk on the board, writing the numbers large and disproportioned. Some of them cannot be made out, and she erases them with a flash and puts up a new set. She finishes, steps back, and waits. It is correct.

Mr. Miller, rather curtly: "Go ahead, erase. You're not through." It's a warning. She starts on the next problem but has difficulty. In a much softer and confiding tone, he adds, "Okay, Sandra, you do it okay on your paper." With real camaraderie, he instructs: "Let's knock that board down. Erase all that and start over again." It is an absurd comment, because she is mad enough to knock the board down if she could.

She only works faster and continues to say nothing. "Sandra, if you would just proceed slowly, you would save a lot of time." He is almost pleading, his voice low and less insistent than it usually is, but in the next breath it is louder, caustic, and accusing: "And mine, too." She works the problem. It is correct, and he adds in the same tone, "All right, erase. Get to your corner and write in the smallest possible space you can." She does just this.

Unexpectedly, he switches problems on her. There is no warning, and she takes a step back and stops momentarily. "All right, right or wrong, put it down."

The answer is wrong, and he corrects her error. There is a hint of pleasure in his voice as he quizzes her further on decimal equivalents. "Okay. That's enough. Go to your desk."

She sits down and actually glares at him. As he assigns new pages she closes her eyes tightly, and only after he finishes does she open them. She flips the book open, making a loud noise, and circles the page number in a quick, efficient gesture and then slams the book shut. I half expect Mr. Miller to get mad, but just at this moment Bob—it seems deliberate—gets up and goes to the teachers desk. It breaks the tension.

Turning to the eighth grade, Mr. Miller, in good humor and in jovial tone, asks them to take out their arithmetic.

What is behind the words and the silence, illusory and perceived only part of the time by the teacher and student and the effects intensely felt by both but never verbalized, governs the course of education. In this incident, which is but one of many, no one wins; teacher and student are pulled farther apart, and the strategies of preaching and silence are refined and made even more destructive.

Mr. Miller is limited greatly by the lack of special training, which can be obtained nowhere in this area of the country. And while he does sense the nature of his problem, he knows no way to clearly define it nor how to correct his errors in teaching. He commented, "Well, you know that [their speaking Cherokee] is one of my problems. They know all the grammar and rules I can teach them in English. They have a hard time telling you what they mean. They need something more than what I can teach them here. Like Sally and William are fairly intelligent students, and they know everything that's in these books. Why, some of them have been having the same things over and over again. I think these students would like something different."

Out of the long periods of silence, and during his repeated attempts to get them to talk, Mr. Miller would hit upon a way of talking or a word that would get a visible student reaction. It never lasted long, because in the next word or sentence he would cut it off, with the exception of the session reported below. It then became clear that the many modes of student silence were highly refined means of selective interaction, subtly ensnaring the teacher in order to teach him those forms of teaching and learning with which they were comfortable and with which they could work. In doing this they religiously maintained one fast and democratic rule: we do not change unless you do. On those rare occasions when teacher and students found a way of working together, he was in fact "giving them something different." But he either did not know it was happening or else he did not know how he had brought it about.

In the following current events lesson about presidents of the United States, Mr. Miller started by using the word "golly." No one anticipated it. The word is used frequently by Indian people in this area of the country and is expressive of a multitude of emotions—exasperation, disbelief, perplexity, awe—but most often it is used to express the humor for that which is more than inane, absurd, or ridiculous. He said it in a long-drawn-out manner, stressing the last syllable so that no one could miss the meaning. It certainly was not a part of his formal manner and there were a few smiles in the room, guarded and some hidden by a hand covering the mouth, but they were there.

Mr. Miller: "Any of you want to be President, you got to get your gall bladder removed."

Sue actually laughs, and Sandra has the noiseless giggles, but this time she doesn't cover her mouth. I find it amusing. Mostly it is in his tone. He is hitting today—a little smug, a little amazed, a little teasing. He is putting them on.

As he talks, he reaches into his desk and takes out a piece of paper, tears a piece off and hands it to Sue, tears another off and hands it to Sandra, and does the same with the other students. He doesn't say what it's for, but he is relaxed and his actions seem to say, "I'm the teacher and I can do this." It is exciting, and one can accept this strange behavior.

He sits down. "I am going to make you think now . . . ." The suspense is maintained and the silence has a new quality—excitement. "I want you to vote yes or no. Now, I want you to vote whether France—now, I want to word this right . . . ." He stops for a moment and the students watch and wait. He is actually silent, thinking—he is going to give them something, and it will be good because he is working on it. He asks them to vote whether they think France was right in withdrawing from NATO. "Now this is a secret ballot. You don't have to put your name on it. Just write yes or no. I'm going to vote myself, and I'm not going to tell you how I voted. I have to borrow a pencil . . . ."

As soon as he finishes, the students whisper and make signs across the room. As they vote, some make a pretense of covering their work.

Mr. Miller: "Bob, you be our ballot counter."

Bob is a little stunned. He grins and then collects the ballots and places them on the teacher's desk. There is a pause while Bob waits for more instructions, but there are none, and he begins counting.

Mr. Miller tallies them on the board. Two ballots have names, which he casually mentions were not needed. There is nothing behind it except the explanation of a secret ballot. The students take the counting seriously, and it is very quiet. Three students voted no. "I am quite pleased to see that. This means you're thinking and you must have a reason. Now, if I asked you to defend your vote, could you do that? Now, I want you to write your defense, tell me why you voted yes or no. Who doesn't have paper . . . ?"

There is a good deal of talking. They are trying to figure out what to do and what to write. He adds, "You can begin by writing, 'I voted yes or no because . . .' and give your reason." He walks around for a few minutes and then, in a quite jovial tone, tells a joke that is beyond the students, but they smile. He adds, "I just thought that was a good joke to tell you." He knows that it wasn't, but his tone is good spirited. Usually he has a marked tone of condescension, implying, "I'm a good guy, a teacher you can really like."

As they begin to work on their answers he asks me to go outside and have a cigarette with him. There is something of awe and surprise in his voice as he explains that he just wanted to leave them alone to write out their answers. When he returns the students are still talking about their assignment. He collects the papers and begins reading. They have not only read, but they have listened closely to his lecture on NATO. In the middle of his reading, he stops. "These are mature and relevant answers . . . they are brilliant." He gushes, pushing it much too far. When the last one is finished he adds, "I'll have to give you extra credit. That's the little secret. It won't hurt you. The extra A will just be put into your average when I give out the grades. I'm going to give you an extra reward. It's not a reward . . . ." But the damage is done and the magic disappears. They turn to science.

"Did you boys turn in your science tests?"

Silence.

"Did you know the answers?"

Silence.

"You'll have to start studying or there will be a little less basketball."

English is supposedly the language of the classroom, but it serves most often as a medium of conflict. Everyone wants more than words and simple definitions; they want to know how words work and how they can be made to work to solve problems. Language is a nerve center, and it is the only means by which they can resolve the cultural conflict. Students want to learn English, but they can do so only superficially and with nowhere near the competency they desire because they cannot talk. The teacher wants to teach, but he cannot because he preaches and talks too much.

Mr. Howard

Mr. Howard's fifth- and sixth-grade class is radically different; they talk. One of my Indian associates remarked, "I didn't know Indian students talked so much." Another commented, "Those kids are crazy," meaning they did the unexpected, something new and different but appropriate and pleasing. In the classroom it was quite typical to hear the question, "What does that mean?", which I had rarely heard Indian students ask before.

Compared to Mr. Miller, Mr. Howard is subdued, calm, and almost sluggish. Behind it all is an amazing vitality exercised in finding ways of getting students to work together. He said one day that one of the most important things he had to do was to get the students to cooperate. At first I was confused, because one of the myths that has grown out of the education of Indian children is that they are much too cooperative, almost to the exclusion of any competitive activity. After watching his class at work it was clear that he was not talking just about students but about the classroom as one unit, or a "team" of which he was a part. Quite often he used the analogy of a basketball team, which he had once coached, to talk about his teaching. Some players, he said, were skilled in technique, while others, perhaps skillful, too, approached the game more through the use of intellect than technique. Both kinds of players were important, and to get them to work together was a matter of training to be handled largely by the coach. Here the difference ended; he could neither teach nor coach his class in techniques about surmounting cultural and language differences, but he could assist them in finding acceptable ways of working together. Cooperation was lodged within this framework, and the development of it required an environment in which choice and compromise were the norms.

Mr. Howard is talking to Mr. Miller's class, who joined his class while Mr. Miller is at a meeting. "We're going to do our history and you can either follow along or do your assignments. We use the same book here. Now, if you're like Joan" (all of the students Mr. Howard talks about here are in his room), "you'll play possum, pretending like you're following along; or if you're like Jake, you'll sit there and look like you're working but do nothing; but if you're like Harry, you'll just sit there and do nothing."

Jake smiles and Joan looks aghast—someone has caught on to her act. There is a silent smirk on her face. Harry smiles and looks a little astonished. The rest of the students smile and turn to look at those singled out.

Mr. Howard reaches in his desk and pulls out some cards. "We have some cards here for those who do nothing. You can read about gunfighters and Indians, and then you'll know why this became known as a bad land. I'll let you look at these, if you're interested. The fifth and sixth already looked at them . . . . Now, don't cop them or run off with them."

How easy it would be to dismiss these newcomers, but he does not. He welcomes them by telling them what his class is like and what to expect. It is done in a matter-of-fact, understated manner—this is the way things are—that imputes no judgment of right or wrong. He points this out by telling about some of his students; what comes across is that he has considerable respect for those students he named. In admitting they act in this way he is also saying that by conventional standards he may have a poor class and may be a poor teacher—certainly by Mr. Miller's criteria—but those standards don't apply because the students are different. He commented, "The difference with Cherokee kids is their power to associate different things. You got to find out what interests them and run with it . . . I kind of teach by ear."

It is the right to choose from a set of already existing alternatives (but which may not be readily perceived because of cultural difference) that is basic to this class. It allows movement and experimentation that are crucial to the intercultural classroom. When the field of discourse is not predefined but is left open, there is every possibility that students left to their own resources can find the ways to work out the problems and difficulties in alien and foreign modes of learning or work. This is true in the following session— children from tribal societies have great difficulty working in the highly individualized atmosphere of the classroom. Here they are given a choice to change it to a group activity. Their resistance is a form of silence, denoting feelings for which there are no words but that can be acted out.

The discussion is about building split-rail fences without nails. Mr. Howard asks John to demonstrate at the board. At first John is reluctant but goes up, shuffling along. He grabs the chalk, turns around, and smiles uneasily.

Problems cover the blackboard, and Kathyrn says in a stern tone, "Don't erase those problems." The class discusses it, and they decide the first one can be erased.

John begins, starts a triangular figure, erases it, and starts again. He draws some lines very quickly and adds, "Get something to tie the top and the end of the posts there." He goes back to his desk with an uneasy smile.

Kathyrn: "I wouldn't do it that way. You can do it this way." She goes to the board.

Mr. Howard: "Is that the way you would build yours, Harry?"

"Just like John's," Harry states quietly, and then reluctantly goes to the board. He is uneasy, starts several times, erases, and looks around the room with an embarrassed smile. He turns back to the board, shuffles a bit, and then starts to diagram.

Mr. Howard: "Show me an old way."

Harry: "Use nails." He smiles, and I am surprised by his shy humor. He does not know English very well and misses much of what goes on in the class.

John jumps up and draws another diagram. "I think that's the way."

"Kathyrn: "I think I know," and she returns to the board.

John: "There's some near Townsend."

From his desk Harry adds, "I know," and returns to the board. All three work on the diagram.

Kathyrn: "It looks like this at the top," and she tries to draw it.

Finally they get it, but it is only after a good deal of effort. Throughout the exercise the teacher stayed in the back of the room.

Choice is allowing Cherokee methods of teaching and learning to become a part of the educational process. Mr. Miller excludes them; Mr. Howard allows them to operate to the degree that it changes his style of teaching. To understand this, it is necessary to go outside of what is going on in the classroom. It can best be explained by the Cherokee people themselves. From Cherokee parents we learned that what Mr. Howard achieved was what they wanted in the classroom but was seldom achieved. One parent stated:

> We would like to see our children that go to school do something like the teacher has done when they went to school. They learned how to be teachers and then the children could go in the footsteps of what they have done, trying to be teachers. So we would like to have good teachers in our school for our children where they can be good students.
>
> All I am asking is to have a good teacher in our community school where our children go, because they sure do have a hard time in school. They have a hard time to learn anything that they should. The Cherokee Indians—it's hard to understand the English to start with. The teacher has to explain well—understand because they are Cherokee. We send the children to school to read and write and talk English—not to just get punished.

Parents used the word "love" to describe the way teachers should work with the children. "Love all the students alike, Indian and white." In addition, common words and phrases were "trust," "teach them until they understand," and "teachers gave out to teach the children." Another parent remarked:

> Some teachers are unable to love the Cherokee Indian. I wish they would love both Cherokee and white the same. They should. Because

I know some teachers, they don't like the Indians. Seems like they have to care more for the white than they do the Indian. Whenever they are qualified to teach, they have to love their kind of people. When I went to school, I knew the teacher love more the white than the Cherokee. When I ask my problem she wouldn't teach me like she ought to.

It is an impressive statement. Like many of the other Cherokee parents, this person sees the act of teaching as culturally prescribed; and when it is held in that framework, it is of dubious value and relevancy for people of another culture.

Reflected in these statements is the Cherokee belief that the ways in which people relate to each other, including the words, are all part of a highly moral transaction. Subject and content are as important as the way in which they are said. The difference can be seen in Mr. Miller's statements; it is what he is saying, the subject content, that he considers to have moral weight, but hardly the way in which he says it. Even with strangers, which teachers most often are balanced and harmonious relations with others. Caution and between people: individual autonomy is greatly valued but so, too, are balanced and harmonious relations with others. Caution and restraint, respect and choice are recurring themes within the interdependent Cherokee families and communities.

Teaching is considered an art in the working out of social relations; secondarily, it is meant to convey academic materials. Because of this, what we commonly think of as a teacher's authority is open to scrutiny from a Cherokee point of view. What the teacher uses for guides for learning, and usually without question—matters quite simple, such as recitation in front of the class, demonstrations at the board, raising hands, and even the way desks are arranged—are in the Cherokee view restricting the boundaries of social relations and imposing a structured relationship on the conversation that has not been worked out within the needs and wants of the participants. A person who does this is acting in a wholly unethical manner.

The teacher is to assist, order, and clarify the unknown, and avoid disharmony and bad feelings. What is taught or learned is achieved within the obligation and responsibility developed in the classroom. "You must or you have to learn" is as alien as "I will teach you this because you say you want to learn" is at the center. It is a radical shift in values, and how one learns, requiring the many and varied forms of social interaction, is more important than academic subjects or skills.

In the classroom it is mediated and worked out through language, and in Mr. Howard's room through English, although it could also be Cherokee. Whatever language is employed, it is necessary that one does not deal simply with words and definitions and rules of grammar, but that a conceptual basis of words and language be conveyed. It is only this that offers one of the few bridges of cultural difference. As such, words and their use hold special and new meanings that evolve and are defined within the dialogues between teacher and students. Mr. Howard allows this to take place—he participates as the students' equal and does little in the way of instructing and structuring conversation through the use of authority.

John: "I'll tell you what I would like to do is just sit back and earn money with cows . . . ."

Kathyrn: "But you got to work, though."

The discussion turns to women's rights, and Mr. Howard begins, "Women had no votes . . . ."

John, with a big smile: "It must have been good back then."

They continue on this subject, and Kathyrn adds, "It's just because we do our work."

Mr. Howard: "In what areas do women have no equal rights?"

Kathyrn: "Control the children."

Jim: "That's women's work."

Kathyrn: "The children belong to the men, too."

Mr. Howard asks Kathyrn, "Do women of today have equal rights?"

John: "Yes, I think so."

Mr. Howard: "Do you have the floor? Hold up your hand."

John smiles and throws his hand in the air in an exaggerated gesture. Students are rarely asked to hold up their hands. Several other students talk, and then John is recognized. "Drink highpowered whiskey." He demonstrates the equivalent of a gallon with his hands.

Everyone laughs. "Now, are you saying more men are alcoholics than women?"

Abruptly, John turns around and looks at Joan. "Her mom was."

Joan: "She used to be."

John: "Ya, she used to be."

Mr. Howard, "Okay, John always has some money-making scheme, let's hear how he could make money."

John: "Borrow money from the bank. That's a man's job."

"My mother gets money from the bank," volunteers Karen, who does not talk very often. The rest of the girls offer suggestions.

Jake has his hand up and is recognized. "Working on a bridge." He is a sixth-grader, barely knows English, and rarely talks. Many students who do not normally talk are participating. Stanley adds, "Get to Vietnam."

Mr. Howard: "What would say if you saw a woman carpenter?"

John holds out his arm in a gesture of holding the woman. The laughter is very open and Mr. Howard adds, "No one is safe around John."

They start to read in the social studies book. Karen reads and has a good deal of difficulty, and the students sitting next to her help her. Mr. Howard occasionally gives a word that no one else is able to get.

"How many know what an insane person is?"

Jim: "What's that?"

Mr. Howard explains as best he can, and John volunteers, "They are retarded?" Mr. Howard corrects him and adds a further explanation.

Karen: "When my mother was at Oswego [state asylum] she said there were two young boys. They had to put them by themselves and keep guards on them with guns . . . ."

Mr. Howard: "How many think that insane people should be kept in hospitals?" Most of the students say they should, but there are a few dissenters.

John: "Some just act that way."

Mr. Howard: "Why?"

Kathyrn: "Just because they want to act that way."

"They could be faking like some people do in the draft," John adds.

Kathryn: "They could be cowards. I wouldn't do that."

John: "Chickens."

Jim: "Roosters sometimes." He is the youngest in the class, and he has not quite learned the intricacies involved in the plays on words that the Cherokee often use.

Mr. Howard: "It's almost time for science."

Kathyrn: "In five more minutes."

About ten minutes later they start science.

Mr. Howard's class has created an alternative rarely, if ever, present in the school. Students can learn English; they can participate without fear, restraint, or caution; and they can develop competency in academic subjects. Language, a knowledge and use of it, is central to the development of this alternative. By being able to talk with each other they have found a way to learn how words work and further use them to solve problems of cultural difference as they exist in the classroom. However, it is achieved at a high cost, for there are no institutional supports or structured means by which this can be an integral and basic part of education.

What happens to the students when they leave this room and go into Mr. Miller's or into the consolidated schools? The answer is, perhaps, too painfully evident. What I did not find out until after the studies were finished was that Mr. Howard's class, with the freedom to talk and to learn about the use and function of words, was a leave-taking, a momentary pause in a long school career of silence.

At the end of the study, a questionnaire was given to the students that was intended to supplement the classroom observations. It was a series of questions about subjects, schools, language, and teachers that students liked or disliked and why. Because of a number of administrative-research problems teachers administered the schedule; they read the questions out loud and the students, who also had the questions, wrote their answers. Mr. Miller's and Mr. Howard's classes were combined.

Before reaching question 14 (Would you like it if your teacher taught in Cherokee?), Mr. Howard came over and asked me if it was necessary to give this question. "I know what they'll say," he stated flatly. In making up the question, I had taken into account the fact that the Cherokee speaker was in the majority, teachers did not speak it, there were no bilingual programs, and many students, even in the later grades, had little proficiency in English. Under these conditions, it seemed students would welcome a teacher who spoke their language. Quite naïvely I replied to Mr. Howard that the question would do no harm.

As he read the question he blushed. The students were indignant, outraged. John blurted out, "Not everyone would understand." Jim added, "He [Mr. Howard] wouldn't understand." Kathyrn and another student said as loudly, "We wouldn't learn English." I had expected none of this. Mr. Howard brusquely broke into the middle of it. "It's a yes or no answer."

They continued to talk among themselves, mostly in Cherokee. Better than anyone else, they understood the exclusiveness of a language not shared by everyone in the classroom. It prescribed, defined, and limited the boundaries of teaching and learning over which one had little control under normal circumstances. Even to raise the question, that they would have to consider it, fragmented and could break down that delicately balanced system of teaching and learning they had worked out. To even suggest they would want the teacher to speak Cherokee was an insult because Mr. Howard did not.

In Conclusion

In the system of forces at work in this intercultural setting, Cherokee students control much of what goes on in the classroom, but in the school and larger community that control is meaningless. They know all too well—like most of the adult members of the Cherokee communities—that they are powerless. To learn and to be taught in Cherokee would excluude them from participation in the larger community, and it would be antithetical to what the Cherokee community has come to hold as the value of formal education (to learn English and to acquire a means of achieving economic stability). At the same time, the ways in which teaching-learning are transacted in the school are of such a nature that they keep the Cherokee student from learning English, thus blocking him from meeting the most basic requirements necessary for using education as a tool in achieving economic stability.

Education for most students is an either-or proposition: participate by teacher-school established norms or withdraw. It is either being able to speak English or silence. Under different social conditions the problems of silence could be attacked. The question of whether a teacher should speak Cherokee should not even have to be raised, but it is. It is the only viable means to get at English and the other academic subjects. However, the conditions of silence continue, and are further developed and refined only because the teacher knows virtually nothing about the Cherokee, neither their language nor their life styles. In the absence of that we can only speak about whether students do or do not talk in the class, and to even suggest anything about the functions of language in discourse, conversation, or dialogue within the classroom is useless, because it does not exist except on rare occasions.

Bibliography

Dumont, Robert V., Jr. "Oglala Sioux Community-School Project Report." 1964. Mimeographed.

Dumont, Robert V., Jr.; and Wax, Murray L. "Cherokee School Society and the Intercultural Classroom." *Human Organization* 28, No. 3 (1970): 217–226.

Wax, Murray L.; Wax, Rosalie H.; and Dumont, Robert V., Jr. *Formal Education in an American Indian Community.* Social Problems Monograph No. 1. Kalamazoo, Mich.: The Society for the Study of Social Problems, 1964.

Participant Structures and Communicative Competence: Warm Springs Children in Community and Classroom

Susan U. Philips
University of Pennsylvania

Introduction

Recent studies of North American Indian education problems have indicated that in many ways Indian children are not culturally oriented to the ways in which classroom learning is conducted. The Wax-Dumont study (Wax *et al.*, 1964) of the Pine Ridge Sioux discusses the lack of interest children show in what goes on in school and Wolcott's (1967) description of a Kwakiutl school tells of the Indian children's organized resistance to his ways of structuring classroom learning. Cazden and John (1968) suggest that the "styles of learning" through which Indian children are enculturated at home differ markedly from those to which they are introduced in the classroom. And Hymes (1967) has pointed out that this may lead to sociolinguistic interference when teacher and student do not

This paper originally appeared, in a slightly different form, under the title "Acquisition of Rules for Appropriate Speech Usage," in James E. Alatis (ed.), *Bilingualism and Language Contact: Anthropological, Linguistic, Psychological, and Sociological Aspects.* Monograph Series on Languages and Linguistics, No. 23. Washington, D.C.: Georgetown University Press, 1970.

recognize these differences in their efforts to communicate with one another.

On the Warm Springs Indian Reservation in central Oregon, where I have been carrying out research in patterns of speech usage, teachers have pointed to similar phenomena, particularly in their repeated statements that Indian children show a great deal of reluctance to talk in class, and that they participate less and less in verbal interaction as they go through school. To help account for the reluctance of the Indian children of Warm Springs (and elsewhere as well) to participate in classroom verbal interactions, I am going to demonstrate how some of the social conditions governing or determining when it is appropriate for a student to speak in the classroom differ from those that govern verbal participation and other types of communicative performances in the Warm Springs Indian community's social interactions.

The data on which discussion of these differences will be based are drawn, first of all, from comparative observations in all-Indian classes in the reservation grammar school and non-Indian or white classes in another grammar school at the first- and sixth-grade levels. The purpose here is to define the communicative contexts in which Indian and non-Indian behavior and participation differ, and to describe the ways in which they differ.

After defining the situations or social contexts in which Indian students' verbal participation is minimal, discussion will shift to consideration of the social conditions in Indian cultural contexts that define when speaking is appropriate, attending to children's learning experiences both at home and in the community-wide social activities in which they participate.

The end goal of this discussion will be to demonstrate that the social conditions that define when a person uses speech in Indian social situations are present in classroom situations in which Indian students use speech a great deal, and absent in the more prevalent classroom situations in which they fail to participate verbally.

There are several aspects of verbal participation in classroom contexts that should be kept in mind during the discussion of why Indians are reluctant to talk. First of all, a student's use of speech in the classroom during structured lesson sessions is a communicative performance in more than one sense of "performance." It involves demonstration of sociolinguistic competency, itself a complex combination of linguistic competency and social competency involving knowledge of when and in what style one must present one's utterances, among other things. This type of competency, however, is involved in every speech act. But in the classroom there is a second sense in which speaking is a performance that is more special although not unique to classroom interactions. In class, speaking is the first and primary mode for communicating competency in all of the areas of skill and knowledge that schools purport to teach. Children communicate what they have learned to the teacher and their fellow students through speaking; only rarely do they demonstrate what they know through physical activity or creation of material objects. While writing eventually becomes a second important channel or mode for communicating knowledge or demonstrating skills, writing, as a skill, is to a great extent developed through verbal interaction between student and teacher, as is reading.

Consequently, if talk fails to occur, then the channel through which learning sessions are conducted is cut off, and the structure of classroom interaction that depends on dialogue between teacher and student breaks down and no longer functions as it is supposed to. Thus, while the question "Why don't Indian kids talk more in class?" is in a sense a very simple one, it is also a very basic one, and the lack of talk a problem that needs to be dealt with if Indian children are to learn what is taught in American schools.

Cultural and Educational Background of the Warm Springs Indians

Before embarking on the main task of the discussion outlined above, some background information on the setting of the research, the Warm Springs Indian Reservation, is necessary to provide some sense of the extent to which the cultural, linguistic, and educational situation there may be similar to or different from that of North American Indians in other parts of the country.

Today the reservation of 564,209 acres is populated by some 1,500 descendants of the "bands" of Warm Springs Sahaptin, Wasco Chinook, and Paiute Indians who gradually settled there after the reservation was established in 1855. The Warm Springs Indians have always been the largest group numerically, followed by the Wasco, with the Paiutes so small in number that their influence in the culture of the reservation has been of relatively small significance. Although they spoke different languages, the Warm Springs and Wasco groups were geographically quite close to one another before the reservation was established and were culturally similar in many respects. Thus, after over a hundred years together on the reservation, they presently share approximately the same cultural background.

The "tribe," as the Indians of Warm Springs now refer to themselves collectively, today comprises a single closely integrated community with strong tribal leadership, which receives the full backing of the people. Until after World War II the Indians here experienced considerable poverty and hardship. Since that time, however, tribal income from the sale of reservation timber has considerably improved the economic situation, as has tribal purchase of a sawmill and a small resort, which provide jobs for tribal members.

With the income from these enterprises, and drawing as well on various forms of federal aid available to them, the tribe has developed social programs to help members of the tribe in a number of ways. Chief among their concerns is the improvement of the education of their children, whom they recognize to be less successful in school than their fellow non-Indian students. Tribal leaders have taken numerous important steps to increase the educational opportunities of their young people, including the establishment of a scholarship program for college students and a tribal education office with half a dozen full-time employees supervising the tribally sponsored kindergarten, study halls, and community center courses as well as the federally sponsored programs such as VISTA, Head Start, and Neighborhood Youth Corps. The education office employees also act as liaisons between parents of children with problems in school and the administrators and teachers of the public schools the children attend. In sum, the tribe is doing a great deal to provide the Warm Springs children with the best education possible.

Despite their efforts, and those of the public school officials, who are under considerable pressure from tribal leaders to bring about changes in the schools that will result in the improvement of the academic performance of Indian students, the Indians continue to do poorly in school when compared to the non-Indian students in the same school system.

One of the most important things to know about the schools the Indian children attend is the "ethnic" composition of their classes. For the first six grades, Warm Springs children attend a public school that is located on the reservation. Here their classmates are almost all Indians and their teachers are all non-Indians or whites. After the first six grades, they are bused into the town of Madras, a distance of fifteen to thirty miles, depending on where they live on the reservation. Here, encountering their fellow white students for the first time, the Indian students are outnumbered by a ratio of five to one. From the point of view of tribal leaders, it is only when they reach the high school, or ninth grade, that the Indian students' "problems" really become serious, for it is at this point that hostility between Indian and non-Indian is expressed openly, and the Indian students' failure to participate in classroom discussions and school activities is recognized by everyone.

There is, however, abundant evidence that Indian students' learning difficulties begin long before they reach the high school. The statistics that are available on their educational achievements and problems are very similar to those which have been reported for Indians in other parts of the country (Berry, 1969). On national achievement tests the Warm Springs Indian children consistently score lower than the national average in skills tested. Their lowest scores are in areas involving verbal competencies, and the gap between their level of performance on such tests and the national averages widens as they continue into the higher grade levels (Zentner, 1960).

Although many people on the reservation still speak an Indian language, today all of the Warm Springs children in school are monolingual speakers of English. The dialect of English they speak, however, is not the Standard English of their teachers, but one that is distinctive to the local Indian community, and that in some aspects of grammar and phonology shows influence from the Indian languages spoken on the reservation.

In addition, there is some evidence that many children are exposed to talk in the Indian languages that may affect their acquisition of English. Because older people on the reservation are very concerned about the Indian languages' dying out, many of them make a concerted effort to teach young children an Indian language, particularly the Warm Springs Sahaptin. Thus some infants and young children are spoken to consistently in both Warm Springs and English. Every Indian child still knows some Indian words, and many informants report that while their children refuse to speak the Warm Springs Sahaptin—particularly after they start school—they understand much of what is said to them in it.

The effects of the acquisition of a very local dialect of English and the exposure to the Warm Springs language on classroom learning are difficult for local educators to assess because children say so little in the presence of the teachers. Observations of Indian children's verbal interactions outside the classroom indicate a control and productive use of linguistic rules that is manifested infrequently in classroom utterances, indicating that the appropriate social conditions for speech use, from the Indians' point of view, are lacking. It is this problem with appropriate social contexts for speaking that will now be considered in greater detail.

Conditions for Speech Use in School Classrooms

When the children first enter school, the most immediate concern of the teachers is to teach them the basic rules for classroom behavior upon which the maintenance of continuous and ordered activity depends. One of the most important of these is the distinction between the roles of teacher and student. In this there is the explicit and implicit assumption that the teacher controls all of the activity taking place in the classroom and the students accept and are obedient to her authority. She determines the sociospatial arrangements of all interactions; she decrees when and where movement takes place within the classroom. And most important for our present concern with communication, she determines who will talk and when they will talk.

While some class activities are designed to create the sense of a class of students as an organized group with class officers, or student monitors carrying out various responsibilities contributing to the group, actual spontaneous organization within the student group that has not been officially designated by the teacher is not encouraged. It interferes with the scheduling of activities as the teacher has organized them. The classroom situation is one in which the teacher relates to the students as an undifferentiated mass, much as a performer in front of an audience. Or she relates to each student on a one-to-one basis, often with the rest of the class as the still undifferentiated audience for the performance of the individual child.

In comparing the Indian and non-Indian learning of these basic classroom distinctions which define the conditions in which communication will take place, differences are immediately apparent. Indian first-graders are consistently slower to begin acting in accordance with these basic arrangements. They do not remember to raise their hands and wait to be called on before speaking, they wander to parts of the room other than the one in which the teacher is conducting a session, and they talk to other students while the teacher is talking, much further into the school year than do students in non-Indian classes. And the Indian children continue to fail to conform to classroom procedure much more frequently *through* the school year.

In contrast to the non-Indian students, the Indian students consistently show a great deal more interest in what their fellow students are going than in what the teacher is doing. While non-Indian students constantly make bids for the attention of their teachers, through initiating dialogue with them as well as through other acts, Indian students do very little of this. Instead they make bids for the attention of their fellow students through talk. At the first-grade level, and more noticeably (with new teachers only) at the sixth-grade level, Indian students often act in deliberate organized opposition to the teacher's directions. Thus, at the first-grade level, if one student is told not to put his feet on his chair, another will immediately put his feet on his chair, and he will be imitated by other students who see him do this. In non-Indian classrooms, such behavior was observed only at the sixth-grade level in interaction with a substitute teacher.

In other words, there is, on the part of Indian students, relatively less interest, desire, and/or ability to internalize and act in accordance with some of the basic rules underlying classroom maintenance of orderly interaction. Most notably, Indian students are less willing than non-Indian students to accept the teacher as director and controller of all classroom activities. They are less interested in developing the one-to-one communicative relationship between teacher and student, and more interested in maintaining and developing relationships with their peers, regardless of what is going on in the classroom.

Within the basic framework of teacher-controlled interaction, there are several possible variations in structural arrangements of interaction, which will be referred to from here on as "participant structures." Teachers use different participant structures, or ways of arranging verbal interaction with students, for communicating different types of educational material, and for providing variation in the presentation of the same material to hold children's interest. Often the notion that different kinds of materials are taught better and more efficiently through one sort of participant structuring rather than another is also involved.

In the first type of participant structure the teacher interacts with all of the students. She may address all of them, or a single student in the presence of the rest of the students. The students may respond as a group or chorus in unison, or individually in the presence of their peers. And finally, student verbal participation may be either voluntary, as when the teacher asks who knows the answer to her question, or compulsory, as when the teacher asks a particular student to answer, whether his hand is raised or not. And always it is the teacher who determines whether she talks to one or to all, receives responses individually or in chorus, and voluntarily or without choice.

In a second type of participant structure, the teacher interacts with only some of the students in the class at once, as in reading groups. In such contexts participation is usually mandatory rather than voluntary, individual rather than chorus, and each student is expected to participate or perform verbally, for the main purpose of such smaller groups is to provide the teacher with the opportunity to assess the knowledge acquired by each individual student. During such sessions, the remaining students who are not interacting with the teacher are usually working alone or independently at their desks on reading or writing assignments.

A third participant structure consists of all students working independently at their desks, but with the teacher explicitly available for student-initiated verbal interaction, in which the child indicates he wants to communicate with the teacher by raising his hand, or by approaching the teacher at her desk. In either case, the interaction between student and teacher is not witnessed by the other students in that they do not hear what is said.

A fourth participant structure, and one that occurs infrequently in the upper primary grades, and rarely, if ever, in the lower grades, consists of the students' being divided into small groups that they run themselves, though always with the more distant supervision of the teacher, and usually for the purpose of so-called "group projects." As a rule such groups have official "chairmen," who assume what is in other contexts the teacher's authority in regulating who will talk when.

In observing and comparing Indian and non-Indian participation or communicative performances in these four different structural variations of contexts in which communication takes place, differences between the two groups again emerge very clearly.

In the first two participant structures where students must speak out individually in front of the other students, Indian children show considerable reluctance to participate, particularly when compared to non-Indian students. When the teacher is in front of the whole class, they volunteer to speak relatively rarely, and teachers at the Warm Springs grammar school generally hold that this reluctance to volunteer to speak out in front of other students increases as the children get older.

When the teacher is with a small group, and each individual must give some kind of communicative verbal performance in turn, Indian children much more frequently refuse, or fail to utter a word when called upon, and much less frequently, if ever, urge the teacher to call on them than the non-Indians do. When the Indian children do speak, they speak very softly, often in tones inaudible to a person more than a few feet away, and in utterances typically shorter or briefer than those of their non-Indian counterparts.

In situations where the teacher makes herself available for student-initiated communication during sessions in which students are working independently on assignments that do not involve verbal communication, students at the first-grade level in the Indian classes at first rarely initiate contact with the teachers. After a few weeks in a classroom they do so as frequently as the non-Indian students. And at the sixth-grade level Indian students initiate such relatively private encounters with teachers much more frequently than non-Indian students do.

When students control and direct the interaction in small group projects, as described for the fourth type of participant structure, there is again a marked contrast between the behavior of Indian and non-Indian students. It is in such contexts that Indian students become most fully involved in what they are doing, concentrating completely on their work until it is completed, talking a great deal to one another within the group, and competing, with explicit remarks to that effect, with the other groups. Non-Indian students take more time in "getting organized," disagree and argue more regarding how to go about a task, rely more heavily on appointed chairmen for arbitration and decision-making, and show less interest, at least explicitly, in competing with other groups from their class.

Observations of the behavior of both Indian and non-Indian children outside the classroom during recess periods and teacher-organized physical education periods provide further evidence that the differences in readiness to participate in interaction are related to the way in which the interaction is organized and controlled.

When such outside-class activity is organized by the teachers, it is for the purpose of teaching children games through which they develop certain physical and social skills. If the games involve a role distinction between leader and followers in which the leader must tell the others what to do—as in Simon Says, Follow the Leader, Green Light Red Light, and even Farmer in the Dell—Indian children show a great deal of reluctance to assume the leadership role. This is particularly true when the child is appointed leader by the teacher and must be repeatedly urged to act in telling the others what to do before doing so. Non-Indian children, in contrast, vie eagerly for such positions, calling upon the teacher and/or other students to select them.

If such playground activity is unsupervised, and the children are left to their own devices, Indian children become involved in games of team competition much more frequently than non-Indian children. And they sustain such game activities for longer periods of time and at younger ages than non-Indian children. While non-Indian children tend more to play in groups of two and three, and in the upper primary grades to form "friendships" with one or two persons from their own class in school, Indian children interact with a greater number of children consistently, and maintain friendships and teams with children from classes in school other than their own.

In reviewing the comparison of Indian and non-Indian students' verbal participation under different social conditions, two features of the Warm Springs children's behavior stand out. First of all, they show relatively less willingness to perform or participate verbally when they must speak alone in front of other students. Second, they are relatively less eager to speak when the point at which speech occurs is dictated by the teacher, as it is during sessions when the teacher is working with the whole class or a small group. They also show considerable reluctance to be placed in the "leadership" play roles that require them to assume the same type of dictation of the acts of their peers.

Parallel to these negative responses are the positive ones of a relatively greater willingness to participate in group activities that do not create a distinction between individual performer and audience, and a relatively greater use of opportunities in which the point at which the student speaks or acts is determined by himself, rather than by the teacher or a "leader."

It is apparent that there are situations arising in the classroom that do allow for the Indian students to verbalize or communicate under or within the participant structures their behavior indicates they prefer; otherwise it would not have been possible to make the distinctions between their behavior and that of non-Indians in the areas just discussed. However, the frequency of occurrence of such situations in the classroom is very low when compared to the frequency of occurrence of the type of participant structuring in which Indian students fail to participate verbally, particularly in the lower grades.

In other words, most verbal communication that is considered part of students' learning experience does take the structure of individual students' speaking in front of other students. About half of this speaking is voluntary insofar as students are invited to volunteer to answer, and half is compulsory in that a specific student is called on and expected to answer. In either case, it is the teacher who establishes when talk will occur and within what kind of participant structure.

There are many reasons why most of the verbal communication takes place under such conditions. Within our particular education system, a teacher needs to know how much her students have learned or absorbed from the material she has presented. Students' verbal responses provide one means—and the primary means, particularly before students learn to write—of measuring their progress, and are thus the teacher's feedback. And, again within our particular educational system, it is not group but individual progress with which our teachers are expected to be concerned.

In addition, it is assumed that students will learn from each others' performances both what is false or wrong, and what is true or correct. Another aspect of this type of public performance that may increase educators' belief in its efficacy is the students' awareness that these communicative acts *are* performances, in the sense of being demonstrations of competency. The concomitant awareness that success or failure in such acts is a measure of their worth in the eyes of those present increases their motivation to do well. Thus they will remember when they made a mistake and try harder to do well to avoid public failure, in a way they would not were their performances in front of a smaller number of people. As I will try to demonstrate further on, however, the educators' assumption of the validity or success of this type of enculturation process, which can briefly be referred to as "learning through public mistakes," is not one the Indians share, and this has important implications for our understanding of Indian behavior in the classroom.

The consequences of the Indians' reluctance to participate in these speech situations are several. First of all, the teacher loses the primary means she has of receiving feedback on the children's acquisition of knowledge, and is thus less able to establish at what point she must begin again to instruct them, particularly in skills requiring a developmental sequencing, as in reading.

A second consequence of this reluctance to participate in speech situations requiring mandatory individual performances is that the teachers in the Warm Springs grammar school modify their teaching approach whenever possible to accommodate, in a somewhat ad hoc fashion, what they refer to as the Indian students' "shyness." In the first grade it is not easy to make very many modifications because of what teachers perceive as a close relationship between the material being taught and the methods used to teach it. There is some feeling, also, that the teaching methods that can be effective with children at age six are somewhat limited in range. However, as students go up through the grades, there is an increasing tendency for teachers to work with the notion, not always a correct one, that given the same body of material there are a number of different ways of "presenting" it, or in the terms being used here, a range of different participant structures and modes of communication (e.g., talking versus reading and writing) that can be used.

Even so, at the first-grade level there are already some changes made to accommodate the Indian children that are notable. When comparing the Indian first-grade classes with the non-Indian first-grade classes, one finds very few word games being used that involve students' giving directions to one another. And even more conspicuous in Indian classes is the absence of the ubiquitous "show and tell" or "sharing," through which students learn to get up in front of the class, standing where the teacher stands, and presenting, as the teacher might, a monologue relating an experience or describing a treasured object that is supposed to be of interest to the rest of the class. When asked whether this activity was used in the classroom, one teacher explained that she had previously used it, but so few children ever volunteered to "share" that she finally discontinued it.

By the time the students reach the sixth grade, the range of modes and settings for communication has increased a great deal, and the opportunity for elimination of some participant structures in preference to others is used by the teachers. As one sixth-grade teacher put it, "I spend as little time in front of the class as possible." In comparison with non-Indian classes, Indian classes have a relatively greater number of group "projects." Thus, while non-Indian students are learning about South American history through reading texts and answering the teacher's questions, Indian students are doing group-planned and -executed murals depicting a particular stage in Latin American history; while non-Indian students are reading science texts and answering questions about how electricity is generated, Indian students are doing group-run experiments with batteries and motors.

Similarly, in the Indian classes "reports" given by individual students are almost nonexistent, but are a typical means in non-Indian classes for demonstrating knowledge through verbal performance. And finally, while in non-Indian classes students are given opportunities to ask the teacher questions in front of the class, and do so, Indian students are given fewer opportunities for this because when they do have the opportunity, they don't use it. Rather, the teacher of Indians allows more periods in which she is available for individual students to approach her alone and ask their questions where no one else can hear them.

The teachers who make these adjustments, and not all do, are sensitive to the inclinations of their students and want to teach them through means to which they most readily adapt. However, by doing so they are avoiding teaching the Indian children how to communicate in precisely the contexts in which they are least able but most need to learn if they are to "do well in school." The teachers handicap themselves by setting up performance situations for the students in which they are least able to arrive at the evaluations of individual competence upon which they rely for feedback to establish at what level they must begin to teach. And it is not at all clear that students do acquire the same information through one form of communication as they do through another. Thus these manipulations of communication settings and participant structures, which are intended to transmit knowledge to the students creatively through the means to which they are most adjusted, may actually be causing the students to miss completely types of information their later high school teachers will assume they picked up in grammar school.

The consequences of this partial adaptation to Indian modes of communication become apparent when the Indian students join the non-Indian students at the junior and senior high school levels. Here, where the Indian students are outnumbered five to one, there is no manipulation and selection of communication settings to suit the inclinations of the Indians. Here the teachers complain that the Indian students never talk in class, and never ask questions, and everyone wonders why.

It does not necessarily follow from this that these most creative teachers at the grade school level should stop what they are doing. Perhaps it should be the teachers at the junior and senior high school levels who make similar adaptations. Which of these occurs (or possibly there are *other* alternatives) depends on the goals the Indian community has for its youngsters, an issue that will be briefly considered in the conclusion of the paper.

Conditions for Speech Use in the Warm Springs Indian Community

To understand why the Warm Springs Indian children speak out readily under some social conditions but fail to do so under others, it is necessary to examine the sociolinguistic assumptions determining the conditions for communicative performances, particularly those involving explicit demonstrations of knowledge or skill, in the Indian community. It will be possible here to deal with only some of the many aspects of communication involved. Attention will focus first on the social structuring of learning situations or contexts in which knowledge and skills are communicated to children in Indian homes. Then some consideration will be given to the underlying rules or conditions for participation in the community-wide social events that preschool children, as well as older children, learn through attending such events with their families.

The Indian child's preschool and outside-school enculturation at home differs from that of many non-Indian or white middle-class children's in that a good deal of the responsibility for the care and training of children is assumed by persons other than the parents of the children. In many homes the oldest children, particularly if they are girls, assume these responsibilities when the parents are at home, as well as when they are not. Frequently, also, grandparents, uncles, and aunts assume the full-time responsibility for care and instruction of children. Children thus become accustomed to interacting with and following the instructions and orders of a greater number of people than is the case with non-Indian children. Equally important is the fact that all of the people with whom Indian children form such reciprocal nurturing and learning relationships are kinsmen. Indian children are rarely, if ever, taken care of by "babysitters" from outside the family. Most of their playmates before be-

ginning school are their siblings and cousins, and these peer relationships typically continue to be the strongest bonds of friendship
through school and adult life, later providing a basis for reciprocal
aid in times of need, and companionship in many social activities.

Indian children are deliberately taught skills around the home
(for girls) and in the outdoors (for boys) at an earlier age than
many middle-class non-Indian children. Girls, for example, learn
to cook some foods before they are eight, and by this age may be
fully competent in cleaning a house without any aid or supervision
from adults.

There are other areas of competence in which Indian children
are expected to be proficient at earlier ages than non-Indian children,
for which the means of enculturation or socialization are less visible
and clear-cut. While still in grammar school, at the age of ten or
eleven, some children are considered capable of spending afternoons
and evenings in the company of only other children, without the necessity of accounting for their whereabouts or asking permission to
do whatever specific activity is involved. At this same age many are
also considered capable of deciding where they want to live, and for
what reasons one residence is preferable to another. They may spend
weeks or months at a time living with one relative or another, until
it is no longer possible to say that they live in any particular household.

In general, then, Warm Springs Indian children become accustomed to self-determination of action, accompanied by very little disciplinary control from older relatives, at much younger ages
than middle-class white children do.

In the context of the household, learning takes place through
several sorts of somewhat different processes. First of all, children
are present at many adult interactions as silent but attentive observers. While it is not yet clear how adult activities in which children
are not full participants are distinguished from those in which children may participate fully, and from those for which they are not
allowed to be present at all, there are clearly marked differences.
What is most remarkable, however, is that there are many adult
conversations to which children pay a great deal of silent, patient
attention. This contrasts sharply with the behavior of non-Indian
children, who show little patience in similar circumstances, desir-

ing either to become a full participant through verbal interaction, or to become completely involved in some other activity.

There is some evidence that this silent listening and watching was, in the Warm Springs culture, traditionally the first step in learning skills of a fairly complex nature. For example, older women reminisce about being required to watch their elder relatives tan hides when they were very young, rather than being allowed to play. And certainly the winter evening events of myth-telling, which provided Indian children with their first explicitly taught moral lessons, involved them as listening participants rather than as speakers.

A second type of learning involves the segmentation of a task by an older relative, and the partial carrying out of the task or one of its segments by the child. In household tasks, for example, a child is given a very simple portion of a job (e.g., in cleaning a room the child may begin by helping move the furniture) and works in cooperation with and under the supervision of an older relative. Such activities involve a small amount of verbal instruction or direction from the older relative, and allow for questions on the part of the child. Gradually the child comes to learn all of the skills involved in a particular process, consistently under the supervision of an older relative who works along with him.

This mode of instruction is not unique to the Warm Springs Indians, of course; many non-Indian parents use similar methods. However, there are aspects of this type of instruction that differ from its use among non-Indians. First of all, when it occurs among the Indians it is likely to be preceded by the long periods of observation just described. The absence of such observation among non-Indian children is perhaps replaced by elaborate verbal instructions outlining the full scope of a task before the child attempts any part of it.

A second way in which this type of instruction among the Warm Springs Indians differs from that of non-Indians is the absence of "testing" of the child's skill by the instructing kinsman before the child exercises the skill unsupervised. Although it is not yet clear how this works in a diversity of situations, it appears that in many areas of skill, the child takes it upon himself to test the skill unsupervised and alone, without other people around. In this way, if he is unsuccessful his failure is not seen by others. If he is successful, he can show the results of his success to those by whom he has been taught, whether it be in the form of a deer that has been shot, a hide tanned, a piece of beadwork completed, or a dinner on the table when the adults come home from work.

Again there is some evidence that this type of private individual's testing of competency, followed by public demonstration only when competency is fully developed and certain, has been traditional in the Warm Springs Indian culture. The most dramatic examples of this come from the processes of acquisition of religious and ritual knowledge. In the vision quests through which adolescents, or children of even younger ages, acquired spirit power, individuals spent long periods in isolated mountain areas from which they were expected to emerge with skills they had not previously demonstrated. While some of these abilities were not fully revealed until later in life, the child was expected to be able to relate some experience of a supernatural nature that would prove that he had, in fact, been visited by a spirit. Along the same lines, individuals until very recently received and learned, through dreams and visions, ritual songs that they would sing for the first time in full and completed form in the presence of others.

The contexts described here in which learning takes place can be perceived as an idealized sequence of three steps: (1) observation, which of course includes listening; (2) supervised participation; and (3) private, self-initiated self-testing. It is not the case that all acquisition of skills procede through such phases, however, but rather only some of these skills that Indian adults consciously and deliberately teach their children, and which the children consciously try to learn. Those which are learned through less deliberate means must to some extent invoke similar structuring, but it is difficult to determine to what extent.

The use of speech in the process is notably minimal. Verbal directions or instructions are few, being confined to corrections and question-answering. Nor does the final demonstration of skill particularly involve verbal performance, since the validation of skill so often involves display of some material evidence or non-verbal physical expression.

This process of Indian acquisition of competence may help to explain, in part, Indian children's reluctance to speak in front of their classmates. In the classroom, the processes of *acquisition* of knowledge and *demonstration* of knowledge are collapsed into the single act of answering questions or reciting when called upon to do so by the teacher, particularly in the lower grades. Here the assumption is that one will learn, and learn more effectively, through making mistakes in front of others. The Indian children have no opportunity to observe others performing successfully before they attempt it, except for their fellow classmates who precede them and are themselves uninitiated. They have no opportunity to "practice," and to decide for themselves when they know enough to demonstrate their knowledge; rather, their performances are determined by the teacher. And finally, their only channel for communicating competency is verbal, rather than non-verbal.

Turning now from learning processes in the home to learning experiences outside the home, in social and ritual activities involving community members other than kinsmen, there is again considerable evidence that Indian children's understanding of when and how one participates and performs individually, and thus demonstrates or communicates competence, differs considerably from what is expected of them in the classroom.

Children of all ages are brought to every sort of community-wide social event sponsored by Indians (as distinct from those sponsored by non-Indians). There is rarely, if ever, such a thing as an Indian community event that is attended by adults only. At many events children participate in only certain roles, but this is true of everyone. Sociospatially and behaviorally, children must always participate minimally, as do all others, in sitting quietly and attentively alongside their elders.

One of the social features that characterizes social events that are not explicitly kin group affairs, including activities like political general councils, social dinners, and worship dances, is that they are open to participation by all members of the Warm Springs Indian community. While different types of activities are more heavily attended by certain Indians rather than others, and fairly consistently sponsored and arranged by certain individuals, it is always clear that everyone is invited, both by community knowledge of this fact and by explicit announcements on posters placed in areas where most people pass through at one time or another in their day-to-day activities.

A second feature of such activities is that there is usually no one person directing the activity verbally, or signaling changes from one phase to another. Instead the structure is determined either by a set procedure or ritual, or there is a group of people who in various complementary ways provide such cuing and direction. Nor are there any participant roles that can be filled or are filled by only one person. In dancing, singing, and drumming there are no soloists, and where there are performers who begin a sequence, and are then joined by others, more than one performer takes a turn at such initiations. The speaking roles are handled similarly. In contexts where speeches are appropriate, it is made clear that anyone who wants to may "say a few words." The same holds true for political meetings, where the answerer to a question is not necessarily one who is on a panel or council, but rather the person who feels he is qualified, by his knowledge of a subject, to answer. In all situations thus allowing for anyone who wants to to speak, no time limit is set, so that the talking continues until everyone who wants to has had the opportunity to do so.

This does not mean that there are never any "leaders" in Indian social activities, but rather that leadership takes quite a different form from that in many non-Indian cultural contexts. Among the people of Warm Springs, a person is not a leader by virtue of holding a particular position, even in the case of members of the tribal council and administration. Rather, he is a leader because he has demonstrated ability in some sphere and activity, and many individuals choose to follow his suggestions because they have independently each decided they are good ones. If, for example, an individual plans and announces an activity, but few people offer to help him carry it out or attend it, then that is an indication that the organizer is not a respected leader in the community at the present time. And the likelihood that he will repeat his efforts in the near future is reduced considerably.

This type of "leadership," present today among the people of Warm Springs, is reminiscent of that which was described by Hoebel for the Comanche chiefs:

In matters of daily routine, such as camp moving, he merely made the decisions himself, announcing them through a camp crier. Anyone who did not like his decision simply ignored it. If in time a good many people ignored his announcements and preferred to stay behind with some other man of influence, or perhaps to move in another direction with that man, the chief had then lost his following. He was no longer chief, and another had quietly superseded him (Hoebel, 1954, p. 132).

A final feature of Indian social activities, which should be recognized from what has already been said, is that all who do attend an activity may participate in at least some of the various forms participation takes for the given activity, rather than there being a distinction made between participants or performers and audience. At many Indian gatherings, particularly those attended by older people, this aspect of the situation is reflected in its sociospatial arrangement: People are seated in such a way that all present are facing one another, usually in an approximation of a square, and the focus of activity is either along one side of the square, or in its center, or a combination of the two.

And each individual chooses the degree of his participation. No one, other than, perhaps, those who set up the event, is committed to being present beforehand, and all participating roles beyond those of sitting and observing are determined by the individual at the point at which he decides to participate, rather than being prescheduled.

In summary, the Indian social activities to which children are early exposed outside the home generally have the following properties: (1) they are community-wide, in the sense that they are open to all Warm Springs Indians; (2) there is no single individual directing and controlling all activity, and, to the extent that there are "leaders," their leadership is based on the choice to follow made by each person; (3) participation in some form is accessible to everyone who attends. No one need be exclusively an observer or audience, and there is consequently no sharp distinction between audience and performer. And each individual chooses for himself the degree of his participation during the activity.

If one now compares the social conditions for verbal participation in the classroom with the conditions underlying many Indian events in which children participate, a number of differences emerge.

First of all, classroom activities are not community-wide, and, more importantly, the participants in the activity are not drawn just from the Indian community. The teacher, as a non-Indian, is an outsider and a stranger to these events. In addition, by virtue of her role as teacher, she structurally separates herself from the rest of the participants, her students. She places herself outside the inter-action and activity of the students. This encourages their cultural perceptions of themselves as the relevant community, in opposition to the teacher, perhaps much as they see themselves in opposition to other communities, and on a smaller scale, as one team is in opposi-tion to another. In other words, on the basis of the Indians' social experiences, one is either a part of a group or outside it. The notion of a single individual being structurally set apart from all others, in anything other than an observer role, and yet still a part of the group organization, is one that children probably encounter for the first time in school, and continue to experience only in non-Indian-derived activities (e.g., in bureaucratic, hierarchically structured occupa-tions). This helps to explain why Indian students show so little interest in initiating interaction with the teacher in activities involv-ing other students.

Second, in contrast to Indian activities where many people are involved in determining the development and structure of an event, there is only one single authority directing everything in the class-room, namely the teacher. And the teacher is not the controller or leader by virtue of the individual students' choices to follow her, as is the case in Indian social activities, but rather by virtue of her occupation of the role of teacher. This difference helps to account for the Indian children's frequent indifference to the directions, orders, and requests for compliance with classroom social rules that the teacher issues.

Third, it is not the case in the classroom that all students may participate in any given activity, as in Indian community activities. Nor are they given the opportunity to choose the degree of their participation, which, on the basis of evidence discussed earlier, would in Indian contexts be based on the individual's having already ascertained in private that he was capable of successful verbal communication of competence. Again these choices belong to the teacher.

Conclusion

In summary, Indian children fail to participate verbally in classroom interaction because the social conditions for participation to which they have become accustomed in the Indian community are lacking. The absence of these appropriate social conditions for communicative performances affects the most common and everyday speech acts that occur in the classroom. If the Indian child fails to follow an order or answer a question, it may not be because he doesn't understand the linguistic structure of the imperative and the interrogative, but rather because he does not share the non-Indian's assumption in such contexts that use of these syntactic forms by definition implies an automatic and immediate response from the person to whom they were addressed. For these assumptions are sociolinguistic assumptions that are not shared by the Indians.

Educators cannot assume that because Indian children (or any children from cultural backgrounds other than those that are implicit in American classrooms) speak English, or are taught it in the schools, that they have also assimilated all of the sociolinguistic rules underlying interaction in classrooms and other non-Indian social situations where English is spoken. To the extent that existing cultural variation in sociolinguistic patterning that is not recognized by the schools results in learning difficulties and feelings of inferiority for some children, changes in the structuring of classroom learning situations are needed. Ultimately the nature of the changes to be made should be determined by the educational goals of the particular communities where this type of problem exists.

If, as may be the case on the Warm Springs Indian Reservation, the people's main concern is to enable Indian children to compete successfully with non-Indians, and to have the *choice* of access to the modes of interaction and life styles of non-Indians, then there should be a conscious effort made in the schools to teach the children the modes for appropriate verbal participation that prevail in non-Indian classrooms. Thus, rather than shifting away from situations in which children perform individually in front of their peers only with great reluctance, conscious emphasis on and encouragement of participation in such situations should be carried out in the early grades.

If, on the other hand, as also may be the case in Warm Springs (there are strong differences of opinion here on this issue that complicate the teachers' actions), there is strong feeling in the community that its culturally distinctive modes of communication should be maintained and encouraged to flourish rather than be eliminated through our educational system's apparent pursuit of cultural uniformity throughout the country, then quite a different shift in the orientation of classroom modes of instruction would be called for. Here an effort to adapt the community's conditions for appropriate speech usage to the classroom should be made, not in an ad hoc and partial fashion as at Warm Springs, but consistently and systematically. And where the classroom situation is one in which children of more than one cultural background come together, efforts should be made to allow for a complementary diversity in the modes of communication through which learning and measurement of "success" take place.

Bibliography

Berry, Brewton. *The education of American Indians: a survey of the literature.* Prepared for the Special Subcommittee on Indian Education of the Committee on Labor and Public Welfare, United States Senate. Washington, D.C.: Government Printing Office, 1969.

Cazden, Courtney B.; and John, Vera P. "Learning in American Indian children." In *Styles of learning among American Indians: An Outline for Research.* Washington, D.C.: Center for Applied Linguistics, 1968.

Hoebel, E. Adamson. *The law of primitive man.* Cambridge, Mass.: Harvard University Press, 1954.

Hymes, Dell. "On communicative competence." In Renira Huxley and Elizabeth Ingram (eds.), *Mechanisms of Language Development.* London: Centre for Advanced Study in the Developmental Science and CIBA Foundation, forthcoming; article first appeared 1967.

Wax, Murray; Wax, Rosalie; and Dumont, Robert V., Jr. *Formal Edu-*

cation in an American Indian Community. Social Problems Monograph No. 1. Kalamazoo, Mich.: Society for the Study of Social Problems, 1964.

Wolcott, Harry. *A Kwakiutl Village and School.* New York: Holt, Rinehart and Winston, 1967.

Zentner, Henry. *Oregon State College Warm Springs Research Project.* Vol. II: Education. Corvallis: Oregon State College, 1960.

5549